Transforming China's Economy in the Eighties Volume I

Transforming China's Economy in the Eighties

Volume I:
The Rural Sector, Welfare and Employment

Edited by
Stephan Feuchtwang
Athar Hussain
Thierry Pairault

WESTVIEW PRESS
Boulder, Colorado

Zed Books Ltd
London, England

Transforming China's Economy in the Eighties, Volume I:
The Rural Sector Welfare and Employment and
Volume II: Management, Industry and the Urban Economy
was first published in 1988 by:

In the UK
Zed Books Ltd
57 Caledonian Road
London N1 9BU

In the USA
Westview Press
Frederick A. Praeger, Publisher
5500 Central Avenue
Boulder, Colorado 80301

In India
Oxford University Press India,
Oxford House,
Apollo Bundar, P.O. Box 31, Bombay 400 001

Cover designed by Andrew Corbett.
Typeset by EMS Photosetters, Rochford, Essex.
Printed and bound in the United Kingdom
at The Bath Press, Avon.

British Library Cataloguing in Publication Data

Transforming China's economy in the eighties.
  1. China — Economic conditions — 1976–
  I. Feuchtwang, Stephan II. Hussain, Athar
  III. Pairault, Thierry
  330.951'058   HC427.92

  ISBN 0-86232-602-8 v.1
  ISBN 0-86232-603-6 v.1 Pbk
  ISBN 0-86232-604-4 v.2
  ISBN 0-86232-605-2 v.2 Pbk

Library of Congress Cataloguing-in-Publication Data

Transforming China's economy in the eighties.
  Bibliography: p.
  Includes indexes.
  Contents: v.1. Rural economy — v.2 Urban economy
  1. China — Economic conditions — 1976–
I. Feuchtwang, Stephan.
  HC427.92.C4674   1988   330.951'058   87-10631
  ISBN 0-8133-0555-1 (v.1)
  ISBN 0-8133-0556-X (Pbk.: v.1)
  ISBN 0-8133-0557-8 (v.2)
  ISBN 0-8133-0558-6 (Pbk.: v.2)

Contents

Tables

Figures

Contributors

Philippe Aguignier Doctoral graduate at the University of Paris with a thesis on the political economy of China. Research fellow at CNRS (Centre National de la Recherche Scientifique)

Claude Aubert Agronomist and sociologist, presently a director of research at the Institut National de la Recherche Agronomique, Paris. Author, in collaboration with Mrs Cheng Ying, of *Les Greniers de Nancang; Chronique d'un Village Taiwanais* (Paris, 1984), and of numerous articles on the rural economy of China

Lucien Bianco A director at the Ecole des Hautes Etudes des Sciences Sociales, and author of *The Origins of the Chinese Revolution 1915–1949* (Stanford, 1971)

Michel Bonnin Researcher at the Centre Chine (Centre de Recherches et de Documentation sur la Chine Contemporaine, Ecole des Hautes Etudes en Sciences Sociales, Paris). Co-author of a book on 'educated youth': *Avoir 20 Ans en Chine . . . a la Campagne* (Paris, 1978)

Jean-Pierre Cabestan Graduate in Law, Chinese and Japanese; doctoral graduate in political science; now researcher at the Comparative Law Research Institute of CNRS

Michel Cartier Historian of pre-modern China originally; since the 1970s has devoted more attention to the demographic parameters of Chinese economy and society, at the Centre Chine

Yves Chevrier Co-director of the Centre Chine; co-editor of *Dictionnaire Biographique du Mouvement Ouvrier International – La Chine* (Paris, 1985); researches the intellectual history of late Qing and early Republican China as well as the reforms and society of post-Mao China

Elisabeth Croll Research fellow in the sociology and anthropology of contemporary China at SOAS (School of Oriental and African Studies, University of London); author of *The Politics of Marriage in China* (Cambridge, 1980); *The Family Rice Bowl* (London, 1983) and *Chinese Women Since Mao* (London, 1983)

Delia Davin Lecturer in History at the University of York; author of *Women Work; Women and the Party in Revolutionary China* (Oxford, 1976)

Stephan Feuchtwang Senior lecturer in Sociology and Principal of the China Research Unit at The City University, London; co-editor of *The Chinese Economic Reforms* (London, 1983)

François Gipouloux Research Officer at the Ministry of Industry, Paris, on Chinese industry, and at present resident in Beijing, PRC. Author of *Le Monde Ouvrier Chinois et la Crise du Travail Syndical en 1957* (Paris, 1983)

Paul Hare Professor of Economics at Heriot-Watt University, Edinburgh; co-author of *Alternative Approaches to Economic Planning* (London, 1981) and of *Hungary; A Decade of Economic Reform* (London, 1981)

Hua Chang-ming Researcher at the Centre Chine and author of *La Condition Feminine et les Communistes Chinois en Action; Yan'an 1935–1946* (Paris, 1981)

Athar Hussain Senior Lecturer in Economics at the University of Keele; co-author of *Marxism and the Agrarian Question* (London, 1981) and co-editor of *The Chinese Economic Reforms* (London, 1983)

Richard Kirkby China Consultant and Town Planner, Sheffield City; author of *Urbanisation in China: Town and Country in a Developing Economy 1949–2000AD* (London, 1985)

Martin Lockett Research Fellow at Templeton College, The Oxford Centre for Management Studies, and author of many publications on cooperative organisation of industry and the cooperative movement, in Europe and China, and on Chinese enterprise management and industrial organisation

Thierry Pairault Director of Research on China at CNRS, economist, and author of *Politique Industrielle et Industrialisation en Chine* (Paris, 1983)

Michael Palmer Visiting Research Fellow at The City University, London; graduate in sociology, anthropology and law; author of a number of recently published articles on family law and on mediation in the PRC

Gordon White Fellow of the Institute of Development Studies, University of Susex; co-editor and co-author of *China's New Development Strategy* (London, 1982) and author of many articles on urban–rural relations, industrial management and labour allocation in the PRC

Wojtek Zafanolli Research associate at the Centre Chine

Abbreviations

CCP: Chinese Communist Party
CHCDC: China Housing Construction and Development Corporation
         (Zhongguo Fangwu Jianshe Gongsi)
FYP: Five Year Plan
PLA: People's Liberation Army
PRC: People's Republic of China
NEP: New Economic Policy
NPC: National People's Congress

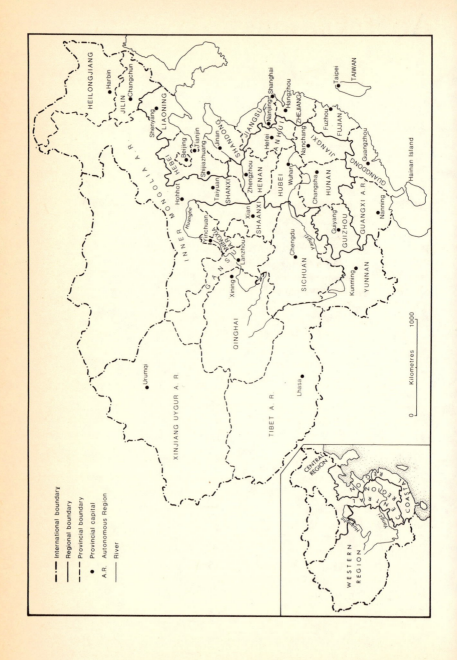

Preface

This is the first of two volumes on the transformation of China since 1978. The second volume concentrates on the government administration of the reforms which have brought changes in economic organization; it deals with the urban economy. The focus of this volume is on changes in the rural economy, provision for basic needs such as nutrition and housing, the population and the new legal structure. The broad coverage of its chapters reflects the wide ramifications of the changes which have taken place since 1978. Information now available on China is far more comprehensive, detailed and reliable than before. As an example, the conduct of the 1982 population census and the release of census returns has opened up a rich seam of research on Chinese demographic trends.

It has been a general presumption that, as compared to large developing economies (India in particular), China has been more successful in providing for the basic needs of its population. However, until recently this has been based on no more than fragmentary evidence and the impressions of travellers. Most of the rural communes which have been visited and written about have been in the vicinity of large towns and tended to be among the more prosperous. But now we have a lot more evidence. In 1981, the SSB released the time series on grain production dating back to 1949. And yearly production figures for grain and other agricultural commodities are no longer a mystery needing to be solved by painstaking and detailed detective work. The regular flow of statistical information from China has widened the scope of studies on the Chinese economy. Rather than piecing together fragments of evidence from newspapers and broadcasts, we can now start to detect patterns of change and regional diversity from official figures. The chapters by Hussain and Feuchtwang and by Aubert do this for nutrition and social welfare. Such studies provide a basis for future comparative studies of China and other developing economies.

Generally speaking, in present-day China, the average level of nutrition in terms of calories and protein is more than satisfactory and is a vast improvement over the 1949 level. But nearly all of that improvement took place either in the 1950s before the great famine or since 1978. This is now widely acknowledged in China and is taken as evidence of the toll of the two revolutionary decades spanning the Great Leap and the downfall of the Gang of Four. However, what is also interesting is that there is a marked discrepancy between the time patterns of various indicators of provision for basic needs. For example, while during the period 1958–77 grain per capita (the usual indicator of food intake) fluctuated wildly and for the most part remained below the 1957 level, the crude death rate in 1962 following the recovery from the famine was not only below the pre-famine level of 1957 but fell steadily from then on. We may attribute this downward trend to public health campaigns and the institution of the primary health care system; but they alone do not account for the whole of the fall. For when a sizeable section of the population subsists at the brink of serious undernutrition, as was the case in China in the 1960s, health care and hygiene need the complement of adequate nutrition to accomplish a downward trend in the death rate. Here circumstantial evidence suggests that the shift towards a more equal distribution of available grain (now termed the 'iron rice-bowl') in the aftermath of the famine furnished that complement.

The 'iron rice-bowl' consisted of two elements: first, the system of distribution of the internal grain supply within rural communes and, second, the use by the government of the marketing network to supply rural units which were not self-subsistent. The insurance mechanism of these two prevented the recurrence of another large famine and averted starvation and severe malnutrition. But it did not and was not meant to eliminate undernutrition and poverty. Pockets of chronic undernutrition and poverty have always existed in China. The present leadership, unlike the former, is candid in acknowledging their existence. According to Deng Xiaoping there are still 100 million people (around 10% of the population) in need of adequate nutrition and clothing. At least a part of what is being revealed now was undoubtedly known to the previous leaders; but it is not clear that they had the means to fathom the depths of destitution in the countryside. Up to the late 1970s, the statistical system was in a state of disarray. Sample surveys of nutrition and household income are recent innovations in China and they still fall short of established statistical norms.

Now that the average level of nutrition is more than satisfactory, pockets of chronic poverty have come to the fore as the main problem in the provision for basic needs. The spectacular increase in agricultural production and rural incomes since 1978 has reduced the extent of poverty but the increase has not been evenly distributed. The north-west, the south-west and some of the northern provinces have lagged behind. Moreover, there still are many poor areas within prosperous provinces. The main issue now is not the non-recognition of the problem of poverty but the lack of effective instruments at the disposal of the government to deal with the problem. Some of the usual mechanisms for reducing economic inequalities are weak in China. For example, the movement of the population is severely restricted. And the budgetary problems of the central government limit the transfer of resources to poor areas.

Agriculture has been the site of most radical changes. They are discussed by Croll, and Davin looks at their implications for women. Briefly, collective cultivation by the production team has been replaced by family cultivation. Formally, the land still belongs to the collective but it has been parcelled out to households, predominantly in proportion to their labour force, and the size of private plots has been increased. With the household as the unit of cultivation, the difference between the private plots and the rest is now reduced to the fact that the former are not subject to taxes and contribution to the local collective fund. The land parcelled out to households is granted to them for a period of 15–20 years, which implies that the present land tenure is regarded as temporary. But, subject to some restrictions, the parcelled land can be sold and passed on to heirs. Michael Palmer shows how the new inheritance law extends and amplifies the systems of contracts and welfare.

In the past, the provision of services in rural areas such as supplying the non-self-subsistent households with basic necessities, water and land management, the maintenance of agricultural machinery, primary health care and education, was interwoven with collective cultivation. The end of collective cultivation has undermined the institutional base of public services. As a result, the irrigated area has decreased, the rural collective health insurance system is nearly extinct and there have been problems with maintaining the system of support for non-self-subsistent households. A decline in school attendance in certain rural areas has also resulted. The general point is that until the reforms, the three tiers of the rural commune combined together to organize economic activities and local government and to provide services. The problem has been that while collective cultivation has been dismantled very quickly, alternative institutions of government and for the provision of services have been slow in emerging. The consequence of this discrepancy is a certain disarray in the countryside. A fundamental reorganization of rural government at lower tiers is now under way. Not only is there a new tier of government in the form of township (or *xiang*) but also a re-delineation of functions of the county and the prefectural government. For example, provision of social welfare is increasingly becoming a responsibility of the prefecture.

As for agricultural production, the rate of increase since 1978 has been outstanding by both Chinese and international standards. The average yearly growth rate for gross agricultural output (including sideline production) has (until 1986) been 9.4%. This has brought in its wake a massive rise in rural disposable incomes, which have increased faster than urban personal incomes. That rise is due to the growth of production, on the one hand, and to increase in the procurement prices of agricultural commodities on the other. The sources of rural incomes have changed as well. The proportion from sideline activities has steadily increased; and within agriculture there has been a steady shift from grain to other crops. The growth rates for non-grain crops such as cotton have been spectacular; as a result, China is, for instance, no longer a large net importer but is self-sufficient in raw cotton. Although the area devoted to grain has decreased sharply, grain output has, with the exception of the two dips in 1980 and 1985, been growing.

The outstanding rates of growth in rural incomes and agricultural output have made the reforms popular and rule out a reversion to the previous institutional structures. But given that present land tenure is still temporary, a further radical change is possible. The rates of growth of the rural economy inevitably raise the question of their causes. As they have coincided with a shift to family cultivation, *prima facie* they seem entirely due to the incentive effect of the dismantling of collective cultivation. Undoubtedly that has been a central cause; but we cannot neglect the role of technical factors. Among them we may single out the development of high-yield variety seeds for grain and non-grain crops, which dates back to the early 1960s, the massive investment in the large-scale fertilizer plants in the mid-1970s and the Herculean exercise in hydraulic construction during the collectivist period. It has to be acknowledged that the pre-1978 revolutionary period left behind a legacy of technical preconditions for a take-off in agricultural production.

As for the future prospects, the rates of growth witnessed from 1978–84 are too high to be sustained. Independently of any policies or measures, a deceleration is bound to set in. And the decrease in the grain output in 1985 is a reminder that the weather, if not political upheavals, still remains a recurring source of fluctuations in agricultural production. As compared to the recent experience the government's growth targets for agriculture up to the year 2000 are decidedly modest. But what are the possible consequences of the expected deceleration? The average level of nutrition now is more than satisfactory; and at just above 1% per annum the rate of population growth is low. It will be easily surpassed by even the most modest target of growth in grain output. Thus maintaining and even slightly improving upon the present level of nutrition is no longer a problem. However, the slowing rate of growth of agricultural production does constrain the speed of shift in the Chinese diet from grain to meat and dairy products.

The structural changes in the rural economy have increased economic inequalities in two dimensions: between the households within a village and between larger units such as the prefectures and the provinces. The former was low during the period of collective cultivation. The latter has always existed, but it is now accentuated and has come to the fore as a major feature of the Chinese countryside. With the increase in rural relative to urban personal incomes, we may argue that it is not the urban–rural inequality but inequalities within the countryside which now deserve special attention.

The growth in rural incomes has not been evenly distributed because, first, the quality of land, climate and the availability of water are not distributed uniformly. Secondly, the possibilities of sideline production and non-agricultural activities depend crucially on location. They are greater in densely populated areas and in the vicinity of large towns. The underdeveloped state of the transport network and the pressure of demand on it limits the radius of the accessible market. The implication is that intra- and inter-provincial inequalities are due to a conjunction of diverse factors; they cannot be altered by simple policy measures and are thus likely to remain as one of the major problems of the Chinese economy.

A shift from agricultural to non-agricultural activities is a common feature of economic growth. Departing from the experience of both socialist and capitalist economies, successive Chinese leaderships have been committed to accomplishing this shift without a massive migration of rural population to urban areas. The restrictions on the movement of the population have been draconian and the emphasis has always been on the expansion of non-agricultural employment within rural areas. Before 1978, aside from the government and public services, rural collective industry was almost the only source of such employment. The reforms have swept aside all the earlier restrictions on sideline activities and have encouraged rural households to engage in non-agricultural activities. Rural markets are now allowed to flourish. As a result, collective rural industry is no longer the sole source of non-agricultural employment in rural areas. Thus, side by side with a shift to family cultivation there has been a massive proliferation of ancillary and non-agricultural activities. Households are now allowed to own a wide variety of capital goods and the increase in rural personal incomes has furnished them with the financial means to do so. One important effect of the change is the emergence of so-called 'specialized households'; that is, those whose principal source of income is not the cultivation of the land but other activities. They now constitute up to 15% of the rural households. However, the government target for the redeployment of the rural labour force from cultivation to other activities is ambitious. The plan is that, as compared to over 60% now, by the year 2000 only 40% of the rural labour force should be engaged in cultivation as a principal livelihood. It is an open question whether the Chinese economy can sustain the rate of economic growth implied by this massive redeployment.

Aside from changes in agriculture and provision for basic needs, the population and urban unemployment are another focus of this volume. In 1982 China had its third population census since Liberation. Up to then, the size of the total population was a mystery, but now Chinese demographic statistics are as good as any for a developing economy. At just over a billion, the size of the Chinese population is staggering. And the cultivable land per head of the population or the agricultural labour force in China is low by international, though not by East Asian, standards. The boom in housing the population since 1978 has itself reduced cultivable land substantially; this is just one of the many problems of housing described by Richard Kirkby. Such problems immediately direct attention to the growth of the population and birth control measures such as limiting newly married couples to one child, discussed in this volume by Bianco and Hua.

Even though birth control measures are severe, the Chinese population is likely to keep on increasing well into the 21st Century. According to the World Bank projections it is unlikely to stabilize before reaching a figure of 1.2 billion. This may seem alarming but it is well within the capacity of the Chinese economy to sustain a population of that size. The total size of the population is important; but an exclusive concentration on limiting it distracts from other demographic features such as the age structure of the population. An increase or a decrease in the fertility rate has an important effect on this. In particular, a decrease implies an increase in the median age of the population and in time poses the problem of supporting the aged. In the Chinese context this problem assumes a special importance because the aged are supported by and large not by pensions but by their children, usually male. Limiting the number of children per couple and provision for the aged should therefore be considered jointly. Birth control has a cost as well as a benefit. It is not clear that the ration of one child per couple was either necessary or justified in terms of its future effects on the age structure of the population. The government now realizes this and a relaxation in the child ration has resulted.

Until the reforms, unemployment was not a problem for the Chinese economy. Rural economic activities were organized taking the labour force as a given. Rather than unemployment, the pressure of the population on the available land and poverty were, and still are, the major problems in the countryside. In the urban areas, the state sector was the principal source of employment. The restriction on migration kept a check on the growth of the urban labour force. The practice of sending urban youth to the countryside and the maintenance of a huge standing army reduced the problem of absorbing the new entrants to the labour force. The control on migration remains, but a number of other factors have changed. With the emphasis on improving the efficiency of the state sector, the growth of employment there is now restricted. The size of the army has been reduced and the urban youth sent to the countryside during the Cultural Revolutionary period have been allowed to return. The result is the problem of absorbing the new entrants into the employed labour force. The government's assumption is that the non-state sector (the urban collective sector), now freed from restrictions, will take care of the problem. As Bonnin and Cartier point out, urban unemployment is a problem in China. But it is nowhere as serious as it is in other developing economies. And the main reason why it is not larger is the restriction on the migration of population from the countryside to the cities. In fact, in some of the cities it has created the reverse problem of labour shortage.

Previous investments and works, as well as continuing constraints such as those of transport and the location of key economic areas, set the limits and the pace of the reforms. There are also ideological and political constraints as well as spurs to the current transformation of China. In Chapter 1, Yves Chevrier gives a broad view of the transformation and its political implications. The view is comparative, historical and necessarily takes in both urban and rural China. The subsequent chapters on more closely specified topics each provide their own perspectives on the extent and limitations of the transformation. And the preface and opening chapters of Volume 2 provide further comparative and historical overviews.

1 NEP and Beyond: The Transition to 'Modernization' in China (1978–85)

Yves Chevrier

NEP minus non-NEP = modernization?

Since Deng Xiaoping snatched the Chinese leadership from Hua Guofeng in December 1978, China's economic reforms have gone hand in hand with demaoization. And they have gone much further under this banner than Khrushchev's reforms ever did under that of destalinization. That is to say that Deng's political and ideological return to orthodoxy, as it existed in China during the 1940s and 1950s, has been coupled with structural changes unparalleled in the Soviet Union or, for that matter, in China before 1978.

To be sure, none of the elements of this breakthrough in the previous Soviet-style or Chinese practice of economic reform is unprecedented. Deng's 'readjustment' (*tiaozheng*) and 'reform of the economic structure' (*jingji tizhi gaige*) has unfolded along three main axes: 1) rural reforms; 2) Western trade, financial and technology transfers; and 3) industrial and urban reforms. China, the Soviet Union, Yugoslavia, the Soviet East European satellites, Cuba and Vietnam, have all explored these paths (Hussain, 1983 and Knight, 1983). But whereas they shuffled along and stopped short of any coherent achievement, Deng's policies – for all their shortcomings, compromises and counter effects, have created a *set* whose scope, depth and range of implementation is unmatched, except perhaps in tiny Hungary or breakaway Yugoslavia. And what is more, these reforms have not stopped at systemic changes. Ten years after Mao 'went to see Marx' (as he was fond of saying), they have begun to change the face of Old China.

This change is perhaps deeper than the transformations brought about by Maoism during the first thirty years of the People's Republic. Maoist policies, and the backlash that followed them, *de facto* froze and preserved old structures and old ways, especially but not exclusively in the countryside. Mao was certainly as adamant as Stalin in his determination to destroy them, in order to make way for the New Man and Woman. But the edge of Maoism was blunted, if only because more than four Chinese out of five were kept out of the cities and the modern sector of the economy. The sweeping impact of Stalinism in the Soviet Union had much to do with the addition of a stark modernization drive to the generalization of a totalitarian rule. This generalization was 'the one leg' on which Maoism walked in the countryside and it was hamstrung by economic constraints, peasant inertia and cadre adhesion to local communal interests. In the cities and within the intellectual and bureaucratic élite, the patriarchal structure of authority (to quote only one example) betrayed the lingering shadow of the past. China's societal sluggishness was one factor (among many) of the 'cultural' leap in the Cultural Revolution: the shadow was to be erased in spite of inappropriate social and economic trends.

The ancient social structures and the tradition-oriented mix of old and Maoist ways, are now exposed to the disruptive influence of the reborn market economy, as well as city and Western-oriented models. To be sure, the relaxation of controls started by giving them a new chance. Old China is coming back to the fore – but perhaps only to die for good. In Skinner's words (1985): 'It is almost as if China's pragmatic leaders were letting commercial capitalism run its course in the countryside, bringing the economy very quickly to where it would have been had the Maoist experiments not intervened.' In many ways, Deng's policies – not just his economic reforms – have bridged the gap. China's society and development were blocked by Mao's failed attempt at socialist construction and uninterrupted revolution. Modernization, on the other hand, builds on historical continuities.

This process of historical rebirth and transition between old and new is a politically significant process, whereby society is coming back to life. Chinese society is still far from being fully-fledged and integrated, with independent economic élites. But it is no longer part of the power structure, or crushed by it. Whatever their economic significance, Deng's economic reforms, bolstered here by the post-Mao return to the rule of law, as well as other non-economic reforms, did alter the balance of the regime. Since the mid-1950s, Chinese society was not so much beheaded – deprived of its natural economic élites (by the land reform and collectivization drive) – as kept lifeless because it was deprived of economic blood at the infra-capitalist layers of the socio-economic pyramid (in Braudel's architectural view of the economic and social order). Although the imposition of a Stalinist-type ideological and organizational monism was marred at rural grassroots levels by lack of support for a complete modernization drive, Maoism did achieve party domination of the whole and, most particularly, of the urban nexus, through economic as well as political means.[1]

Deng Xiaoping has now taken the risk of discarding this weapon, because it has proved unable to achieve the other goal of communism: that of economic growth and country-strengthening which goes beyond mere party-building and political control. He needs to treat society *as it is* as a partner where Stalin and Mao viewed it as a dangerous challenger and saw social transformation as the prime lever of economic progress (with differing points and degrees of emphasis).

Using capitalist means, however, does not necessarily mean discarding socialist ends. There exists a median term, whereby the latter can be obtained through a careful sifting of the former: an up-to-date version of the Tongzhi self-strengtheners' strategy, whose motto was *Zhongxue wei ti, Xixue wei yong* (take Chinese ways as the basis and Western learning as means), often rendered, in Deng's China, as *gongchan zhuyi wei ti, zichan zhuyi wei yong* (communism as basis, capitalism as means).

It is possible to read in two ways the resulting post-Mao pattern of historical mending and non-political pluralism aimed at maximizing state initiative for economic development. In a non-communist regime, it would be a clear-cut modernization programme. Within the communist world, it can be viewed as another New Economic Policy (NEP), on the lines of the Soviet experiment of the 1920s and the Chinese version of that experiment in the early 1950s (called the New Democracy).

There is one essential difference, however. The NEP was a political strategy meant to bolster the grip of the party in the wake of the civil war, when the Soviet leadership realized that their dictatorship was suspended in a social and political void (Lewin, 1968). And it was overridden by non-NEP (under Stalin) for the task of modernization, in a climate of pristine ideological faith and virgin enthusiasm for system-building. Hence the efficiency of the Stalinist *mix* (command structure + modernization) in establishing an absolute and unchallenged rule. The fact that this mix was constructed in one country added the unifying power of nation-building to the building of the system: the latter became identified with the former. The victory over Germany and the building of Soviet military power and empire legitimized the whole process in spite of growing frustrations with the economic result of Stalin's construction.

Deng's NEP, on the other hand, is conceived as the very instrument of modernization, not of system-building through modernization: the system, after all, has *already* been built, in spite of the many structural weaknesses in the Chinese building process. Post-Mao China, therefore, is not in the same situation as the Soviet Union at the end of Lenin's life. Neither is it, however, in the position of the USSR at the end of Stalin's rule: the very reason why Deng's reforms could not be restricted to a banal and superficial imitation of post-Stalin reforms.

As with the Soviet NEP, the goal of the reforms has been primarily political. They have aimed at strengthening the party (*and* the system) in the wake of Mao's cataclysmic end. In this sense, the Cultural Revolution and post-Cultural Revolution succession struggles played the part of war communism and the civil war (rather than that of their model: Stalin's Great Terror). In addition, whereas Leninism and Stalinism ended in victory, Maoism backfired in failure. The intra-party criticism that spread in 1978 and after stemmed from a tremendous sense of loss, which reached much wider and deeper than the frustrations voiced against Stalin's or the system's economic shortcomings after 1956, in the 1960s or after Brezhnev and Chernenko's demise. These Chinese frustrations can be summed up in this way: not only is China *not* a rich and strong country because the socialist growth of the industrial economy has failed to modernize the whole, but the system has been built at the *expense* of modernization (Chevrier, 1983).[2]

It would be inaccurate, however, to think that Chinese clocks were set back to pre-Stalin time, giving only a short life expectancy to the new direction that has developed since 1978. Although the theoretical fig-leaf of the 'Four Modernizations' drive, in Deng's version, is definitely NEPian ('temporarily making use of, and adapting, capitalist ways and means to Chinese socialist needs'); although the political, social, economic and even ideological framework of the 1980s often recalls the ill-fated New Democracy model, strategic clocks and historical time seem to have changed. The readily avowed necessity of readjusting and reforming the economic system, as well as repositioning the whole power structure (in relation to society), does not simply translate short-term political and economic difficulties (which are also admitted). It betrays an underlying but unavowed weakness, which is more than ideological wear: the very impossibility of a second Stalinian spurt which, according to party logic – but not to the Chinese historical experience – would be the best cure for these difficulties. The creation of a new legitimacy for the regime in China is a process similar to the one which started after the Great Terror and during the anti-German war in the Soviet Union. But since it rests on a negative, not triumphant, experience, the Chinese process entails a fair degree of 'illegitimate' (but *de facto* legitimized) means: a bitter cup which the Soviet leadership, so far, has succeeded in keeping at a safe distance.

It should not come as a surprise, then, if the *other* path followed by Deng's new economic policy recalls the strategy with which Bukharin opposed Stalin *after* 1927: to continue NEP after NEP instead of resorting to a non-NEP.[3] Bukharin's model for economic regulation and social pluralism within an overall strategy of balanced development and gradual change (as against the imposition of a voluntarist and destructive command structure) rested on key assumptions, which are clearly echoed in the post-Mao Chinese economic policies and economic policy debates. Of paramount importance were the answers to the crucial questions raised by the difficulties (the so-called 'crisis') of the NEP. How to plan? How much planning? How to finance accumulation? What part should social differentiation and dynamics play? And, above all, what to do with the peasantry (Nove, 1969)? Other similarities can be found on the tactical level (as we shall see below), namely in the leading part played by the rural sector in the reformist drive, as well as in the use of Lenin's and Bukharin's commanding heights principle which gives some leeway to the private play and intercourse of economy and society (provided the party retains control of the strategic points which control the whole).

The gradual and pluralistic perspective of Bukharinism was nothing other, after all, than a communist translation of non-communist modernization strategies (such as Bismarck's in Prussia, or the anti-Bakufu forces in Meiji Japan), where state power also led and controlled the overall process of change in spite of, and above, the liberated interplay of economic, social and societal forces (non-centralized or micro-political and domestic institutions).[4]

Bukharin's scheme, however, rested on two interrelated ideological assumptions which raised many questions in the real world of reforms and politics. First was a peasant grassroots capitalism compatible with socialist structures. A head-on contradiction could be avoided, Bukharin believed, since the countryside was not central to the overall political balance of the regime (commanding heights, in other words, were mostly urban strongholds), and as long as the peasant economy provided food and funds for the cities whose growth, in the long run, would solve the problem by drawing to them a large fraction of the peasant population and modernizing those who remained in the villages. Would this very process, however, not reinforce conflicts and contradictions in urban society where they could not be by-passed so easily? What if modernization did not generate more proletarians, as Engels and Kautsky had said, but more urban and rural petty bourgeois – a Bernsteinian 'middle class'? A moot point, Bukharin believed, since the admittedly questionable hegemony of the proletariat in the socio-economic process of growth would be supported by party organization, socialist state-building and an uninterrupted (albeit 'civilized') political and ideological struggle aimed at conquering non-proletarian classes. Because of the profound complementarity between his modernistic outlook and his ideological faith, Bukharin believed that party retrenchment would not disturb the teleology of revolution. The proletariat and the party could play the part of the capitalist bourgeoisie and the central modern state, ensuring their domination over a pluralist, dynamic and altogether compliant polity: a truly socialist (that is, at once proletarian and modern) civil society.

The post-Mao, post-Hua Guofeng Chinese leadership may not share this ideal vision in steering the country away from Mao's rash short cuts and unbalanced emphasis on cultural factors. They believe more strongly in the unabashed dynamics of capitalism, Western capital and technology imports, as well as relying on patriotism and some basic tenets of Confucianism to mobilize the Chinese people around the goals of modernization and alleviate the 'atomizing' effects of recent transformations in family structures and social behaviour. Authoritarian modernization strategies are more readily referred to (in Japan, Hong Kong, Taiwan and the experiments of the Tongzhi era) than Bukharinism. Emphasis is laid on state-building rather than party-building. However, Bukharinism and, for that matter, socialism, are not forgotten. The modernization scheme has to work within the framework of party hegemony. We can safely assume, therefore, that for all practical purposes – and for legitimation purposes as well – Deng Xiaoping's NEP has already gone beyond NEP, not into non-NEP, but into modernization. And the crucial issues of the relationship between the power of the party, state integration and professionalization, as well as those of élite formation and circulation, are far from being solved.

My goal in the following sections is to show that systemic constraints were not such that the modernization process could not have included some more drastic changes than the minor, post-1978, political shake-ups, with some room given to management professionalization and autonomized socio-economic processes. These constraints remain, however, and could halt the whole process or, at the very least, bring about counter effects damaging to both the integrity of the socialist system and the processes of modernization. The last section will look in this light at the difficulties and prospects of the 'New Course'.

Reforms within the System: a Tentative Ecology

Following the 'revolution–restoration' of 1868, the transition from traditional order to modernization in Japan entailed drastic political and organizational changes. Not so with Deng's own revolution–restoration of 1978 which, as we have said, restored communist orthodoxy everywhere except in economic matters (and related organizational areas). In this light, the Chinese experience conforms to the common post-Stalin reformist experience, which appears to have depended on two main factors: a succession at the top providing a (usually narrow and short-lived) political opportunity, in which some factions and established groups find it useful to shake bureaucratic inertia; the resulting reforms grow and survive within the dynamics of the system, which should not be viewed as a frozen monolith. Indeed, far from opposing reforms to system, or society to system, we should look for an historical and systemic continuum in which reforms help build a low-grade organizational and social pluralism. The reforms occupy, legitimize and tend to enlarge a systemic 'ecological niche', which goes a long way towards explaining their initial successes and later fading; the niche is neither large nor capable of much expansion. In sum, reforms and system add up not to a zero sum but to a limited dialectic.

The Chinese record of the past eight years would seem to confirm this analysis. The Chinese breakthrough, however, raises two related questions. The conventional one is: how did the post-Mao reforms grow beyond the 'normal' stage without overthrowing the system (or without being overthrown by the system)? A more difficult issue is to know why the system + reforms dialectics achieved a higher measure of success in China.

A general overview shows that the Chinese reforms and their socio-economic consequences grew by fitting in with the environment, thanks to the concurring acceptance by the system (established power networks and social interests) of certain structural changes up to certain levels. In other words, the mutual acceptance of system and reforms rested on a double basis, one general, one specific. The first basis was the post-Mao decision to retreat from the all-out command approach of Stalinism and Maoism. This allowed social pluralism and ideological withdrawal, exemplified in the introduction of economic levers and market mechanisms within the formerly non-economic sphere of economic organization. The second, more specific, basis amounted to a secondary, or complementary, legitimacy for reforms, built around three main pillars: 1) economic performance and expediency; 2) the appeal to private and group interests within and without the power structure; and 3) the relative harmlessness of the reforms and their consequences to the overall political balance of the system.

The birth and growth of the post-Mao Chinese reforms have much to do with Deng Xiaoping's intra- and extra-party charisma, and with his skill at political manoeuvring. But a good example of Deng's (and his associates') pragmatism is provided by the building of a working consensus around these three pivots. This likewise exemplifies the limits of their pragmatic approach. Indeed, while the consensus seemed to work well from 1978 to 1984 because Deng could buttress his policies against one or two of the pillars when the third one seemed to falter, difficulties have been cropping up since 1985 on all three fronts, resulting in social tensions and renewed political conflicts. While consumer prices have gone up in city markets, urban blue- and white-collar workers have complained about rural wealth and bureaucratic corruption. And while economic performance in agriculture has faltered, industrial growth has faced a rising tide of price inflation, 'blind' investments, trade and budget deficits. In September 1985 the national conference of party delegates heard a bitter indictment of the runaway reforms by an angry Chen Yun. Since then an unadmitted economic readjustment has been under way (coupled with an anti-corruption campaign), although the more reformist groups in the central leadership and their local supporters (*gaigepai*) are far from being tamed.

These difficulties cannot be blamed on failed foresight (as in Zhao Ziyang's meek apology in the spring of 1985), or on the waning of Deng Xiaoping's ascendancy (with the successors of the successors already in place, and even in charge). Clearly, the basis for the initial consensus outside and inside the power structure has been eroded.

A good way to answer the second question – why did post-Mao China achieve more reform than post-Stalin Soviet Union and Eastern Europe – would be to look more closely into the building of this consensus. The Chinese pragmatists' initial reforming success is easily explained by their original approach. Deng's reforms were built gradually, from the bottom up and from the rural periphery to the urban and industrial core – in sharp contrast with the standard practice which, like the system, and in China as well as elsewhere in communist regimes, is urban-oriented and anxious to avoid what Alec Nove (1977) has termed the 'failure of gradualness'.

The Chinese approach emerged in a pragmatic way. From 1978 Deng Xiaoping steered a sinuous course by playing one factor (in the triangular combination outlined above) against the others, depending on political and economic circumstances. When economic difficulties arose at the end of 1980 and during 1981 (with price increases, runaway investment, erosion of state revenue and budget deficits), the Chinese leadership progressively switched to rural reforms and scaled down a rebuilt open door policy to establish a stronger basis for private interests while complying with the basic rules of system acceptance (Chevrier, 1983). In 1984, in the wake of the campaign against 'spiritual pollution', Deng could build on the still unmixed economic performance of these reforms in order to stifle political dissent at the top and launch further reforms in the urban sphere (Schram, 1984).

A few rules of thumb seem to emerge from the Chinese practice beyond the decentralized and trial and error process (*zou yi bu, kan yi bu*) readily admitted by the Chinese authorities and already pinpointed by some Western scholars (Aubert and Chevrier, 1983, Lee, 1986). The basic rule is that, as in guerrilla warfare, reforms advance more where there is more space for them in the political and organizational web of the system. They also take advantage of social support from various segments, avoiding – or retreating from – areas where there is more resistance and/or no support. A second rule, then, becomes apparent. In a mosaic-like, continent-size country, with low state and economic integration, good reforms are divided reforms. The decentralized and marginal approach – exemplified, for instance, in the special status granted to Guangdong or in the relative advance of rural reforms after 1980 – had a structural edge over the centralized and urban orientation of the USSR and Eastern European satellites, at least so long as cumulative economic effects did not overflow the urban core (which happened in 1985), and as long as the centrifugal organizational effects inherent in the structural avoidance process did not threaten party and country unity (a threat also felt in 1985).

Let us pay more attention to the differential analysis stemming from this approach. The conventional wisdom about reforms of the Soviet model is that, although the logic of the command system is monopolistic through and through, some monopolies (such as the production and circulation of ideas and the distribution of power) are more monopolistic than others (like the concentrated control of the economy). Economic demonopolization is therefore conceivable, if not always implemented, with the unavoidable consequence of social autonomizations. But it would seem that the same principle holds true within the economic and social sphere. Economic demonopolization (including rural decollectivization, industrial deplanification, price deregulation, management decentralization, specialization of functions and deconcentration of power) is comparatively easier where it is profitable and safe and, above all, where it is *de facto* prepared for by structural weaknesses in the fabric of the system: gaps in the integration and transformation of the previous social and economic structures and fractures, nodes and conflicts in the bureaucratic command structure.

The balance between the communist system and ancient social patterns, as well as with social formations created by but alienated from the system, is therefore a factor of paramount importance. The fact that a strong peasant society survived the Maoist onslaught was a key component in establishing rural reforms. Another factor is the well-known phenomenon of bureaucratic pluralism (see Waller in Goodman (ed.), 1984). A loose organizational mesh and factional and centrifugal tendencies in the Chinese power network offered good opportunities both for bureaucratic resistance and for by-passing resistance. The system's weaknesses were the strength of the reforms.

In other words, reforms appear to be linked not just to the limits and deficiencies of monopolistic command structures and to differences in the degree of social and bureaucratic integration, but to the manner – certainly not that of a modern centralized state and society – in which bureaucratic and social formations are connected. And just as Chinese guerrilla warfare in the 1930s exhibited a reverse connection to the geography of modernization,[5] so a differential linkage connects the reforms to areas of sharper systemic underdevelopment – or faster erosion. In order to understand how the Chinese reforms succeeded in growing through the armour of the command structure, let us not ask why but where they occurred.

We should not look at reforms from the economic or institutional angle only, and as short-term (if short-lived) phenomena, but as complex symptomatic events pointing to the uneven long-term dynamics of communist systems, including their uneven articulation with the precommunist past. It is usual to make comparative studies of economic and institutional changes as well as bureaucratic and social reactions and compare these to corresponding evolutions in other socialist countries. At this level, the post-Mao experience in China would not appear drastically original, with the sole exception of its rural appendix – the mixture of post-Lenin NEP and post-Stalin (post-system-building) reforms. But to follow the approach suggested here does more justice to each country's specificity in adjusting to – after adapting – the Soviet model. Comparative studies should compare systems rather than reforms *per se*, that is, various levels of society–system and systemic integration over time and between different countries. Finally, it is in this light that we should reconsider the issue of China's originality, beyond sheer tactical skill and political circumstances. Were there more reforms after Mao because there had been less system under him?

Such a comprehensive comparative approach is barely feasible now, because we know too little about the articulation of communist systems with precommunist history. What we can reasonably do is use the Chinese reforms as a way of catching a glimpse of the long-term and more recent dynamics of the system in China, so as to evaluate the prospects of modernization. Because it draws a clear line between cities and countryside by contrasting economic, social and bureaucratic reactions, the argument helps us understand the most salient feature of the immediate post-Mao era: namely, the fact that the reformist breakthrough was a *rural* breakthrough.

Rural Decollectivization: Market or Communal Breakthrough?

This sectoral breakthrough was achieved thanks to the convergence of the three conditions spelled out above: economic performance and expediency, appeal to private interests and the relative lack of damage to the regime's overall political balance. In economic terms the Chinese rural reforms, as NEP policies always do, built on a short-term production and productivity boost. Whereas the large-scale industrial reforms trumpeted after 1978 have run into difficulties (in 1980–81 and in the cities), the 'silent revolution' of *de facto* decollectivization achieved immediate and impressive successes (as indicated in Chapter 4).

Clearly, these results could not have been achieved without the support of the peasantry. By the same token, the decollectivization drive rested on the domestic structure of the ancient rural society, preserved in spite of Mao's attempt to replace it by an *artificial* community pattern. The reforms recognized and gambled upon the institutional failure of collectivization, the major deficiency in Mao's adaptation of the Stalinist monopolistic scheme (Aubert, 1986). The pragmatist leaders could thus replace, in a few years, a low efficiency system of corvée labour, political mobilization and compulsory (albeit hidden) extraction of agricultural surplus by a highly efficient formula of economic incentives appealing to individual households' interests.

Economic expediency was further displayed in the dismantling of the quota system (for compulsory grain purchases) in 1984–5, when the peasants – who had formerly been reluctant sellers because of low official prices – flooded government purchasing agencies with more grain bought at higher (subsidy) prices. The price reform in urban markets in 1985 was the direct outcome of the two-stage rural reforms (first land tenure, then distribution networks), with the government switching the burden from the state budget to urban consumers (who do get food bonuses, however).

If we look at the political dynamics of the rural reforms, the same rule of expediency, the same convergence between party power and peasant private interests seems to have prevailed. I need not emphasize that party power means the interests of the anti-Hua Guofeng, pro-Deng Xiaoping coalition which came together in 1978 but had been in the making for a few years, even before Mao's demise. The rural breakthrough was made possible not only because factional struggles occurred at the top, but because, given the loose geography of China's bureaucratic integration, factional politics became oppositional provincial policies, with the new policies rejuvenating some provinces (Sichuan as early as 1975, Anhui in 1977) while Hua Guofeng was still practising old Maoist policies from Beijing (Donnithorne, 1984). In the USSR of the 1920s and 1930s neither Trotsky nor Bukharin could have experimented with anti-Stalinist economic policies in the Ukraine or even the Far East.

The picture, however, is not complete if we speak only of peasant support or even of mass pressure. To be sure, the general and moderate will of the pragmatist leadership to restore village society as an economic partner for modernization was not only met, but pushed forward by the peasants as far as it entailed land decollectivization and the dismantling of the quota system. These peasant inroads, however, did not mean that party power was completely routed. A peasant society is a fragmented body, not an integrated whole able to negotiate with or even challenge state power. The peasants could thus push forward without endangering the overall political balance of the system. The same strategic consideration explains official acceptance of social differentiations – the emergence of rich peasants (*funong*) – in the villages. The Chinese rural breakthrough plainly illustrates the truth of the NEP principle: a communist system can live with a non-integrated peasant society but not with an integrated, urban, civil society, which it must not just control, but conquer. Being a society (not a 'dead body' as Montesquieu describes social groups under 'oriental despotism'), but not a modern civil society, has been a decisive asset in the historical breakthrough of the Chinese countryside during the past few years. In sum, the breakthrough has rested on the political advantages of backwardness.

Further evidence that the withdrawal of party power from the villages was voluntary and selective – not an overall retreat – may be found in demographic controls. Central urban authorities (admittedly in the name of the state and modernization, not under the guise of a revolutionary party mobilizing the people for the sake of socialist construction) still find their way not only to villages, but to the very heart of the renewed peasant society: to the family, which they try to reshape. The fact that they must do so in a *rash* way (see Chapter 6) epitomizes the limits of the reform-making convergence between urban power and rural communities, as well as the erosion – or continuing inconsistency – of state authority in the Chinese countryside.

As a result of decollectivization competitive violence has arisen, not merely in local communities (villages, kinship and traditional cults), but with local cadres leading the competition (Perry, 1985). These cadres, who were thought of as potential obstacles to the reforms, thus appeared to go overboard (much as a previous generation did in the wake of the Great Leap Forward), although at higher but still local levels many take advantage of their remaining power financially to pressure villages and wealthy 'specialized households' (*zhuanye hu*).[6] State intervention, when it comes, must come from without. Altogether, the atomization of the lower, local strata of the bureaucracy matches the atomization of peasant communities. Rural voices need intercessors to be heard at higher levels. As Alexander Yanov (1983) has pointed out in the case of Russia and the Soviet Union, they cannot aggregate in power networks able to bear on interest groups and factional struggles at the top. The countryside is a near non-entity on the political chessboard not just because it does not harbour a modern civil society, nor because it is subjugated by a strong, centralized, modern state, but because local leaders do not count in the established political society which runs the premodern command structure.

In sum, the communal dynamism of rural society and the erosion of party power in the villages, as well as the marginal position of the countryside in the distribution of *actual* power, made the cities vs countryside division the prime opportunity for the kind of structural detour – a tactical NEP – which materialized in the early 1980s (Chevrier, 1985). Did Khrushchev's reforms fail because he failed to see the wisdom of peripheral, rural reforms avoiding urban economic difficulties and bureaucratic strongholds (Yanov, 1984)? Did China succeed because of the existence of a rural society (to an extent unknown in the Soviet Union since the late 1920s), and, furthermore, a working, economically dynamic peasant society? Did the NEP fail because Russian peasant communities did not respond with as much enthusiasm?

The Chinese response, however, has not been completely positive. The tendency in Chinese history for society to revolve (and rebound after times of crisis) around local communities, thus by-passing the state, is an asset in decollectivization but a liability for modernization. Not only is state intervention required in the countryside to coordinate production and stimulate productive investments – as the 1985 setbacks have made clear – but also to check the new potential baby boom and to dam the rising tide of rural emigration to the cities. The building of state structures upon societal and cultural transformations is also a necessity. Despite important differences in their bureaucratic and social ecology, urban reforms have laid bare similar weaknesses and point to the same necessity.

Urban Economic Reforms: the Threat of Entropy

Putting rural reforms ahead was a cunning recognition of the system's differential reactions to change. But command monopolies are also *de facto* broken in the urban–industrial core in two ways. The first is linked to gaps and nodes in the chain of command betraying past difficulties in the establishment of the system as well as later wear. The second stems from social reactions to the new economic deal.

De facto deplanification of vast sectors in the command economy is an intrinsic and perennial contradiction in centrally and administratively managed economies on the Soviet model. As Alex Nove has shown for the Soviet Union, the centre never actually manages to control distribution efficiently. Distortions are compounded by the 'parallel economy' (or 'black markets' linking firm managers to local and sectoral bureaucracies) which, in the first place, aims to alleviate them. Berliner (1968), Kornai (1980) and others have shown how the non-economic command structures only function through a mix of low-grade economic and highly developed bureaucratic exchanges (see Volume 2, Chapter 8). Such a situation obviously does not generate a 'capitalist' mentality; but it does maintain some principles and even realities of the market economy, albeit faint and distorted, on the reverse side or in the interstices of the command system.

The return of the 'economy' to its prereform state not only betrays intrinsic limitations in the Stalinist command scheme, it also reflects the history of industrialization, and state–economic integration both before and after party takeover and the start of the 'socialist transformation'. The pattern of socialist industrialization, with priority emphasis on heavy infrastructure and large-scale projects, links the command economy at a high level to heavy industry, while light industry, distribution and services remain less integrated (and less developed).[7] In China, management of these sectors was devolved to a comparatively wide margin of scattered and small units, under both state and collective ownership. In the latter case, these units remained unintegrated in the state sector until the Cultural Revolution.[8] Administrative integration, however, led by no means to economic or even bureaucratic integration. The Maoist worship of decentralization and self-sufficiency contradicted the other and more conventional Maoist emphasis on completing the command structure. Thus, the drying up of urban retail trade and the total extinction of economic incentives and regulators in enterprise management were paralleled by the full blooming of subbureaucratic layers fuelled by the bureaucratic–economic mix outlined above.[9] The ascendancy of comradeship was (contrary to Ezra Vogel (1965), who thought economic transformations and fear made it a deep phenomenon) a surface structure resting on the deep structures of systemic distortions and unabated Chinese traditional networks of kinship and interpersonal relationships (*guanxi wang*).[10]

The differential geography of state and economic organization is paralleled by the uneven sociological integration of the urban population. Beyond the kernel of privileged *zhigong* (wage-earners) integrated in the wealthy *danwei* (work units) in the priority sectors (the bureaucracy, large industrial enterprises, etc.), are circles of lesser integration where the benefits of the *danwei*-man (such as housing) tend to dwindle, together with his employment status. At the periphery of the *zhigong* galaxy, even beyond the far circles of temporary jobs and contractual labour, are the unemployed – especially but not exclusively the young – and cross-border elements, who must rely on kinship, *guanxi* and *banfa* (ways), as well as geographical mobility, to make ends meet. Despite severe constraints on rural emigration and mobility, the post-Mao era has multiplied these elements, fuelling official fears of social unrest. Also out of the *danwei* network, the self-employed (in the private sector authorized by the reforms) appear as a new addition to these 'unorganized' marginals, calling for state organizational efforts.[11]

The striking feature of industrial management and other urban economic reforms is not that they improve the low degree of economic, state and social integration in the cities (although they may develop neglected sectors, such as the services, and provide jobs). Quite the contrary, they thrive in less integrated areas, legitimize and widen the interstitial 'black markets', which they tend to give back to the free play of the market economy although, as we shall see, they do not free them from bureaucratic encroachment.[12] Weakly integrated sectors are more likely to produce management and price reforms which, in fact, reduce but do not deconstruct centrally controlled networks anchored in heavy industry and large-scale projects. Thus, smaller enterprises in these sectors are no longer given input–output quotas, although they still negotiate a production plan with supervising (i.e. local) authorities on a contractual basis integrating 'floating prices' (the margin being assigned by the state). This 'guidance planning' functions with a busy inter-enterprise market which tends to replace the former 'back door' (*hou men*) market.[13] In some areas, such as Sichuan or Wuhan, the difference between fixed, floating and free (market) prices (reflecting the three sectors of integration, from high-degree and centralized supervision and resource allocation to zero planning) gives way to a system of indicative prices (*zhidao jiage*) reflecting the changing relationship of supply and demand on the market under minimal state intervention. In these experiments goods which are centrally allocated at fixed prices under mandatory (national) planning (such as iron and steel products) are allowed to pass on to the market.

However, whereas the tendency is to generalize municipal management of state enterprises, and to multiply these experiments, the inner sanctum of central departments' (*bumen*) supervision of resource allocation and management is far from being dismantled. While many enterprises, some goods and some areas have been granted a certain measure of freedom, many still remain under direct central control. It is difficult to form a precise idea of the range of the reforms given the *piecemeal* Chinese approach.[14] The first spate of reforms in 1979–80 was altogether micro-economic. Synchronized and comprehensive (*tongbu*, *chedi*) reforms (integrating management, price and resource allocation reforms, as well as labour management, welfare and housing reforms) are now the official goal, but on an experimental and local basis.[15] In so far as general impressions are legitimate, it would seem that the evolution in recent years has entrenched the structural fact of urban industrial *de facto* demonopolization rather than the universal application of economic regulations. The prime reason for the pragmatic selection and gradual advance of Chinese urban reforms is that they fit an uneven organizational geography. Alec Nove has long recommended this kind of reform 'by default' as a practical working compromise, allowing information to flow through separate markets in transit to the central planners. Joseph Berliner (1983), who calls it a 'neo-NEP', commends its flexibility in terms of price regulation.

Indeed, the Chinese economy has become more economic, and controls less direct (less political) over the past few years. If shortages and bottlenecks have not disappeared completely, goods are flowing more smoothly. Non-political macro-economic regulation, still in its incipient phase (many consumer prices, and even some industrial prices, have been adjusted by the market), is in jeopardy because of weak central state control over the regulators (taxes, monetary mass, credit, wages) rather than sheer lack of market information. If anything, there are too many markets. From inter-sectoral avoidance (the rise of the rural reforms in 1980–82) to intra-sectoral avoidance (the rise of industrial–urban reforms since 1983), the guerrilla principle (good reforms are divided reforms) has allowed the encirclement and penetration of the urban fortress. The obvious failure of this approach, however, is that the growth of a reformed urban sector tends to erode the system further while reforms are not allowed to go far enough to give a decisive start to a new kind of integration.

We know that the cautious, piecemeal approach could not avoid economic flooding of the market in 1985. Runaway small-scale construction projects, wages, prices and imports increases were fuelled by the rapid swelling of extra-budgetary funds.[16] Easy, decentralized reforms have led to a centralization of difficulties. This development is paralleled by the appearance of acute economic and social imbalances, also made plain in the course of the 1985 crisis. Flexibility seems to have been gained at the expense of integration. By playing the game of the system, the reforms appear to contradict modernization. Thus, many features of the Maoist Great Leap Forward seem to have plagued the economic overheating of 1985. A large number of small urban and rural collective enterprises, created because of the growing availability of funds and local price distortions, are not profitable, are technologically backward and not needed (*RMRB*, 4 October 1985). Subsequent local attempts at further market integration and pressure on floating industrial prices has added a geographical component to the irrationality of the price structure, with developed areas going ahead faster while the others remain under tighter controls.[17] The reduction of central state intervention has aggravated the very regional imbalances which central planning had somewhat alleviated (see Volume 2, Chapter 5). We do not know how the price situation will develop: the obvious example of rural reforms may not serve as a precedent. Central authorities tend to check the rising tide of regional and sectoral imbalances by promoting horizontal links. But reforms which would be essential for the full play of market integration, such as a transgression of the taboos on dismissals and bankruptcy, even though discussed and put into regulation, are far from being implemented. The establishment of a market for manpower is clearly linked to that of a social security net, which means making social reintegration a precondition for economic integration at a time when disintegration is increasing.

Social disintegration is plainly seen, not only in the renewed ascendency of interpersonal relations and the collapse of Maoist comradeship, and the rising influence of the new consumer habits and individualistic societal models of the 'me' (*ziwo*) generation. It is not limited to changing marriage patterns and group attitudes towards old age or to the crime wave which is now reported to engulf not just large cities, but small towns and even villages (where it is often associated by the official media with feudal cults and witchcraft). The new economics of the post-Mao era have generated genuine class tensions; urban blue-collar workers and students, whose wages and benefits lag behind inflation rates, as well as those who come to the cities in growing numbers without being integrated in the *danwei* safety net of employment and social benefits, confront the new wealth of the countryside and bureaucratic profiteering. The fact that no national protest emerged from repeated local clashes in 1985, the fact also that no dissident movement appears to be in the making, despite the modernist outlook of post-1978 literature, is not only testimony to the sophistication of control techniques. It is a clear sign of weak social integration. The power structure is able to divide and rule because urban social groups are divided and so are their protests, geographically, organizationally and politically. The past few years have seen the autonomization of social (as well as economic) agents, not the integration of a modern civil society.[18]

These imbalances can be regarded as a sign of the transitional disorder (pending reorganization) inherent in any reformist process. Indeed that is how they are seen by the most articulate among the Chinese reformists, who have no doubts that only more reforms will counter entropic economic and social trends. Should the 'invisible hand' be trusted so far? A more decisive question, however, is whether it can be allowed to play its part fully. Because economic forces are tied to social development, and social development to the rebirth of economic élites and to pressures to restructure the polity (although not necessarily to democracy and liberalism), the probable answer is a qualified no. At the very least, the issue of systemic constraints – of limited reforms – has to be raised anew, with that of the established polity: the party–state and bureaucratic framework of the reforms.

Expansion of the Bureaucratic Universe

It would be misleading, indeed, to analyse the movements of post-Mao China as the free play of economic and social forces contradicted or restricted by a rigid bureaucratic grid. The grid itself is changing, in ways which only serve to maximize entropic tendencies.

While workers have complied with the expected counter pattern (by pushing wages and bonuses higher and resisting new rules and standards of discipline and productivity), party, state and military cadres, at all levels, have *not* displayed the overall resistance to reforms which analysts expected from their privileged status. They might well have been expected to use their opportunities to act in vertically structured networks articulated through ministerial departments (*bumen*), metropolitan organizations (such as the military) and power channels (the party). But the NEP is supposed to appeal to private interests. It is not supposed to cajole cadres, whose interests are not supposed to be private. In the actual world, however, Chinese local cadres and higher bureaucrats did support the reforms in so far as they realized that the official principle of a planned commodity economy (*you jihua de shangpin jingji*), in which planning retains priority (*wei zhu*), allowed them to keep their privileged positions on the commanding heights while turning to profitable activities in the new sphere of the commodity economy. While social initiatives are indeed restricted by this unequal bureaucratic competition, the economic opportunities of the bureaucracy have been extended far beyond the former black market activities. The Chinese reforms owe much to their indirect appeal to bureaucratic interests and to the connected fact that the Chinese decentralizing process gave more room to local power networks.[19]

To be sure, party and army are expected to give way to state administrators, the rule of law, professional management and technical expertise and even to private ownership (including ownership of knowledge and expertise) and entrepreneurship. But the official goal of deconcentration of power (the specialization of functions within the enduring communist system) has been contradicted by decentralization. Whereas some analysts detect a shift in the overall balance of groups (with the established groups of party, army and ideology giving way to state administrators and professionals), it would seem, as far as we can assess a very complex situation, that actual power has not been taken away from existing power networks below the higher levels of central authorities (where the shift is indeed tangible).

The prime reason for this stability is that cliques and lobbies at local and intermediary levels were of a mixed nature. It is these groups, as entities, using their various connections to power outlets, which tap (by taxes, extortions and other underhand means) a good proportion of the new economic channels and start their own projects, even their own private businesses. The largest fraction of the swelling extra-budgetary funds is thus rechannelled into local ventures, forcing many enterprises to rely on bank loans in order to fulfil their contracted investment and production goals. If anything, adding the economy to the system of bureaucratic fiat has not resulted in better integration, but in bureaucratic management of the economy through generalized competition.

> In spite of the rectification campaign of 1985 which implemented managers' individual responsibility, factory heads still have to enter the competition if they want to assert their authority. They must use their state-given rights and become part of the locally based and often faction-ridden informal government of the enterprise, or face opposition and even demotion (Chevrier, 1986b).

Detrimental to economic integration, this bureaucratic competition is responsible for redundancy, low profitability – and corruption.

Corruption is not due to a sudden ethical collapse, as the Chinese central authorities would have us believe. The price to pay for divided reforms, it should be read as a chemical, not moral, phenomenon, translating the emergence and growth of previous black market activities and, in China, the horizontal, centrifugal strength of the communities (structured by kinship and *guanxi*) as opposed to the lasting weakness of the vertical state. Whereas bureaucratic resistance is supposed to follow the lines of integration in an industrial organization shaped by the Stalinist model, bureaucratic acquiescence is structured by the age old defective state–society integration in China: the feudal (*fengtian*) tradition of rapprochement between local lords and communities confronted and contained by the bureaucratic estrangement fostered by the imperial government in the name of the common good (*gong*). Multi-purpose interest groups, of course, are not unknown in the West. In many ways, enterprises where workers' inertia (to raise bonuses and keep productivity low) is effective only through the complicity of unions and management, could be described as nodes of communal solidarity.[20] What the Chinese reforms have brought to light, however, is the superficial hold of the imported state model and the historical deficiency of indigenous supra-communal structures, be they state or society. Although we are mainly concerned here with urban networks, we must recall the fact that China has remained predominantly agrarian. When the Stalinist model was implemented by Mao with lasting communal features and low rates of urbanization and exchange activities (despite a high rate of industrial growth), this only compounded the legacy of history.

With hindsight, it is apparent that the retreat of central command structures was organized in compliance with this legacy. The first wave of reforms, which granted rights (of autonomy) to enterprises in 1979–80, slowed down from the end of 1980 because central authorities were faced, among other difficulties, with declining revenues, a circumstance which led to the spread of fiscal and contractual reforms as a sounder basis for further advances (which actually took place in 1984–5). The primary purpose of the generalization in 1982–3 of the taxation of benefits in lieu of remittances to the state (*yishui daili*) and of the industrial responsibility system based on contracts (*gongye jingji zeren zhi*) was not so much to consolidate enterprise autonomy as to guarantee central state revenues in the wake of the profit-sharing reforms. Central authorities thus secured stable revenues and, increasingly through the contractual links of guidance planning rather than through a shrinking imperative plan, what they deemed essential investment and production, leaving the remaining share – that is a sizeable part of the recent economic growth – to the unorganized competition of infra-state communities and groups. (The same case could be argued by analysing, in investment channels, the concentration and reduction of state resources on key projects, as if central planners took account in advance of uncheckable excesses by local units managing extra-budgetary funds.) We shall see that this pattern, which recalls the attitude of the central authorities in late imperial times, is only one side of the picture – state-building being the other side or, rather, the long-term strategy. Once the tactical step was taken, however, the entropy of the bureaucratic universe could not but tend towards a maximum. Disintegration, under the circumstances, translates as bureaucratic erosion and, historically, as dynastic decay.

Although widespread (as widespread as the myriad intersections of the bureaucratic grid with the new or renovated flows of economic activity), competition evidently depends on the actual opportunities, for individuals in local and/or functional groups, to enter and control the economic field. Thus, it has been easily won by the parts of the establishment most closely connected to the richest pools of activity (such as the Special Economic Zones in the south) and to the higher strata of the *nomenklatura*. Indeed, the magnitude of business (licit and illicit) seems to be in direct proportion to the status of patronage, with central party and state nomenklaturists, as well as the offspring of high level cadres, playing the essential role of intermediaries. It is only by means of these far-flung connections that vast business networks can flourish beyond the narrow limits of divided markets and local protections (see for instance *Zheng Ming* 4, 1 April 1985). Could money – big money and influence – do what more diffuse social changes in the cities, sectoral protests, and even economic transformations in the countryside, do not seem to do – that is provide some reintegration outside the system's framework along the horizontal and vertical mesh of the counter market? Are we witnessing the birth of a capitalist élite, however bureaucratized? Is this possibility reinforced by the open door policy which has brought in capital and capitalist entrepreneurs from the Chinese overseas communities, while some former 'national capitalists' (or their scions) are allowed to resume management of their former businesses?[21]

We should not make too much of this evolution. The open door policy is a divided reform – Deng Xiaoping saw to it that it would be piecemeal and allowed to spread only in an insular fashion – ruled because it is divided and divided because it is ruled. However much change it brings to the ruling bureaucracy and to certain regions such as the Pearl River delta and Guangzhou near Shenzhen and Hong Kong, capitalism in the kernels of change has to change even more in order to adapt to the rules of the game: much more so than with bureaucratic capitalism elsewhere in the Far East (e.g. Taiwan). Hong Kong, a new square soon to be added to the Chinese chessboard and already fallen under its influence, is undergoing a covert but telling normalization.

The 'one country, two systems' approach should not be regarded as a blueprint for allowing the coming of age of a new capitalist élite. The only legitimate élites recognized beyond the party are experts whose groups, in the post-Mao New Deal, are viewed as major vehicles of the party and party policies. For this reason, one of the priority goals of the 1985 rectification campaign was not just to promote experts in economic management and state administrations, but to integrate them into the party within an unaltered framework operating according to different rules. Such recruitment, of course, results in changes. These, however, are not detrimental to party identity and even contribute to the stabilization of the system as long as the party code is painstakingly maintained. Stalin's aim, when he conceived the grand design of drafting the Soviet technical intelligentsia, was to bring it closer to the proletariat. In fact, he brought it closer to the regime, the outcome being party gentrification and bureaucratization of those drafted but without any deep structural change in the system's basic framework (Bailes, 1978). For all the official talk of capitalism, the likely strategy of the post-Mao leadership, including the more overt reformists, is to organize such a Stalinist–Brezhnevian circulation of élites, even though they resort to a non-Stalinist mode of modernization allowing a decisive autonomization of the economy. The task of maintaining party identity through change will therefore be more difficult since bureaucratic structures will have to be kept separate from economic structures – a most useful feature, which was instrumental in preserving bureaucratic hegemony over merchant trading and merchant society in late traditional China.[22]

Nowadays in China, these limits to élite formation and circulation are a direct consequence of systemic constraints. The Chinese bureaucracy is not just a bureaucracy eager to control and to squeeze. It does stem from a command structure and a totalitarian power (however abated) which not only controlled but destroyed the former social formation, especially at élite levels. The inheritors, with their different goals and methods (and even bureaucratic manpower) may have no reason to reconstruct the ancient social pyramid fully. But they do have some reasons for allowing partial, spatially and structurally limited, reconstructions. I believe that, in order to understand the overall social evolution in post-Mao China, we should link several facts: systemic pre-emption of the social field, bureaucratic invasion of the economy, partial reconstruction of a capitalist élite whose goal, obviously, is not to restore a class, but whose ecological niche is, once again, the uneven integration of the system, not integrated structures outside the system. Speaking of a capitalist transition in post-Mao China is as much a misrepresentation as speaking of a modern civil society in Chinese cities.

Indeed, capitalism, even bureaucratic capitalism, are probably inadequate terms for describing the warped social formation the system has allowed to grow out of a divided and congruent market economy. Capitalism means a radically new kind of integration of state, society and the economy. But the Chinese reforms are only adding some socio-economic layers generated by market relationships to a Stalinist social formation (which, as we saw, lacked neither infra-economic practices, nor non-socialist societal structures). There is no reason to believe that the command structure, once it has been built, cannot live without its economic trappings, provided structural social and political limits (organizational more than ideological constraints) are respected. Are there further reasons, in the longer history of modern China, for believing that a transition from a non-economic to an economic society *must* lead to the development of a modern state and to capitalism? Post-Mao China is best understood as still belonging to the conventional dynamics of socialist systems. Interests and groups formed or multiplied and enlarged by the new economic deal are also best understood in the light of bureaucratic group formation and relative autonomy, that is within the framework of bureaucratic pluralism: the counter system consubstantial to and coeval with the system.

All together, the growth of the reforms within the system, and the limits set to this growth by the system, remind us of the economic development as well as increased social mobility and pluralism within the stable framework of Confucian China. As exemplified in the Ming–Qing dynastic cycles, the main risk entailed by such a situation lies in the contradiction between the requirements of stability and the logic of development, not between the power structure and a (questionable) civil society (or, in present terms, between socialism and an equally questionable capitalism). And the likely outcome is bureaucratic erosion by intra-power competition and the prospect of a dynastic restoration – behind shut doors – rather than modernization.

Thus, post-Mao China displays not so much a vertical, one-dimensional confrontation, as horizontal, multi-layered conflicts detrimental to state efficiency and unity as much as to party authority, which, indeed, is imperilled more by its own inbred weaknesses than by a social challenge *per se*. Dynastic decay, however, is a distant possibility. The present power structure is far more resilient (although hardly less flexible) than its imperial counterpart. Because China is a proud sovereign nation, the crisis of socialist values is less destructive than the crisis of Confucianism at the end of the Qing dynasty, when the urbanized and modernized élites created power networks of their own before turning against the embattled empire. In fact, despite their failure to check the centralization of difficulties in 1985, decentralization and division are still useful. The Chinese mosaic does fragment protest as well as incorrect tendencies, and while it also divides and distorts state policies and agencies, the party still remains the unique overall network.

The political order created after 1949 is, therefore, not threatened by imminent collapse. But it is undermined, at a time when ideology has lost its power, precisely where the communist regime had fared better than the other regimes which tried but failed to modernize China from the end of the 19th Century: that is, state unification. The Chinese authorities, then, could be content with managing the status quo by rectifying what needs rectification, by checking economic growth, bureaucratic and social entropy, and above all by plugging holes in party dams. China would in this way fail to achieve in a decisive, Japanese or Taiwanese manner, the elusive goal of modernization. It would after all be one of Stalin's heirs, although at the upper stratum of reformist practice. The post-Mao era, then, would amount to a transition not to modernization *per se*, but to an economically regulated (and corrupted) bureaucratic command structure: the structural equivalent to the Ming–Qing dead end in developmental terms.

There are signs, however, that the regime is not content with keeping abreast of the reforms, that is, keeping the reforms within its margin of flexibility – giving them their ecological niches. Modernization is still on the agenda. But since an integrated economy and society would be detrimental to the system, and since modernization has been historically linked to strong states and strong ideologies – not just to dynamic economies and integrated societies – where can modernization come from? How is it to be achieved and mastered?

State-building: the Challenge of Modernization

According to this dilemma, the first rule of modernization stems directly from the premodernization logic – the privilege as well as the power – of the system. If the system's weaknesses are the reforms' strengths, its strength is the reforms' weakness. Social, organizational brakes, therefore, will be applied to *their* power to integrate a civil society, a modern polity. Above all, free play will not be given to economic forces, if only to check the growth of centrifugal and proto-capitalist tendencies. The 1985 measures to scale down capital construction investments, the pledge to strengthen central state controls in the new Five-Year Plan, should be viewed in the light of a socio-political (not just economic) stop and go, alternating phases of relaxation (*fang*) and restriction/repression (*shou*) in line with Keynesian attempts at macro-economic regulation. Thus, without going to an all out reversal (which *ad hoc* steps taken since 1985 were not), central authorities will see to it that unhealthy tendencies are controlled and that the party, while it oversees modernization, remains a communist organization, by using the available techniques of population control and management of cadres (such as rectification of work style, anti-corruption and anti-pollution campaigns, etc. – also on a stop and go basis). Although some of these measures (against crime and demographic misbehaviour) are very harsh, the strategy is not to eradicate deviance, as it was under Mao, by pursuing utopian changes in human nature and society. However, since the more realistic transformations of modernization have to be both controlled and pressed (family planning has to be pressed because society is not changing fast enough), and since some of their consequences may threaten the balance of power, I would agree with scholars who conclude that cycles of relaxation and restriction are the only way pragmatically to implement authoritarian societal transformations and to reconcile the monistic ideological roots of the system with social pluralism.[23]

The global regulation of the system under Deng Xiaoping's new deal must follow a cyclical pattern as it did under Mao, but for other reasons. Overseeing modernization also means a permanent, if selective, disengagement. For the party must of itself do what economic and social forces may not do (are not allowed to do and/or not capable of doing), and what Chinese history has not done yet: nothing less than building a modern state (and a modern society, since state-building, through the state–society relations, addresses societal and even collective mental structures, beyond central state structures). In other words, the party–state system should become an integrated state–society complex under flexible party supervision. Hence the crucial role played by the scheme to separate party and state affairs and to integrate expertise within party ranks, so as to modernize the bureaucrats and enfranchise the vanguards of modernization. As the Chinese media repeat endlessly, the party must 'take the lead in mastering the skill of modernization'; to make sure that it does so while remaining the master, it must co-opt the technocrats. State-building reforms have therefore overtaken economic reforms *stricto sensu* and overtaken measures aimed at party and population control as strategic priorities of the regime. This evolution had clearly emerged by 1985, when reforms aimed at reshaping the party and creating new socio-mental patterns to supersede traditional communal structures (such as the promotion of law, the upgrading of the education system, the commercialization of housing, etc.), formed a first round of administrative and 'deconcentration' reforms, which institutionalized the state–party functional split in rural *xiang*, urban enterprises, intellectual life, research and education.

Economic reforms were the easy step in party redeployment on the commanding heights. That state-building would be the difficult but even more necessary step to be taken now, in the perspective of modernization, may seem somewhat paradoxical in the country of statecraft. The Chinese state, however, including the post-1949 restored state (since Maoism, as we saw, enhanced communal structures both as a means for the socialist transformation and as a way for the precommunist community patterns to duck it), is an old-fashioned command structure which never integrated the myriad communities which have supported it for two millennia. In the resulting balance, which was far from unsatisfactory as long as developmental and international pressures were not too strong, central controls were at times properly asserted (the ascending or active phase in the pattern of dynastic cycles), but it was not merely by chance that centrifugal tendencies, organizational decay and central paralysis were recurrent. The enemy of modernization in post-Mao China is not just bureaucratic inertia, or the iron law of the system (which precludes the free rise of capitalist élites), but the legacy of the past, in which communal societal and cultural patterns resting on the patriarchal links of lineage have been closely intertwined with recurrent interventions from above, at times strong and destructive, but never sustained enough or targeted enough to give a decisive historical edge to the state against communal entropy.

To some historians, this legacy is linked to the ritual rather than legal tradition of the Chinese political culture, which created an administrative order, not a political construction (see Vander-Meersch, 1965). Nor should we equate this administrative command structure to Wittfogel's oriental despotism: the traditional Chinese state allowed much space for decentralized socio-economic relationships and micro-politics not only beyond its control, but beyond its concerns.[24] Nor should we believe that the integrated societies of the Western nation states developed on their own. They may have grown against the state, but they did not grow without it. That is, certain societal, juridical, political and economic patterns shaped them and the state. What the Chinese authorities are trying to do is to create conditions for these patterns to grow in China.[25]

In their attempts at building the bedrock of modernization, and at checking the concomitant rise of entropy, the Chinese authorities must face another challenge:

the utter collapse of the ideological link, leaving the organizational party–state as the only trans-communal structure. In other words, they cannot rely on history-given ideological integrators, such as nationalism in Prussia or the *tennō sei* (imperial system) in Japan, which were so instrumental, together with strong states, in successful modernizations. The post-Mao leaders must build the culture of modernization at the same time as they build a new Chinese state and society. Socialism remains a code of party identity and behaviour, as well as the generic code (a socialist spiritual civilization) under which the new culture should take shape; patriotism is a major element, in connection with China's rediscovered maritime and open door traditions, as exemplified in Zheng He and Sun Yat-sen.[26] But patriotism, an important raw material, and a working slogan for the party as the embodiment of national unity,[27] hardly qualifies as an ideological *integrator*. Some would claim that Confucianism may be called on to fill the void.

Confucian moral community ideals are indeed used in order to alleviate the social tensions and societal disruptions of old age and marriage customs generated by the new economic policies,[28] as well as to control the potential contradictions between unhealthy trends centred on self-interest and the ultimate socialist order. So are Confucian *state* ideals – public virtue (*gong*) vs selfishness (*si*) – promoted in order to castigate official corruption and centrifugal tendencies. That traditional morality is put to use in order to place the whole above the parts, or to save the parts from a painful disintegration process, is natural enough since Confucianism has been recognized (against Weber's view) by many historians and sociologists – and now in China[29] – as a powerful cohesive factor capable of binding together traditional societies during the accelerated modernizations of the East-Asian late-comers (such as Japan and Taiwan). Given the defective situation of the state in China, however, is Confucianism a better integrator than patriotism?

It would appear from the Japanese experience that a strong state was more necessary for Confucianism to perform its cohesive role than Confucianism was necessary to build a strong state. While weaknesses in the pre-Meiji Japanese state may have been more feudal in the European sense of the word than community-based, it is questionable that Japanese Confucianism allowed a higher measure of state–social integration, as some historians suggest (see Morishima Michio, 1985). If not structured by a strong, cohesive framework, Confucianism fosters disintegration more than it checks it. Japan's state-building during the Meiji era achieved such a strong framework by relying on administration, conscription and education reforms, as well as the all important restoration of the imperial system (*tennō sei*) at the centre of the national polity (*kokutai*). Traditional rural communities and communal structures found a new equilibrium, although not without painful adjustments, in this renewed framework, and could efficiently contribute to Japan's modernization.

Being devoid of any historical assets on a par with the Japanese national honour (*kokutai*), post-Mao China must build the state more at the expense of the traditional communal pattern. In this light, the social and mental strategy of the Chinese modernization drive becomes clearer: a more modern economy, based on individual contractual relationships, demands a better integrated society based on educated and disciplined individual entities. The reforms and measures already quoted (individualization and contractualization of economic relationships within a legal frame, *ad hoc* upgrading of education, population and cadres control techniques and campaigns) all point to this goal. Beyond these, the major state–society building policy – given the objective and systemic constraints on economic development in post-Mao China – may very well include the authoritarian remodelling of the Chinese family and the replacement of the age old pair of kinship and local community by the new pair of nuclear families and the country-wide state. This transformation is of paramount importance; successive marriage laws and campaigns to emancipate women have only just started, mainly in the cities. It would be the consequence of the voluntarist family planning programme initiated during the 1970s and relaunched after 1979 in an even more voluntarist fashion with the one child policy.[30]

It is worth noting that, contrary to conventional assumptions on the linkage between modernization and liberalization, the attempt to destroy traditional communal links and replace them with the nuclear family and the forces of the market – in a modern nation state – does not necessarily bring decline in the power structure, but transforms the state into one less crippled by communal disruptions and more capable of intervention. This state-making process relying on a voluntarist demographic/societal policy, as well as on emancipated but still controlled economics, can go a long way in modernizing the countryside without a cataclysmic rural to urban shift. Controlling such a shift not only calls for state intervention, as already suggested. It is part of the same authoritarian strategy. Social and mental patterns should be changed with the development of small towns and industries. It will be interesting to measure the impact of this programme as opposed to the Maoist scheme (of small rural industries), which worked within the artificial solidarities of the commune system and did not radically alter the ancient societal patterns of the Chinese countryside.[31] The planned development of a state social security programme should also be seen in this light. The new system would not serve obvious economic and social purposes only. It would of course help enterprises to get rid of surplus manpower, and small collective and private firms to hire more freely, by providing welfare, unemployment, and retirement benefits; it would also help local state authorities to integrate the marginal elements. But more covertly, the whole system of social protection would be moved from the state as communities (enterprises, workshops, *danwei*) to the state as state (through municipalities and provinces). Urban tax and housing reforms should be related to this conception in order to be understood properly.

In more general terms, the economic part of the global regulation already alluded to clearly depends on a better efficiency of macro-economic regulators whose control is necessary for the satisfactory implementation of Keynesian economics. One of the top priorities of the Seventh Five-Year Plan, connected to the objective of bringing economic growth under control, is precisely to organize the transition from deplanification to a state-controlled market economy, where prices, investments, etc., would faithfully respond to the 'stop' and 'go' signals given by central authorities through the manipulation of taxes, bank rates, monetary mass, wages, etc. Moving from direct (or political) controls to market regulations (indirect or economic controls) does not imply the free play of Adam

Smith's invisible hand, but the sort of market economy under flexible state intervention which the Chinese authorities seem to identify with the French model of planning. Given the unsatisfactory results of the earlier total planning in terms of economic coordination and state structures, and considering the counter effects of the decentralized withdrawal of central authorities, the successful shaping of such a mix would be a decisive achievement of the new state-building strategy.

However, routinization, ritualization and inertia already plague the ideological and even organizational sides of the Chinese modernization drive. Besides the perennial problem of the economy, whose disorderly growth is far from being tamed, good examples would be the anti-corruption campaign, the promotion of moral heroes, and campaigns to discipline and improve the morality of the Chinese people by emphasizing the three loves (motherland, socialism, party) and five stresses (discipline, morals, manners, decorum, hygiene), or setting apart an 'anti-spitting month' or a 'socialist courtesy month' which seem neither more efficient, nor more efficiently promoted, than parallel moves in the Soviet Union or similar features in Chiang Kai-shek's 'New Life' movement during the 1930s.[32]

Actual transformations will thus depend mainly on the linkage between authoritarian societal building (centred around demographic controls, education and repression) and the slow progress of state-regulated market relationships. Once the traditional communal horizon is by-passed, patriotism can effectively displace parochialism. The measures based on traditional community ideals can be retained, even after the transitory stage is over, as necessary ingredients for forging new patterns of authority and responsibility. Ancient ways will not be allowed to die if and as long as they are useful to state-building. In this perspective, the routines, rituals and cycles which seem hardly useful to state-building appear as essential elements helping to shape an adequate polity by preventing the unwelcome growth of the mental and political consequences of the desired individualization in social and economic relations. At the beginning of the century, in his blueprint for China's modernization (borrowed from Western and Japanese models), Liang Qichao called for a more active and independent public spirit while private (kinship and interpersonal) relations were to remain structured by the traditional community ideals of reciprocity and hierarchy central to the Chinese national character (*guoxing*).[33] The post-Mao transition to modernization – that is from system-building to state-building – depends on the reverse: active and independent private family members, consumers and tax-payers as workers, peasants, entrepreneurs, writers, artists, experts, officials; dependent and submissive citizens.

Conclusion

Since 1978, Chinese economic reforms have filled and exhausted the fault lines created in the borrowed Soviet model by the communal patterns and weaknesses in state–society integration born out of the Chinese past and unwittingly furthered by Maoism. They have not really risen above the resulting mix (the system in Chinese terms). It is not surprising, then, that the second stage of reforms which was delineated in the midst of the crisis of the first stage, in 1985, should address this crucial matter in non-economic terms. The post-Mao leadership has come to conceive modernization as a comprehensive process of state-building carrying with it self-coordinated powers to transform, integrate and regulate, to check disorders inherent in the reorganization stage as well as to prevent possible challenges to the ultimate socialist order due to the growth of new economic and social forces. This strategy gives a new breathing space to the reforms, no longer within the system, but not necessarily against it, although the goal is to transform the system's performance and Chinese society more deeply than Mao had been able to do.

There may be some wisdom after all in the official claim that the Chinese reforms do not imperil the former political status quo because the country is so distant from its Western and Japanese models, as long as we take the post-Mao reforms at face value, that is as a modernization programme, now centred on transferring authority and controls from system to state. State-building reforms tower above the spectacular but localized re-emergence of capitalist ways and even of some segments of the bourgeoisie. And without them, the prospect of a sharp increase in per capita income by the beginning of next century would be meaningless. The real issue, then, is not the capitalist transformation of China. It is whether the present power structure can build a state and a society no longer, or at the very least less, based on and bound to extra-state solidarities and interests. In principle at least, no system-related action should interfere with party–state relations, as they do for the articulations of party and state with socio-economic factors. But state-building is not system-building. The accumulated weight of the system did not hinder the decentralization process as long as it meant bureaucratic management of a thriving economy. What if the statecraft of modernization keeps the new economy but changes the rules of the game and even transforms some of the players? What if groups and interests centred around the party do not function within the state structure, or if the new state–society integration, however authoritarian, does not sufficiently respect the privileged status of the party and its ideological monopoly. These contradictions can be resolved, with tactical flexibility and some delay, because the strategic goal does not mean more economic and social freedom for the Chinese, but more state intervention (although of a different kind) and a better integrated society.

Yet, neither the authoritarian nature of these policies (which are unabashedly voluntarist in demographic matters), nor the pragmatic management of contradictions, have been able to preclude bitter power struggles at the top. To be sure, much room is left within the formula for strong disagreements, such as the ones dividing the leadership on the extent of state controls and even on their nature (that is, in the last analysis, on the role individualized economic relations and self-interest should play in a socialist system). Factional struggles are not absent from modern states and polities. It would be foolish to consider them as a sure sign of failure. And, I suggest, it would be helpful to regard them in the light of state-building. The ideological cleavage between reformists and conservatives is not an opposition of capitalism to socialism; the reformists are far removed from the concerns of Western, society against state, liberalism. But it does seem to oppose those who are ideologically within the perspective of state-building, to those who are not (or not completely, or not yet). Such a classification should be completed, of course, by localizing the actual status of individuals and groups in relation to the new distribution of influence and affluence entailed by the party–state reorganization. From this vantage point, the situation is much more complex, if not hopelessly confused.

Yet the policy alternative is clear enough. One should therefore witness the gradual emergence of either a sustained policy of state-building requiring further reforms on all fronts (but not excluding the sort of political and economic stop and go which has prevailed since 1978) or, given the amount of change already introduced, a cycle of bureaucratic erosion and reaction leading to a stronger and longer stop. It would seem that the liberating shock of demaoization and some hard facts – population pressure, economic backwardness and state inadequacies – marginally favour the state-builders in their confrontation with historical liabilities against the more cautious approach of the so-called conservatives. Whatever comeback they make should in any event be viewed more in the manner of Liu Shaoqi than as a Maoist restoration.

Will Deng Xiaoping's demise provide the opportunity if not for a decisive reaction, at least for a reassessment, possibly connected to a rapprochement with the USSR? At any rate, one is far from Bukharin's ideal vision of history and society marching forward of their own accord towards the utopian paradise of a proletarian modernity. One is equally far from the goal, and even from some of the crucial means (such as the liberation of capitalist forces, ideological and state integration) of the Meiji breakthrough. Once Mao had become a dead body and symbol (it took two years, from 1976 to 1978, to go from A to Z), reforms were easy enough to initiate: it was playing practice against theory, history against the superimposed model of Soviet communism. Modernization, that is theory against practice, state-building against system conservation and entropy, will be much more difficult.

Notes

1. The substitution of a non-economic command structure for the organic networks built throughout history ranks, together with ideological monism, as the superior weapon of communist totalitarianism, making non-economic totalitarianism weaker in comparison. Some authors think that Nazi Germany and Fascist Italy were not actually totalitarian for that very reason. The case for the failure of the Guomindang to reorganize economy and society in Shanghai between 1927 and 1931 is argued by Fewsmith (1985).

2. The Central Committee's decision on the reform of the economic structures of October 1984 states clearly that, because of the way in which the economy had been planned and managed, socialism had not been able to prove its superiority in China for some thirty years (*Renmin Ribao*, 21 October 1984).

3. As far as it can be known, Bukharin's programme for the continuation of NEP is analysed in Cohen (1974).

4. I am indebted to Stephan Feuchtwang for suggesting this definition of societal forces. Below, I refer to them as interacting, in the Chinese context, within the community framework structured by kinship and interpersonal relations.

5. A point made by Selden (1971).

6. This, of course, counters the official policy of separating party affairs from *xiang* administration and the connected policy of *paying* peasant services. On rural bureaucratic squeeze, see Ts'ai Ming-ch'in (1984). The term 'burden' is used in Chinese sources (*NYJJ*, no. 8, 1983).

7. Here, I must disagree with Dernberger (1982), who argues that 'there is no reason, in theory at least, why the central planners cannot use (their) power to favour agricultural development, increases in the standard of living, light industrial production, investment in social overhead capital, or any other sector they choose.' The limits to the *theory* are of the essence.

8. Tang Jianzhong and Ma (1985) show that weak integration continued despite overhauling attempts during the Great Leap Forward.

9. The case that Maoism did not deter, but increased, back door practices, and indeed replaced socio-economic processes with decentralized bureaucratic processes and micro-politics is brilliantly argued by Walder (1982). See also Shirk (1982).

10. See Gold's criticism and study of *guanxi* (1985). The weakness in Gold's argument, however, is to look at the *present* definition of *guanxi* as a rebirth linked to new economic opportunities. While the new economic activities of the post-Mao period certainly flow through the grid of *guanxi*, as we shall see below, the permanence and prosperity of this grid under the non-economic aegis of Maoism should not be overlooked.

11. This description is admittedly too sketchy. On the differential integration of the workers in the command structure of 'industrial society', see, for an up-to-date analysis of the Chinese case, Roland Lew (1986). On unemployment, see Chapter 8. On 'loose' urban elements, see William Parish and Martin Whyte (1984). Official concern about unorganized self-employed elements in the cities has been voiced, for example in *Liaowang*, 4 November 1985.

12. Such was the case already with the 1979–80 experiment, notably in Sichuan. See Aubert and Chevrier (1982–3).

13. Author's survey of enterprises in Sichuan, October–November 1985 (see Chevrier 1986b).

14. The best index of the *actual* (that is differential) scope of demonopolization is certainly not given by the share of state enterprises in industrial output value compared to that of collective enterprises and individual businesses, enterprises under contract from the state, joint ventures, etc. A better index would be the distribution of the circulation of raw materials and goods between plan and market. National averages, such as the ones found in *Jiage lilun yu shijian* (*Price Theory and Practice*) or *Wuzi guanli* (*Handling of Goods and Materials*), are deceptive, however, because local authorities manage their own additional quotas and because there are wide regional discrepancies in plan/market relationships. See Citoleux, 'Le rôle des prix dans l'allocation des ressources', *Tiers-Monde*, forthcoming issue on the Chinese reforms.

15. The transition from the initial piecemeal approach to the later comprehensive approach is analysed by Halpern (1985) somewhat too optimistically. The author fails to see the regional unevenness of the systematic approach.

16. Extra-budgetary funds are funds managed by local authorities' units and enterprises outside the state budget. In 1986, they were roughly equivalent to those

managed under state budgets (*Beijing Information*, no. 8, 24 February 1986).

17. Market prices under light coordination and supervision became local norms because competition between market and plan (fixed or floating prices) for raw materials and intermediate goods has made it impossible to keep the distinction. Hence, the system of double prices with a constantly readjusted orientation price (*zhidao jiage*) in Sichuan. On the experiment of Shijiazhuang in Hebei, see *Hong Qi*, 1 November 1985.

18. The complex issues of urban society, social protest and ambiguities in the status of the intellectuals (including official patronage at the cost of self-inflicted censorship) are dwelt upon at some length in Chevrier (1986a).

19. The point is made in the case of the open door reforms by Barbara Krug in 'China's Foreign Trade: Socialist Construction, Profit and Rent' (paper presented at the Second Sino–European Conference, University of Oxford, August 1985).

20. Classic statements about interest groups, however, do not follow such an integral approach (see Skilling and Griffiths, 1971). The dimensions of economics and micro-politics are more pervasive than admitted in this approach, also followed in the recent collection on China edited by Goodman (1984).

21. On the return of the bourgeoisie, see Bergère (1986).

22. This division did not preclude local lateral links, although perhaps not as much to the merchants' advantage as it would appear from Rowe's study of the late-Qing Hankou community (1984).

23. The alternation between go and stop phases and the related switches of emphasis between economics and politics are analysed by Schram (1984) and Chevrier (1985). Bianco and Hua Chang-ming explain (in this volume) the characteristic mix of voluntarism and pragmatism in family planning. On the cyclical management of the balance between the logic of the system and that of pluralism, see Myers (1985).

24. The case for minimal state intervention in economic matters in traditional China is made in two unpublished papers by Pierre-Etienne Will, 'Appareil d'Etat et infrastructure économique dans la Chine prémoderne' and R. Bin Wong, 'The Chinese State and Economy, Past and Present'.

25. The case is argued by default about the failure of the Shanghai bourgeoisie in the 1920s by Bergère (1986).

26. There is something like a cult of Sun Yat-sen in Deng Xiaoping's China. On the official celebration in July 1985 of the 580th anniversary of Zheng He's first naval expeditions, see *RMRB*, 15 July 1985.

27. In checking student unrest during the fall of 1985, central and local authorities appealed successfully to student patriotism.

28. On old age, see Hua Chang-ming (1986).

29. See the conference on Confucius and education held in Shandong from 21 to 26 September 1984 (*Jiaoyu yanjiu* (*Education Research*), November 1984, pp. 27–33).

30. Bianco (1985) has contrasted the societal and socio-economic implications in the voluntarist demographic transition on the Chinese mainland with the Taiwanese evolution, which responded more to economic and social changes than to state initiatives.

31. Many surveys should provide materials for answering this question. See for instance Fei Xiaotong et al. (1986).

32. See, for instance, *RMRB*, 21 January 1984. What I call moral heroes are (besides former Maoist models still in use, such as Lei Feng) good peasants who donate money (earned in private farming or businesses) to village schools, or to relieve poverty, etc.

33. I admittedly collapse two stages in Liang's thought: the *xinmin* (new people) period around 1902 and the later, more statist and conservative period of *guoxing*. Liang's growing reliance on traditional solidarity did not prevent him from maintaining his initial ideals of a new family pattern emancipating women, and of a new state pattern in which state institutions would establish a political construction above the traditional communities. The difference is that he no longer viewed these patterns as egalitarian emancipation and democracy. See his 'Zhongguo daode zhi dayuan' ('Basic principles of Chinese Morality'), *Yongyan* (Justice), vol. 1, nos 2 and 4, December 1912 and February 1913.

2 The People's Livelihood and the Incidence of Poverty

Athar Hussain and Stephan Feuchtwang

The object of our investigation is the level and the structure of provision for the basic needs of China's rural population, which in 1983 constituted 76.5% of the total population (*TJZY*, 1984, p. 15). Before listing the basic needs and the guarantees for their provision, we must draw attention to the particular connotation of the term 'rural' in the Chinese context. 'Rural' designates the place of residence and not the source of livelihood. A fair proportion of the population designated as rural obtains its livelihood not from agriculture but from the extensive range of rural industries, social services and government administration.

An interesting feature of China is that even after the spurt of urbanization in the 1980s, it remains more rural than many other comparable developing economies. The main reason for this is that in China the place of residence has been administratively controlled. Citizens are required to register with the local police and not change their place of residence without prior permission. In addition, basic commodities have been rationed in urban areas since 1953 and an urban ration card is available only to permitted urban residents. Rationing has been such a central feature of Chinese life that the term 'peasant' has largely been used to denote those not entitled to rationed grain. Thus rationing has been used in China not only to ensure the provision of basic consumption goods at low prices but also to regulate the geographical distribution of population (see Parish and Whyte, 1978, pp. 53–4). Food rationing is now regarded more as an emergency measure than a permanent fixture, but migration still remains subject to strict control and is likely to remain so.

In the 1950s the Chinese government formally guaranteed to its population provision for its basic needs. The list of guaranteed basic needs has varied from time to time but it is commonly referred to as the 'five guarantees' (*wu bao*). Initially, there were four: food, clothing, fuel and school fees – medical care was added later on. Housing was usually not included, though housing aid has sometimes been provided (Dixon, 1981, Chapter 7). The guarantee for basic needs is now enshrined in the 1982 constitution as part of an array of rights (*quanli*) and duties of citizens. The ones concerned with welfare include the right and duty to work, the right to rest and the right to livelihood for the aged, the sick, the disabled and the families of killed and disabled soldiers. But the right to material assistance is indirectly circumscribed by the duty to practise family planning, the duty of children to support their parents and, not least, the duty to work.

The constitutional guarantee for basic needs is neither an empty promise nor an entirely new principle. It is a formal rendition, as we shall see, of a medley of governmental and non-governmental (collective) and interpersonal measures to aid non-self-subsistent units, families as well as larger units. Most, though not all, analysts agree that China as compared to other developing economies has been notably successful in reducing, if not entirely banishing, the threat of starvation and destitution to its citizens (*China 1985*, p. 16). This success has not been without blemish. As the Chinese authorities themselves admit, the calamities of 1959–61 on top of the upheavals of the Great Leap Forward condemned tens of millions to a premature death. One estimate drawing upon recently compiled series puts the figure at 30 million, thus making it a major social catastrophe (Ashton et al., 1984). Besides, pockets of temporary destitution have always existed in China and continue to do so even now after the massive increase in grain production and rural incomes since 1978. The Chinese experience of providing for the basic needs of its population raises two types of question, one factual and the other analytical. What in fact have been the levels of provision for basic needs such as nutrition, clothing, housing and health care? What social and economic relations determine their levels and what mechanisms are there for providing support to non-self-subsistent units? Given the vast improvement in qualitative and statistical information on China, we are now able to answer these questions on the basis of something more than the fleeting and piecemeal impressions of travellers.

Here we restrict ourselves to nutrition, leaving the rest for a larger study. And we answer these two questions by first setting out the food–population balance at the national level and then looking at various types of evidence of the incidence of undernutrition. In the final section we analyse the various mechanisms of assistance to food-deficit rural units.

Food accounting is a well established and straightforward exercise. As a basic need, nutrition concerns an individual or a family. Since food balances are usually compiled for economies or smaller supra-familial units such as provinces, by their very nature they overlook the distribution of food within the accounting unit; hence the incidence of undernutrition and even starvation among families and individuals within the unit. Following Sen's trenchant critique of the availability of food as the exclusive framework for analysing the incidence of famines, we pay attention to entitlement relations determining the availability of food to families and individuals (Sen, 1981). For empirical evidence we rely on both statistical data and qualitative accounts. While the data on food availability (grain in particular) is fairly comprehensive and reliable in China, surveys of consumption patterns are sparse and piecemeal. Therefore an analysis of poverty in China has to rely on selective reports and sporadic observations.

Before discussing the food–population balance, we must first draw attention to some general features of the institutional framework for ensuring basic guarantees and to the structure of families. China is not a welfare state in the Western sense of the term. Although, as we shall see, there is in place a multi-tiered system for supporting non-self-subsistent units, there is no formal social welfare system. In rural areas, welfare or public welfare (*gong yi*) has been financed out of the collective fund dating from the formation of advanced cooperatives in the 1950s.

As a proportion of the net income of the collective (production teams after the formation of the commune) it has varied between 1 and 2% (*SYB*, 1983, p. 209). It has been used not only to provide assistance to destitute families within the unit but also to finance the local health service, nurseries, old people's homes, cultural activities and a wide range of miscellaneous amenities. The provincial government reports for 1983 included the following among non-government welfare expenditure by collective units: house repairs, mending of roads and building a new school, cinema and children's park (*Ban Yue Tan*, no. 3, 1983, p. 18).

The general point is that provision of assistance is not a distinct category of policy measures. Moreover, in line with the usual practice in socialist economies, assistance to individuals and families is provided by economic units such as enterprises and production teams rather than by a special government agency. The government, in turn, restricts itself to providing assistance to non-self-subsistent units entrusted with the welfare of households. More importantly, both the level and methods of provision to needy households vary locally. Although basic needs have been guaranteed, there have been no national standards of provision for rural areas. In fact, as we hope to show, the institutional arrangements and policies are concerned less with providing assistance than minimizing the numbers needing assistance by instituting a formidable array of social and economic imperatives for self-sustenance. Principal among these are participation in labour up to physical capacity and the maintenance of family and kin solidarity. Public assistance is seen and projected as the safety net of last resort. Given China's level of economic development, this preventive strategy and the makeshift character of support mechanisms are understandable; but they do impart a very specific connotation to provision for basic needs and create problems which could become increasingly important in the future. Thus the World Bank report on long-term development issues and options singles out social security as one of the areas in need of reform (*China 1985*, pp. 163–4).

A central component of the strategy to minimize the numbers in need has been the maintenance of family cohesion and filial obligations. In rural China, when possible, the developmental cycle of a household (*hu*) includes a span of three generations: the old, working adults and children (Wolf, 1985, p. 184). Households with a narrower inter-generational span are more the result of the demographic cycle or unavoidable contingencies such as deaths, the history of births, marital separations and emigration than choice. In China, custom binds the young to the old by filial obligations, normally along the male line. That is, the norm is for the aged to live with their grown-up sons; failing that, they may live with their married daughters. Although filial obligation is traditional, the communist government has sought to sustain and indeed strengthen the tradition. Filial obligation was enunciated in the 1950 marriage law and is reiterated in the 1980 marriage law and the 1982 constitution. Thus by tradition and government policy, households consisting of the aged alone are rare, especially in rural areas, and receiving the 'five guarantees' from 'strangers' is a last and shaming resort (Wolf, 1985, p. 226).

In economic terms filial obligation is an arrangement for sharing incomes within a group with blood ties. It extends beyond the sharing of the same roof to mutual assistance across households. Although of primary importance in respect of support from children to parents, it often covers other relations as well. Filial obligations reduce claims on public assistance, leaving it to cater for the exceptions bypassed by the net of filial support. As a result, the number supported by rural collectives has been remarkably small: around 0.3% of the rural population in 1981 and 1982 (*SYB*, 1983, pp. 103 and 510). As for the aged, a survey of over 2,000 persons over 65 in Henan province found that 95% of them either lived or depended upon their children rather than local collective assistance (Liu Jinji, *Shehui*, 1983, no. 3, p. 6). Old age pensions are still rare and are an innovation pioneered by a few rich brigades (Rossi, 1985). So too are houses of 'respect for the aged'.

Although the obligation to support parents in old age reduces claims on public funds, it is not without its attendant problems. For it provides an incentive to parents to accumulate sons as a source of sustenance in old age. In rural areas especially this conflicts with birth control policies (see Aird, 1981, pp. 165–6). In China now old age pensions are under discussion not because the aged are a relatively deprived group, as they are in some economies, but as an instrument for keeping the birth rate low.

Nutrition

Although the focus here is on nutrition, culinary patterns are of some importance. They specify the range of socially acceptable diet and may themselves be a barrier to achieving a nutritionally satisfactory diet. From the nutritional point of view, a diet is a combination of energy (calories) and nutrients. A nutritionally adequate diet is simply a combination of these varying with age, sex and physiological states such as morbidity, pregnancy, lactation and physical exertion. Malnutrition is the non-conformity of diet with nutritional requirements. There is not one but a range of norms of adequate nutrition. Undernutrition is usually defined as energy or calorie deficiency (not having enough to eat) and protein deficiency (dietary imbalance). The consensus seems to be that calorie deficiency is primary and, except in a few areas dependent on staples such as cassava or plantain, protein deficiency is positively correlated with it (see Schmitt, 1979 and Latham, 1984). Therefore, we take daily calorie intake as the principal index of nutrition.

Broadly speaking, there are two principal approaches to assessing undernutrition: directly in terms of food available or consumed or indirectly with reference to the effects of undernutrition. And the two approaches, in turn, can take a number of forms, as outlined in Table 2.1.

Although the data on China permits the application of all four approaches, its reliability and coverage is highly variable. Some of the time series needed for compiling the annual balance sheets of food availability (such as domestic production and net imports of cereals in particular) are, by usual standards, reliable and comprehensive, while the others on animal feed, the rates of extraction of edible from harvested food, stocks and wastage are not. The World Bank has already compiled annual food balance sheets for 1950–81 on the basis of available information (Piazza, 1983). There are a few food consumption surveys for recent years, but the sampling technique is often not reported.

Table 2.1
Approaches to Assessing Undernutrition

Unit of Observation	Type of Data	
	Direct	*Indirect*
Economy or regions	Food balance sheets	Death, birth and infant mortality rates and causes of death
Individuals or households	Food consumption surveys	Archetypical abnormalities due to undernutrition. Anthropometrics of height and weight

Following the 1982 census and the work by Chinese and foreign demographers, the time series of rates of deaths, birth and infant mortality are now as reliable as any for a developing economy (Banister, 1984). There is a fair amount of information for recent years on the causes of death, abnormalities due to undernutrition and malnutrition (including anthropometric sample surveys of children, see, *China – The Health Sector*, 1984). In sum, now as compared to before 1978, many more pieces of the jigsaw puzzle on the nutritional status of the most populous country in the world are available. The problem is how to cope with a surfeit of data of variable quality.

Our main concern here is with the nutritional status of the rural population, which has not been on a par with its urban counterpart. For, since the early 1950s to 1984, essential items of food in urban areas have been rationed to scales fixed by the government. As a consequence of this, urban inhabitants have been cushioned from fluctuations in supplies, except in times of grave shortage. The rural population, in contrast, has borne the brunt of fluctuations. There has been rationing in rural areas too, but with the essential difference that the scales of ration have been fixed locally (by the production team, for the most part) in accordance with local supply. The food balance sheet is therefore more directly relevant to the nutritional situation in rural than urban areas. In contrast, for the latter the analysis is best conducted in terms of the ration scales and the non-rationed market for food, prices and incomes.

In China, as elsewhere, grain, vegetables, meat and fat are the principal categories of food. Recent years have witnessed a trend away from grain, more pronounced in urban than in rural areas. However, grain still remains by far the most important item. For example, between 1978 and 82, plants furnished around 93% of the calorie intake, most of which came from grain (*SYB*, 1983, p. 509). The shift towards meat does not decrease the importance of grain. On the contrary, given that for its production meat requires grain several times its weight, it increases it. Therefore, by themselves, grain balances are a sufficient basis for analysing the nutritional situation.

The principal entries in China's national grain balance sheet are shown in Table 2.2.

Table 2.2
China's National Grain Balance Sheet

Sources	*Uses*
Domestic production	Direct human consumption
Net imports	End stocks
Beginning stocks	Animal feed
	Seed and wastage

In food accounts, grain available for human consumption is usually calculated as the residue of supplies left after all other uses and the processing of grain. The problem is that the figure for 'all other uses' and the extraction rates of edible from harvested grain range from reliable figures through informed estimates to rough guesses. The Chinese government puts the sum at 20%, while the World Bank at 30% by weight (Piazza, 1983, p. 4). This difference points to a wide margin of error and its implication is that there is little point in trying to calculate 'grain available for human consumption' from the figures.

The analysis here is concerned with the following two related but distinct questions: 1) what has been the pattern of evolution of the nutritional level since 1949 and 2) how high is the level of nutrition in China now? The first question is adequately answered in terms of changes in grain supplies per capita without any reference to the extraction rate and 'other uses'. And to answer the second question we rely on the World Bank and the Chinese estimates.

Grain-Population Balance
Grain per capita is defined here as the sum of grain production per capita and net exports or imports per capita. Changes in stocks are not taken into account because of the lack of reliable national figures. Its time series is shown in Figure 2.1.

What inferences can we draw from this time series? Although even large increases in grain per capita do not rule out the persistence of pockets of undernutrition, there is no doubt that there has been a massive improvement in grain availability and hence the nutritional status of the population. However, from a longer historical perspective extending back to strife-ridden Republican China, the choice of 1949 may well exaggerate the improvement. We would expect the grain production that year to be low by historical standards because of the civil war and the organizational upheavals in the wake of the new regime. The peak grain production reached in 1936 was not surpassed until 1952 (*SYB*, 1983, pp. 158 and 185). One possible implication of this fact is that the improvement during the first few years of the regime were due more to civil peace than the new rural order. Leaving this aside, the striking feature of the series is that improvements in nutritional status have not been monotonic but highly cyclical, with precipitous falls in 1959–60. In fact, the two fat periods span only 19 out of 36 years up to 1984 and have included all the improvements. If we employ the classification rule that a fat period extends over those years with grain per capita higher than the peak attained in the previous fat period, we can summarize the periods as in Table 2.3.

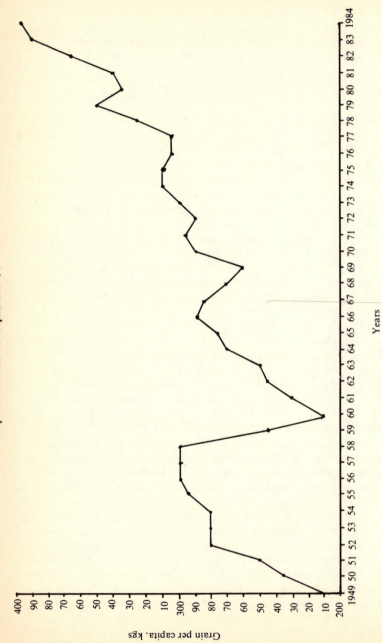

Figure 2.1
Unprocessed Grain Per Capita 1949–84

Grain per capita, kgs

Years

See Appendix 1 for the numerical data and the sources.

Table 2.3   Rising Grain Production

Periods	*Main Features*
1949–56	
1949–54	Land reforms and the formation of producer and marketing cooperatives.
1955–6	Rising rural collectivization.
1974–84	
1974–6	Relative calm after the tempestuous years of the Cultural Revolution.
1977–84	First a partial and then a complete rejection of the Cultural Revolution and partial decollectivization.

This periodization does not quite conform to the now current Chinese view that, during the wasted two decades spanning the Great Leap Forward and the Cultural Revolution (1958–77), there was no perceptible improvement in the nutritional standard of the population. However, the data does not decisively reject that view either. It points to a slightly different hypothesis: that the spectacular improvement witnessed since 1978 represents not so much a radical break from the revolutionary decades as a sharp improvement in a trend which began earlier in 1974. By itself, this alternative hypothesis is no more than a minor statistical quibble; but it is a stepping stone towards a more fruitful perspective that the improvements witnessed since 1978 have been partially due to factors dating from the preceding period. To give one example: but for the historically low rate of population growth brought about by a steady deceleration during 1971–8, the observed increase in grain per capita would not be so striking. This suggests the need to decompose the observed pattern of changes in grain per capita into its constituent elements.

A change in grain per capita ($\triangle F$) could be written as:

$$\triangle F = X\,(g{-}n) + \triangle\,(M/N)$$

$\triangle$ denotes change, X is grain production per capita, g is the rate of growth of grain production, n the rate of growth of population and $\triangle\,(M/N)$ the change in net import or export per capita. We look first at the changes in grain production balance $(g{-}n)$, and then turn to net imports or exports.

As Figure 2.2 shows, and indeed as expected, g is a far more volatile series than n. To start with, what it shows is that the striking characteristic of the two 'wasted' revolutionary decades is, in fact, not stagnation but large fluctuations in the rate of growth of grain production, g. Although these fluctuations could be attributed to a diverse range of factors, foreign as well as Chinese analyses have tended to pile the main burden of explanation on to the twists and turns of politics, which were indeed the most striking feature of the period. To redress the balance we may point to the influence of the weather. Notwithstanding the massive dislocation due to the hurried leap into rural collectivization the two ominous falls in the grain production one after the other in 1959–60 were also due to the exceptionally adverse weather which seriously affected 33–43% of the cultivated area. Similarly, the troughs in 1972 and 1980 either coincided with or immediately followed poor

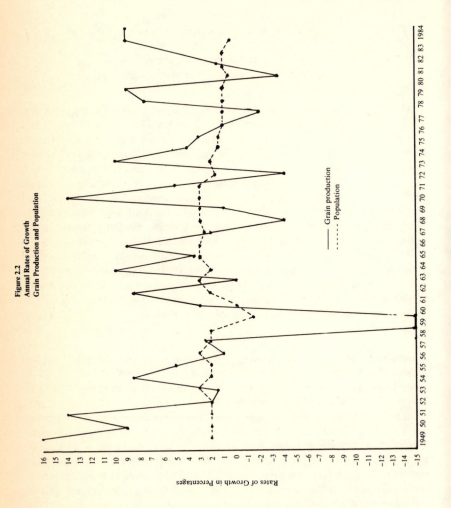

Figure 2.2
Annual Rates of Growth
Grain Production and Population

climatic periods. By the same token, the peaks of 1970 and, more recently, of 1982 coincided with fair weather (*SYB*, 1983, p. 212). The general argument to be drawn from these observations is that even if, perhaps prematurely, we rule out further recurrences of the political twists and turns which characterized the period 1958–77, many other factors leading to fluctuations in the rate of growth of production still remain. As a consequence, further improvements in the food–population balance, which the Chinese government justifiably expects, may still follow a stormy path. Thus, at the economy-wide level, food policy faces the twin problems of deciding upon the target of improvement in the nutritional status of the population by, say, the end of the century and coping with fluctuations in the grain production–population ratio. In relation to the latter, it may be interesting to point out that the 1985 grain harvest was significantly lower than those of 1984 and 1983.

What role did political factors play in the variations of the rate of growth in grain production? After the two successive falls of 15% each in 1959 and 1960, which took grain production back to a lower figure than 1951, it took as long as six years to surpass the 1958 peak. The slow pace of recovery has to be ascribed to the resumption in 1962 of rural collectivization. There was a retreat into family farming at the height of the famine. In the same vein, the fact that during 1967–9 grain production at best failed to keep pace with the population, and at worst fell by 4%, has to be attributed to the rising tide of the Cultural Revolution. When the tide receded in 1969, grain production was lower than it had been five years earlier. Therefore, in sum, revolutionary advances in the 1960s were at the expense of the nutritional level. But this pattern was, arguably, broken not in 1978 but earlier in 1970. In fact, during 1970–77, the average rate of growth of grain production was 3.9%, marginally higher than the average for the whole of 1949–84. It would have been even higher but for a negligible and a negative rate during 1976–7 – the interregnum between the fall of the Gang of Four and the final rehabilitation of Deng Xiaoping.

So much for the adverse effects of political shifts and the organizational transformations that came in their wake; but they had favourable ones as well. The rapid recovery to the 1936 peak followed by sustained growth up to 1958 can be ascribed to, first, land reform and, second, the development of cooperative institutions. That the average rate of growth up to 1958 was 6.6% singles out China as an exceptional case which managed to combine sustained growth with radical changes in land tenure and agricultural organization. The same, perhaps with a greater force, holds for the period since 1978. Since then the average rate of growth has been 5.4% representing a sharp acceleration over the 3.4% growth rate until then. This acceleration is all the more remarkable, if puzzling, because it has been accompanied by a steady decrease in the area devoted to grain (*SYB*, 1983, p. 154). However, it is an open question how much of this acceleration is permanent. A part of it can be attributed to the once-for-all impact of a shift in the regime of cultivation. The Chinese government itself expects the long-term growth rate of grain production to be 2% a year and the rate of population growth up to the end of this century to be around 1% per year (*China 1985*, Chapters 3 and 8).

To turn now to the second term in the grain production–population ratio, we may divide the rates of growth of population into three phases: 1950–57, 1958–70 and 1971–83. The first phase, but for a single dip in 1956, exhibits an upward trend, which could well be attributed to the restoration of civil peace, and a steady improvement in grain per capita. The second phase (1958 – 70) is marked by a large fluctuation followed by ripples. The first simply mirrors the onset and the recovery from the great famine of 1958–61. What singles out the period after the famine is the unparalleledly high rate of population growth. Except once in 1967 the rates of growth remained higher than the 1957 peak in the first period. As we shall discuss later, this cannot be attributed to improvements in grain per capita. For, starting from the trough of 1960, when grain per capita was only marginally higher than that in 1949, until 1969 grain per capita for the most part remained significantly below the levels common between 1952 up to the eve of the famine in 1957. Figure 2.3 brings out the contrast between the respective patterns of grain per capita and the rates of population growth in the first and second phases. The third phase (1971–83) exhibits a steady downward trend up to 1978, and then minor fluctuations. This is the period which in its later stage has witnessed a significant improvement in grain per capita.

On the face of it the period 1949–62, straddling the first phase and the famine part of the second, conforms to a loose Malthusian relation between changes in the availability of food and the rate of population growth. The third phase, 1971–83, corresponds in turn to the 'tertiary demographic phase', where declining or low rates of population growth exist side by side with an improvement in the nutritional level of the population. As is usual in Chinese studies, it is tempting to explain the high rate of population growth in the remaining period in terms of political factors: birth control had fallen from grace with the political leadership. However, the evidence in terms of the birth and the death rates is not quite in keeping with this simple political explanation. (Their pattern is shown in Figure 2.4.)

The interesting feature brought out by the graph is that during 1953–7 there were fluctuations in the birth rate but no sustained trend. Moreover, if we leave aside the high birth rates of 1962–3 on the grounds that they partially represent births delayed by the famine, then the average birth rate in 1964–70 was in fact lower than that for 1953–7 (38 as compared to 42), and the same is true of the fertility rate. Therefore a shift in the government attitude did not imply a higher birth rate. It is, however, true that had the regime persisted with the birth control policies inaugurated in the mid-1950s, the birth rates of the 1960s would have been lower. But the question still remains as to why the rates of population growth were higher after than before the famine. It is at this point that the historical pattern of death rates becomes relevant. Aside from the famine period (1958–61), the death rates, in contrast to the birth rates, exhibit a remarkably steady downward trend up to 1978, then a marginal reversal thereafter. The explanation for the high rates of population growth in the 1960s lies partially in, first, a sharp fall in the death rate to an unprecedented level in 1962, and then the continuation of the downward trend. That fall was remarkable because grain per capita in 1962 was even lower than it was in 1951 (see Figure 2.1). In sum, the responsibility for the high rates of population growth rests as much with egalitarian distribution policies as it does with the neglect of birth control. For, as we shall explain later, those policies, by

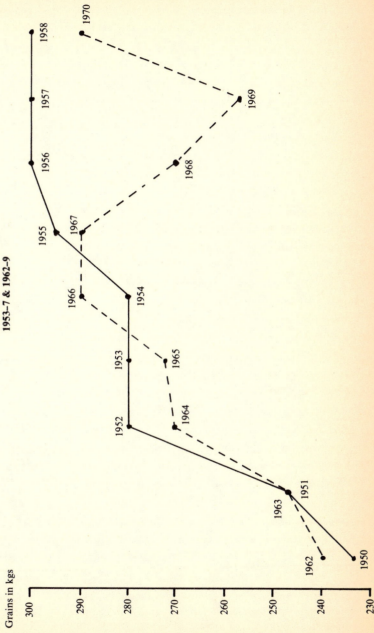

Figure 2.3 part I
Patterns of Grain Per Capita
and Population Growth
1953–7 & 1962–9

Figure 2.3 part II

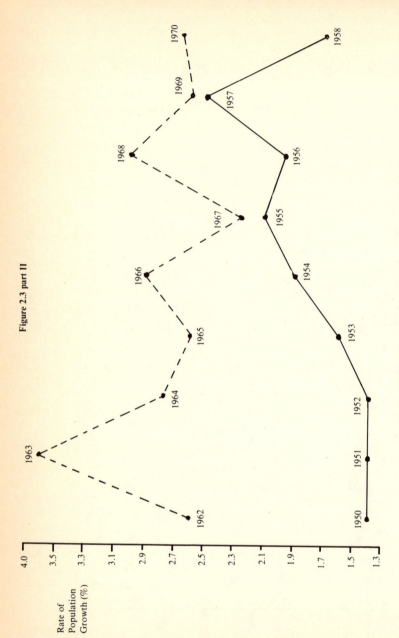

Rate of
Population
Growth (%)

For the numerical data and the sources see Appendix 1 for grain per capita and Appendix 3 for the rates of population growth.

spreading now scarce grain according to needs, brought about successive falls in the death rate.

As can be seen from the figure, birth rates declined from 1971 to 1978. Like the death rate they have shown a marginal upturn since 1978. According to the latest evidence the latter may well turn out to be temporary. From a long-term demographic perspective, but for a hiatus in the middle, the time pattern of the birth and death rates between 1959 and 83 corresponds to the classic pattern of transition from a regime of high birth rates and death rates (as in the period up to 1957) to one of low birth rates and death rates (as in the period since the mid-1970s). Under this schema, the 1960s would figure as the transitional phase in which the decline of mortality preceded the fall of fertility, thus leading to an upward jump in the population growth (on transition see Keyfitz, 1977, pp. 23–5). From an international perspective, China is an outstanding case of demographic transition within a very short period of time (see Keyfitz, 1984 and Aird, 1981).

As the proportion of cultivable to total area in China is exceptionally low (about 10% as compared to India's 57%), the ratio of population to cultivable area is correspondingly high (see *China 1985 – Agriculture to the Year 2000*, p. 28). Although China's rate of population growth is exceptionally low by world standards, it still poses a problem for nutritional policy. What is the likely future pattern of population growth? The Chinese government has set the population target of 12,000 million for the year 2000 – a target which implies population rates of growth of 1.1 to 0.9% and fertility below the replacement level (see *China 1985*, Chapter 8 and Keyfitz, 1984). However, in view of China's draconian birth control policies, the target is regarded as feasible, if hard. Even if the target is achieved, the population will keep on increasing well into the 21st Century because of the further expected decline in the death rate and the echo effects of positive rates in the past. The total is unlikely to stabilize before reaching the figure of 14,000 million, the maximum sustainable limit according to Chinese sources (op. cit.). The implication is that for a long time to come China will still face the twin problems of improving the diet of the existing population and feeding the new arrivals.

International Grain Trade and Food–Population Balance

We turn now to the strategies behind China's international grain trade since 1950. Broadly speaking, international trade bridges the gap between domestic production and the domestic supply of grain: the two need not be equal. In particular, in an economy such as China's, where undernutrition is a potential, if not an actual, problem, international trade opens up the scope for trading other goods for grain, thus for domestic consumption to exceed domestic production. Alternatively, it also provides the possibility for exporting grain in return for other goods, which is what China did initially. As we shall see, China has used international grain trade either as a source of finance for importing capital goods or as an additional source to supplement domestic grain production. These two functions are an alternative way of expressing the balance of trade in grain, which is analysed here in terms of the ratio of net exports or imports to the total supply of grain.

There is, however, an additional way of looking at international trade in grain.

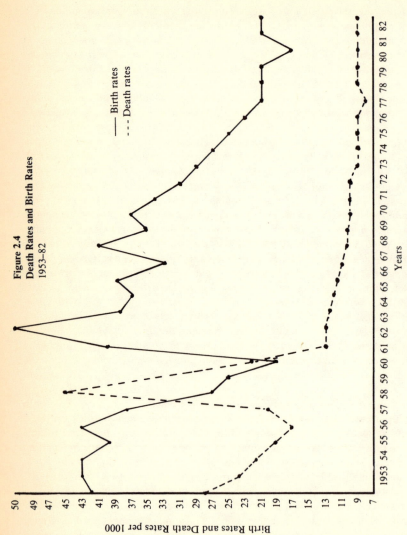

Figure 2.4
Death Rates and Birth Rates
1953–82

—— Birth rates
- - - Death rates

Birth Rates and Death Rates per 1000

Years

1953 54 55 56 57 58 59 60 61 62 63 64 65 66 67 68 69 70 71 72 73 74 75 76 77 78 79 80 81 82

For the numerical data and the sources see Appendix 3

The export of grain in fat years and its import in lean years is equivalent to building up stocks in good years for consumption in bad years. The difference is that in the case of international trade what is stored is not grain but foreign exchange reserves, rising and falling with changes in production. In order to analyse how far China has used international grain trade to stabilize grain consumption we must look at the relation between the direction of changes in grain production per capita and net export or import per capita.

The time series, depicting the broad strategies behind China's international grain trade, indicates two main breaks in the pattern. First, China was a net exporter of grain up to 1960 and has been a net importer ever since. Second, there has been a steady increase in the ratio up from 1977, despite, as we saw earlier, exceptionally high rates of growth in production since 1978. The trade pattern up to 1960 was simply a consequence of predominantly bilateral exchanges with East European economies of grain and other primary commodities for capital goods. The striking feature of the export phase is that the export ratio reached its peak of 2.5% in 1959, the first year of the great famine when grain production fell by 15%, and notwithstanding a fall, it stood at the high of 2% in the year following when grain production fell by another 15%. These figures stand out against the average of 1.1% between 1950 and 58. In fact, the direct export of grain in 1959–60 underestimates the total magnitude, because during these years, meat exports, which constitute an indirect export of grain, were also high relative to those in preceding years (*SYB*, 1983, pp. 422–3). In all, the high export of grain during those two years added to the death sentence pronounced by the precipitous falls in grain production. And the reason for this perverse trade policy was the almost total break in Sino-Soviet economic relations, which forced China to repay immediately all its outstanding debts to East European economies.

Faced with widespread starvation and a death toll in the tens of millions, the Chinese government finally resorted in 1961 to a massive import of grain. Within a year, an export surplus of 2.7 million tons turned into an import deficit of 4.5 million tons. Thereafter up to 1966 the ratio of imports to the total supply remained high: it averaged 2.4% over the range of 2.9% to 1.6%. But, as may be seen, it decreased steadily with the increase in grain per capita. In sum, the pattern of the ratio up to 1976 suggests that the initial surge of imports in 1961 was regarded as temporary and the aim was to keep the dependence on imported grain within a minimal range. None the less, it is interesting that once a net importer China did not revert to being a net exporter of grain.

This brings us to the radical shift in attitude towards grain imports since 1977. One way of bringing out the transformation that has taken place is to note that, in the period prior to it (1961–76), total grain per capita had not surpassed its 1956 peak as late as 1974 (see Figure 2.1). It could be argued thus that until 1976, grain imports, for the most part, did no more than partially bridge the gap between the current level and the past peak. In contrast, the upward trend in the ratio of imports to the total supply since 1978 has largely served to accelerate even further the improvement in the level of nutrition over historic levels.

How permanent are the trends witnessed since 1977? Although no firm figures are available, reports indicate that in the wake of an all time record harvest in 1984

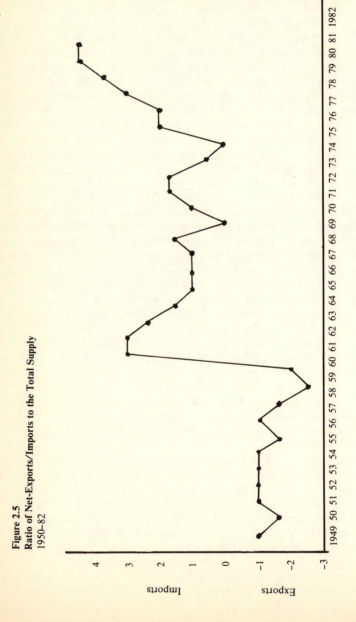

Figure 2.5
Ratio of Net-Exports/Imports to the Total Supply
1950–82

for the numerical data see Appendix 4

imports were negligible and exports high. But, given reports of a poor harvest, the reverse may be true for 1985 (*China Daily News*, 2 December 1985). In sum, a possible prognosis is that in future the ratio of net imports to the total supply will fluctuate within the upper bound of 4–5% reached in 1982–3 (*China 1985 – Agriculture to the Year 2000, passim*).

We turn now to the relation between changes in grain production per capita and net exports or imports per capita (Figure 2.6), with the aim of analysing the effect of international trade on the time pattern of grain per capita. In the Chinese context, these relations fall into three categories: 1) for some years changes in net imports per capita are the opposite of changes in grain production per capita and hence partially stabilize the pattern of grain per capita; 2) for others a decrease in grain production per capita is coupled with either an increase in net exports or a decrease in net imports per capita, thus accentuating the decline in total grain per capita – a perverse trade policy from the nutritional point of view but one that may have a rationale in terms of foreign exchange reserves; 3) finally, some years show an increase in net imports per capita in the face of an increase in grain production per capita.

As can be seen, the exports policy up to 1958 was for the most part stabilizing, though only partially. That is, net exports per capita rose with an increase in grain production per capita and vice versa. One interesting feature of the eight unexceptional years (1951–8) is that, in good years, the rise in exports did not claw back the whole increase; and, more importantly, the fall in exports in bad years merely cushioned but did not completely offset the fall. Therefore international trade policy left room for an improvement in the nutritional level earned by an increase in grain production per capita, but did not completely insure against its deterioration.

But an important feature of the period since 1961, when China became a net importer, is that, in terms of the typology of cases employed here, it has been more varied than the export phase. On numerous occasions, grain imports have been used not to stabilize the pattern of consumption but to increase total grain per capita beyond what was permitted by increases in grain production per capita. This was the case in 1961–4 (when total grain per capita was still very low), in 1973–4 (when total grain per capita was relatively high), and, of course, since 1978. The case of 1973–4 is of some interest because it suggests that the grain import policy since 1978, although exceptional, is not entirely novel.

In historical perspective, China's grain import policy could well be regarded as an end result of a recurrent conflict between the aims of achieving self-sufficiency in food and the recognition that the nutritional level is low and in need of an improvement beyond what is permitted by domestic production. Until 1976, there was an uneasy compromise between these inconsistent aims; but since 1977 the conflict has been resolved in favour of improving the nutritional level. This resolution has to be seen in the wider context of a general increase in China's international trade, which has made it possible to relegate self-sufficiency to a distant aim.

We turn now to the role which international trade has played in altering the composition of grain supplies. Rice is by far the most important grain crop in

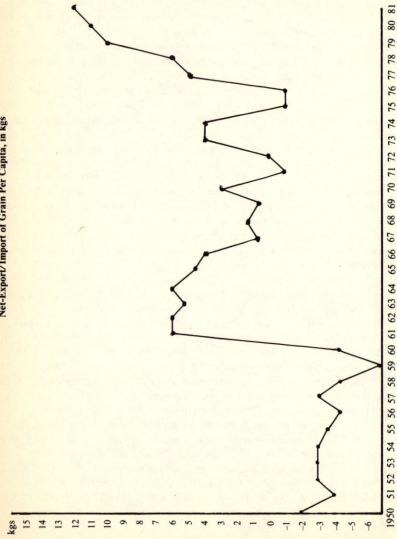

Figure 2.6 part I
Net-Export/Import of Grain Per Capita, in kgs

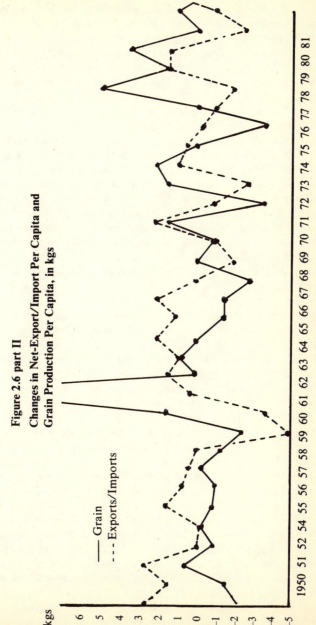

Figure 2.6 part II
Changes in Net-Export/Import Per Capita and
Grain Production Per Capita, in kgs

Grain
Exports/Imports

See Appendix 5 for the numerical data

China, accounting for 45% of total production; and at 20% wheat comes next. In recent years, rice has been the principal export grain and wheat the most important import grain. Therefore, apart from altering the total supply, China has used the international grain market to exchange some relatively abundant rice for relatively scarce wheat. And this transformation through exchange is highly advantageous both from the point of view of consumer tastes and of nutrition. For a number of years the demand for wheat has exceeded the domestic supply; and if China follows the international trend, the proportion of wheat in direct consumption will increase further with a rise in income (see *China 1985 – Agriculture to the Year 2000*, pp. 19–21).

The important point is that trading rice for wheat is not only in keeping with consumer tastes but also highly lucrative. The reason is that, by weight, rice contains marginally more calories (5%) and significantly less protein and fat (around 40%) than wheat (Piazza, 1983, p. 7). But the price per unit weight of rice is over twice that of wheat. Hence, their price ratio is out of line with their respective nutritional composition. As a consequence, for the same expenditure, wheat brings over twice as many calories and nearly four times as much protein and fat as rice (calculated from *China 1985 – Agriculture to the Year 2000*, p. 127). In effect, trading rice for wheat amounts to a highly profitable arbitrage operation in nutrients. However, the price ratio may not remain as favourable to rice as it has been in the past, because, like China, India too plans to increase rice exports significantly. And, in addition, the turnover in the international rice market has been significantly smaller than that in the wheat market (on India see Paarlberg, 1985, Chapter 2).

With the rapid increase since 1978 of personal incomes, especially rural, the direct consumption of grain has decreased, while indirect consumption in the form of meat has increased – a trend which is expected to persist and even accelerate (see Aubert in this volume and *China 1985*, Chapter 3). This shift is tantamount to a substitution of coarse grain (animal feed) for fine grain such as rice and wheat. The achievement of the ambitious targets for meat and dairy production that the Chinese government has set for the turn of the century would imply a substantial increase in the import of coarse grain (*China 1985 – Agriculture to the Year 2000*, pp. 105–9). The implication is that in coming years the exchange of rice for coarse grain and feed concentrates will increasingly displace the past pattern of the exchange of rice for wheat. As the price ratio of rice to coarse grain is very similar to that of rice to wheat, the former offers the same profitable opportunities as the latter. But to the uncertain future of the rice:wheat ratio in international trade should be added some uncertainty about grain and dairy stock production in China. First, there is evidence that overgrazing and unplanned urbanization are reducing the area of cultivable land (see Chapter 6). Second, the expansion of non-grain agricultural production on this diminished amount of land may have been responsible for the sharp drop in grain production reported for 1985. There can be no certainty, therefore, of increases in the output of grain or the value of the output directly produced or, indirectly, via stock.

There is a general conclusion concerning the aim of self-sufficiency to be drawn from the opportunities of trading grain open to China. As indicated earlier, self-sufficiency is not a simple aim. Item by item self-sufficiency is economically unjustifiable. It has a heavy cost in terms of restrictions on diet and nutritional level. Self-sufficiency by weight of all grain taken together is, in China, the most likely connotation of self-sufficiency in grain since grain production and supply are almost exclusively measured by weight. But this too lacks an economic rationale because of the wide differences in the price per unit weight of different types of grain. Finally, there is self-sufficiency by value, or zero balance of grain trade by value. This has ample economic justification and is consistent with the exploitation of profitable opportunities of grain trade open to China. Given international price ratios and the composition of China's grain production, such self-sufficiency implies that China will remain a net importer of grain by weight.

To conclude the discussion of the grain–population ratio, at around 2% the average rate of growth of grain production per capita since 1949 is a reasonable but not an extraordinary performance by international standards. The nutritional level in today's China is impressive, but any historical assessment has to pay particular attention to the massive fluctuations in grain per capita. Although not likely to be of the same amplitude as those of 1959–70, a further recurrence of fluctuations cannot be ruled out. Whatever China's achievements in the field of nutrition may be, the Chinese government has not had a consistent nutrition policy. Providing even a minimal level of grain supply has at times been secondary to other aims. A paradox of Chinese politics since 1949 has been that although banishing hunger and destitution has been a central aim of the revolution, revolutionary ferments have distracted from that aim. Now that China has graduated to the tertiary demographic phase of low death and birth rates, population growth is no longer as serious an obstacle to improving the level of nutrition as it was up to the early 1970s. As for international trade, although relatively unimportant in terms of aggregate indices, it has a crucial role to play in evening out fluctuations in the domestic grain production and matching the composition of supply with that of demand.

Nutrition and Vital Statistics

Ultimately nutrition matters because diet affects the incidence of disease and the physical make-up and the life expectancy of the population. Even though the chains of causation are not precise, the effects are well established. This cause–effect relationship offers the possibility of inferring the nutritional status of a population from its death rate, the pattern of its diseases and the anthropometrics of its members. Such a 'reverse inference' is common in demographic studies of mortality (see Preston, 1976, Chapter 5). This is what we have set out to do here; we look first at the death rate, then the recent data on the pattern of proximate causes of death and anthropometric evidence.

The use of the death rate to infer the nutritional status of the living needs some explanation. Even in extreme famine, still less in a situation of undernutrition, the cause of death is not starvation. Gastro-intestinal disorders (diarrhoea, in particular), respiratory and pulmonary diseases and parasitic afflictions are the most common proximate causes. But infectious diseases and undernutrition are intricately related: they are synergistic. More specifically, undernutrition not only increases the incidence of infectious diseases but also the deaths caused by them. In turn, infectious diseases, by lowering food intake and absorption, give rise to so-called secondary undernutrition (Latham, 1975, *passim* and Grigg, 1985, Chapter 1). In short, undernutrition and infectious diseases are bound together by a cumulative causation.

This vicious circle can be broken by improvements in both food intake and health care. But one without the other loses at least some of its effectiveness. As we have seen (Figure 2.4), China has witnessed a steady downward trend in its crude death rate. The system of preventive and basic medical care in China is acknowledged to be an outstanding success; but it alone cannot be held entirely responsible for the decline in the death rate.

Concerned as it is with broad directions of change, the analysis here needs no more than the assumption that, with a caveat, a decline in the crude death rate is an index of improvement in the nutritional status of the population. Such an assumption ought to be valid for a substantial part of Chinese history since 1949; if we explain the exceptionally high death rates of 1959–61 in terms of precipitously low grain per capita in those years, then by a symmetrical argument the comparatively low and falling death rates before and after that period signify an improvement in the nutritional status of the population. Since not each and every instance of a decline in the death rate is attributable to an amelioration in the nutritional status, how valid is this assumption? Here we must note that the postulated relation is between undernutrition and infectious diseases, especially those in synergistic relation with undernutrition. Needless to say, people also die of diseases other than infectious diseases (which rank low among the causes of death in developing economies and high in developed ones). The answer, therefore, is that the prevailing pattern of causes of death itself indicates the validity or otherwise of the assumption. When infectious disease begin to rank low – as they do in the well off regions of present-day China – the assumption starts to lose general validity, though it may still hold for particular sections of the population, as indeed it does in some rural areas of China (on cause patterns of mortality, see Preston, 1976).

Finally, it may be asked what an indirect assessment in terms of vital data adds to a direct assessment in terms of grain per capita. Grain consumption is a statistical distribution and grain per capita is no more than a measure of its central tendency. It does not tell us anything about actual distribution. Since the death rate and other vital data are sensitive to the distribution of available food, they, in conjunction with grain per capita, can be used as qualitative indices of inequality in the distribution of food. In the discussion here, we focus more on this aspect than on food availability.

Since the focus here is on the link between the nutritional status and the crude death rate we must first of all draw attention to a striking contrast between the two series (see also Figure 2.1). Unlike grain per capita's recurrent fluctuations, the crude death series exhibits a steady downward trend (apart from a hiatus in the middle and a slight upturn at the end). This discord may be regarded as an essential feature that needs to be analysed together with the downward trend in the crude death rate.

Grain exports were at a record level during the first three years of the famine, 1958–60 (see Figures 2.5 and 2.6). What this perverse configuration suggests is that the Chinese government was slow in grasping the magnitude of the unfolding catastrophe. Arguably, it was not so much advance warnings from the plummeting grain production as reports of widespread starvation and deaths which finally prompted the Chinese government to import grain and embark on other corrective measures. Notwithstanding the break with the Soviet Union, what other factors may be held responsible for this delayed recognition? A brief answer is past history and the system of reporting. The usual under-reporting of deaths (especially in rural areas) was made worse by the organizational upheavals wreaked by the famine, the massive flight of rural population in search of food and, not least, deliberate under-reporting by local cadres. However, once the government introduced emergency measures, the death rate fell dramatically.

Unlike in the past, the present leadership is now candid about the deaths from the famine and the numbers presently living in abject poverty (see Deng Xiaoping in *BR*, 1985, no. 4). What is now being revealed has indeed in part been known to the leadership; but taking into account the disarray in statistical services during 1958–78, it could just as easily be argued that the deaths from the famine and the proportion of population suffering from undernutrition were in the past not obvious to the leadership.

Yet the downward trend in the crude death rate in China is remarkable by international standards. Expressed in terms of life expectancy at birth, the Chinese population has extended its lease of life since 1949 by an average of 1.5 years per calendar year; that is, according to the UN estimates, three times as fast as the average for comparable countries over the same period. China's achievement is matched by only a few, much smaller economies such as Taiwan, Chile and Sri Lanka. The first two are in a higher income bracket than China. What is more relevant is that China outshines the achievements of populous developing economies such as Brazil, India, Indonesia and Bangladesh (see UN, 1984, pp. 126–45, Banister and Preston, 1981 and *China – The Health Sector*, 1985, pp. 8–9). According to the World Bank, the life expectancy of 67 years for the Chinese population puts it among the ranks of upper middle-income economies – two classes above its income per capita rating (*WDR 1985*, pp. 174–5). The figure is for 1983 and the Chinese estimate is higher (*China Daily News*, 27 March 1984).

Although it seems that China has been a super-performer in terms of vital indices since the early 1960s, in terms of average nutritional level it has not until recently been far ahead of its income peers. It is at this point that we must refer back to the discord between the series on grain per head and the death rate, especially during the 1960s, when, for the most part, grain per capita was significantly lower than before the onset of the famine.

To bring out the significance of this discord, we plot in Figure 2.7 the combinations of the crude death rate and grain per capita for the period 1953–7 (i.e., up to the sharp jump in the death rate) and for 1962–9 (i.e., from the steep fall in the death rate up to the eve of the steep increase in grain per capita – for which see Figure 2.1). The contrast is striking. Following the recovery from the famine, the whole configuration markedly shifts downwards: now a lower grain per capita is associated with a lower and not a higher death rate. It is as if the trade-off between grain and death underwent a radical change. Drawing upon the circumstantial evidence, this suggests that government measures such as tight rationing and the mulcting of grain over the minimum requirements of the peasants on the one hand, and the egalitarian distribution implicit in the rural communes on the other, succeeded well in offsetting the effects on deaths of the shortfall in grain per capita but, as we shall see later, not on undernutrition. In sum, although grain per capita was slow in regaining its pre-famine peak, a more egalitarian distribution of now more scarce grain compensated for it. Moreover, the network underlying that distribution was robust enough to withstand a short but sharp fall in grain per capita during the high tide of the Cultural Revolution in 1967–9, when the death rate still continued to decline. Arguably more than the much cited Dutch famine during the Second World War, the China of the 1960s furnishes an example of the success of an egalitarian distributive framework in keeping at bay the threat of death posed by an historic fall in the food supply (on the significance of the Dutch case, see Sen, 1981). But this very success may have taken some of the urgency out of the task of increasing grain per capita, hence opening the possibility of vacillation between the aims of self-sufficiency and improvement in the level of nutrition, which, as we argued earlier, has been a characteristic of Chinese nutritional policy since 1949.

We may now ask, granted China's achievements in terms of national vital indicators since the early 1950s, and the current nutritional level of its population taken as one unit, how these fit in with the now ample evidence of abject poverty and even severe undernutrition in parts of rural China. For a start, Wu Xiang, Vice-Director of the Centre for Rural Development Studies of the State Council, revealed at the 1985 National Party Congress that there were still 100 million persons (concentrated in the north-west and the south-west of the country) with incomes less than 120 yuan a year – a threshold that signifies poverty rather than destitution (reported in *Liaowang*, 9 September 1985; see also Deng Xiaoping, *BR*, 1985, no. 4, p. 15, Cui Naifu, *BR*, 1985, no. 4, p. 9 and Du Rensheng, *BR*, 1984, no. 4, p. 9). Relatively speaking, 100 million was around 10% of China's population in 1983. More importantly, this is the most recent estimate and considerably higher than the percentage of the poor in sample surveys (see Du Rensheng in *BR*, 1984, no. 18, p. 16 and no. 21, p. 9). No less important is the fact that Wu Xiang's estimate refers to a time after several years' record increases in personal incomes.

In fact, there is now a whole mosaic of data all pointing to substantial pockets of poverty, undernutrition and even destitution. The data is disparate and piecemeal. First of all there are sample surveys of income and food consumption. But they fall short of statistical standards in terms of both their method and the manner of reporting. Then there is the data on provincial mortality rates provided by the 1982 census, which by all accounts was well conducted. In keeping with the evidence used so far, we concentrate on the provincial mortality rates, all of which relate to recent years.

We rely here on official data, which have been shown to underestimate the true rates. The data are for 1981 and the figure for the national death rate is 6.36 per

Figure 2.7
Combinations of Grain Per Capita (kgs) &
Death Rates (per 1000)
1953–7 & 1962–9

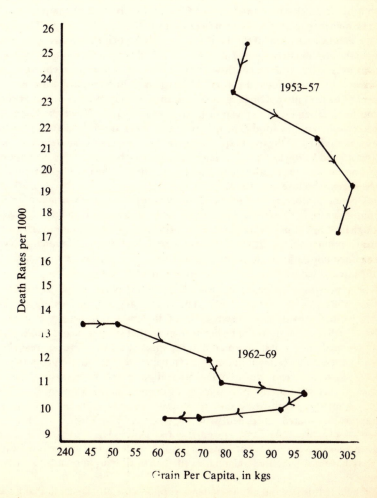

For the numerical data see Appendix 1 for grain per capita and Appendix 3 for death rates.

1,000, which is around 17% lower than Banister's figure of 7.7 for 1981 (Banister, 1984). But this has no serious consequence, since we are concerned with distribution and not the absolute level. The grouped data are shown in Table 2.4, which has some interesting features. To start with two provinces stand out: at 9.92 Tibet has a death rate about twice as high as Heilongjiang's 4.95. Outliers aside, the observations are heavily clustered around the national rate of 6.36. More specifically, the range between 7 and 5.5 includes the provinces with 55% of the total population. To give an idea of the scale, we may note that the distribution of provincial death rates for China is significantly less than that of the national rates for the low-income and the middle-income economies (*WDR 1985*, Table 20). As the provinces with high crude death rates tend to have high birth rates as well, the distribution of death rates standardized for the age structure of the population would be higher than that for the crude death rate. Nevertheless, large disparities are not a significant feature of the data. What *is* significant is that the five provinces falling in the high death range of 7.7–10 (18–57% higher than the national rate) are all in the north-west and the south-west of China – a feature which corroborates Wu Xiang's observation cited earlier. The provinces in question, in descending order, are Tibet, Yunnan, Guizhou, Xinjiang and Qinghai and they do have below average food expenditure per capita (*SYB*, 1983, p. 503). However, there are provinces with very low food expenditure but with low death rates (compare the death rate ranking and the food expenditure ranking in *China – The Health Sector*, 1984, p. 115 and *SYB*, 1983, p. 503). The implication is that low food consumption is only one cause of the death rate and that the quality of the local health services and the social structure are others.

The Chinese authorities themselves admit that the fruits of growth have not been distributed evenly: economic inequalities at various levels have increased. Although helping the poor rural units was a principal justification for overhauling the rural economy, there is little evidence to suggest that the acceleration in growth has benefited poorer areas more than richer ones. (There are some cases where it has; the ones which have been cited are shown in Table 2.5 below.)

All these provinces were poor and with the exception of Anhui they still are (see Vermeer, 1982 and *SYB*, 1983, p. 505). The piecemeal evidence does suggest that the accelerated growth has raised some of the poor counties to a state of comfortable living. But it has to be borne in mind that success stories make news, while failures do not. If it is accepted that the spurt of growth in rural areas since 1978 is due less to investment and more to a better exploitation of geographical location and the local endowment of land and labour, then it follows that the fruits of economic growth have by-passed many of the poor areas. Many of the areas, especially in the north-west and south-west, are poor because they are geographically isolated, burdened with low resources and adverse weather and lacking in organizational and entrepreneurial skills. The very fact that the leadership has singled out the north-west and south-west as problem areas indicates that they have not benefited as much as the North China plain and the eastern region.

To conclude this section, all the evidence supports the official claim that a vast majority of the Chinese population has attained the stage of *wenbao* (basic needs

Table 2.4
Provincial Mortality Rates (per 1,000, 1981)

Provinces	Mortality Rate Range	Ratio in the Population	Cumulative Ratio
Tibet	10–9.5	00.186	00.186
Yunnan	9–8.5	03.233	03.419
Guizhou Xinjiang	8.5–8	04.126	07.545
Qinghai	8–7.5	00.387	07.932
Hubei Hunan Shaanxi Sichuan	7.5–7	22.87	30.759
Shanxi Jiangxi	7–6.5	05.804	36.563
Shanghai Zhejiang Tianjin Shandong Jiangsu Ningxia Hebei Henan	6.5–6	32.236	68.799
Fujian Beijing Nei Mongol Gansu Guangxi Guangdong	6–5.5	16.846	85.645
Liaoning Jilin Anhui	5.5–5	10.701	96.346
Heilong- jiang	5–4.5	03.231	99.577

Source: *China – The Health Sector*, 1985, p. 115.

satisfied) and that a section of it has graduated to *xiaokang* (is comfortably off). But taking Wu Xiang's estimate as a guide, around 10% of the population is still trapped in poverty (*jihan*). As important as the quantitative estimate of poverty is the fact that it is publicly recognized by the leadership. Since poverty and undernutrition do not advertise themselves until they sink to the extreme, the

Table 2.5
Areas benefiting from Chinese rural reforms

Province	Beneficiary in the Province
Guizhou	Mountainous areas
Gansu	Dingxi prefecture
Anhui	Chuxian prefecture
Ningxia	Guyuan prefecture
Shandong	The North-west
Henan	Kaifeng prefecture

Source: Li Chengrui and Zhang Zhongji: *BR*, 1982, no. 17, pp. 15–18 (on Gansu's Dingxi prefecture see also *China 1985*, pp. 20–30).

recognition of poverty is a precondition for tackling it. Rapid economic growth makes it all the easier for the present leadership to banish destitution. As Deng Xiaoping has put it, rich areas can now spare a little to help the poor areas (see *BR*, 1985, no. 4, p. 15). It is perhaps an historical irony that a departure from a revolutionary course has at least hastened, even if it has not achieved, the realization of one of the central aims of the Chinese revolution, i.e.: banishing destitution and hunger.

Nutritional Insurance

We turn now to an analysis of the diverse mechanisms for providing grain to non-self-subsistent rural units. We treat them as insurance mechanisms and are concerned with assessing their effectiveness in alleviating, if not eliminating, undernutrition among China's rural population. For this purpose we may distinguish between the following: 1) the nature of nutritional contingency; 2) the mechanisms for dealing with the contingency and the forms of relief; and 3) the agencies responsible for providing help. The nature of nutritional contingency depends crucially on the level of analysis. For an economy predisposed towards self-sufficiency, as China has been, the principal contingency is a crop failure; but for a household the relevant contingencies depend crucially on its usual sources of supply. The second and the third items also vary with the unit in question. For rural China, the village (or *cun*) and the household are the two most relevant units. The recent organizational changes have emasculated the production team (but it still remains useful for registering the changes). We take the production team and the rural household in turn.

Until the beginning of the so-called responsibility system in 1980, the production team was both the unit of cultivation and the lowest tier of local self-government. A production team could be regarded as a small to medium size village consisting of some 30 households (36 was the national average in 1980, see *SYB*, 1981). Since the emergence of the rural commune in 1962, production teams have, with a few exceptions, been the elementary cells of Chinese rural structure. They have been entrusted with the welfare of their constituent households.

The grain balance sheet for a production team or, as now, village would look as follows:

Table 2.6
Grain Balance Sheet for a Team or Village

Sources	Uses
1. Own production	1. Grain tax
2. Beginning stocks	2. Quota sales (compulsory until recently)
3. Purchase from the government (conditional)	3. Above quota sales (obligatory until recently)
4. Purchase from the market (only possible recently)	4. Seeds and end-stock (normally non-discretionary)
	5. Own consumption
	6. Discretionary sales to the government
	7. Sale on the market (only possible recently)

Until the recent changes, for most teams, the first two sources were meant to cover at least the first five uses. In principle at least, the total government procurement from a team (i.e., grain tax, quota and above quota sales) was fixed for no less than five years at a level based on the normal supply situation of the team (on the details of government procurement see Maxwell and Nolan, 1980). The teams were pressured into keeping enough stocks to smooth minor fluctuations in current production. 'Production for self-relief in bad years' and 'persist in storing grain and be prepared against war and natural disasters' have been common slogans in rural China; and they were heeded (see Croll, 1983, p. 142–4). As we shall see, self-insurance has been and still is a central feature of the Chinese social welfare mechanism at all levels.

Production teams were the lowest level in a three-tiered structure, with the production brigades and communes above them. The intra-communal redistribution, which varied, supplemented the team's own insurance mechanism. The governmental mechanism only came into the picture when the contingency was beyond the scope of the intra-communal insurance mechanisms. The whole rural economic organization has been geared to minimizing the chances of such a contingency occurring. Under the slogan of 'taking grain as the key-link', coined in the early 1960s, each team was supposed to devote enough of its crop area to provide for its own consumption and meet its procurement target. The only exceptions were teams assigned to specialize in non-grain crops such as tea and the teams located in regions officially designated as poor.

The past policy of according near total primacy to grain has been much criticized since 1978 and there has been a massive shift in the cultivable area away from grain (mainly because of the price structure). Up to 1984, the government went along with the shift; but the low 1985 grain crop has been partially blamed on the neglect of grain (see *BR*, 1981, no. 9, pp. 8–9 and *BR*, 1985, no. 49, p. 4) and measures to remedy the neglect are indicated. Although applied less rigidly than in the past, grain still remains the key link and local self-sufficiency a norm.

Given the emphasis on local self-sufficiency, the principal nutritional contingency for a village is a decrease in its own grain supply due to natural factors. In any year there have always been teams or villages faced with such a contingency. In such cases, government intervention has fallen into two categories: first, increasing the disposable grain of the team by total or partial exemption in the descending order from above quota sales, quota sales and grain tax; second, supplementing the grain production of the team or village by sales from the state marketing network. Now that private markets are allowed there is an alternative source of supply. But since the price in the private market is higher, permission to buy from the state marketing network carries an element of subsidy (on the present structure of grain prices see Du Rensheng, *BR*, 1985, no. 25, pp. 15–17). Apart from private grain markets, which were curbed in 1953 when the state marketing network was established, none of the above measures is new. They date from the days of the First Five Year Plan (1953–7) and are all based upon the marketing of grain by the government which, as we shall argue, has been the node of all its relief measures.

Although relief measures are not new, there has been an important change in their usage. They are now governed more by general rules and less by the discretion of cadres. In 1979 the State Council decided to exempt from grain tax entirely the teams endemically short of grain for three years and for one year the teams with a temporary shortage in one year (*BR*, 1980, no. 29, p. 5). The longstanding principle that grain procurement quotas are to be set at a fixed level for five years was reiterated (*BR*, 1980, no. 12, pp. 14–20). In the past when the grain purchased from peasants was the index of performance, local officials at times revised the already set quota upwards when grain production rose (see Hsu, 1984, p. 1232). As a result, the rapid increase in grain production in the last few years has led to a decrease in the ratio of quota procurement to grain production, hence an increase in the disposable grain of rural areas.

The government argues that reducing the burden of procurement has removed a cause of undernutrition in the past. But by the same token those measures have also reduced the possible effectiveness of grain tax and quota remissions as policies for providing relief from temporary shortages. Moreover, they also imply a reduction in grain sales from the state marketing network to rural areas, which have been an important component of the supply network in rural areas. In fact, grain-deficit rural units, unless classified as poor, are now expected to rely on higher price private markets rather than the lower price state marketing network. But it must be acknowledged that, as relief measures, tax and quota remissions have always been more relevant to well off rather than endemically poor teams or villages. As they are meant to be set with reference to the local grain–population ratio, chronically poor teams or villages would have relatively low tax and quota liabilities and thus stand to gain little from their remission.

Let us turn now to the relief mechanism of sales to rural areas from the state marketing network ('return sales' in Chinese parlance). Even after the remission of its quota liabilities, a team or village may still not have enough for its own consumption. It is only at this point that a resort to the state marketing network becomes relevant. Access to the network has always been restricted to teams or villages deemed to be in difficulty and purchases from it have been rationed to the amount needed to bring the team or village up to a grain per capita threshold, which has varied geographically. In recent years, the national averages have been as shown in Table 2.7 below.

Table 2.7
Annual Thresholds per capita

Grain	*In kgs*	*In nutrients*		*% of Adequate Levels*	
		Kcal	*Protein, gms*	*Kcal*	*Protein*
Rice (unmilled)	200	1,400	25	64	69
Wheat etc (unhusked)	150	1,250	35	57	97

Source: *China – The Health Sector*, 1985, p. 80.

These are typical levels; the threshold can vary between and even within a province. The main importance of the thresholds is that they provide a floor to food consumption. But as the last column shows, they are set to alleviate but not eliminate undernutrition. Although there is no doubt that the thresholds have been important in averting starvation, we must keep in mind that resort to the state marketing network has carried a stigma in the past, especially during the period of the Cultural Revolution (Hsu, 1984). As a consequence, many teams or villages either willingly or unwillingly subsisted on a grain ration less than the local threshold. Thus in 1979, there were still 100 million peasants with food consumption less than the thresholds (Vermeer, 1982, pp. 18–19).

But now the thresholds carry a greater weight. On what terms have the grain deficit teams been able to acquire grain from the state marketing network? The terms fall into three categories, each applying to a particular class of teams. An otherwise solvent team pays in cash the lower quota price. Teams short of alternative forms of income have been supplied on loan to be repaid in grain. A cash loan from the Agricultural Bank would be more common now (see *BR*, 1983, no. 38, pp. 23–7 and *BR*, 1984, no. 46, p. 26). Although advanced for a year only, grain or cash loans can be rolled over. Default on loans has always been a problem in China. Apart from applying political pressure, the government has periodically written off the loans of poor teams. Finally, chronically poor teams or those struck by natural calamities may receive an outright grant of grain.

Looked at from the point of view of an individual team or village, the state marketing system appears coercive in purchasing grain from peasants and niggardly in supplying it to them. Restricted by this partial perspective, it is easy to slip into attributing this to bureaucratic cussedness. But there is a perfectly good economical rationale to this stance which is easily brought out by the balance sheet of inflows and outflows from the state marketing network (Table 2.8).

Table 2.8
Balance Sheet of State Marketing Network

Inflows	*Outflows*
1. Taxes	1. Urban consumers
2. Quota purchases (until recently)	2. Grain deficit rural units
3. Above quota purchase (obligatory until recently)	3. Exports
4. Negotiated purchases	
5. Imports	

Although small in relation to the total supply, grain imports are a large item in this balance sheet and are crucial in determining the stance of the marketing network. If the government policy is to keep net imports low, as it was up to 1977, then the main burden of adjustment falls on quota and above quota sales on the inflow side, and on sales to rural units on the outflow side. In most years, negotiated purchases have applied to only a few areas, and sales to urban consumers were determined by the urban population and the scale of the food ration. Under these circumstances an immediate consequence of a taut grain situation is to coerce peasants into supplying more and restricting their access to the network. This stance notwithstanding, the state marketing network has not simply been a mechanism for siphoning grain from rural to urban areas. Since its establishment in 1953, it has re-sold a quarter to a third of its purchases in rural areas themselves (*SYB*, 1983, p. 393). And the ratio has increased to around 40% in recent years because of a greater specialization in non-grain crops. Moreover, the re-sale ratio has been high when grain per capita has been low. What this suggests is that, as well as providing for urban areas, the state marketing network has played an important part in averting starvation in rural areas. Therefore, at least in part, the coercive purchase policies of the network have simply been a counterpart of readiness to supply grain to grain-deficit rural units.

Given the various government decisions on grain procurement since 1978, the extent of coercion is now much less. In fact, after the record crop of 1984, the common complaint in rural areas was that the state marketing network was not willing to buy up all that was offered to it. No doubt successive increases in grain output since 1978 have helped in the relaxation. But no less important is the change in the stance towards a greater reliance on the international grain market. As we saw earlier, from 1978 to 1983 net imports outpaced fast growing grain production. The implication is that this change of stance provided the state marketing system with an extra balancing mechanism. Now the government could relax the hold of coercive purchase policies and allow private markets to boom and still maintain, to a large degree, its commitment to supply the cities and grain-deficit areas.

Thus the central feature of all the measures to relieve temporary or chronic grain shortages in teams or villages is that they are all centred on the state marketing network. Hitherto, the network has combined commercial mediation with relief. The recent measures to reform the network could well be regarded as attempts to separate these dating from the days of the Great Famine (on the reform see Zhao Ziyang, *BR*, 1985, no. 1, p. 15 and no. 6, pp. 7–8, Du Rensheng, *BR*, 1985, no. 25, pp. 15–17; for a general discussion see Lardy, 1983). Leaving aside the mounting losses of the network and the urban dimension, the successive increases in the purchase prices of the network imply an increase in the real income of the net sellers of grain, but also, by the same token, a decrease in the real income of the net purchasers of grain. The latter in many cases has been offset by an increase in cash income from other sources. But opportunities for earning a cash income are not evenly spread over rural China; there must therefore be many teams or villages that have experienced a net decrease in real income. More importantly, such teams are likely to be in remote areas and chronically poor. The implication is that the recent changes in grain commerce within China have grossly reduced the effectiveness of the usual measures in coping with undernutrition in chronically poor teams. In the spirit of the present reforms what is needed are cash transfers to grain-deficit rural units with little or no cash income. There are signs of changes in that direction; but as the Chinese sources themselves admit, they are still groping towards an effective system for relieving chronic poverty (on the new measures to help poor areas see *BR*, 1981, no. 3, pp. 21–2; *BR*, 1982, no. 15, p. 25; *BR*, 1984, no. 46, p. 26 and *BR*, 1985, no. 27, pp. 14–15).

We now turn briefly to the problem of poor households in rural China. They need to be analysed separately because they raise specific problems. The problem of the poverty of teams or villages is regional; but that of poor households is not. They are geographically dispersed. There have always been poor households in well off teams. Secondly, the causes of the poverty of rural households are not the same as those for teams or villages. While the endowment of land, remoteness, the weather and organizational factors are important in accounting for the poverty of a team or village, the poverty of a rural household is mainly a result of a low hands-to-mouths ratio. Poor households are the result of either a depletion of family labour force – due to age, illness, disability and death – or a large number of children. Unlike elsewhere in developing economies, landlessness is not yet an attribute of poor households in China.

Historically, assistance to poor households has been intertwined with the collective ownership of land (which still exists in principle) and the collective cultivation of land (which no longer exists). The centrepiece of the public assistance network has been the guarantee to meet the basic needs of the destitute (on the history of the five guarantees see Dixon, 1981, Chapter 7). The responsibility for providing resources and implementing the guarantees has rested in the past with the team or village and still does so. The levels and methods of provision have therefore not been uniform. They have varied greatly both in time and space and so too have the criteria of eligibility for assistance. It has been less an organized system of social welfare and more a network of mutual aid with many of the features of charity. It has always been intended to complement rather than supplant intra-familial and intra-kin support networks (see Dixon, 1981 and Parish and Whyte,

1979, *passim*). Moreover, it has been permeated by the distinction between deserving and non-deserving poor (see, for example, *BR*, 1981, no. 52, p. 7).

As far as nutrition is concerned, up to the introduction of the responsibility system in 1980, the central node of the team-level grain network was the division of the disposable grain of the team into two funds, the basic and the workpoint grain. Although the antecedents of this division can be found earlier, it was written into the Commune Charter of 1962, when the structure of the rural commune was formalized (Ahn, 1975). Basic grain had the first claim on disposable grain and it was to be distributed to the constituent households according to the number of mouths. In effect, it was a local rationing system. Over and above the floors provided by the mechanism of support for grain-deficit teams, the level of ration varied. The division of disposable grain into basic and workpoint grain was left to the teams; the ratio 7:3 has been cited as the norm (see Ahn, 1975, Parish and Whyte, 1978 and Croll, 1983 for case studies). Except to households lacking the capacity to earn workpoints, basic grain was not free. It was an advance against workpoints to be earned by the household during the course of the year. But the lending system was lax, debts were rolled over and many households fell heavily in debt (see Vermeer, 1979). As basic grain claimed an overwhelming proportion of the team's disposable grain (the principal source of grain for rural households), the level of nutrition within a team varied little. In contrast, the differences between teams and even more so communes were always large.

By replacing collective by family cultivation, the new responsibility system has unravelled the network of mutual aid and local agro-technical and social services. From a distributive point of view, the team was like a bank: it advanced basic grain and distributed whatever was left over after various deductions according to remaining workpoints. The situation is reversed now; income in cash or kind accrues first to the constituent households, who are supposed to hand over a precontracted amount to the village to cover local services. The net effect is a considerable weakening in the authority and the resources at the disposal of the village.

Initially it was hoped that local services including the system of support for poor households would continue as before. But things have turned out differently. In the teams where collective organization and spirit were not strong to start with, local services broke down (see Bernstein, 1985; *China 1985*, no. 30, pp. 92–3 and 164 and *BR*, 1982, no. 9, p. 9). What is more important is that the breakdown is more likely to have happened in areas where the number of poor households is likely to be high. The government has been aware of these developments and has issued various circulars on help to poor households (see *BR*, 1981, no. 3, p. 22; 1981, no. 43, p. 3; 1981, no. 52, p. 7; 1983, no. 38, pp. 23–7; 1984, no. 9, p. 9; 1984, no. 46, p. 26; 1985, no. 4, p. 9; 1985, no. 27, pp. 14–15). Some villages have developed mechanisms for helping poor households, but these new mechanisms, like the old, are varied, and they are informal (on mechanisms of help see *BR*, 1982, no. 9, p. 9 and 1983, no. 38, p. 23).

The change to the responsibility system was not planned. Although the system was first introduced in 1980, it was only in 1984 that the government drew up a blueprint of new rural organizations (see *BR*, 1985, no. 20, p. 15). The government's reaction to the unravelling of the local networks centred on collective cultivation has been piecemeal. There are, however, some pointers to the system likely to emerge. It seems that responsibilities of production teams, especially of providing help to poor households, are being passed on to the newly created lowest tier of government (*xiang*) and the next tier, the county (*xian*) (see the issues of *BR* cited above and the chapter by Croll in this volume).

To conclude, there has been in place a makeshift multi-tiered mechanism for coping with nutritional contingencies. The guiding principle of that complex could be summarized in the slogan 'self-reliance, local mutual aid, assistance from a higher tier only in the last resort'. In effect, it has been a co-insurance system anchored in the state marketing system and collective cultivation. The latter no longer exists and the scope of the former is much reduced. The responsibility system has destroyed the network built around these two. As we have seen, the government is now more aware of the dimension of rural poverty and committed to eliminating destitution and undernutrition. But it is still groping towards an organizational structure for achieving this aim.

There are two perspectives on the Chinese system of coping with nutritional contingencies. One assesses the system as a social welfare and insurance mechanism and concludes that it has been makeshift and highly variable in coverage and method. Alternatively, we can start with China's achievements in keeping at bay the threat of starvation and severe undernutrition which has historically hung over its population and then conclude that achieving this aim does not require a sophisticated social welfare system.

Appendix 1
Rates of Growth of Population and Grain Production and Average Cumulative Rates of Grain Production (in percentages)

Year	Population	Grain	Average Cumulative Rates
1950	1.90	16.74	14.00
1951	2.00	08.74	10.45
1952	2.09	14.07	10.79
1953	2.29	01.77	07.79
1954	2.50	01.61	06.03
1955	1.98	08.50	06.14
1956	2.22	04.78	05.66
1957	2.90	01.19	04.66
1958	2.07	02.53	04.21
1959	1.83	−15.00	01.92
1960	−1.49	−15.58	00.36
1961	−0.53	02.78	00.57
1962	2.18	08.47	01.01
1963	2.79	00.06	01.19
1964	1.92	10.29	01.61
1965	2.89	03.74	01.55
1966	2.76	10.00	01.87
1967	2.45	01.78	01.72
1968	2.83	−04.02	01.27
1969	2.72	00.91	01.12
1970	2.88	13.74	01.54
1971	2.70	04.24	01.54
1972	2.29	−03.86	01.21
1973	2.33	10.17	01.47
1974	1.85	04.09	01.50
1975	1.72	03.36	01.49
1976	1.40	00.62	01.41
1977	1.34	−01.25	01.27
1978	1.35	07.79	01.45
1979	1.33	08.97	01.64
1980	1.19	−03.48	01.43
1981	1.38	01.39	01.39
1982	1.47	09.07	01.57
1983	0.94	09.25	01.76
1984	1.00	05.12	01.82

Source: *SYB* 1985.

Appendix 2
Unprocessed Grain Per Capita (kgs; all figures rounded)

Year	Level	Change
1949	209	—
1950	237	28
1951	252	15
1952	283	31
1953	281	–02
1954	278	–03
1955	296	18
1956	303	07
1957	299	–04
1958	299	00
1959	247	–52
1960	213	–34
1961	231	18
1962	245	14
1963	252	07
1964	273	21
1965	274	01
1966	292	18
1967	287	–05
1968	269	–18
1969	263	–06
1970	293	30
1971	294	01
1972	278	–16
1973	302	24
1974	308	06
1975	309	01
1976	306	–03
1977	304	–02
1978	324	20
1979	351	27
1980	337	–14
1981	338	01
1982	364	26
1983	391	27
1984	394	03

Sources:
1. 1949–82 from *SYB*, 1983;
2. 1983 from *TJZY*, 1984 (does not include exports);
3. 1984 from *BR*, 1985, no. 25, p. 15 (does not include exports or imports, and the population is estimated).

Appendix 3
Crude Birth and Death Rates 1953–82 (per 1,000)

Year	Crude Birth Rate	Crude Death Rate
1953	42.2	25.8
1954	43.4	24.2
1955	43.0	22.3
1956	39.9	20.1
1957	43.3	18.1
1958	37.8	20.7
1959	28.5	22.1
1960	26.8	44.6
1961	22.4	23.0
1962	41.0	14.0
1963	49.8	13.8
1964	40.3	12.5
1965	39.0	11.6
1966	39.8	11.1
1967	33.9	10.5
1968	41.0	10.1
1969	36.2	9.9
1970	37.0	9.5
1971	34.9	9.2
1972	32.5	8.9
1973	29.9	8.9
1974	28.1	8.3
1975	24.8	8.1
1976	23.1	7.8
1977	21.0	7.7
1978	20.7	7.5
1979	21.4	7.6
1980	17.6	7.7
1981	21.0	7.7
1982	21.1	7.9

Source: Banister, 1984.

Appendix 4
Ratio of Net-Export/Imports to Total Supply (in percentages)

Year	Ratio
1950	−0.88
1951	−1.39
1952	−0.94
1953	−1.10
1954	−1.00
1955	−1.13
1956	−1.315
1957	−0.100
1958	−1.35
1959	−2.50
1960	−1.88
1961	2.93
1962	2.90
1963	2.56
1964	2.47
1965	2.00
1966	1.63
1967	0.78
1968	0.945
1969	0.73
1970	1.34
1971	0.22
1972	0.755
1973	1.57
1974	1.60
1975	0.325
1976	0.21
1977	1.97
1978	2.23
1979	3.12
1980	3.55
1981	4.00
1982	4.02

Source: calculated from *SYB*, 1983.

Appendix 5
Levels of and Changes in Net-Import/Export Per Capita and Changes in Grain Production Per Capita (in kgs)

Year	Net-Imports	Changes in Net-Imports	Changes in Grain Production
1950	−02.1	−02.1	+30
1951	−03.50	−01.41	+16
1952	−02.65	+00.85	+30
1953	−03.08	−00.43	−01
1954	−02.79	+00.29	−03
1955	−03.34	−00.55	+18
1956	−03.98	−00.64	+08
1957	−02.98	+00.10	+05
1958	−04.03	−01.05	+01
1959	−06.18	−02.15	−50
1960	−04.00	+02.18	−36
1961	+06.76	+10.76	+07
1962	+07.12	+00.36	+14
1963	+06.45	−00.67	+08
1964	+06.74	+00.29	+20
1965	+05.50	−01.24	+02
1966	+04.76	−00.74	+19
1967	+02.23	−02.53	−02
1968	+02.54	+00.31	−19
1969	+01.92	−00.62	−04.5
1970	+03.94	+02.02	+27.5
1971	+00.65	−03.29	+04
1972	+02.10	+01.45	−17
1973	+04.75	+02.65	+20
1974	+04.93	+00.18	+07
1975	+01.00	−03.93	+05
1976	+00.64	−00.36	−02.5
1977	+05.99	+05.35	−07.5
1978	+07.23	+01.24	+19
1979	+10.79	+03.74	+23
1980	+11.97	+01.00	−15
1981	+13.54	+01.57	00
1982	+14.64	+01.1	+24

Source: calculated from *SYB*, 1983.

3 The New Peasant Economy in China

Elisabeth J. Croll

One of the most important dimensions of the recent rural reforms in China has been the new interest in and focus on the peasant household as the basic economic, political and social unit in the countryside.[1] Indeed, during the past five years or so the peasant household has virtually replaced the collective as the dominant unit of production in rural China. The peasant household itself has consequently become a much more complex unit engaging in a number of wide-ranging economic activities which in turn have placed new and important resources at its disposal and given rise to the most significant increases in peasant income since the 1950s.

The process by which the peasant household has become the major unit of production is the reverse of that of the 1950s when the means of production, including land, were gradually collectivized. Then, the resulting shift in responsibility for production, accounting, planning and distribution from the household to the collective, either the commune, production brigade or production team, reduced both the property base and the production responsibility of the individual peasant household. As a result, the peasant household economy had become a much simplified economy and its autonomy and control over resource allocation and production output had been much diminished. However, despite its encapsulation by the collective, the peasant household economy did remain a more important unit of production than was generally recognized and it constituted a much underrated and under-studied fourth tier of the rural production system. Within the collective it was a subsidiary, though important, unit of production. Nevertheless, important though it was then, its significance as an economic unit pales when we look at the fundamental shifts in the balance of production responsibility between the individual peasant household and the collective that have taken place since 1978. As a result of recent shifts in responsibility for production, in the balance of production for the plan and for the market and between private and public forms of resource allocation, the attention of planners and analysts has increasingly focused on the new attributes of the peasant household economy.

After the death of Mao Zedong, the new leadership initiated a number of rural economic reforms designed to alter inter-sectoral relations in favour of agriculture, increase rural production, improve the management of the rural economy, diversify agriculture and furnish incentives to raise productivity and to increase peasant income. To achieve these ends, the government has contracted land and production quotas to the peasant household under the responsibility system, developed domestic sideline production and encouraged diversification and specialization in commodity production.

The Rural Responsibility System

The original aim of the rural responsibility systems was to introduce a new form of management in the collective sector, reduce the size of the labour group and provide incentives to promote production and link reward more directly to performance.[2] Initially it was not intended either to increase the autonomy of the peasant household as a unit of production – and so radically alter its relationship with the collective – or to extend responsibility for production to all households throughout the country. Rather a responsibility system was primarily conceived as a means by which the production team was to enter into a contract with a small labour group, individual labourer or household which imposed a new set of rights, obligations and responsibilities for production on both parties. There was to be a good deal of variation in the degree of responsibility assigned downwards by the production team, the parties to whom this responsibility was to be delegated and the means by which reward or remuneration was to be calculated. For instance, the party contracting with the production team might be a small work team, a peasant household or even an individual, and the degree of responsibility assigned to them might range from responsibility for individual production tasks to responsibility for the entire production process based on allocated lands, with payment negotiated according to the demands of the labour process or according to output. In all these responsibility systems, the production team was to remain the overall unit of production, planning, management and accountancy and maintain its former economic and political controls.

The government had anticipated that the type of responsibility system instituted in any one region would be determined by the fertility of the area, its natural assets, the degree of mechanization, its proximity to markets and its existing levels of livelihood. Where conditions of production were large-scale and highly mechanized and where commune members already had a high standard of living, as in the suburban communes surrounding the cities and the rich arable areas of the eastern seaboard, then the government recommended that the production team allocate agricultural tasks to small work-teams. In intermediate areas less well endowed, and described as neither rich nor very poor, the production team was encouraged to contract land and output quotas to individuals. Only in poorer inland and infertile areas was land to be contracted to the peasant household and payment to be negotiated according to output.[3] However, far from constituting such a graduated continuum, it became increasingly apparent that the distribution of land to the household with payment made according to output had taken place over most of China. Whereas at the end of 1982 it was reported that 79% of China's production teams had adopted this system, a year later at the end of 1983 it was estimated that in 98% of China's production teams land had been contracted out to peasant households.[4] This responsibility system in one form or another is now prevalent in almost all of China including the richer suburban communes.

In the most common form of the responsibility system in operation, usually referred to by its Chinese term *bao gan dao hu*, 'contracting everything with the peasant household', the village government contracts out land and output quotas to each household. The household is thus allocated land for cultivation, draught animals and small- and medium-sized equipment for its use. These responsibility lands are allocated to the household on a per capita or per labourer basis; to ensure fairness of distribution where land is variable, portions of good, average and poor lands are equally distributed to each household (*RMRB*, 1 August 1983). The responsibility lands are not privately owned, but are allocated for use over a fixed period of time. In most areas this is likely to have recently been extended to a minimum of 15 years or even longer for waste land and other lands that require high initial investment to bring them into production. On the land each household contracts to grow specified crops and provide a portion of the harvest set according to the expected yield of the land and the total crop harvest. Any surplus over and above these quotas may be retained by the household for its own use, be sold in the market, or it may be sold to the state at above quota prices. The household takes responsibility for all field management from sowing to harvesting and for the costs of production including the hire or exchange of animal labour and small machines. In addition to cropping based on contracted lands, peasant households may also contract to undertake a variety of domestic sideline activities.

Domestic Sideline Production

A marked characteristic of rural economic policies in the late 1970s was the legitimation and promotion of household or domestic food production based on the cultivation of the private plot and the raising of domestic livestock such as pigs, sheep, rabbits, chickens, ducks and geese.[5] Policy regulations formulated at the time of the establishment of communes in 1958 clearly allowed for the rights of peasant households to undertake these sideline activities. Indeed, peasant households soon came to depend on their domestic production to provide the majority of their non-staple food supplies – especially of vegetables – and to generate a substantial portion of their cash income with which to purchase additional supplies. However, despite the importance of domestic production to the domestic and national economy, the very existence of this private sector within the collective economy constituted a source of tension and debate; domestic production has been the subject of marked policy changes. Indeed, before the late 1970s, government policy towards domestic production was marked by several attempts to either eliminate it or impose limits, but on each occasion these attempts were followed by a restoration of domestic production which was an essential source of non-staple food and cash income. Since the late 1970s, however, the government has not only legitimized and stabilized this sector but it has actively encouraged the expansion of domestic production by the household.

In the current search for every available means to expand the rural economy it is clear that domestic sidelines are one of the areas of the economy most immediately extended in scope. Domestic sidelines have the advantage that their labour and capital are chiefly provided by the individual peasant household and that they provide, at little cost to the state or the collective, quick returns, rapidly increasing supplies of food and small consumer goods for subsistence and exchange and make raw materials available for industry. In the past, domestic sideline production has mainly been limited to cultivating private plots, the raising of small numbers of domestic livestock, the gathering of wild plants, the production of handicrafts and other small-scale activities which chiefly provided for subsistence. With the exception of a period in the early 1960s, the government has never encouraged the expansion and diversification of these private and individual sidelines; it has rather preferred that any expansion and diversification of production should take place at the collective level. Now any doubts that the government may have had previously seem to have taken second place to the more immediate priorities of finding employment for surplus labour, providing for and developing the market and improving peasant livelihoods. For instance, the development of family-based industries seems to constitute an ideal solution to the most pressing problem of reducing surplus labour and of finding jobs for the unemployed, the numbers of which are increasing in the countryside today. The government thus plans that with 'the full development of the individual industries of thousands upon thousands of peasant households, the surplus labour of thousands and thousands of individuals will be absorbed' (*RMRB*, 8 October 1981).

To encourage the peasant household to increase the production of domestic sidelines, the government has expanded the area allotted to private plots and fodder lands. From 1980 onwards there have been a number of regulations enlarging private plots and abolishing restraints on their use (Walker, 1984, p. 789). According to official figures the area of private plots increased by 23% between 1978 and 1980 with the area allotted to private plots accounting for 5.7% of arable lands in China in 1978 and 7.1% in 1980. A State Council directive in March 1981 raised the maximum allowed to 15% of arable land but this was only deemed appropriate in areas where the per capita land ratio was relatively favourable. In addition to private plots, private fodder and waste lands may also be allocated to peasant households. To provide an additional outlet for sideline products and to encourage peasant households to produce a wide variety of goods over and above those necessary for family subsistence, the government has re-established rural fairs or markets where goods, foods, local handicrafts and daily necessities can be exchanged between the producer and purchaser at a negotiated and agreed price according to local supply and demand.

In addition to the revival of local handicrafts, the production of foods and small goods for daily use and the local market, the government has encouraged the home-based production of goods for export. In poorer provinces where land is scarce or infertile, county offices have distributed materials for handicraft goods and organized the production and purchase of finished products according to fixed schedules, quality and quantities.[6] Provincial administrations may now negotiate contracts directly with foreign agencies to buy these goods, and in a few localities the present government has formed special economic zones where joint Chinese and foreign capital have established enterprises which also distribute raw materials to peasant households for processing and the purchase of the finished products.[7] As a result of these policies encouraging domestic sidelines, the household has once more become the substantial producer of goods for subsistence and exchange. In these activities, too, the contract system, whereby production quotas for raising animals, cultivating vegetables and fruit and producing small goods for the state are distributed to individual households with the household retaining control of the surplus, is becoming a major form of production.

Diversification and Specialization

The diversification of the rural economy is one of the current platforms in China which has been developed with a view to broadening the previous and narrower emphasis on grain production, developing cash cropping, specializing, providing employment for surplus labour, increasing rural industry and developing the rural economy generally and with it peasant purchasing power and livelihood. The present government has thus revised the former slogan of 'taking grain as the key link' in favour of effecting 'the all-round development of agriculture', and it has done so most especially in areas where natural conditions are more favourable to the development of cash cropping, forestry, animal husbandry, fishing and other activities. The present leadership's policy aims to abandon the traditional small-scale rural economy undertaken mainly for subsistence in favour of diverse, specialized and commodity production. This substitution is thought to be the prerequisite to developing the wealth of the country.

> The experiences of many years have proved that we can never extricate ourselves from self-sufficiency or a semi-sufficient economy if we simply rely on tilling the land, concentrate all labour power in the fields and have all 800 million peasants growing food crops (*NCNA*, 16 June 1981).

The government has encouraged diversification and specialization of commodity production at both inter-regional and intra-regional levels. It has increasingly emphasized that areas which are quite unsuitable for growing grain should be encouraged to develop other agricultural activities. Thus, hilly and mountainous areas which are more suitable for forestry and pasture are to engage in these activities. Similarly, regions such as the Pearl and Yangtze river deltas which are better suited to the production of cash crops such as sugar-cane, flowers, vegetables and bananas and to breeding fish are to develop these products for both internal and external markets. As a recent policy statement suggested, these regions 'should not necessarily try to achieve self-sufficiency in grain much less should they engage in building bases for producing commodity grain'.[8]

Likewise, within regions, a degree of diversification and specialization is encouraged and there is an increasing division of function between village households. This is the result of a second and increasingly important development in which peasant households are being encouraged to move outside agriculture for employment and to develop specialized production that may be non-agricultural in nature.

Gradually over the past five years, the development of specialized commodity production has become one of the main platforms of the present government.

> The rural economy is now being transformed from a self-sufficient and semi-self-sufficient economy to a commodity economy, and the business of engaging in specialised jobs and in a multiplicity of occupations besides farming and socialised production has developed in varying degrees (*RMRB*, 1 August 1983).

The introduction of specialized households marks the beginning of a new type of household economy – one that is 'small and specialized' as opposed to one that is 'small and complete'.[9] A rural household is said to be specialized if it is a family-managed unit characterized both by a certain high proportion of commodity production and by specialization in product or service. In practice within a village it is often the size of the enterprise that determines its categorization. In some localities a household is said to be specialized if the main labour force works or manages some form of specialized commodity production with the income from commodity production accounting for 50% or more of the total household's income.[10] In other localities it is simply the number of rabbits, poultry or other products which determine its classification.

Specialized households need not contract responsibility lands; indeed they are increasingly encouraged to disengage themselves from working in the fields. Thus in 1984 the government permitted the subcontracting of responsibility lands between peasant households so that those households which were engaged in non-agricultural pursuits might subcontract out their lands to neighbouring peasant households with surplus labour and agricultural skills who in turn will farm their lands on their behalf. The government anticipates that as few as 30% of China's 800 million peasants may be engaged in crop cultivation in the future.[11]

Types of Peasant Household Economy

As a result of the new rural policies there has been an increasing differentiation of function and division of labour within rural villages although some 85% or so of peasant households continue to operate a much expanded mixed economy. They cultivate lands allocated to them by the village government and undertake domestic sidelines both for subsistence and for purchase by the state or in local markets. A typical peasant household will thus either produce grains for subsistence, for purchase by the state or the market or it will cultivate cash crops for state purchase and local markets on the responsibility lands and also produce vegetables, pigs, poultry and poultry products and handicraft goods for its own use as well as for the local or export market. It is still something of a self-sufficient unit and the main difference compared to the past is that it now has more control over both its produce and the allocation of its resources. In one group of villages in Shanxi province in 1983, approximately one-third of the peasant households remained in diversified farming activities, one-third specialized in industrial and sideline production or in providing services such as transport, commerce and water conservation and the remaining third specialized in commodity grain production. The latter third cultivated almost 58% of the responsibility lands allocated and supplied grain to most of the households specializing in services and in non-grain commodity production (*NYJSJJ*, November 1983).

The proportion of specialized households within any one region is likely to be higher in coastal areas rather than inland and on the plains and hilly areas rather than in mountainous regions and in localities where the average arable land per capita is low. At the beginning of 1984 it was estimated that between 34 and 35 million or 13 to 14% of all peasant households had specialized in activities other than crop growing and that in some provinces this proportion had risen to 17%.[12] These numbers continue to rise and since peasant households are increasingly being encouraged to specialize in commodity production the characteristics of this second type of household are important in setting the trend for the future. A third type of peasant household economy is one that seems to be emerging in the suburban communes where part-time farming households are becoming more common. Normally one worker on the land, frequently a retired person, remains in agriculture while the other members, employed elsewhere, confine their farming activities to the evenings and to their days off. For all these types of peasant households the resultant changes in productive structures and the division of labour have fundamentally altered the economic and political relations between the peasant household and the collective, between peasant households within the village and relations within the peasant household itself.

The Peasant Household and the Collective

The relationship between the peasant household and the collective has been largely redefined by the introduction of the rural responsibility system, the expansion of domestic sidelines and commodity production and by the reduction of the political and socio-economic role of the collective in arranging for production, consumption and welfare of the individual peasant household. The government anticipates that a new partnership between the collective and the peasant household will evolve in which the collective, instead of being the main unit of production as in the past, will encourage and support the peasant household by providing goods and services which will enable the household to better fulfil its role as the main unit of production of crops and sidelines.[3]

Collective Services for Production

Under the new system of *bao gan dao hu*, the village government has remained responsible for distributing land and drawing up the terms of the production contracts with individual households. In this it is advised by the state planners who set the cropping patterns, the overall timetables for production and the expected yields for the administrative unit. The collective was responsible for the purchase of the production output quotas at a fixed price and a portion of this produce was then transferred to the state either in the form of agricultural taxes or as the fixed production quotas set for the collective. However, the role of the collective or village government and the state in fixing production quotas is likely to be reduced in the future, for the state is gradually reducing its control of cropping design and the disposal of agricultural products. In May 1984, the State Council announced that individual peasants and rural supply and marketing cooperatives were permitted to buy, transport and sell grain on the markets both in and outside of their counties and provinces so long as taxes and quotas were first fulfilled (*XH*, 5 August 1984). This was a major change, but it marked only a beginning in the redefinition of the relationship between the market and state in grain supply. In 1985 the state abolished the state monopoly on the purchase of grain and from then on peasant households were to depend largely on contracts and the market to determine what grain they would grow rather than, as previously, on mandatory state production and purchase quota plans. In the first few months of 1985 each province thus abandoned its planned mandatory purchasing quotas of grain and instead arranged for local grain bureaux to enter into contracts with peasants to supply various types and amounts of grain. In total the state plans to purchase 120–160,000 million *jin* of grain or 15 to 20% of the harvest on a contract basis (Zhao Ziyang, 1985). The price paid for grain purchased by contract is to be fixed according to state regulation and the remaining surplus grain will be sold at market prices and subject to market fluctuation.

The village government is thus being increasingly relegated to a supportive role whereby it arranges for the supply of technology, capital, raw materials, provides transport, storage and processing facilities and gives market information and management guidance. These are all areas where the infrastructure has been weak in the past and which are frequently beyond the resources of the individual peasant household. The government recognized this problem when it recently stated that the new focus of the collective economy at all levels from the production team to the township or commune levels should be the servicing of the peasant household and more particularly the peasant household specializing in commodity production in order to both facilitate production and more particularly to ease circulation, distribution and consumption.

The main aim of the collective economy is thus to establish service units to guarantee supplies of seeds, fodder, fertilizers, oil and other means of production, capital loans to invest in stock, equipment and other services and to make available storage, processing and transport facilities to enable produce to reach the market. It is the collective which is to develop the infrastructure to facilitate the circulation of commodities and advise the individual peasant household in establishing a new relationship between production and demand and demand and marketing. The experience of collectives which have established these services has been reported in the press as an example to others. In the case of Heilongjiang province, 500 service stations have been established which offer technical and other services to meet the demands of specialized households which produced 86% of the city's eggs, 60% of the milk and 95% of the pork.[14] These service stations provided a whole range of pre- and post-production services, including facilities for artificial insemination, disease prevention, fodder processing and marketing. Elsewhere in another report, a production brigade in which as many as 60% of peasant households were specializing in commodity production established nine service companies including some dealing with agricultural machinery and water irrigation (*HQ*, 28 March 1984). Where households specialized in raising cattle and sheep, it was the collective which had established milk powder processing plants and was responsible for the marketing of the milk. Where it was the cultivation of mushrooms which was the speciality, the collective organized the spore-raising and made available funds, equipment and technical services to aid the peasant household.

However, in diversifying and developing specialized commodity production, much will depend on the effectiveness of local government and so far not all village governments have been as assiduous in providing such support and services; there have been a number of reports of peasant households bankrupted because of lack of supplies of fodder or fertilizer or because of difficulties in selling their produce even in relatively wealthy Jiangsu (*BR*, 28 November 1983). Thus much of the success of the responsibility system rests on the development of a new division of labour between village or production team and the peasant household, with the one engaged in production and the other in servicing production.

The Welfare Services of the Collective

The collective is not only to provide new services in support of peasant household production. It is also to continue to accumulate public welfare funds and to be responsible for providing local welfare services as before. Both now and in the past, peasants who are old, weak, widowed, disabled, orphaned or handicapped are always primarily the responsibility of their immediate family and kin. But the collective and the state, in the absence of this support, have provided for basic needs in the form of the 'five guarantees' of food, clothing, medical care, housing and burial expenses. Since the introduction of the responsibility system, the collective welfare funds may have been at risk because of the new economic arrangements whereby peasant households retain the control of their surplus produce and make their own separate contributions to the collective welfare fund after the harvest. This contrasts with the previous practice whereby the production team extracted its welfare funds before income distribution. Local cadres have also found that their time is increasingly taken up with the administration of the responsibility system and cultivating their own lands and that they have less time or indeed even inclination to get involved in accumulating and distributing public welfare funds or the cultivation of produce for distribution to the needy. So the authority of the collective to extract individual household contributions for such funds will become very important, and the collective itself will have to maintain strong controls if the large and wealthy individual households are not to contract out.

The government has made some effort to ascertain the scale of the demand for welfare by instituting the first ever national survey of households requiring 'the five guarantees',[15] and by directing collectives to continue to support those who require assistance either by accumulating and distributing public welfare funds or by arranging for the cultivation of produce for distribution. Nevertheless, it is clear that the government favours some form of self-help or community care although organized on an *ad hoc* basis. The press ran a series of articles praising a county government in Anhui province which had developed its own networks for social relief (*BR*, 19 September 1983). During a 'help-the-poor' campaign, it had compiled a register of the needy and issued them with certificates entitling them to preferential consideration in regard to loans and access to means of production, reduction in medical expenses and free education for their children. Groups of willing cadres and peasants were then organized into 'help-the-poor' committees to give practical assistance to those in their immediate vicinity by helping them either to cultivate their lands or plots or develop their domestic sidelines such as pig-raising. On the basis of this and other examples, the government has very recently compiled a list of recommendations for helping the poor which is based on the establishment of similar 'help-the-poor' committees (*XH*, 25 March 1984). Such welfare provisions seem to imply a degree of voluntarism and self-help and in the absence of more formal institutions the welfare of the needy individual may well come to depend on the labour and material resources of their families even more than in the past. Moreover, informal provisions are unlikely to be sufficient in any drought or flood situation when welfare is demanded on a larger scale.

Two-Tier Management

In sum, the government has recommended that the collective undertake the unified management of services beyond the capacity of the individual peasant household in a new two-tier system that combines both collective and household management of the economy (*HQ*, 28 March 1982). That is, activities such as the distribution of land, the planning of crop cultivation, the construction of irrigation works, the purchase of heavy duty machinery and the establishment of collective welfare facilities remain the responsibility of the collective. Smaller undertakings within the capacity of the single domestic units are to be left to individual peasant households.

The government anticipates that this new division of labour between the collective and the peasant household will strengthen both the collective and peasant household economies and their interdependence. For the long term, the government has outlined a three-stage development cycle beginning with the responsibility system and contracting out of land and the diversification of the economy with the development of a specialized commodity production. The concentration of land use and development of specialized households marks the development of a second stage in which some peasant households remain in agriculture while others develop specialized non-agricultural occupations. The third stage will be marked by a new level of cooperation between households based on specialization and the division of labour, which is to be managed by the collective but on the basis of mutual support and equality (*NCNA*, 9 March 1982). However, already in rural areas the decentralization of management and production responsibility to the peasant household has proceeded faster than the central government originally intended and reports suggest that the collective economy, far from being strengthened, is weakening to a point where a significant degree of decollectivization is taking place. Collective assets such as heavy farm machinery have been dismantled and distributed to individual households by the collective and in some areas, collective property has even been disaggregated without the approval of the authorities. For instance, some small factories, schools and clinics have been dismantled and divided among peasant households.[16] From such spasmodic reports it is difficult to ascertain the scale of such unofficial decollectivization; but what is clear is that the intended division of labour between the collective and the peasant household has been altered in favour of the peasant household.

There is evidence to suggest that the peasant household has acquired greater independence in its use of land, greater access to the means of production and a greater role in defining the division of labour and managing the labour process. It has acquired greater control of planning, investment and resource allocation and its produce and can participate in the wider economy through exchange. There is also evidence to suggest that peasant households themselves perceive the balance of power in both production and reproduction to have been altered in their favour and to have increased their own bargaining power vis-à-vis the collective and the state. In one commune, peasants had apparently bared the fields of topsoil to make mud bricks for house building. When they were reproached, they were reported to have replied that 'now that the land has been contracted out for use to peasants, you can mind your own business. What's the harm anyhow in taking a bit of earth to make bricks' (Gittings, 1984). In other cases reported, peasants also argued against the implementation of the single-child family policy in similar terms.

We cultivate our land, eat our own grain and bring up all our children on our own.[17]

We have taken responsibility for the land and there is no need for you to bother about our childbirth.[18]

Reports from China increasingly suggest that the balance of power favours the peasant household and that the new bargaining power of the households within the collective may well have increased beyond the point where the previous balance of controls over produce and labour in favour of the collective can easily be regained.

Relations between Peasant Households

Before 1978 it can be argued that the traditional exchanges of goods and services between neighbouring peasant households had been institutionalized and encouraged by the process of collectivization. By this process all kinds of exchange had moved from what had been an informal and *ad hoc* basis to one that was institutionalized and officially prescribed on the basis of a common neighbourhood and common economic, political and social interests. The peasant households within the rural villages were thus required to co-operate and maintain a high degree of intimacy or frequency of contact between kin and neighbourhoods who, within the framework of the collective, were responsible for the common accumulation, allocation and distribution of resources within the village. Although an exchange of goods and services may continue it seems likely that the new independence and autonomy of each peasant household will cause new and increasing divisions and income differentials between peasant households and therefore some fragmentation of the village community.

Peasant Incomes
One of the main aims of the rural economic reforms has been to improve peasant livelihood by altering the relationship between accumulation and consumption in

favour of consumption and raising standards of living. Indeed a major policy document of 1984 stated that the main criterion for judging the 'correctness' of the government's new agricultural policies was not whether they furthered socialist or national development but whether they enriched the peasants rapidly.[19] In the long term the government is aiming for an average annual income in the countryside of Y1,000 per capita; but in the short term this seems very ambitious despite the substantial rises in peasant incomes. Throughout the countryside a combination of economic reforms and new pricing policies have caused the largest overall rise in peasant incomes since the 1950s (Travers, 1984). There have been a number of surveys of peasant cash incomes over the past few years which, although little is known about their sampling techniques and the definition and categorization of income, do illustrate the general trend of rising peasant household cash incomes. One survey undertaken in 1982 suggests that the proportion of peasant households earning a cash income of between Y200 and Y500 annually has risen substantially (see Table 3.1).

Table 3.1
Peasant Per Capita Income, 1978 and 1982[a]

	Percentage of Households	
	1978	*1982*
Earning more than Y500	0.6	6.7
Earning between Y500 and Y200	27.4	66.5
Earning less than Y200	72.5	26.8
	100	100

[a] Based on a survey of 22,000 peasant households in 589 counties.

Source: *BR*, 16 May 1983, p. 7.

One of the most detailed household surveys undertaken in China recently suggested that average per capita peasant incomes may have more than doubled between 1979 and 1982, rising from Y133.6 to Y270.11 (*BR*, 24 October 1983, pp. 22–3). Lee Travers has made adjustments to these figures to compensate for the bias in selection of households, and his revised figures show a less dramatic but still significant rise in incomes from Y108.24 in 1978 to Y165.96 in 1981 (Travers, 1984, see Table 3.2).

In 1983 another sample survey suggested that the increase in the average annual per capita income was continuing quite substantially, although like earlier surveys it does not take into account the simultaneous rise in prices.[20] However in 1984 a more sophisticated survey did take these into account. It calculated that although the average per capita income of Y355 in that year represented an increase of 160% over 1978, the percentage rise would be reduced to 100% if price rises were allowed for (*SWB*, 6 April 1985).

However there is a wide range in household incomes both inter- and intra-regional, and within rural villages there are marked differences in the degree to which peasant households have been able to expand their economies and take

Table 3.2

Sample Survey of Peasant Per Capita Income 1978–82 (Y)

	Sample Survey	Travers' adjustments
1978	133.57	108.24
1979	160.17	127.76
1980	191.33	145.75
1981	223.44	165.94
1982	270.11	—

Sources: 'Sample Survey of Peasant Household Income', *BR*, 24 October 1983, pp. 11–12; Travers, 1984, pp. 241–60.

advantage of the new economic reforms. At the outset the government anticipated that in the next few years 30 to 40% of peasant households would become rich, 40 to 50% would achieve considerable improvements while 15 to 20% of peasant households with little or no labour power, no technical qualifications and no planning or business acumen would still encounter difficulties in meeting basic needs (*NCNA*, 9 March 1982). In a similar vein, the government has forecast that within any one collective it is likely that on average the richer households will earn two to three times the income of poorer households (although even greater differentials are probable in some localities); these are seen to be an inevitable consequence of the greater household control of production. At the present time the government seems prepared to tolerate the rising differentials in the interests of promoting riches for some.

Within the villages there is a strong correlation between the wealth of a peasant household and its labour resources, its skills and management qualities and the degree to which it has been able to diversify its economy into sidelines. Most of the new and very rich or so-called '10,000-yuan households' are reported to be large households with access to much family labour (Zhang Huaiyu, 1981) and a high degree of educational and management skills (*RMRB*, 1 August 1983). Almost without exception it is the specialized households and households whose domestic sidelines furnish a high proportion of their income which have earned the highest incomes over the past five years. Where peasant households have widely diversified their economies or specialized in the production of a commodity then the proportion of their income derived from field cultivation has declined quite dramatically. Table 3.3 thus shows that only 20% of the total income of the richer specialized households derives from field cultivation while poor peasant households obtain more than 65% of their income from field cultivation.

Reports suggest that those which undertake full-time commodity production and earn the highest incomes are more likely to be cadres or ex-cadres of production brigades or communes or young educated persons and ex-servicemen who may have had some experience in management, developed their own networks for communication or acquired technical or specialist skills.[21] At the other end of the continuum there is a proportion of peasant households within any one village which have not been able, or indeed are not in a position, to take advantage of the new

Table 3.3
Sources of Peasant Income, 1983

Types of household in order of wealth	Proportion of total income from field cultivation (%)
Specialized households	20
Well off households	33.5
Poor peasant households	66.5

Source: Results of 1983 Survey of Rural Economy, *RMRB*, 1 August 1983.

policies. These include both 'five guarantee' households and those officially classified as 'impoverished'.

Today the poorer members within rural communities are those lacking able-bodied members, funds or technology. The proportion of households with low incomes has declined (see Table 3.1); but nevertheless the figures available at provincial and local levels suggest that about 7% of peasant households are still officially classified as 'impoverished'.[22] A preliminary enquiry in one of the counties of Anhui province in 1983 showed that 5,300 or 6.7% of the county's rural households were in need of some assistance (*BR*, 19 September 1983). In another county study in Jiangsu province, the average per capita income of the 200,000 peasant households in 1982 was Y260, but while some 80 of these earned more than Y1,000 and 3,400 had a per capita income of more than Y500, approximately 10,000 households had an income of Y100 or so which was considered to be below the poverty line (compared with Y40 or less which had been the official poverty line before 1978). Thus at one extreme in the county, a chronically ill husband, his wife and four young children had a debt of Y69 at the year's end; at the other, a husband, wife and their two children raised more than 2,000 chickens which netted an annual income of Y5,000 (*BR*, 28 November 1983).

It is not only the increase in the range of incomes which suggests that there is a new degree of differentiation within the village. Reports on the quality of inter-household relations within the rural community also suggest that there may be a new degree of polarization within the village, recognized by rich and poor alike. There is increasing evidence to suggest that the richer, and particularly the specialized households, with outstanding wealth feel their position in the village to be threatened not only should there be a change in government policy but by the attitudes and actions of their fellow villagers. Many have therefore expressed doubts as to the wisdom of expanding their economy and becoming richer than their neighbours: 'Although we are willing, we dare not become well off. We fear that if we become well off we may suffer.'[23]

The government has made every effort to persuade peasants that the newly rich households have achieved their wealth by legitimate means through their own labour and the acquisition of skills and that they are merely paving the way for their fellow villagers who will follow in their footsteps and also become rich. However, it seems that their poorer neighbours remain unconvinced, for one of the main problems facing the richer households, and particularly specialized households in many villages, has been the threats to and attacks on their crops, property and persons.[24] There are numerous reports in the media which exhort collectives to take special measures to protect specialized households from violence.

So far an important element underlying these divisions within the village remains a household's access to labour resources and particularly its family labour resources. The increased demand for labour by the individual peasant household has led to some restructuring of the division of labour and of gender and age relations within the peasant household.

Within the Peasant Household: Labour Resources

A rich and complex peasant household economy not only demands new material resources but also access to and control of new labour resources so that it can deploy its labour in different sectors of the economy and in a wide variety of occupations. For the past twenty years the labour resources of a peasant household have been one of the most important determinants of a peasant household's income and welfare. Previously, as a result of collectivization, the peasant household no longer relied on the exploitation of family lands or estates so much as on the waged and domestic labour of each member of the household. Labour was the chief means by which a household fulfilled its obligations to the collective production unit, cultivated its private plot, raised livestock, undertook domestic sideline handicraft production and serviced family members. The performance of all these activities, whether collective, private or domestic, relied on the accumulation of labour resources by the household and on its management and distribution between these three sectors. The peasant household also aimed to ensure a plentiful and steady supply of labour by having at least three to four children, and timing their marriage and births so that potential labourers might be recruited into the labour force at about the same time as the older generation or grandparents retired. In the 1970s, it became increasingly clear that peasant households had become more elaborate in form than at any time during the recent past. The expansion in size of the peasant household and the establishment of extended or joint families for at least one stage in its developmental cycle had been encouraged by a number of economic and demographic factors. In rural areas where post-marital residence was still patrilocal, marriage usually immediately occasioned the expansion of the domestic group. It was this phase which offered a unique opportunity for the household to make use of its expanded labour resources to diversify its economy and develop a number of specializations. As a result some large families did not divide (or *fenjia*) and in other cases, household division might be delayed until sufficient wealth had been accumulated to facilitate it.

Now that the peasant household has become the main unit of production with individual responsibility for cultivating land and unlimited domestic sideline production, the demands of the labour resources of the peasant household are even greater than before (see Table 3.4).

The government has recognized this new demand for labour by the peasant household and in a radical new policy it now permits the hiring of labour by peasant households. There seems to be some uncertainty as to the details of the new policy, for instance in the number of labourers that any one peasant household may employ, for reports suggest a ceiling of anywhere between five and nine persons. There also seems to be a wide variation in the extent to which the practice is presently encouraged; but one of the reasons why it may become more widespread in the future is the new government's family planning policy which in principle at least limits the number of children permitted to be born to each peasant family to one child per couple.

Table 3.4
Demands on the Labour Resources of the Peasant Household

Before 1978

Collective Sector Production	Domestic Sector Sidelines	Servicing	Welfare
Cropping, live-stock, industries	Private plot Livestock Handicrafts (mainly for subsistence)	Sewing Cooking Laundry Shopping Cleaning	Child care Care of elderly

After 1978

Collective Production	Production for the Collective	Domestic Sector Sidelines	Servicing	Welfare
Some live-stocks, industries	Cropping and livestock	As above but expanded, mainly for the market	As above	As above

Family Size

That peasant households have traditionally perceived there to be a direct correlation between the size of the family and its income and welfare is reflected in many an old folk saying which linked the idea of greater family size and more children to more wealth and blessings. This link still holds sway in much of rural China where many of the 'thousand-yuan and ten-thousand-jin' households are recognizably larger than their neighbours'. The results of a recent survey in China also suggested a strong correlation between the size of family and level of income (see Table 3.5).

The continuing desire to maximize family labour resources to take advantage of the new income-generating opportunities is likely to affect fertility decisions and decisions concerned with family structure and division. Families may continue to delay division in the interests of maximizing their labour and the economic cooperation of their members and it is possible that if division does take place, economic partition may not be so complete as in the past when the peasant household was more fully incorporated into the collective structures and economy.

Table 3.5
Size of Family and Income

No. of Family Members	Per Capita Household Income	
	Less than Y100	*More than Y100*
	(%)	*(%)*
1–2	92	8
3–4	74	26
6–8	69	31

Source: Based on a survey of 396 peasant households in 1980 (reported in analysis of reproduction of rural population in *JJYJ*, 20 June 1984).

In other words, at the same time as household division with the establishment of separate budgets for consumption occurs, exchanges of labour and means of production and other forms of mutual economic support to do with production may be maintained. In rural China today, not only has the exchange of goods and services between households been encouraged, but households have also been encouraged to contribute to the joint purchase of and share in means of production and cooperation in enterprises. It is a fair guess and there is some evidence to suggest that kin ties have once more become a very important basis for these forms of exchange and cooperation.

The present and continuing desire to maximize family labour resources has also led to much opposition towards the new single-child family policy. The single-child policy, as its name suggests, is distinguished by its novel, universal platform – one child. Only in exceptional circumstances are two children to be permitted (Croll *et al.*, 1985; Croll 1983; Croll 1984). From its inception in 1979 there have been reports of increasing difficulties and problems in the implementation of the single-child family policy in the countryside. This is largely because of the conflicting demands on the peasant household as a unit of production and reproduction which have probably never been greater than in contemporary China. At the same time as peasant parents are to have just one child, the value of the labour resources of the peasant family has been maximized by the new economic policies. Because of the new income-generating activities, two to three children per couple are even more welcome additions to the labour force of the individual peasant household than previously. Recent surveys of preferred numbers of children and the factors determining family size in rural areas suggest that almost half the peasant women surveyed still want three or more children and that for the large majority, children's labour was still the primary form of insurance in their old age (see Table 3.6).

The importance attached to a family's labour resources in maximizing its income and supporting the elderly is also the reason why peasant couples continue to prefer to have a son who, because of post-marital residence patterns, will remain with them in the same neighbourhood if not the same household. The limit of one child has meant that the sex of the first born has become very important to households. In a recent survey of peasant households, a mere 2.2% preferred to have a daughter as an only child (*JJYJ*, 20 June 1983) and indeed, since the introduction of the single child family policy, there have been reports of rising female infanticide. If a peasant household has only one daughter then parents foresee a situation in which they will have no direct economic support. Even those with single sons look forward to a future in which a young married couple may have to support up to seven persons: two sets of grandparents, themselves and one child. The premium placed on family labour resources by the new economic policies and its direct conflict with the single child policy is probably a major reason why the government has recently relaxed its rules prohibiting the hiring of labour (see Bianca and Hera, this volume).

Table 3.6
Preferred Number of Children

No. of Children	Percentage of Women
1	4.81
2	51.24
3	28.43
4	15.52
	100.00

Based on survey of 728 women of child-bearing age (reported in *JJYJ*, 20 June 1982).

One means by which the peasant household can presently maximize its labour resources is to intensify the demands on the labour of each member and even the younger members of the household. That all family members are pressed into some form of income-generating activity, from grandparents to grandchildren, is evidenced by the decline in middle and even primary school rolls in the past five years as a result of the new demand on family labour. Peasant girls in particular have been withdrawn from full-time education in order that they can earn income for the peasant household.[25] For older peasant women who divide their time between production and reproduction, the expansion and reorganization of production has made new demands on their labour and affected the sexual division of labour within the peasant household (See Davin, this volume).

Divisions of Labour
The new economic reforms have affected the way in which peasant women structure their daily lives, the intensity of their labour and their relations with other members of the household. Again and again in interviews, peasant women noted that in the past, production team leaders who had responsibility for the production timetable allocated production tasks each morning and the work points they earned had been directly related to and dependent on their presence in the fields. Now however, they exercised a degree of daily control over the arrangements of production and enjoyed a new flexibility. Instead of staying in the field for set times regardless of the actual demands of the labour process, the peasants now laboured in the fields when crop production necessitated it and turned their attention to alternative activities at other times. They enjoyed this new flexibility although they also recognized that

many of them were now working harder than ever before. The degree of control which they exercised over their own labour was primarily determined by both the sexual division of labour and range of economic activities undertaken by the peasant household and the division of labour within it.

Where a peasant household continues to operate a mixed economy and combine agricultural cultivation on its contracted lands alongside the production of domestic sidelines, the contracting out of lands to peasant households and the diversification and unlimited expansion of domestic sideline production has increasingly brought about a new division of labour in which men undertake the field work and women the domestic sidelines.

Previously both the men and the women of the peasant household would have had to be present in the fields in order to earn sufficient work points. Now the new division of labour has come about as a consequence of two concurrent trends; the rise in surplus labour in the countryside and the diversification of the rural economy. The new calculation of remuneration according to output and the more efficient use of labour in the fields have led to a significant decline in the demand for labour in the fields. In one village for example, the field group responsible for the production of grain and vegetables on 300 *mu* of land was reduced from 70 in the first year of contract to 45, and by the third year the group numbered a mere 25 workers (Ma Ping, 1983). According to recent national reports, surplus labour has risen by a third or so over the past five years, and it is forecast that in the future the number of persons engaged in agriculture may be reduced by some two-thirds (Kong Keqing, 1980). Much of this surplus labour is likely to be made up of women, whether they were previously the main or auxiliary field workers. In one or two counties in Zhejiang province, for example, it is already estimated that more than 90% of the female workforce has no regular field work assignments, and even in busy seasons only a small percentage of this workforce is still required (Xu Dixin 1981, p. 6). Developing income-generating activities for this surplus labour has become an important and urgent problem, and collectives with surplus labour have thus encouraged peasant women to allocate more and more of their labour to domestic sideline production.

It has long been one of the characteristics of domestic sideline production that its scale of operation was almost exclusively determined by an individual household's access to women's and especially to older women's labour. Occupations such as cultivating vegetables, tending livestock and producing handicrafts have traditionally been performed by the women of peasant households. Consequently the expansion of domestic sidelines and diversifying the economy by raising pigs, chickens and other animals, fish-farming, the cultivation of vegetables and fruit, and the establishment of handicraft industries have all broadened the scope of women's income-generating activities so that the pattern whereby women stay at home and are engaged in various side-occupations is increasingly a characteristic of households in which the males are employed in full-time agricultural field work. Reports describing the way in which peasant households have taken advantage of the new economic reforms to expand their economies beyond field work frequently display this division of labour.

In the case of one peasant household located on the hills of Jiangxi province which earned an annual income of Y7,240, the men of the household were perfectly able to cultivate the fields once the responsibility system was in operation. By 1981 the husband and two sons cultivated 10.8 *mu* of paddy field yielding 9,300 catties of rice and 5 *mu* of dry lands which yielded 1,400 catties of tobacco (600 of which was sold to the state and the rest sold on the free market). They had also contracted to care for an orchard of fruit trees and 6.5 *mu* of small fish farms in which they kept a variety of carp. The 47-year-old wife no longer worked in the fields but devoted herself to tending three or four grown pigs, two litters of young pigs, numbers of chickens and the family vegetable garden which between them provided a fifth of the total annual cash income of the household (Liu Fanrong, 1983, p. 2). Elsewhere another peasant woman turned to the production of noodles as her main occupation once it was evident that her husband was able to take exclusive and meticulous care for their 6 *mu* of contracted land. Except in the harvesting and planting seasons, when there was still some demand for her labour, she processed noodles for her fellow villagers and raised a number of pigs and rabbits all of which enabled her to make a contribution of several hundred *yuan* to the household income. She thought her experience was not unusual and that peasant women were increasingly turning to side occupations now that they and their husbands did not both have to be in the fields merely to earn a minimum number of work points (Xiao Ming, 1983).

A quite different division of labour has been established in peasant households where the men of the household are employed in non-agricultural occupations. It was not uncommon before 1978 in regions where there was a range of employment opportunities outside agriculture for the men of the village to move into rural industries, capital construction projects, mining, fishing, forestry and other similar occupations. In such regions, the proportion of women employed in the agricultural field labour force was consequently much higher than elsewhere. Now these women cultivate the contracted lands in addition to expanding their domestic sidelines and undertaking domestic labour. It is commonly reported that many households in the countryside have become 'half-side' families, that is those in which the husband works in occupations other than agriculture and either commutes from the village on a daily basis or is absent for long periods. Combining the management and cultivation of contracted lands and expanding domestic sidelines is likely to increase the demands made upon the labour of those peasant women who already, before 1978, laboured from dawn to dusk to fulfil their collective and domestic obligations. In the last few years several women in these 'half-side' circumstances, and particularly younger women with small children, have noted their lives have become much busier as a result of the economic reforms; although they usually also add that as a result they now enjoy higher incomes.

Intensity of Female Labour

In one report from the poorer Yanbei region of northern Shanxi province, one young mother of three small children described how she alone farmed the land and undertook domestic sidelines. Her husband worked as a miner and lived away from the village so that once the responsibility system had been introduced she was allocated 17 *mu* of land on which to grow grains. After fulfilling her production quota for the state of 1,400 catties of grain, she managed to produce a surplus of 5,000 catties and indeed as a result of this increase the household had changed from a 'deficiency' household, or one that produced insufficient grain for subsistence, to a surplus household characterized by its own stores of reserve maize, rice and flour and a substantial cash income. In addition to the field work, domestic chores and caring for three children she also cultivated cucumbers, broad beans and tomatoes in her courtyard and raised a pig, three sheep and a dozen or so chickens. She thought that although she had had to work hard in the past, the recent expansion of domestic sidelines had made her daily routine even more demanding.

> Though it's hard work, we peasant women have been accustomed to work in the fields since we were children. Women continue to undertake field and household work but we have become even busier in the last two years mainly, because of keeping domesticated animals at home on the side (Xiu Ling, 1983, pp. 18–19).

In another village, as many as one-tenth of the households were for all practical purposes female-headed and operated in that the men of the household worked and resided away from the village (Xiao Ming, 1983). One wife with two young children whose husband worked and resided in a nearby town had contracted to work 4 *mu* of land after the introduction of the responsibility system. In order to support herself and her two children, she was kept busy in the fields cultivating wheat (3.5 *mu*) and cotton (0.5 *mu*). Because she was on her own she was often to be seen in the fields applying fertilizer, weeding, spraying and doing other jobs while keeping an eye on her children playing nearby. Her plot had one of the highest yields in the village and after putting aside 1,000 catties of wheat for her family's consumption, she was able to earn several hundred *yuan* from selling the remaining 1,800 catties of wheat to the state. In addition she earned a considerable income by raising pigs and chickens. She was very proud of the fact that she by herself had managed the household economy in such a way that it not only supported the family but also allowed them a surplus to accumulate for a new house. In the village as a whole, it was jested that several such wives held up not just 'half the sky' but 'all the sky'. As one husband ruefully remarked on his return to help with the harvest, 'Now that she [his wife] handles everything in and outside the house, I've been reduced to her farmhand' (Xiao Ming, 1983).

It is also one of the characteristics of specialized households that their operations are frequently planned and managed by the woman of the household. Many pig and chicken farms are managed by the peasant woman of the household, and the most successful chicken farm in China was established by a fifty-year-old peasant woman who had previously worked in the fields and whose husband worked away from the village. She decided to establish a chicken farm to supply eggs to the nearby market of Beijing which for years had chronically suffered a shortage of eggs. For this purpose she had applied for a state loan of Y7,500 to supplement family savings of around Y3,500 to build a four-roomed chicken house and the purchase of coops, ventilation and light equipment. After buying 1,000 chickens for breeding purposes, she signed a contract with the county animal husbandry bureau in which they supplied the chickens and feed and a local state chicken farm sterilized the coops and provided an inoculation service. She tended the chickens herself, and as a result of some experimentation her enterprise had proved to be very profitable. Within a year or so she had not only repaid the original loan but had been able to expand the enterprise to employ her teenage son on a full-time basis and earn a cash income of more than Y10,000 (Li Zhenying, 1983, p. 2).

Distribution of Rewards

The calculation of remuneration according to output probably on balance favours women workers and may well mean that they receive more equal pay and make a more equal contribution to the household budget than in the past. When both men and women laboured in the fields previously, the average number of workpoints allocated to women by the production team, whether they were calculated according to either female labour capacity or the type of agricultural task performed, was consistently two to three points lower than those awarded to men. Women's share of the earning may be equal now that remunerations made on the basis of fulfilling output quotas and rewards are distributed irrespective of the sex of the producer. But much will depend on them also receiving an equal share of the land and it is by no means clear that this is the case. Moreover where both men and women undertake field work there is the danger that women's individual contributions may become less visible; any payment due to the household will be calculated on the basis of output quotas regardless of the number and identity of the family members whose labour contributed to its production (see Davin, this volume).

Overall, the economic and social status of agricultural field workers, including women agricultural workers, has increased within the village as a result of the new economic policies. Previously they were disadvantaged in terms of income and other benefits compared to those employed in rural industry, the army and other occupations which took them beyond the village. Because of the higher prices paid for agricultural produce and the opportunities for combining field work with other income-generating activities, field workers in many regions have been placed in a better income-earning position than those on fixed wages outside agriculture. It is this factor which has done much to increase the status of the agricultural field workers within the village, and when it is the woman or the women of the peasant household who are the agricultural field workers this rise has increased their contribution to the household budget vis-à-vis other members of the peasant household employed outside agriculture.

Neither need the new division of labour, whereby women take responsibility for domestic sidelines and commodity production, necessarily be to their detriment; it is likely to increase their contribution to the household budget. But the degree to which this separate contribution is recognized and thus affects a woman's bargaining power within the household is probably largely determined by gender divisions within the household. Where the men of the household are employed in agricultural production, then in all probability it will be the male head of the household who will decide the organization of labour, the distribution of tasks within the household and receive the remuneration due to it from the collective. In these conditions the traditional relations of authority within the household may well be reproduced in production and affect a woman's share of rewards. Where the men of the household are engaged in pursuits other than agricultural field work, then women may well have gained a new flexibility and acquired a large measure of control over the peasant household economy in what for economic purposes have virtually become female-operated and headed households. However, female-headed households are commonly discriminated against in most agricultural systems and it remains to be seen how these households will fare in the new rural economy that is emerging in China.

Conclusion

The return to the peasant household as the basic unit of production means that it is the degree to which the household has access to and can deploy its labour resources which will primarily determine its overall income and welfare. In these circumstances, individuals are increasingly dependent on the peasant household to provide for their basic needs and well-being and much will therefore depend on the performance of each peasant household economy in meeting those needs. If a significant group of peasant households do not participate in the general rise in peasant incomes and see no way in which they will be able to take advantage of the new economic reforms, then divisions between peasant households may well affect intra-village relations to the point where some form of collective political controls and welfare provisions will have to be reinstituted in the interests of individual welfare, social order and stability. Within the peasant household it is largely the division of labour which will determine the role, status and authority of individuals within it. What is a very striking feature of all the literature on the devolution of responsibility to the household is that there seems to be little or no reference to the distribution of tasks and labour or rewards within the household itself. Although it has moved from the fourth to the first tier of the rural production system, the peasant household still remains a much under-studied institution.

Notes

1. A first draft of this paper was written while I was a visiting fellow at the Institute of Social Studies, The Hague, Netherlands. I would like to express my gratitude to the Institute for providing research facilities and particularly to Ashwani Saith for his discussions on the peasant household economy and his comments on this paper.

2. For articles on the rural responsibility system see 'Quota Fixing at Household Level', *SWB*, 28 December 1979 (FE 6305/B11/7, 8); 'Discussion on the Systems of Responsibility for Output Quotas by Production Teams in Rural People's Communes', *JJYJ*, 20 October 1980; 'Fixing Output Quotas for Individual Households', ibid., 20 January 1981; 'Communist Party Central Committee discusses Agriculture', *NCNA*, 19 May 1981; 'Prospects for Development of Double-contract System', *RMRB*, 9 March 1982 (*SWB*, 19 March 1982, FE/6982 B1158).

3. *NCNA*, op. cit., 19 May 1981.

4. 'Results of 1983 Survey of Rural Economy', *RMRB*, 1 August 1983; 'New Achievements in Rural Economy', *BR*, 5 September 1983; 'Rural Economic Reforms', *HQ*, 23 November 1984.

5. For discussion on domestic sidelines see Croll (1982); 'Defence of Domestic Sideline Production', *SWB*, 27 April 1978 (FE/5799/B11/9); and 'The Encouragement of Domestic Sideline Production'. *JJYJ*, 20 August 1979, pp. 28–33.

6. *NCNA*, 14 June 1980, 16 August 1980 and 30 August 1980.

7. 'Home Processing Industry in Shenzhen', *Nanfang Ribao* (Southern Daily), Guangzhou, 15 June 1980.

8. Zhao Ziyang, 'Reorganising Agriculture and Loosening Price Control', *SWB*, 2 February 1985; *XH*, 30 January 1985.

9. 'Developing Specialised Households is a Major Policy', *RMRB*, 23 January 1984.

10. 'Anhui Regulations on Specialised Households', *SWB*, 28 April 1984 (FE/7629/B11/7).

11. Du Runshung on 'Rural Development Plans', *XH*, 13 March 1984.

12. 'Expansion of Rural Production', *SWB*, 1 February 1984 (FE/W1272/A/2).

13. For articles on the new service role of the collective see: 'Report of Guangxi Rural Work Conference', *SWB*, 28 January 1984 (FE/7552/B11/10); 'Report of Agricultural Work Conference in Beijing', *SWB*, 2 February 1984 (FE/7556/C/1); 'Household-Based Responsibility System', *HQ*, 15 February 1984.

14. 'Rural Specialised Households in Heilongjiang', *SWB*, 21 January 1984 (FE/W1271/A/1).

15. 'Survey of Five Guarantee Households', *SWB*, 4 February 1984 (FE/7558/B11/5).

16. See William Hinton, reported in Schell, 1984, pp. 43–86 and John Gittings, 1984, pp. 3–6.

17. 'Rural Population Policy', *SWB*, 18 February 1982 (FE/6957/B11/4).

18. 'Population and Education in Family Planning Work', *RMRB*, editorial, 29 September 1981.

19. See Central Committee's Document No 1, 1984; 'Making Peasants Rich', *Shanxi Ribao*, 4 February 1984 translated in *SWB*, 8 February 1984 (FE/7561/B11/3).

20. See 'Report on 1983 Economy', *SWB*, 1 May 1984 (FE/7631/C/10).

21. 'Questions and Answers on Rural Work', *Shanxi Ribao*, 11 February 1984 translated in *SWB*, 24 February 1984 (FE/7575/B11/5).

22. See Report on Heilongjiang Province in *SWB*, 16 May 1984 (FE/7644/B11/6).

23. 'Shanxi Calls for Support for Specialised Households', *SWB*, 15 February 1984 (FE/7567/B11/5). See also *RMRB*, 23 January 1984; CCP Document No. 1 in the Countryside, *SWB*, 16 May 1984 (FE/7644/B11/4).

24. E.g. 'Ningxia County Police Protect Specialised Household', *SWB*, 28 February 1984 (FE/7578/B11/7).

25. 'The Women's Movement in China', *China Reconstructs*, 1 March 1979.

4   China's Food Take-Off?

Claude Aubert

Communist China used to be the object of the most contradictory judgements. Some saw it as the site of an original socialist path to development, while others saw it as a mere oriental variant of a Stalinist dictatorship. Until recently, however, whatever their political differences, all were agreed in recognizing that the new China had at least solved the centuries old problem of hunger and finally put an end to the past ravages of famine.

But even that image was destroyed when, in recent years, the Chinese authorities admitted that famine still affected almost 100 million people and when the population figures now available revealed an excess mortality due to famine of at least 15 million victims for the three dark years of the Great Leap Forward (1959–61).

What are we to believe? Fortunately, it is now possible to form a more considered opinion, based on better facts, thanks to the statistics that the Chinese themselves have begun to publish in recent years, and which, each year, are becoming more numerous and more detailed. It is these statistics that we shall present and analyse here. The figures are sometimes contradictory and interpreting them remains a delicate matter. But they do throw a new and often unexpected light on the food situation in China. And above all, they make it possible to understand better the reasons that have recently driven the present leaders to embark on an abrupt change in their agricultural policy, thus transforming the food strategy that has been followed in China for almost thirty years.

The Change of Direction

Before looking at the figures, it will help to recall the institutional framework of that earlier food strategy and set out briefly the changes that have recently occurred.

By the beginning of the 1950s, when collectivization had not yet been extended to the whole country, the state had already established its monopoly over rural commerce in agricultural and food commodities through the promulgation (in November 1953) of the Unified Purchase and Supply system. All the surpluses of essential crops – grains, edible oilseeds and cotton – had to be compulsorily sold to the state on the basis of administratively set quotas and prices; private transactions in these so-called 'first-category' commodities were prohibited (or very severely curtailed) and the state took responsibility for supplying families (or units) that were short. Later, other commodities, called 'second-category', such as pigs, poultry, eggs, etc., were also subjected to compulsory sale quotas; but surpluses of these remaining after delivery could be sold on the free market. There were no delivery quotas or any restrictions on the private sale of the remaining commodities, which were less important.

This state control of the marketing of crops, which was total in the area of foodgrains, obviously discouraged private speculation and helped to weaken the resistance of rich peasants to the later movement of collectivization. Indeed, the difficulties, already appearing by the autumn of 1954, of allocating quotas to millions of individual producers, made the formation of collective units more logical. In these circumstances it was not at all surprising that collectivization was not long in following, with the generalization of 'producers' cooperatives' during the winter of 1955-6. In 1958, the cooperatives were merged into 'people's communes' comprising several thousand families. The breaking of the peasant's link with his own land (as a result of the increased scale of work collectives), combined with the frantic mobilization of labour for hydraulic works and other non-agricultural activities, provoked such chaos that, in 1961-2, the government was forced to revert to simpler production structures. Henceforth – and this level of collectivization was to be maintained for some twenty years – agricultural work was organized, and crops distributed, in the framework of 'production teams' of some thirty families forming a hamlet or a village neighbourhood.

This dual institutional framework – compulsory deliveries of surpluses of the main crops and collective structures of production and distribution in the countryside – was the basis of a strategy of sharing basic products aimed at ensuring a minimum of food security for the whole population (see Chapters 2 and 3).

In the cities, rationing of the same basic commodities, mainly grains, ensured city-dwellers very cheap food, closely controlled by the state bureaucracy. In the countryside, every member of a production team was entitled to a 'basic ration' of grain. For foodgrains, the most flagrant disparities in consumption within a single village community were thus eliminated and the state could use its commercial monopoly to carry out the necessary equalization. For other commodities such as meat and vegetables there was less food security because these items were less subject to collective distribution or state control. Most of the pork and vegetables consumed, in small quantities, by the peasants came from their private plots (5–15% of the cultivated area depending on the place and the period). The supply of these latter commodities to the cities was much more unreliable than for grains; rationing was often synonymous with shortage. Nevertheless, given that, in the countryside as in the cities, grains constituted more than 80% of the caloric intake (see below), most consumption was the object of institutional mechanisms ensuring a minimum of security and equality for all.

Such a food policy seemed well conceived and the upheavals of recent years, questioning its foundations, therefore appear all the more astonishing, and even, to some, scandalous. The retreat of collective institutions and state monopolies since 1978 appears as the exact opposite of the evolution observed during the 1950s, decollectivization this time preceding the lifting of the monopolies.

In the beginning, in 1979, land was divided among small work-groups which made a 'production contract' with the team, allowing for the free disposal by the group of production surpluses over and above the contracted quantity of the crop (this latter being subject to collective distribution). Then production contracts were made directly with individual families during 1980. The 'division of budgets' soon followed the 'division of land', and, during 1981, 'farming contracts' with families gradually replaced 'production contracts': these 'farming contracts' limited the obligations of families over and above the compulsory sale to the state of quotas of the main crops at administrative prices to simply handing over to the team various taxes and expenses. Collective distribution, workpoints and basic rations were abolished. This latest 'responsibility system', which is rather like a sort of tenant farming, was generalized in 1982 and applied to 94% of peasant households by the end of 1983 (Aubert, 1984).

De facto decollectivization (the land remains collectively owned, but is now allocated for 15 years or more to individual families), has been accompanied, or rather followed, by an unprecedented liberalization of rural commerce. At the end of the 1970s, fairs and petty trading, which had been severely restricted, or even suppressed, during the last Maoist campaign 'of learning from the Dazhai brigade' (1975–7), made their reappearance and the peasants could again sell the products of their private plots (vegetables, etc.) as well as their over-quota surpluses of second-category products (pigs, poultry, etc.). This liberalization advanced slowly, and people were reminded, at the beginning of 1981, that private wholesale trade in all these products remained prohibited, and that peasants were only permitted to market their own produce, transported over short distances by their own means, without using mechanized or public transport (*RMRB*, 20 December 1980; *XH*, 15 January 1981).

Two years later, at the beginning of 1983, when the return to family farming had largely been achieved, commercial policy was further relaxed. The authorities recognized the advantage of increasing the variety of 'channels of commodity circulation', private or cooperative commerce making up the deficiencies of the state network. The peasants were now allowed to sell on the free markets the surpluses of all their commodities, including grains (but excluding cotton and tobacco), after delivery to the state of compulsory quotas. Wholesale commerce by private traders was permitted as well as long-distance transport for business purposes with hiring of lorries, boats or railway waggons. Peasant traders simply had to take out a licence and pay the commercial taxes.[1]

At the same time the state began of its own volition to reduce the scope of its monopolies by reducing the number of 'second-category' commodities subject to compulsory deliveries. These dropped from about 30 to fewer than 20 during the spring of 1983, and then to only 7 by the autumn of 1984 (Radio Guangdong, 5 April 1983; *SWB*, p. 1233; *JJRB*, 6 October 1984). For the basic first-category commodities (grains, cooking oils, etc.), while not removing the delivery quotas, the state encouraged private traders and cooperatives to share in marketing them whereas, hitherto, wholesale trading in them had been the sole prerogative of the state depots (marginal quantities being released on to the free market).[2]

As the logical conclusion to this slow relinquishment by the state of its prerogatives in the area of rural commerce, the *People's Daily* of 31 December 1984 proclaimed on its front page that it was time 'to put rural production on the road to the mercantile economy', and hence to extend the area subject to regulation by the market and that, consequently, 'an end will gradually be put to the system of compulsory deliveries, by 1985'. Provincial regulations, introduced since, have in fact suppressed compulsory deliveries of grains and replaced them by contracts made between the state and the individual producers, purchases by the state being made at a price that is very advantageous for the peasants. All the surpluses after these purchases have been made can be sold on the free market (the state limits its obligations to the eventual repurchase of these surpluses at a very low intervention price in the event of a collapse of prices on the free market). The delivery quotas for pigs have likewise been suppressed and replaced by contracts negotiated each year, the price paid by the state being the market price at the time of the transaction.[3]

Thus, with a return to family farms after collectivization and a return to the market after an almost total state monopoly, the change of direction was radical. Its implications for the present food strategy are no less fundamental. The elimination of collective distribution within the teams signifies that a minimum ration is no longer automatically ensured to families that are now autonomous. Of course, the team is still supposed, in theory, to come to the help of needy households, through the welfare fund formed by contributions specified in the contracts. In practice, however, it seems that the poor in the villages must rather count, for help in their distress, on family or clan solidarity or on handouts by the new village bosses. The reappearance of private traders has also opened the way to every sort of speculation, to the disadvantage of those at the bottom of the ladder. In the cities, the rationing of cereal products, sold cheaply, has not yet been eliminated. On the other hand, price readjustments have already begun for other foodstuffs, with rises in the spring of 1985, ranging from 35% (pig meat) to over 100% (beef, fish, vegetables).[4]

Manifestly, the quest for food security, through the use of institutional mechanisms for equalizing consumption or through state intervention, is no longer being pursued by the Chinese authorities. What then were the reasons impelling the authorities to make such a drastic revision of a policy that seemed to be one of the pillars of socialism in China?

They must be sought in the novel conditions for consumption resulting from the recent rapid growth of output, itself linked to decollectivization and the rises in agricultural prices that followed. That at least is what we shall attempt to show in the analysis of Chinese statistics to which we now turn.

The Double Revolution in Production

After more than twenty years of statistical silence, leaving the field open to the lucubrations of propagandists or the estimates of CIA experts, China has recently begun to publish its first yearbooks: an agricultural yearbook (1980), a statistical yearbook (1982), with new editions each year. So far as agriculture is concerned, the figures now available are extremely detailed, with provincial breakdowns of crops, areas cultivated, yields etc. The question is, are they reliable?

The figures do not appear to suffer from any detectable political biases. Their weakness arises rather from the rudimentary character of the Chinese statistical apparatus, scarcely recovered from the upheavals of the Cultural Revolution, and confronted with the enormous task of gathering data in a continent-size country which is still underdeveloped. The figures concerning cultivated areas are, as the Chinese themselves admit, under-estimated because of concealment of facts by peasants. Yields are probably over-estimated. Crop volumes are full of uncertainties for the most recent years since the detailed accounts of teams are no longer available; it may therefore be that, with the help of official optimism, they too are somewhat inflated.

Yet on the whole, it is not possible, or reasonable, to reject all these official statistics when it is difficult to see what could replace them. We must simply take the greatest care in using them and look wherever possible for verifications and crosschecks.

Thanks to the official information in the yearbooks, we now have available the corrected series,[5] for every year from 1952 to 1983, of the overall outputs of foodgrains (paddy rice, wheat, maize, soybean, secondary cereals and tubers counted at one-fifth of their dry weight). This series (Table 4.1) shows both the scale of the catastrophe of the Great Leap Forward – producing a fall of almost 30% in cereal output between 1958 and 1960 – and the very steady growth of agriculture both before and after this catastrophic episode, with an average increase in grains of 3.5% a year from 1952 to 1957 and 1964 to 1977. This rapid growth rate shows that, unlike the giant communes of the Great Leap Forward, collectivization restricted to a small number of families within teams had been able to preserve the 'territoriality' of peasant labour [6] and had not therefore constituted a major brake on the growth of output. However, it seems certain that the collective structures did not permit total efficiency of the factors mobilized and – and this is a second important point – that the decollectivization of recent years has been accompanied by an unprecedented acceleration of the growth rate of grain harvests, which grew by 5% p.a. on average between 1977 and 1983. Chinese agriculture has probably suffered in the past (although in a much more attenuated way than in the Soviet Union) from the same diseconomies of scale and lack of adequate incentives for the peasants as are found in other collectivized agricultures. And it is precisely this argument, which is quite accurate, that the Chinese authorities have put forward, with many examples, to justify the introduction of 'responsibility systems' and the return to a family mode of agricultural exploitation.

Only the future will tell whether this recent acceleration will continue for long or whether it will run out of steam, once the potential released by decollectivization has been exhausted. More fundamentally, the spectacular character of what amounts to a revolution in the structures of production represented by the return to family farming must not lead us to overlook another, more long-term revolution underway in Chinese agriculture. The growth observed in the 1950s (and interrupted by the Great Leap Forward) and the growth manifested in the 1960s and 1970s are not of the same kind. The growth of the 1950s was based on the

Table 4.1
Foodgrain and Meat Production, Population, 1952–83

	Official grain production[a]	Corrected grain production[b]	10⁶ tonnes	Meat production[c]	10⁶ tonnes	Population[d]	+%	10⁶ persons
1952	163.9	160.7	} 162.1	(3.39)	} 3.82	574.8	} 23	} 581.4
1953	166.8	163.5		3.82x		588.0	25	
54	169.5	166.1	an. inc.[e] 3.5%	3.89x	an. inc. 2.2%	602.7	20	an. inc. 2.4%
55	183.9	180.2		3.27x		614.7	22	
56	192.8	188.4		3.40		628.3	29	
1957	195.1	190.7	} 192.1	3.99	} 4.17	646.5	} 21	} 653.2
1958	200.0	193.5		4.34x		659.9	18	
59	170.0	165.2	decline 26%	2.60x	decline 71%	672.1	–15	an. inc. 0.4%
1960	143.5	139.4	} 141.3	1.27x	} 1.22	662.1	–5	} 660.3
1961	147.5	143.2		1.17x		658.6	22	
62	160.0	155.3		1.94		673.0	28	
63	170.0	165.7		3.70x		691.7	19	
1964	187.5	187.5	191.0	4.96x	5.24	705.0	29	715.2
1965	194.5	194.5		5.51		725.4	28	
66	214.0	214.0		5.96		745.4	28	an. inc. 2.7%
67	217.8	217.8		6.12x		763.7	28	
68	209.1	209.1		6.01x		785.3	27	
1969	211.0	211.0	an. inc. 3.4%	5.55x	an. inc. 3.4%	806.7	29	
1970	240.0	240.0		5.97		829.9	27	818.3
71	250.1	250.1		6.96x		852.3	23	
72	240.5	240.5		7.65x		871.8	23	
73	264.9	264.9		7.91x		892.1	18	an. inc. 2.1%
74	275.3	275.3		8.09x		908.6	17	
75	284.5	284.5	} 284.5	7.97	} 7.81	924.2	14	} 943.4
1976	286.3	286.3		7.81		937.2	*14*	
1977	282.7	282.7		7.80		949.7	*13*	
78	304.8	315.6		8.56		962.6	14	
79	332.1	332.1	an. inc. 4.5%	10.62	an. inc. 9.9%	975.4	13	an. inc. 1.3%
80	320.6	320.6		12.05		987.1	12	
81	325.0	325.0		12.61		1,000.7	14	
1982	354.5	354.5	} 370.9	13.51	} 13.77	1,015.4	} 15	} 1,020.1
1983	387.3	387.3		14.02		1,025.0	9	

a Official grain production: tubers counted at one-quarter of dry weight from 1952 to 1963, one-fifth from 1964 to 1983, in *SYB*, 1984, p. 141.
b Corrected grain production: tubers counted at one-fifth of dry weight, derived from ibid. p. 141; figure for 1978 in *NYNJ*, 1980, p. 99.
c Meat production: pig meat, beef and mutton (excluding poultry) in *SYB*, 1984, p. 160; figure for 1952 pork only; figures with an 'x', estimates.
d Year end population figure, in *SYB*, 1984, p. 81.
e an. inc. = annual growth.

Table 4.2
Factors of Production, 1952–83

	1952	1957	1965	1978	1983	83/78
Chemical fertilizers[a], 10^6 t.f.e.	—	0.4	1.9	8.8	16.6	1.89
(as % of total manure)		(3)	(14)	(35)	(50)	
Irrigated area[b], 10^6 ha	20.0	27.3	33.1	45.0	44.6	0.99
of which power irrigated	0.3	1.2	8.1	24.9	25.3	1.02
Agricultural machinery[c], 10^6 hp	0.3	1.7	14.9	159.8	245.0	1.53
of which tractors and cultivators	—	—	—	39.8	69.3	1.74
(of which cultivators, 10^6 units)				(1.37)	(2.75)	2.01

[a] Chemical fertilizers: in millions of tonnes of fertilizing elements (t.f.e.), in *SYB*, 1984, p. 175; as a percentage of total manure estimates.
[b] Irrigated area: in millions of hectares in *SYB*, 1984, p. 175; of which power irrigated, ibid.
[c] Agricultural machinery: in millions of horsepower in *SYB*, 1984, p. 169; of which tractors and cultivators, ibid., pp. 169–70.

application of pre-modern factors of production: at that time the irrigated area under cultivation recovered and even surpassed its pre-war level and the application of organic fertilizers grew proportionally to population and the number of pigs, agricultural intensification being the result, as previously, of increased human population density. The strength of this growth testified to the possibilities still latent in traditional Chinese agriculture once civil peace and maintenance of infrastructures were assured; these were precisely what the new regime brought to China, after half a century of war and destruction.

The growth inaugurated in the 1960s was altogether different. It was based on the increasingly widespread employment of modern factors of production, of industrial and scientific origin and thus not generated by the agricultural sector itself. Chemical fertilizers, virtually non-existent before the Great Leap (four kg of fertilizers per cultivated hectare in 1957), became preponderant with high levels of application: 166 kg of fertilizers per cultivated hectare in 1983, at least equal to the amount of fodder and night-soil (see Table 4.2). Irrigation was gradually mechanized, and half the irrigated areas are now irrigated by electric or diesel pumps. Tractorization has also made great progress with about 70 horsepower available per 100 hectares; however, tractors and cultivators are mostly used for transport and most field operations remain manual (61 oxen or horses are used per 100 cultivated hectares). The steady progress of the last 20 years is in fact the result of a real green revolution, pumps and chemical fertilizers having accompanied the introduction of new improved seeds that have come directly from the research laboratories. These improved varieties are used for over 70% of sowings of wheat, maize (hybrids), groundnuts or rapeseed; dwarf varieties of rice, similar to Filipino 'miracle' rices, were popularized in China during the 1960s and, most recently, even more productive hybrid rices, invented by the Chinese, have made their appearance, applied in 20% of paddyfields in 1983 (*NCNA*, 30 January 1984).

The very nature of this green revolution makes it possible to understand how the increase in grain output, in the last twenty years, has occurred solely through an increase of yields (almost double for rice, more than triple for wheat); the areas cropped have been diminishing (see Table 4.3).[7]

For foodgrains, the present revolution in agricultural structures has thus simply accelerated the progress that started earlier with this other revolution, a technical one, represented by the introduction of improved seeds and chemical fertilizers. Conversely, for industrial crops (cotton, oilseeds, sugar, etc.) the changes of these last few years have been much more radical, the volume of crops having more than doubled between 1976 and 1983 (see Table 4.3). Unlike grains, the volume of these crops had in fact grown very little previously, with stagnation of rapeseed yields, collapse of groundnut, sugar-cane, and sugar-beet yields and a large decline in the area under cotton. Since 1976, for all these crops, there has been both a leap forward in yields (doubled for rapeseed and sugar-beet) and a large increase in the areas cultivated (the latter increasing by virtue of the amount of land devoted to foodgrains).

Collectivization, with the very tight control that it made possible on what was grown and the priority then given to cereals, was in fact harmful to industrial crops. The spectacular advances of recent years, obtained without diminution of the availability of foodgrains (indeed quite the reverse) are one more justification for the dismantling of the people's communes and the decision to put an end to the collectivization of agricultural work.

The same strides can also be found in the production of meat (Table 4.1).[8] Whereas production had increased at a rate similar to that of grains during the period of stable growth from 1965 to 1977, progress has been even faster than that of grains in recent years: almost 10% annual growth between 1977 and 1983, double that of cereals. As we shall see, this more marked growth of meat production is linked to the growth in the availability of animal fodder (availability increasing even faster than the rations) along with an increased efficiency of family husbandry. In contrast to the steady progress observed at the time of the restricted collectivization of the 1960s and 1970s, and the rapid growth that appeared with the recent decollectivization, the production of meat suffered greatly from the early extremes of collectivization: there was a fall in the very first year of the cooperativization of agriculture (1955) and a collapse at the time of the Great Leap (a drop of over 70% between 1958 and 1961).

Generally speaking, comparison of the growth of grain and meat production with that of population (Table 4.1) shows that, for the 'stable' periods of 1952–7 and 1964–77, the rate of increase of food production has been higher (just) than the growth of population. The advantage thus achieved was, however, largely eliminated by the losses of the Great Leap Forward, grains in particular taking five years to recover their previous production level. The scale of the catastrophe of the Great Leap can be verified by observing the (net) fall in population of almost 14 million people in two years (1959–61) whereas previously China's population growth had been stable (official population figures, Table 4.1).[9]

Since 1978 the situation has completely changed; we now have the favourable and novel combination of a strong increase of grain and meat production and very low population growth, resulting from an energetic, even brutal, birth control policy in the countryside (abortions and sterilizations, in particular, made it possible to halve

Table 4.3

Crops (Areas,[a] Yields,[b] Harvests[c]) 1983/76/57/52

	10⁶ha	%	83/76	83/57	57/52	t/ha	83/76	83/57	57/52	10⁶t	%	83/76	83/57	57/52
Cultivated area	(100)													
Harvested area	144.0		0.96											
Foodgrains	114.0	100	0.94	0.85	1.08	(3.40)	1.47	2.39	1.12	387.3	100	1.35	2.03	1.19
of which rice	33.1	29	0.91	1.03	1.14	5.10	1.47	1.89	1.16	168.9	44	1.34	1.95	1.27
of which wheat	29.1	26	1.02	1.05	1.11	2.80	1.58	3.28	1.16	81.4	21	1.62	3.44	1.30
of which corn	18.8	16	0.98	1.26	1.19	3.62	1.45	2.53	1.07	68.2	18	1.42	3.18	1.27
of which soybean	7.6	7	1.13	0.59	1.09	1.29	1.30	1.64	0.96	9.8	3	1.47	0.97	1.06
of which tubers	9.4	8	0.91	0.90	1.21	3.11	1.21	1.86	1.11	29.3	7	1.10	1.67	1.34
of which other grains	16.0	14	0.81	0.45	0.94	1.85	1.28	2.12	0.96	29.7	7	1.04	0.95	0.90
Other crops	30.0													
of which cotton	6.1		1.23	1.05	1.04	0.76	1.83	2.68	1.22	4.64		2.26	2.83	1.26
of which oilseeds	8.4		1.45	1.22	1.21		1.80	2.06	0.96	10.6		2.63	2.51	1.00
of which rapeseed					1.17	2.03	3.05	0.76						
of which groundnuts						1.80	1.76	1.77	0.79					
of which sugar crops	1.2		1.33	2.81	1.95					40.3		2.06	3.39	1.50
of which sugarcane						47.6						2.26	2.83	1.26
of which sugarbeet						16.9						1.10	2.06	0.90

[a] Areas: in *SYB*, 1984, pp. 137–9, sown area, figure officially under-estimated, in *JNJ*, 1984, pp. 1–17; surfaces sown to oilseeds in *NYNJ*, 1984, p. 101. *NYNJ*, 1980, p. 35.

[b] Yields: in *SYB*, 1984, pp. 153–4.

[c] Harvests: in *SYB*, 1984, pp. 141–3.

the annual population growth rate in less than ten years during the 1970s). This exceptional combination obviously cannot but confirm the authorities in the change of direction implemented since 1978; the abundance of per capita supplies cannot but facilitate the transition to a different strategy which is less concerned with the equalization of minimum rations than with the increase in the general level of consumption, abandoning authoritarian regulation by the state in favour of the more flexible mechanism of the market and greater variety and better adaptation in the very composition of food.

The Evolution of Overall Consumption

This turnaround of recent years is clearly confirmed by the figures for human consumption of foodgrains which have recently been published in China (Table 4.4, column official intake/per capita). These figures show a sharp take-off of intake at the end of the 1970s, whereas they had failed, until then, to overtake the level of the 1950s.

This series of official figures must, however, be corrected before they are interpreted. Consumption is expressed in 'trade grains' (semi-processed) and it seems that two different conversion factors have been used by Chinese statisticians to deduce 'trade grains' from 'raw grains' (unprocessed).[10] Apart from that, the series seems rather unreliable for the most recent years, peasant intakes in particular being no longer as precisely known as in previous years from team accounts. Using the official series, we have therefore calculated a 'corrected' consumption series expressed in raw grains (comparable with the output figures), using on the one hand the successive conversion factors (raw grains to trade grains) of 0.95 (1952 to 1960) and 0.85 (1961 to 1980), and on the other hand replacing the official consumption figures from 1981–3 by consumption estimated on the basis of surveys on samples of rural and urban households (see below).

The corrected series thus obtained (Table 4.4, column corrected intake/per capita) nevertheless broadly corroborates the conclusions drawn from the official series. A virtual stagnation (or very slight progress, about 0.5% p.a.) of intake during the periods 1952–7 and 1965–77 can be observed, interrupted by the collapse of the Great Leap (a fall of over 20% between 1957 and 1960). Although slightly higher in 1977 (225 raw kg) than what it had been in 1957 (215 kg), the level of consumption of grains had thus not significantly advanced in twenty years. The take-off of the last six years is all the more spectacular, with intake reaching 260 raw kg in 1983, for an annual growth rate of 2% since 1977.

This advance was achieved despite the fact that the share of human consumption in total availability (Table 4.4, column I/A) has diminished. This diminution is, in fact, an old long-term trend, appearing since the early 1960s against the background of the improvement of intake (at first slow and later accelerating). What does it mean?

We have attempted to reconstruct the different uses of grains between 1952 and 1983 (Table 4.5). Such a reconstruction is, of course, partly hypothetical: we had to estimate the shares going to seeds, losses, stock changes, etc., fodder grains

Table 4.4
Total Availabilities and Foodgrain Rations, 1952–83 (in millions of tonnes and kg)

	Corr. Gr. Prs.[a]	Imp.[b]	Exp.[b]	Tot. Av.[c]	Av./cap.[d]	Raw kg/cap.	Off. Rat./cap.[e]	Corr. Rat./cap.[f]	R/A[g]	Raw kg/cap.
1952	160.7		1.5	159.2	277	275	198	208	75	210
53	163.5		1.8	161.7	275		197	207	75	
54	166.1		1.7	164.4	273	*an. inc. 1.1%*	196	206	75	*an. inc. 0.5%*
55	180.2	0.2	2.2	178.2	290		198	208	72	
56	188.4	0.1	2.7	185.8	296		204	215	73	
1957	190.7	0.2	2.1	188.8	292	290	203	214	73	215
58	193.5	0.2	2.9	190.8	289	*decline 29%*	198	208	72	*decline 21%*
59	165.2		4.2	161.0	240	205	187	197	82	170
1960	139.4	0.1	2.7	136.8	207		164	172	83	
61	143.2	5.8	1.4	147.6	224		159	187	83	
62	155.3	4.9	1.0	159.2	237		165	194	82	
63	165.7	6.0	1.5	170.2	246		165	194	79	
64	187.5	6.6	1.8	192.3	273		182	214	78	
1965	194.5	6.4	2.4	198.5	274	275	183	215	78	215
66	214.0	6.4	2.9	217.5	292	*an. inc. 0.9%*	190	224	77	*an. inc. 0.4%*
67	217.8	4.7	2.9	219.5	287		186	219	76	
68	209.1	4.6	2.6	211.1	269		174	205	76	
69	211.0	3.8	2.2	212.6	264		174	205	77	
70	240.0	5.4	2.1	243.3	293		187	220	75	
71	250.1	3.2	2.6	250.7	294		188	221	75	
72	240.5	4.8	2.9	242.4	278		173	204	73	
73	264.9	8.1	3.9	269.1	302		192	226	75	
74	275.3	8.1	3.6	279.8	308		188	221	75	
75	284.5	3.7	2.8	285.4	309		191	225	72	
76	286.3	2.4	2.8	286.9	306		190	225	73	
1977	282.7	7.3	1.7	288.3	304	305	192	224	74	225
78	315.6	8.8	1.9	322.5	335	*an. inc. 4.2%*	195	226	72	*an. inc. 2.4%*
79	332.1	12.4	1.7	342.8	351		207	240	70	
80	320.6	13.4	1.6	332.4	337		214	244	75	
81	325.0	14.8	1.3	338.5	338		219	252	74	
82	354.5	16.1	1.3	369.3	364		225	251	70	
1983	387.3	13.5	2.0	398.8	389	390	232	255	66	260

a Corrected grain production in Table 4.1.
b Imports/exports in *SYB*, 1984, pp. 412, 397.
c total availabilities = Corr. Gr. Pr. + Imp. - Exp.
d Availabilities per capita = Tot. av. divided by population in Table 4.1.
e Official ration per capita, in trade grains, *SYB*, 1984, p. 477.
f Corrected ration per capita, in raw grains = official ration trade grains divided by 0.95 for 1952–60, 0.85 for 1961–80; ration derived from Table 4.7 for 1978, 1981–3.
g Proportion of rations in availabilities is corrected ration/availabilities per capita.

appearing, in our method of calculation, as a balance left after deducting (from total availability) the various uses thus estimated and the human consumption derived from the previously estimated intakes (human consumption, as defined by the Chinese, includes grains consumed directly and those consumed after industrial processing). But this does not mean that the series of figures obtained in this reconstruction is arbitrary, only that we have had to make allowances for technical norms for seeds, delivery constraints for state stocks and Chinese information on the general level of stocks and fodder grains for the most recent years.[11] These norms, constraints or indications in fact leave a very narrow margin of manoeuvre.

Thus reconstructed, the grain-use table is surprising and carries a major lesson. The surprise is the scale of losses. In order to make the fodder grains correspond to other relevant Chinese figures we had to postulate that these losses were as high as 7-8% of total output. This very high rate, higher than that generally accepted by experts or even our own previous estimates, reflects, of course, the inadequacy of means of transport and storage which in China are those of a still underdeveloped country. It is thus officially estimated that rats alone consume, annually, between six and eight million tonnes of grains or 2% of the harvest.[12] To these 'traditional' losses must probably be added, until recently, those relating to the collective organization of distribution in production teams: neglect and waste in the course of the frequent handling of grains, 'wastage' to the benefit of cadres in the management of collective stocks, etc. Special mention should also be made of the losses in the state warehouses (which we have separated out in the 'Losses' column in Table 4.5). According to some surveys, these losses are in fact considerable, partly because of the high level of humidity of grains delivered by the peasants, no one being concerned to ensure respect for the regulation ceilings.[13]

To some extent the size of the losses may thus be the reflection of bad management, both collective and state, of grains, not unlike the problems the USSR experiences in this area. These same problems have probably also influenced the use-rate for seeds; we have postulated that this rate has remained constant for a long time at about 6% of crops, the productivity gains that naturally appeared with the increase in yields having been wiped out by waste in collective operations (sacks of seeds scattered at the edge of fields, etc.) as well as by certain irrational practices imposed by the cadres (seeds planted too close etc.).

The major lesson of the grain-use table concerns fodder grains: the relative diminution of the share of human consumption in total output noted previously corresponds in fact to an increase, notable in recent years, of the share of grains devoted to feeding livestock. Throughout the period studied, the amount of fodder available has varied considerably. After an initial increase between 1952 and 1957, fodder grains collapsed in 1960–61: in that famine period, peasants who had slaughtered their cattle themselves consumed the grains normally set aside for fodder. Conversely, in the 'normal' years from 1965–77, corresponding to the stabilization of collectivization at the limited level of the teams, fodder output increased at a higher rate than that of the production of grains and meat, higher still, it goes without saying, than that of food intakes which rose only slowly. The share of fodder in total output thus rose from 8% in 1965 to 13% in 1977. When, after 1977, human intake took off, the growth of fodder grains also speeded up,

Table 4.5
Grains. Hypothetical Model of Uses, Food and Forage, 1952–83

	T.Av.[a]	Seeds[c]	%	Losses[d] Coll.+State	%	ΔStocks[e] Coll.+State	%	Consum.[b]	%	Forage[f]	%	Unit: million tons
1952	159	11	7	9 (+1)	6	+3	2	120	75	15	10	15 (10%)
53	162	11	7	9 (+1)	6	+8	5	122	75	11	7	
54	164	12	7	9 (+2)	7	+5	3	124	75	12	8	
55	178	13	7	11 (+2)	7	+8	4	128	72	16	9	↕ an. inc. 7%
56	186	13	7	11 (+3)	8	−2	1	135	73	26	14	
1957	189	13	7	11 (+3)	7	+3	2	138	73	21	11	21 (11%)
58	191	14	7	15 (+4)	10	+1	1	137	72	20	10	
59	161	14	9	14 (+4)	11	−8	5	132	82	5	3	
1960	137	10	8	12 (+3)	11	−5	4	114	83	3	2	3 (2%)
61	148	9	6	10 (+3)	9	+1	1	123	83	2	2	
62	159	9	6	10 (+3)	8	+3	2	131	82	3	3	
63	170	10	6	10 (+3)	8	+8	5	134	79	5	3	
64	192	11	6	12 (+3)	8	+5	3	151	78	10	6	
1965	199	12	6	12 (+3)	8	+3	2	156	78	13	5	15 (8%)
66	218	13	6	14 (+3)	8	+6	3	167	77	15	8	↕ an. inc. 8%
67	220	13	6	13 (+3)	7	+7	3	167	76	17	8	
68	211	13	6	13 (+3)	8	+1	1	161	76	20	9	
69	213	13	6	13 (+3)	8	0	0	165	77	19	9	
70	243	14	6	15 (+3)	7	+7	3	183	75	21	10	
71	251	15	6	16 (+3)	8	+9	4	188	75	20	9	
72	242	14	6	15 (+3)	7	+4	2	178	73	28	10	
73	269	16	6	17 (+3)	7	−4	−1	202	75	35	14	
74	280	16	6	18 (+3)	8	+15	5	201	72	27	13	
75	285	17	6	18 (+3)	7	+5	2	208	72	34	13	
76	287	17	6	18 (+3)	7	+3	1	210	73	36	14	
1977	288	17	6	18 (+3)	7	−3	−1	215	74	38	13	38 (13%)
78	323	17	6	20 (+3)	7	+12	4	231	72	40	15	↕ an. inc. 10%
79	343	20	6	21 (+3)	7	+12	3	238	70	49	15	
80	332	19	6	21 (+3)	7	−10	−3	249	75	50	15	
81	339	16	5	20 (+3)	7	+13	4	251	74	36	11	
82	369	18	5	22 (+4)	7	+9	2	259	70	57	16	
1983	399	19	5	24 (+5)	7	+20	5	265	66	66	17	66 (17%)

[a] Total availabilities; cf. Table 4.4.
[b] Direct and indirect human consumption, after industrial processing: derived from corrected rations in Table 4.4.
[c] Estimates.
[d] Collective losses and from state stocks: estimates.
[e] Changes in collective and state stocks: estimates; cumulative, collective and state stocks (1952–83) equal to 100 million tonnes.
[f] Balance.

their share of output reaching 17% in 1983. There was thus a parallel evolution of the output of fodder grains and food intake, the variations of fodder being in the same direction, but infinitely more accentuated, than those of human intake: respective growths (fodder grains/intakes) of 8% (approximately) and 0.5% in the stable periods of 1952–7 and 1965–77, 10% and 2% at the time of the take-off in recent years (and conversely collapse of fodder when intake fell by 20% during the Great Leap). This pattern is to be found in fact in other Asian agricultures and we can thus confirm that China, from this point of view, is no exception to the general rule.[14]

The very rapid increase in fodder grains that has recently emerged is thus in line with the favourable combination of recent years: not only has the human consumption of foodgrains at last been able to increase but, even more importantly, stock rearing can now call on increased resources and the production of meat is able to match a growing demand (corresponding, as we shall see, to a change in food habits). These increased resources are also better used; pig herd management is improving (Table 4.6).[15] Thus herd rotation has been accelerated, the number of pigs slaughtered rising from 60% of the total at year end, in the late 1970s, to almost 70% in 1983. At the same time, carcase weight has increased, rising from 40 to 60 kg. The savings in fodder thus achieved explain how, in recent years, the consumption of fodder grains has grown at the same rate as meat production (about 10% a year), whereas in previous years the increase in fodder grains has been distinctly higher than that of meat.

It must however be noted that these results have been obtained in the framework of family stock raising in which pigs, fed mainly on kitchen waste, consume little grain. The move to a more industrialized type of stock raising (unavoidable eventually for at least part of the herd) will mean an infinitely heavier use of refined foods and thus grains. In view of this prospect of an enhanced use of fodder grains, greater efficiency will have to be sought in the actual composition of concentrated feeds provided to animals: a large proportion of the present 'fodder' grains are in fact made up of surpluses of wheat and rice which are not very effective in increasing meat yields. The problem in coming years is thus likely to be rather the quality of fodder than its quantity and, faced with being unable to alter substantially the structure of cereal production, solutions will no doubt have to involve the use of protein additives in grain-based feeds (composite feeds at present constitute only 10% of the grains used as fodder) (*XH*, 9 January 1985).

Rural and Urban Consumption

The problem of quality also arises, in other ways, with regard to grains destined for human consumption: the fact is that the high-yield varieties of wheat or rice, which have been the basis of the revolution in output, do not really satisfy their users, the flours being of mediocre baking quality and the rice having a disgusting taste (*RMRB*, 28 December 1984; 9 February 1985). Yet the fact that people are now talking of 'quality', and no longer only of 'quantity' as previously, shows clearly that decisive progress has been accomplished in the satisfaction of basic food needs.

Table 4.6
Production of Pig Meat, 1952–83 (in kg, millions of tonnes and millions of pigs)

	C/cap.[a]	Pr. pig[b]	Millions of tonnes	Nb. sl[d]	Pr./p[e]	% Sl.[f]	Nb. Pigs[c] Millions of pigs
1952	5.92	3.40 } 3.48 an. dec. 0.6%		65	52	72	90 } 93 an. inc. 8.8%
1953	6.06	3.56		69	52	72	96
54	6.01	3.62		74	49	73	102
55	4.94	3.04		64	48	73	88
56	4.66	2.93		62	47	74	84
1957	5.08	3.28 } 3.37		71	46	49	*146* } *142* dec. 44%
1958	5.23	3.45		88	39	64	*138*
59	3.08	2.07 } dec. 71%		68	30	57	*120*
1960	1.53	*1.01* } 0.97		43	23	52	*82* } 79
1961	1.41	0.93		33	28	43	*76*
62	2.22	1.49		43	35	43	100
63	4.27	2.95		78	38	43	*132*
1964	5.62	3.96 } 4.26 an. inc. 4.1%		105	38	59	*152* } 160 an. inc. 5.1%
1965	6.29	4.56		122	37	69	*167*
66	7.04	5.25		132	40	73	*193*
67	6.89	5.26		134	39	68	*190*
68	6.57	5.16		131	39	70	*179*
69	5.91	4.77		126	38	73	*173*
70	6.02	5.00		126	40	61	206
71	7.03	5.99		148	40	59	250
72	7.56	6.59 } an. inc. 4.1%		166	40	63	264
73	7.63	6.81		167	41	65	258
74	7.67	6.97		162	43	62	261
75	7.63	7.05 } 6.91		162	44	58	281 } 290 an. inc. 8.6%
1976	7.38	6.92		167	41	58	287
1977	7.25	6.89		168	41	53	292
78	7.67	7.38		161	46	58	301
79	9.66	9.42		188	50	59	320
80	11.16	11.02 } an. inc. 10.1%		199	55	65	305
81	11.08	11.09		195	57	66	294
1982	11.76	*11.94* } 12.30		201	59	67	*301* } 300
1983	12.35	12.66		207	61	69	299

a Consumption of pig meat per capita: in *SYB*, 1984, p. 477.
b Production of pig meat: derives from C/cap. and population in Table 4.1.
c Number of pigs: year end figures, in *SYB*, 1984, p. 160.
d Number of pigs slaughtered during the year: in *SYB*, 1984, p. 160.
e Production of meat per pig or carcase weight: derived from Pr. pig and Nb. sl.
f Percentage of number of pigs slaughtered compared to year end total; derived from Nb. pigs and Nb. sl.

Does this mean that the problem of subsistence has been completely solved in the China of the 1980s? That is not at all certain and our analysis, made at the national level, is too general to be able to answer this question (60 to 80 million people are still said to have difficulty in feeding themselves adequately): answering it would involve breaking down consumption levels by region and by social category (the 'responsibility systems' having in particular had the effect of increasing income disparities within villages).

Part of the detailed picture of the Chinese food situation has been provided in Chapter Two of this volume. It is still necessary, nevertheless, to attempt to distinguish rural and urban consumption. All sociological studies are agreed about the widening gap between the respective evolution – in terms of incomes, customs, social structures, etc. – of cities and countryside over the last twenty years (see Parish and Whyte (1978) and Whyte and Parish (1984)). What is the situation now?

We now have available the results of surveys made by the national statistical bureau on large samples of urban and rural households to help us answer this question. These results, setting out in detail consumption for the years 1957, 1964 and 1981–3 in the urban sample, and for the years 1978–83 for the rural sample, are surprising. They suggest, in particular for grains, lower consumption than the national consumption published elsewhere (for 1983, peasants are said to have consumed 260 kg of unprocessed grains, city-dwellers 144 kg of processed grains, equal to 195 kg of unprocessed grains, [16] whereas total national average consumption, directly derived from the official figure, was given as 273 unprocessed kg). These results are so surprising that most experts have so far refused to accept them, alleging possible biases in the samples (which however include over 30,000 village families and 9,000 workers' and employees' households) or uncertainties of nomenclature.[17]

In fact, if there was bias, it would above all be a bias upwards, the rural households surveyed, particularly, being better off than the average (Travers, 1982). As for the consumption figures in the urban sample, they are quite consistent for recent years with the piecemeal data known for a few large cities in China.[18] It is thus not possible simply to ignore the information provided by these samples; it must be interpreted and not rejected. We have therefore tried to reconstruct rural and urban grain consumption, from 1952 to 1983, trying to integrate the survey data into the overall figures for consumption, deliveries, population, etc. known from other sources. In this model which, once again, remains hypothetical (see Table 4.7), direct urban consumption is as indicated in the samples for 1957, 1964, and 1981–83 (with estimates and interpolations for the missing years); consumption after industrial processing has been estimated, and rural consumption has been derived from total consumption by subtracting direct urban and industrial consumption (except for 1983 for which we have used the consumption indicated in the sample of peasant families).

Given the approximations of this sort of reconstruction, we obviously cannot guarantee the exactness of the figures for urban and rural consumption. The overall picture of evolving consumption patterns, as they emerge from our table, cannot however be fundamentally challenged.[19] And the trends that they bring out provide vital, and previously unknown, information on food consumption in the

Table 4.7
Foodgrains: Hypothetical Model of Rural and Urban Consumption, 1952–83

	T. Cons.[a] 10⁶ t	R. Cons.[f] 10⁶ t	Nb. Rur.[c] 10⁶ p	Rc./cap.[g] kg. br.	Gross kg./cap.	Gross kg./cap.	Uc./cap.[b] kg. br.	Nb. Urb.[c] 10⁶ p	U. Cons.[d] 10⁶ t	C.I.[e] 10⁶ t
1952	120	98	508	195	195	250	250	72	18	4
53	122	97	510	190			250	78	20	5
54	124	99	520	190	an. dec. 2%		240	82	20	5
55	128	103	532	194		an. inc. 1%	235	83	20	5
56	135	109	536	203			225	92	21	5
1957	138	111	547	203	205	225	226	99	22	5
58	137	104	553	188			250	107	27	6
59	132	97	548	177		dec. 22%	230	124	29	6
1960	114	86	531	162	dec. 18%		190	131	25	3
1961	123	97	532	182	160	185	185	127	23	3
62	131	106	556	191			190	117	22	3
63	134	107	575	186			200	116	23	4
64	151	120	575	205			211	130	27	4
1965	156	122	595	209	205	230	230	130	30	4
66	167	132	612	216			230	133	31	4
67	167	133	628	212			225	135	30	4
68	161	126	647	195			225	138	31	4
69	165	130	666	195		an. inc. 0.6%	220	141	31	4
70	183	148	686	215			215	144	31	4
71	188	151	705	214			215	147	32	4
72	178	141	722	214	an. dec. 0.8%		215	149	32	5
73	202	163	739	221			215	153	33	5
74	201	161	753	214			215	156	34	6
75	208	168	764	218			215	160	34	6
76	210	169	774	220			210	163	35	6
1977	215	171	783	235	185	210	210	167	36	7
78	231	186	790	235		an. inc. 2.8%	210	172	38	9
79	238	190	790	240			205	185	38	9
80	249	201	796	253	an. inc. 1.2%		200	191	40	10
81	251	201	799	251			197	202	40	10
82	259	205	804	255			196	212	42	12
1983	265	204	784	260	260	195	196	241	47	14

a Total human consumption: cf. Table 4.5.
b Urban direct consumption per capita: urban sample 1957, 64, 81, 82, 83 in *SYB*, 1984, p. 465 (conversion factor net grains/raw grains: 0.74); other years estimates.
c Number of urban people and number of rural people: in *SYB*, 1984, p. 81.
d Total direct urban consumption: derived from UC/cap and Nb. urb.
e Consumption after industrial processing: estimates.
f Total direct rural consumption: derived from T. Cons., U. Cons. and C.I.
g Direct rural consumption per capita: derived from R. Cons. and Nb. rur.; rural sample 1983 in *SYB*, 1984, p. 474.

countryside and the cities.

It appears in fact, and this confirms the observations made by sociologists, that in the cities, there has been a slight but constant fall for 15 years in the direct consumption of grains, which have fallen from 230 unprocessed kg per person in 1965 to 195 kg per person in 1983. The rate of this fall, about 1% a year, has been scarcely affected by the changes of recent years. Conversely, in the countryside, after virtual stagnation for over ten years, from 1964–76, this same consumption has taken off in the last few years, rising from 220 unprocessed kg to 260 kg. The increase in the average total ration, consequent on the recent growth of outputs, has thus mainly benefited the peasants.

Examination of the respective consumption of meat in the countryside and in the cities deduced in the same way from the results of samples and figures for total consumption (Table 4.8) leads to the same conclusion.[20] In the cities, there has been a steady and rapid increase (about 5% a year) in meat consumption for almost 20 years; meat is replacing cereals in the urban diet (meat consumption, not including poultry, now reaches 20 kg per capita a year). This increase in meat consumption has not changed over the last five years either. On the other hand in the countryside, the quantity of meat consumed, which had not noticeably changed for decades, has greatly increased since 1978, rising from 6 kg per capita a year to 10 kg. Recent advances thus again reflect a considerable and unprecedented improvement in peasant diet. In the countryside, this improvement is a direct result of the improved supply of meat, following the increase in the availability of fodder. In the cities, the substitution of meat for cereals appears as a phenomenon linked to the urban way of life and the fact that its rate has not changed with the wage increases in recent years also shows that the consumption of meat is not at all a direct function of the level of incomes.

Whatever the respective mechanisms of the evolution of rural and urban consumption, it is clear that the food take-off that followed the decollectivization of agriculture has mainly benefited the peasant population. And we are now at a major turning point in the evolution of Chinese food consumption: it seems clear that with about 260 unprocessed kg per capita the ceiling of the grain ration is about to be reached in the countryside. Any further increases in cereal production will, given the slowing down of the population growth rate, go to increasing the availability of fodder, accelerating the production and consumption of meat, if protein additives are added to cattle feed.[21] As it is, the quantities of grain used for fodder have almost doubled in six years. Even more, the state warehouses are full to bursting with excess stocks and the authorities are reduced to recommending use as fodder or as raw materials for agri-business (whereas the total capacity of the collective and state warehouses, at the end of 1983, was only 100 million tonnes, stocks rose to over 125 million tonnes, a large proportion of which were stored in the open air).[22] This is a wholly new situation, since all through the 1960s and 1970s there was, on the contrary, a slow fall in state stocks, forcing the Chinese authorities, in the late 1970s, to embark on massive imports of grains (see Table 4.4).[23] The present turnaround in the situation, the prelude to a major change in the composition of the Chinese diet, thus justifies the concern of the Chinese authorities, in their new food strategy, with facilitating the transition towards a more varied diet, higher in animal proteins.

Table 4.8
Meat: Hypothetical Model of Rural and Urban Consumption, 1952–83 (in kg and million tonnes)

	Tot. Pr.[a]	OP/cap.[b]	Kg/cap.	R.Cons.[e]	RC/cap.[c]	Kg/cap.	U.Cons.[e]	UC/cap.[d]	Kg/cap.	Balance[f]
1952	3.39	5.90		2.63	5.16		0.62	8.0		0.57
1953	3.82	6.50	6.50							
54	3.89		↕							
55	3.27									
56	3.40									
1957	3.99	5.41	6.17	2.61	4.77		0.78	7.92		0.60
58	4.34	6.17	↕							
59	2.60									
1960	1.27									
1961	1.17	1.78	1.78	0.53	1.00		0.26	2.00		0.38
62	1.94	2.88	1.78							
63	3.70									
1964	4.96	7.04	7.04	3.15	5.48	5.50	1.07	8.22	8.20	0.74
65	5.51	8.00	8.00							
66	5.96									
67	6.12									
68	6.01		an. inc. 1.7%							
69	5.55									
70	5.97	7.19	7.19							
71	6.96					an. inc. 0.3%			an. inc. 4.8%	
72	7.65									
73	7.91									
74	8.09	8.62	8.62							
75	7.97	8.33								
76	7.81	8.21								
77	7.80		8.89			5.75			15.90	
1978	8.56	8.89	8.89	4.55	5.76		2.73	15.87		1.28
79	10.62	10.89	an. inc. 9%	5.14	6.51	an. inc. 11.7%	3.33	18.00	an. inc. 4.7%	2.15
80	12.05	12.21		6.17	7.75		3.54	18.55		2.34
81	12.61	12.60		6.96	8.71		3.76	18.60		1.89
82	13.51	13.31		7.28	9.05		3.96	18.66		2.27
1983	14.02	13.68	13.68	7.81	9.97	10.00	4.79	19.86	20.00	1.42

[a] Production of meat, excluding poultry: cf. Table 4.1.
[b] Availability of meat per capita: derived from Tot. Pr. and population Table 4.1.
[c] Rural consumption per capita: rural sample 1978–83 in *SYB*, 1984, p. 474; other years estimates.
[d] Urban consumption per capita: urban sample of workers and employees for 1957, 64, 81–83 in *SYB*, 1984, p. 465; other years estimates.
[e] Rural and urban consumption of meat: derived from RC/cap and UC/cap, and from Nb. rur. and Nb. urb., Table 4.7.
[f] Overconsumption of cadres, derived for 1981–83, estimated for the other years.

Table 4.9
Estimates of Rural and Urban Caloric Rations, 1983

		Official Ration[h]			Rur. + Urb. Ration[g]				Rural Ration[e]				Urban Ration[f]			
	Coeff.[d]	Tot.[d]	Rat.[b]	Cal./d.[c]	Tot.[a]	Rat.[b]	Cal./d.[c]	%	Tot.[a]	Rat.[b]	Cal./d.[c]	%	Tot.[a]	Rat.[b]	Cal./d.[c]	%
Foodgrains	3.62	227	221	*2.192*	200	195	*1.934*	84	165	210	*2.083*	87	35	145	*1.438*	71
Ind. g.[j]							51				21				144	
Oils	8.84	4.2	4.1	99	4.3	4.2	102			3.5	85			6.5	157	
Sugar	3.87	4.6	4.5	48	1.7	1.6	17			1.3	14			2.8	30	
Fruits	0.40	9.5	9.3	10	9.5	9.3	10			3	3			30	33	
Vegetables	0.22	142	139	84	142	139	84			131	79			165	99	
Total Veg.				*2.433*			*2.198*	93			*2.285*	95			*1.901*	87
Meat	3.85	13.5	13.2	139	12.6	12.3	130			10.0	105			19.9	210	
Poultry	1.29	1.3	1.2	4	1.3	1.2	4			0.8	3			2.6	9	
Fish	0.62	3.2	3.1	5	3.2	3.1	5			1.6	3			8.1	14	
Eggs	1.44	3.1	3.0	12	2.9	2.8	11			1.6	6			6.9	27	
Milk	0.65	2.2	2.2	4	2.2	2.2	4			0.5	1			7.7	14	
Total Anim.				*164*			*154*	7			*118*	5			*274*	13
Total Rat.				*2.597*			*2.352*				*2.403*				*2.175*	
Rounded Ration		Offic.		[2.600]	R.+Urb		[2.350]	100	Rural		[2.400]	100	Urban		[2.200]	100

a Total consumed (in millions tonnes).
b Ration per capita p.a. (in kg); grains expressed in net grains.
c Number of calories per day: derived from Coeff.
d Coeff. (caloric coefficient or number of calories per gram).
e R from rural sample in *SYB*, 1984, p. 474 (conversion net grains/raw grains: 0.81).
f R from urban sample in *SYB*, 1984, p. 465.
g Sum of rural and urban ration.
h Official R in *SYB*, 1984, p. 477.
j Grains consumed after industrial processing: alcohols, beer, pasta products, soybean cheese, etc. = estim. at 10% of direct consumption of grains in cities. 1% in the countryside.

Table 4.10
Estimates of Urban and Rural Caloric Rations, 1957, 60, 65, 77, 83

| | 1957 | | | | 1960–61 | | | |
| | Rur.[a] | | Urb.[b] | | Rur. | | Urb. | |
	kg[c]	cal.[d]	kg	cal.	kg	cal.	kg	cal.
Foodgrains[e]								
Cooking oil[g]	175	*1.735*	170	*1.685*	140	*1.390*	155	*1.540*
Other veg orig.[g]	2	50	4	100	1	25	2	50
		100		265		20		120
Total veg. foods		*1.885*		*2.050*		*1.435*		*1.710*
Meat[f]								
Other anim. orig.	5	55	8	85	1	10	2	20
		5		35		—		5
Total anim. food		*60*		*120*		*10*		*25*
Total Ration		1.945		2.170		1.445		1.735
Rounded ration		[1.950 / 2.150]				[1.450 / 1.750]		

[a] Rural ration.
[b] Urban ration.
[c] Annual ration in kg.
[d] Daily caloric ration.
[e] Direct consumption in net grains derived from Table 4.7 (rur.: 1957, *1960*, 1965, 1977, 1983; urb.: 1957, *1961*, 1965, 1977, 1983), conversion factor net grains/raw grains rur. 0.85 (except 1960 and 1965, 0.88; 1983, 0.81), urb. 0.74 (except 1961, 0.85).
[f] Derived from Table 4.8.
[g] Other veg. orig. includes foods coming from industrially processed grains.
[h] Estimates.

The calorific intake, such as it can be calculated from the consumption figures of the rural and urban samples (Table 4.9), shows in fact that a satisfactory level has now been reached: 2,400 calories per person per day in the countryside, 2,200 in the cities.[24] The estimate of caloric intakes for past years (Table 4.10) [35] reveals that, in 1983, the cities had recovered the consumption level of the 1950s, but with a very different composition, products of animal origin having risen from 6% of the caloric total to 13%. For the countryside, on the other hand, the current abundance is a new phenomenon, based mainly on the increase in the availability of grains, which still account for over 85% of calories (as against 90% in the 1950s; in 1983, animal products still accounted for only 5% of calories).

A new abundance in the peasant intake, growing availability of fodder grains, bursting granaries . . . the food situation, such at least as it emerges from the available figures, inspires a (prudent) optimism. The long-awaited food take-off has at last arrived. And the new agricultural policy and the return to family plots, by giving a decisive push to the growth of yields, have played an essential role. No less essential in this take-off has been the role of the new commercial policy which, as we have seen, also accompanied decollectivization.

The Marketing of Agricultural Products

The recent increase in the availability and consumption of foodgrains, meat, cooking oil, etc., have also been accompanied by a distinct rise in the extent to which crops are marketed.

Table 4.11
Purchases of Food Products, 1952–83

	Grains						Oils		Pigs		Aquat. Prod.	
	Gr. Pur.[a] 10^6 t	% Pr.	Net Pur.[b] 10^6 t	% Pr.	Peas. Res.[c] 10^6 t	% Pr.	Pur.[d] 10^6 t	% Pr.	Pur.[e] 10^6 p	% Sl.[f]	Pur.[g] 10^6 t	% Pr.[h]
1952	33.3	20	28.2	17	5.1	3	1.17	81	37.4	57	0.92	55
1953	47.5	28	35.9	22	11.6	7	1.47	97	43.8	63	1.03	54
54	51.8	31	31.6	19	20.2	12	1.58	87	48.6	66	1.24	54
55	50.7	28	36.2	20	14.5	8	1.58	75	41.9	65	1.34	53
56	45.4	24	28.7	15	16.7	9	1.35	79	39.7	64	1.43	54
1957	48.0	25	33.9	17	14.1	7	1.24	63	40.5	57	1.72	55
58	58.8	29	41.7	21	17.1	9	1.45	82	46.7	53	1.53	54
1959	67.4	40	47.6	28	19.8	12	0.78	85	34.0	50	1.92	62
1960	51.1	36	30.9	22	20.2	14	0.60	79	19.9	46	1.90	63
1961	40.5	27	25.8	18	14.7	10	0.48	61	8.7	26	1.39	60
62	38.1	24	25.7	16	12.4	8	0.64	62	19.3	45	1.48	65
63	44.0	26	28.9	17	15.1	9	0.94	68	40.2	52	1.69	65
64	47.4	25	31.8	17	15.6	8	1.06	66	62.7	60	1.82	65
1965	48.7	25	33.6	17	15.1	8	1.06	63	78.6	65	1.83	61
66	51.6	24	38.2	18	13.4	6	0.94	58	86.4	66	1.93	62
67	49.4	23	37.7	17	11.7	5	0.90	57	87.5	65	1.91	63
68	48.7	23	37.9	18	10.8	5	0.83	55	83.5	64	1.62	60
69	46.7	22	33.8	16	12.9	6	0.90	57	76.6	61	1.60	55
70	54.4	23	42.0	18	12.4	5	0.97	57	75.6	60	1.99	63
71	53.0	21	39.8	16	13.2	5	0.90	53	88.2	60	2.14	63
72	48.3	20	33.9	14	14.4	6	0.95	51	105.3	63	2.39	61
73	56.1	21	41.0	16	15.1	6	0.98	52	102.0	61	2.32	62
74	58.1	21	44.0	16	14.0	5	0.98	52	98.4	61	2.53	59
75	60.9	21	43.9	15	17.0	6	1.00	53	102.8	63	2.56	59
76	58.3	20	40.7	14	17.6	6	0.83	51	103.5	62	2.61	58
1977	56.6	20	37.6	13	19.0	7	0.88	53	104.2	62	2.70	58
78	61.7	20	42.7	14	19.0	6	1.15	56	109.4	68	2.69	57
79	72.0	22	51.7	16	20.3	6	1.53	62	135.5	72	2.53	58
80	73.0	23	48.0	15	25.0	8	1.95	71	142.5	72	2.39	59
81	78.5	24	48.8	15	29.7	9	2.79	76	137.2	70	2.44	53
1982	91.9	26	59.1	17	32.8	9	3.08	72	144.6	72	2.88	56
1983	119.9	31	85.3	22	34.6	9	2.63	65	143.1	69	2.71	50

[a] Gross Purchases.
[b] Purchases net of resales to peasants.
[c] Resales to peasants: in *SYB.* 1984. p. 370, expressed in raw grains.
[d] Purchases: in *SYB,* 1984. p. 371.
[e] In *SYB.* 1984. p. 366.
[f] Percentage of pigs purchased in total slaughtered: derived from Nb. sl. in Table 4.6.
[g] Aquatic products purchased: in *SYB.* 1984. p. 367.
[h] Derived from *SYB.* 1984. p. 163.

Table 4.12
Marketing of Agricultural Products, 1952–83

Unit : billion yuan

Year	Val. Agr. Prod.[a] I	Val. Agr. Prod.[a] II	Val. Mar. Prod.[b] Curr. pr.	Val. Mar. Prod.[b] Index	Val. Mar. Prod.[b] Const. pr.	Prop. Mark.[c] /I	Prop. Mark.[c] /II	Free Markets[d] Curr. pr.	Free Markets %P.mar.[e]
1952	41.7	39.6	14.1	83.2	16.9	*41*	*43*	1.2	*9*
1957	53.7	50.5	21.8	100.0	21.8	*41*	*43*	1.3	*6*
1958			23.0					0.8	*3*
1959			27.9					0.4	*1*
1960			22.0					0.8	*3*
1961			20.5					3.0	*15*
1962			21.1					2.7	*13*
1963			23.8					1.9	*8*
1964			27.1					1.4	*5*
1965	59.0	54.0	30.7	128.5	23.9	*41*	44	1.3	*5*
1970	71.6	63.8	34.8	*133.4*	26.1	36	41	1.7	5
1975	120.2	113.1	47.9	107.0	44.8	37	40	2.5	5
1976	119.8	111.6	47.0	107.5	43.7	36	39	2.2	5
1977	119.2	110.8	49.5	107.2	46.2	39	42	2.2	4
1978	128.9	120.2	55.8	111.4	50.1	39	42	3.1	6
1979	138.6	130.0	71.4	136.1	52.5	38	40	4.8	7
1980	140.6	131.2	84.2	*146.8*	57.4	41	44	4.8	8
1981	209.1	189.8	95.5	105.9	90.2	43	48	6.9	9
1982	232.8	210.6	108.3	108.2	100.1	43	48	8.9	10
1983	251.1	226.2	126.5	113.0	111.9	45	49	13.3	*11*

a Value of agricultural production: I (excluding rural industries), II (excluding forests, non-staple products and rural industries) in *SYB*, 1984, p. 133, in constant prices 1957/70/80.
b Value of marketed production: in *SYB*, 1984, p. 364, in current prices; in constant prices, derived from the price index of agricultural purchases in *SYB*, 1984, p. 425.
c Proportion marketed; percentage: in current prices/Val. Mar. Prod. in constant prices/Val. Agr. Prod. I or II.
d In current prices in *SYB*, 1984, p. 364.
e Percentage of production marketed derived from ibid.

For grains (Table 4.11), the relative share of gross deliveries, including grains later resold to deficit peasants, increased by 50% between 1978 and 1983. The relative volume of net deliveries destined for the cities having remained constant (except in 1983 when the excess of purchases led to the well known problems of surplus stocks), most of this growth of deliveries has thus benefited the grain-deficit agricultural zones, making it possible for some regions to specialize in industrial crops; this specialization is not unconnected with the considerable growth of the latter in recent years.[26]

The same evolution, although less marked, can be observed for oilseeds (only half were marketed in the 1970s, over two-thirds now) and for pigs (the proportion of slaughtered pigs marketed rising from 60% to almost 70%, see Table 4.11). Overall, the rate of marketing of agricultural products, as measured by the relationship between the value of deliveries and the value of total output (see Table 4.12), rose from 40 to 50% for vegetable and animal products as a whole. The share of marketed quantities moving through the free markets also rose rapidly between 1976 and 1983.

This evolution contrasts with the previous situation which was marked by a stagnation in sales and by a marked orientation of work collectives towards semi-autarky. The low level of administrative prices formerly imposed on peasants through the state monopolies was obviously not unconnected with such a situation. A survey carried out on a sample of 3,000 production teams showed that in 1978 these prices were in fact lower than the costs of production for the main agricultural products (Table 4.13) (*NYNJ*, 1981, pp. 364 ff.). At a workday pay rate of 0.8 *yuan* and a profit rate of 14.41%, corresponding to the effective average pay in the teams

Table 4.13
Actual Costs (survey of 3,000 teams) and Agricultural Prices, 1978 (yuan/tonne)

	Mac[a]	*WD*[b]	CL_1[c]	CL_2[d]	*AC*[e]	%[l]a
Foodgrains	101.6	166.4	133.1	231.3	234.7	57
of which Rice	94.4	136.8	109.4	190.2	203.8	54
of which Corn	141.2	195.8	156.6	272.2	297.8	53
of which Wheat	84.4	136.2	109.0	189.3	193.4	56
Oil-bearing crops						
of which Rapeseed	260.2	448.4	358.7	623.3	618.9	58
of which Groundnuts	199.4	317.4	253.9	441.2	453.3	56
Cotton	882.8	1,573.4	1,258.7	2,187.0	2,141.5	59

Sources: Costs in *NYNJ*, 1981, pp. 365–7, prices in *NYNJ*, 1980, pp. 380–1 (except groundnuts, derived from *SYB*, 1984, p. 437).

[a] Material costs in fertilizer, etc.
[b] Number of work-days.
[c] Cost of labour at 0.8 yuan/WD.
[d] Cost of labour at 1.39 yuan/WD.
[e] Actual cost 1 (MAC + CL_1).
[f] MAC + CL_2.
[g] Value of production 1 (AC₁ × 1.1441).
[h] Value of production 2 (AC₂ × 1.2).
[j] Procurement prices.
[k] Ratio price/value 1.
[m] Ratio price/value 2.

and the real deductions for agricultural tax and collective accumulation (case I in the table), procurement prices were lower than costs in proportions ranging from 3 to 21%. At a daily wage of 1.39 *yuan* and a profit rate of 20% (conditions similar to those of industry), prices were lower than the value of output in proportions ranging from 34 to 47% (case II).

In such conditions it is not at all surprising that the peasants were unwilling to sell their crops and that the state should have been obliged to use force to secure deliveries. In 1979, when the reports of surveys of agricultural costs were beginning to reach them, the authorities decided to raise the quota prices of the main agricultural products by 20–25% (Table 4.14, columns PP). Deliveries rose sharply at once (Table 4.11). This initial price rise was, however, only a first step in a series of successive rises which were no longer to be simply at the state's initiative. The fact is that the simultaneous spread of responsibility systems marked a sharp decline in control by cadres in the countryside. The state was no longer capable of ensuring respect for the volume of quotas, which, by 1981, represented for grains only 49% of deliveries (Xia Changwen in *Caimao Jingji*, September 1982, pp. 50–51). The bulk of state purchases was thus no longer at the administered quota prices but at much higher 'over-quota' prices (50% higher) or at negotiated prices aligned with those of the free markets. This forced rise of the prices paid by the state was no doubt connected with the possibility now open to the peasants of selling their over-delivery surpluses on the free markets.

However that may be, the rises were spectacular. Taking all deliveries together, the average purchasing price of grains rose by 49% between 1978 and 1983, that of oilseeds by 52%, that of sugar by 56% (see columns GP, Table 4.14). These rises have led to a total reversal of the situation and peasants now voluntarily queue up to sell at the state depots that are often obliged to reject their grain; previously peasants sought to conceal their crops so as to keep them for themselves. This letter from a peasant to a Chinese daily paper sums it up.

> Comrade editor, In the past the comrades in charge of the grains departments used their shoes to run everywhere and their lips were all burned (from trying to convince us) to fulfil the tasks of deliveries to the state . . . Now it is we, the peasants, who earnestly want the state to buy more of our grain. Unfortunately, while we push waggon after waggon and carry sack after sack to the grains depots, the depots no longer want to buy. Their faces covered with sweat, the peasants besiege the staff (of the depots), imploring them to buy their grain, but despite their supplications, they fail to get rid (of their crop).[27]

In these conditions, the maintenance of compulsory delivery quotas, the distinction between quota prices and over-quota prices etc., no longer had any meaning, and, already in some provinces, like Sichuan, in the summer of 1984, the state was paying for all the deliveries at a uniform price, not far removed from the free market prices (*Sichuan Ribao*, 10 August, 1984).[28] The decision at the end of 1984 to gradually put an end to the whole system of deliveries and state monopolies simply ratified the *de facto* situation.

The considerable rises in agricultural purchase prices which made the monopoly of deliveries to the state irrelevant, obviously inspired the peasants to produce more

Table 4.14
Agricultural Prices, 1952, 57, 65, 78–83 (yuan/tonne)

	Grains[e]			*Oil*			*Sugar Crops*[g]			*Cotton*			*Pork*[f]			*Eggs*			*General Index*	
	GP[a]		*P P*	*GP*		*P P*	*GP*		*P P*	*GP*		*P P*	*GP*		*P P*	*GP*		*P P*	*GP*[c]	*P P*[d]
j	*Y*	*ind.*	*ind.*	*Y*	*ind.*	*ind.*	*Y*	*ind.*	*ind.*	*Y*	*ind.*	*ind.*	*Y*	*ind.*	*ind.*	*Y*	*ind.*	*ind.*		
1952	138.4	100	100	605.6	100	100	21.7	100	100	1.830	100	100	658.6	100	100	620	100	100	100	100
1957	162.0	117	116	940.0	155	(155)	25.9	119	(118)	1,796	98	98	1,004.2	152	(139)	942	152	(146)	120	120
1965	229.21	166	157	1,450.0	239	(228)	32.4	149	(155)	2,040	111	108	1,481.5	225	(188)	1,280	206	(180)	155	152
1978	263.4	*190*	*185*	1,746.4	*288*	*(297)*	39.0	*180*	*(174)*	2,278	*124*	*123*	1,674.2	*254*	*(195)*	1,378	*222*	*(208)*	*179*	*170*
		100	100		100	100		100	100		100	100		100	100		100	100	100	100
1979	330.7	126		2,458.2	141		49.6	127		2,680	118		2,149,5	128		1,680	122		122	
1980	360.6	137	121	2,640.8	151	(124)	57.9	148	(125)	3,174	139	129	2,295,6	137	(128)	1,714	124	(121)	131	121
1981	381.7	145		2,818.8	161		59.8	153		3,116	137		2,260.3	135		1,840	134		139	
1982	392.2	149		2,772.9	159		55.5	142		3,236	142		2,198.9	131		1,864	135		142	
1983	392.6	*149*	*126*	2,654.1	*152*	*(125)*	60.9	*156*	*(132)*	3,422	*150*	*129*	2,156.7	*129*	*(128)*	1,886	*137*	*(140)*	*148*	*125*

[a] Average general price, all purchases combines, in *SYB*, 1984, pp. 448–51.
[b] Procurement price, index in *SYB*, 1984, p. 434.
[c] In *SYB*, 1984, p. 425.
[d] Ibid., p. 434.
[e] Price per tonne of trade grain.
[f] Price derived from price per head *SYB*, 1984, p. 448 and from carcase weight in Table 4.6.
[g] Weighted average of cane and beet prices.

for sale. In the case of grains, even though actual sales still represent only a small share of crops, this spur must have played a no less essential role than decollectivization in the growth of production. The phenomenon is even more clear-cut for industrial crops which are much more profitable per hectare than grains and which are largely marketed. The doubling of their output in the last five years cannot be explained in any other way; already the rations of cooking oil and sugar are infinitely less parsimonious than previously (see Tables 4.9 and 10).

The real commercial revolution underway in the Chinese countryside is thus crucially responsible for the improvement of subsistence levels that we have noted earlier. This revolution also lies behind the extraordinary increase in peasant incomes in the last few years; they have more than doubled in five years (but note that the increase is only of part of total income since only half agricultural output is marketed). Before the realignment of agricultural prices, the under-valuation of delivery prices led to a hidden transfer of resources, through the 'price scissors', which Chinese financial experts have attempted to estimate (Table 4.15) (Chen Jialang in Chinese Finance Society 1981). Whereas the relationship between the agricultural price index and the industrial price index has apparently moved favourably between 1952 and 1978, the under-valuation in agricultural prices and over-valuation in industrial prices as compared to output values (a debatable concept) persisted (ΔAV, ΔIV in Table 4.15); the resulting transfer, calculated on the basis of the volume of exchanges between cities and countryside, may thus have been of the order of 20 to 30% of the equivalent of the budgetary resources of the state making a transfer of about 25 billion *yuan* in 1978. Conversely, the gains achieved by peasants since then in their agricultural transactions through price rises after 1978 represented more than 40 billion *yuan* for the year 1983 alone (gains column in Table 4.16). Since the state did not pass on the full amount of the rises to urban consumers (retail food prices in state shops having increased by only 18% between 1978 and 1983) the subsidies made to commercial departments to meet their deficits rose to over 20 billion *yuan* in 1982 (state subsidy, Table 4.16), equal to one-fifth of budgetary resources. It is not surprising in these circumstances that the state should have begun to readjust urban food prices.

At the price, then, of a calling into question the privileges of city-dwellers who have long benefited from abnormally low food prices, the peasants are now enjoying marketing conditions that offer far more incentives than in the past and are favourable to the growth of food production.

Will the marketing of food products be able to advance even farther? That of course raises the question of the extension of urban markets and hence the capacity of the industrial sector to absorb rural labour. But the question can be asked in a different way: will Chinese agriculture, which now feeds the whole population more satisfactorily than in the past, be able in the long run to feed a growing number of non-peasant families with a falling agricultural labour force?

Here an answer is possible. In the survey of the agricultural costs of production in 3,000 production teams that we have already used, the most significant data were not only the high level of costs compared to agricultural prices, but the extraordinary amount of agricultural labour time taken up with food production: 137 work-days to produce a tonne of rice, 448 for a tonne of rapeseed, in 1978 (see

Table 4.15
Price Scissors, 1952, 57, 66, 78

	AGP[a]	IPF[b]	IPR[c]	AGP/IPF	AGP/IPR	ΔVA[d] %	ΔVI[e] %	Scissors	Transf.*[f] 10^6 y	% Budg.[g]	*Transfer in billion yuan
1952	100	100	100	100	100	- 5.5	+8.4	13.9	1.3	7.1	
1957	120	87	102	138	118	-18.8	+21.4	40.2	7.0	22.6	
1966	161	84	105	192	153	-27.3	+37.3	64.6	19.5	34.9	
1978	179	72	100	249	179	-25.9	+15.6	41.5	25.6	22.8	

[a] Agricultural prices index, all purchases combined.
[b] Index of ex-factory industrial prices.
[c] Index of industrial prices, rural retail trade: in *SYB*, 1984, p. 425.
[d] Under-estimate of the value of agricultural production.
[e] ΔVI Over-estimate of the value of industrial production.
[f] Transfer from agriculture to industry brought about by price scissors.
[g] Percentage of state budgetary resources: cf. Chen Jialiang in Chinese Finance Society (1981).

Table 4.16

Agricultural Gains from Price Rises 1979–83/1978 (billion yuan)

| | Value Agr. Pur.[a] | | | Gains[d] | St. Sub.[e] | |
	c.p.[b]	ind.[b]	p. 78[c]		tot.[f]	goc.[g]
1979	71.36	122	58.49	12.9	7.8	n.d.
1980	84.22	131	64.29	19.9	15.9	12
1981	95.50	139	68.71	26.8	20.5	16.3
1982	108.3	142	76.27	32.0	(21)	17
1983	126.5	148	85.47	41.0	n.d.	n.d.

[a] Value of agricultural purchases in current prices: in *SYB*, 1984, p. 364.
[b] Index of agricultural prices (1978 = 100) in *SYB*, p. 425.
[c] Value of agricultural purchases in 1978 prices.
[d] Agricultural gains from price rises.
[e] State subsidies for agricultural prices.
[f] Total.
[g] Of which grains, oils, cotton; cf. official communiques (state sub. tot. 1982: estimate).

Table 4.17); at this rate, agriculture would have great difficulty in feeding a high proportion of non-agricultural workers. This high-level of use of labour, equivalent to 600 days for a hectare of harvested rice, 400 days for a hectare of wheat, etc. is found in other surveys in Jiangsu, Jiangxi, and the suburbs of Shanghai (see Table 4.17).[29]

What is seen here is less a true absorption of agricultural labour than a disguised under-employment. In fact, the real needs of crops, as estimated by official norms (in Henan or Anhui),[30] and as we ourselves measured them in a survey in the autumn of 1981 (Aubert, 1981), are far lower: of the order of only 300 days for a hectare of rice, 100 to 150 days for a hectare of wheat, etc. In other words, without a major change in farming practices, half the present agricultural labour force, provided that it is topped up at times in the crop cycle when extra labour is needed, would be enough to ensure the present level of subsistence. The very scale of present under-employment is in fact the poisoned heritage of 25 years of a collectivization that tied the peasantry to the soil it was cultivating and prohibited any geographical or occupational mobility; the labour unable to employ itself elsewhere was thus absorbed by less and less productive agricultural work (see the stagnation of the productivity of agricultural labour, from 1952 to 1977, in Table 4.18). Until recently, this disguised under-employment weighed heavily in the production cost of food, labour costs forming almost two-thirds of this (see Table 4.13).

The encouragement currently being given to peasants to diversify their activities, the permission given them to settle in county towns to engage in trade or industry (*NCNA*, 13 June 1984) are thus not only the means of enriching the rural economy; they are much more the condition, in the long run, of an increase in the productivity of agricultural labour, and of a reduction in the costs of food production, both essential for the agricultural take-off to be transformed into a true economic take-off.[31]

Conclusion

Assuredly, food security is no longer assured in China, in so far as the minimum

Table 4.17
Absorption and Work Norms for Crops

	Absorpt. Labour Nat. Samp.[a] WD/harv. tonne[b]			WD/ha harv.[c] (Rendt t/ha)		Absorpt. WD/h[d]				Norms/WD/ha harv.[c]		
	1965	1978	78/65 %			Jiading (Shangh)	Jiangsu	Jiangxi	Anhui	Henan	C.A.[f]	Est. a.v.[g]
Foodgrains	160	166	+ 4	(3.13)	520							
of which Rice	165	137	−17	(4.45)	610	542	585	495	375	115	200	*300*
of which Wheat	184	196	+ 6	(2.07)	406	436	570	300	150	160	85	*120*
of which Corn	135	136	+ 1	(3.14)	(427)		435		180	75	90	*140*
of which Soybean	164	255	+56	(1.18)	301							
Oils	372	399	+ 7	(1.18)	471	660						
of which Rapeseed	493	448	− 9	(0.81)	363			285	150	120		
of which groundnuts	315	317	+ 1	(1.50)	476							
Cotton	1,092	1,573	+44	(0.50)	787	856	900		600	225	425	*450*

a National Sample of 3,000 teams, 1965–78.

b Number of work-days per harvested tonne: in *NYNJ*, 1981. p. 366.

c Number of work-days per hectare harvested: derived from yields. t/ha (yields in tonnes per hectare), themselves derived from cereal averages, oils in ibid.. p. 365 and national averages in *SYB*, 1984, pp. 153–4.

d Absorption of labour, in work-days per hectare harvested: observations at Jiading in *NYJJ*, January 1981. pp. 54–9, in Jiangsu in *ZGSHKX*, May 1982, pp. 121 ff. in Jiangxi in *NYJJ*, August 1982, pp. 50–55.

e Norms in work-days per hectare harvested: in Anhui, in *NYJJ*, April 1981. pp. 23–6, Henan, in *SSC*, June 1963. pp. 121 ff.

f Personal observations by Claude Aubert in travel report 1981.

g Estimate of the average of norms.

rations formerly distributed by the teams are no longer now automatically ensured to the villagers. There is a risk that the cleavages between poor households and prosperous peasants will increase again. The cost of food is going to rise too in the cities, making the condition of the poorest all the more difficult.

But perhaps this was the necessary price to be paid for the food take-off, which we are currently witnessing. The collectivization of agriculture and egalitarian distribution within teams turned out to be a brake on a really efficient mobilization of the means of production, even though it did not hinder the green revolution. The state monopolies on trade in agricultural and food commodities, essential to the controls on consumption and the feeding of the cities at low cost, had, for their part, profoundly depressed agricultural output through administered prices that were too low, and paralysed trade without, for all that, succeeding in an effective equalization of food resources. Finally, the total lack of mobility of the peasant population, reduced to the state of serfdom on the soil of the villages that it could not leave, was the source of a basic waste: that of under-employment, in less and less productive work.

It is not surprising, in these conditions, that decollectivization and the ending of the state monopolies should have resulted in a renewed dynamism of agricultural production. This dynamism, linked with the favourable conjuncture of a low population growth rate, has brought about a raising of the general level of rations and led to the emergence of significant fodder surpluses, heralding a basic change in diet, with, for the first time in China, a growing consumption of animal products.

It is of course too soon to know whether the food take-off that is under way will be lasting. Many uncertainties weigh on its future: natural constraints (notably the limits on the possibilities of irrigation) and the possible flattening out of yields, risks

Table 4.18
Productivity of Agricultural Labour, 1952–83

	TAP^b	Ind. Val. Agr. Prod.[a] % indus.[c]	CAP^d	Nb. Ag. W^e 10^6 p	ind.	Prod.[f] ind.	Gr. Pr./Ag. W^g t/mø	ind.
1952	100	—	100	173	100	100	0.93	100
57	125	—	125	193	112	*112*	0.99	*106*
65	137	1	136	234	135	101	0.83	89
1970	166	3	161	278	161	100	0.86	92
1975	202	6	190	295	171	111	0.96	103
76	207	9	188	294	170	111	0.97	104
77	211	11	188	293	169	*111*	0.96	*103*
78	230	12	202	294	170	119	1.07	115
79	249	12	219	294	170	129	1.13	122
80	259	12	228	302	175	130	1.06	114
81	276	12	243	312	180	135	1.04	112
82	307	12	270	320	185	146	1.11	119
83	336	13	292	325	188	*155*	1.19	*128*

[a] Index of agricultural production.
[b] Total agricultural production.
[c] Percentage of rural industry in TAP.
[d] Corrected agricultural production, excluding value of rural industry, *SYB*, 1984, p. 134.
[e] Number of agricultural workers: in *SYB*, 1984, p. 109.
[f] Productivity of agricultural labour: index CAP/Nb. Agr. W.
[g] Production of grains per agricultural worker in tonnes per *mou* (t/mø): derived from Corr. Gr. Pr. in Table 4.1 and Nb. Ag. W.

of anarchy and the collapse of prices with the spread of private trading, climatic vagaries and political vagaries linked above all to who will follow Deng Xiaoping. And the very optimism of official figures might seem suspect. But it still remains true that, so far, all the indicators, and all the reports that reach us directly from the Chinese villages, point in the same direction: that of an undeniable progress. It is to be hoped that China, at last, is embarked on the path of true development.

This chapter was written in the spring of 1985. At that time the take-off in food production based on increases in grain from 1978 to 1983 was confirmed by the record harvest of 1984: 407 million tonnes. It brought annual rural grain harvests to an average level never before reached: 265 kg (unprocessed) for direct consumption. Since then the Chinese countryside has suffered a worse year. Preliminary estimates show a decline of more than 25 million tonnes from the 1984 peak. Has our diagnosis of a food take-off been premature?

In the short run, certainly not. The accumulated surpluses stored during the summers of 1983 and 1984 came to more than 40 million tonnes. They will with ease have made up the short fall of the last harvest and the drop in deliveries which will in all likelihood have followed. Furthermore, it seems that meat production in 1985 did not suffer from a lack of grain for fodder. Farmers drew on their abundant reserves to feed livestock. So, food consumption levels should not in the short term have been affected.

In the longer term there is evidently still a question of whether or not the rises in food production over the past few years will continue. We can only register once more, perhaps at greater length, some of the uncertainties already mentioned.

First are the vagaries of climate. Bad weather, in particular serious floods in the north-east, probably accounted for almost half the drop in production in 1985. Such fluctuation from climatic factors is inevitable; it is possible to observe a drop in grain production every three to five years, interrupting the overall rising tendency since 1965. China experienced poor harvests in 1968–9, 1972, 1977 and 1980–81, each one followed by a spectacular recovery.

More than half of the recent drop in grain production cannot, however, be attributed to intemperate weather. It is the result of the contraction of sown land and the decreased application of chemical fertilizer to grain cultivation. Thus the reduced harvests also stem from farmers' loss of interest in grain production. This could be a much more serious portent for the future.

In fact, this disaffection is a perfectly reasonable response by farmers to the partial release of market forces in the countryside since the elimination of obligatory deliveries (quotas) to the state purchasing agencies. At the end of 1984, in a situation of general surplus – excepting of course pockets of local scarcity and of individual distress – and knowing that the government stations would no longer buy surpluses at advantageous, above-quota prices, cultivators reduced their grain fields. They were further persuaded to do so by the fact that grain production was far less profitable than other crops per hectare because the costs of production had increased and chemical fertilizer was selling at inflated, black market prices. Oil-bearing crops were, for instance, more profitable and their production increased in 1985. Neither was the state able to enforce the cultivation plans included in the farming contracts with individual households. There was therefore a spontaneous adjustment of production.

Such an adjustment was justified in the short term. Rural incomes increased in 1985, despite the fall in grain production. But the adjustment will nevertheless be disturbing if it indicates a reversal of the previous tendency of grain production growth. If it continues, future improvement in the diet – of grains, but even more so of meat – may henceforth be achieved only by substantial imports. Can such an unwelcome outcome, for the Chinese government, be avoided?

Because of the many intervening factors, there is no easy answer to this question. We can be sure that there will be no sudden renewal of grain production after 1985 such as there was in the first half of the 1980s as a result of decollectivization. The gains in productivity from this reorganization have by now been exhausted. Further growth is once more constrained by natural limits such as the difficulties of extending irrigation, yields reaching their ceilings, environmental deterioration, reduction of arable land. It should still be possible however to sustain a growth rate sufficient to consolidate the food take-off begun in the 1980s, and to continue the change in diet with increased meat consumption. But to do so, the government will have to make a success of the second stage of reforms begun with the reintroduction of market-regulated distribution of agricultural products.

Such a success will depend essentially on the authorities being able to implement a price policy with sufficient incentives for grain producers without at the same time further aggravating budget deficits. There is little room for manoeuvre to a government which until now, for obvious political reasons, has avoided readjustment of wheat and rice prices to urban consumers. There is also a question whether inflation of retail meat prices, already taken badly by city-dwellers, will be sufficient to encourage breeders and stimulate demand for grain fodder.

Control of agricultural prices in the new conditions of partial market regulation is a complex and difficult task in which the Chinese administration has had little experience. For three decades the administration has simply managed state monopolies in an authoritarian manner. Will it be able to adapt to its new task? Failure would not merely put in jeopardy the recent food take-off, but could bring into question the very basis of the rural reforms. And this is precisely the time when those reforms are beginning to create new employment. The extraordinary blossoming in these past two years of small rural enterprises has meant a doubling of the number of non-agricultural workers in the countryside, thus relieving the serious under-employment which affected farmers' productivity. In sum, the current modernization of the countryside is at stake in the success or failure to renew the growth of grain production over the next few years.

Notes

1. See *RMRB*, 6 January 1983 (exemplary legitimation of the activities of peasant Wang Quanjing), *XH*, 30 January 1983 (interview with Ren Zhonglin); and 9 February 1983 (details of the regulations).

2. See *ZGNMB*, 29 March 1984 (regulations on private trade); *XH*, 5 December 1983 (free markets in grains in Anhui); *RMRB*, 30 November 1984 (the 'grains shop' of the Li brothers, Wangshi county, Lixin district, Anhui).

3. For the new grain delivery contracts, see the regulations in Sichuan (Radio Sichuan, 12 February 1985, in *FBIS*, daily report 034-1985), in Shandong (radio broadcast of 27 February, in *FBIS* 040-1985), etc; see also *Ban Yue Tan*, 10 February 1985, pp. 5–8. Generally speaking, 30% of the average price of cereals is fixed on the basis of the former quota prices and 70% of it on the basis of above-quota prices. The intervention prices (in the event of a collapse of the market) are those of the former quota prices.

For the freeing of the price of pork, see the interview with Cheng Zhiping, in *XH*, 12 April 1985; see also note 28.

4. See *NCNA*, 9 May 1985 for the prices of meat, poultry and eggs in Beijing. The readjustment of food prices in the cities had been announced already in the decision of the 3rd Plenum of the Twelfth Congress of the CCP, in *RMRB*, 21 October 1984.

5. The official series of figures in the *SYB*, 1984 is not homogeneous: until 1963 tubers are counted at one-quarter of their dry weight, then at one-fifth for the following years. We have therefore carried out the necessary correction by counting tubers at one-fifth of their dry weight from 1952 to 1963. Another correction: the 1978 figure published in the statistical yearbook omits part of the secondary cereals; we have replaced it with the corresponding figure from the agricultural yearbook (*NYNJ*, 1980, p. 103) which contains no such omission.

6. For this notion of 'territoriality', see de Koninck (1985).

7. It is reasonable in fact to believe that the under-estimate of cultivated areas and the consequent over-estimate of the level of yields scarcely affect the long-term trends revealed by the evolution of official figures of areas and yields.

8. The official figures for this production of meat (pork, beef, mutton, excluding poultry) are known for the years 1952, 1956, 1957, 1962, 1965, 1970 and 1975 to 1983 (see *SYB*, 1984, p. 160). The volume of production for the missing years has been estimated on the basis of figures for the slaughter of pigs and consumption known from other sources.

9. The official series of population figures given in the statistical yearbook (*SYB*, 1984, p. 81) is not altogether consistent with the birth/mortality rates published in this same yearbook (1984, p. 83). The excess famine mortality derived from the official mortality rates alone (1957, 10.8%; 1958, 12%; 1959, 14.6%; 1960, 25.4%; 1961, 14.2%; 1962, 10%) would suggest about 14 million extra deaths, compared to a normal mortality of 11% for the three dark years 1959–60–61. See Chapter 2 of this volume for further discussion.

10. The conversion factor to be applied to obtain the quantities consumed in terms comparable to those of the quantities harvested ought to depend only on the composition of the rations and the extraction rates of the different grains (broadly trade grains differ from unprocessed grains in that rice and millet are counted as having been husked, other grains being counted unprocessed). However, it seems that the Chinese statisticians have used conventional conversion factors, the conventions having changed between the 1950s and 1960s. Using the figures derived from deliveries, known from 1952 to 1983, both in terms of 'trade grains' and 'unprocessed grains', we have adopted the following factors (trade grains/ unprocessed grains): 0.95 for 1952–1960; 0.85 for 1961–1980.

11. For 1980, fodder grains amounted to 36 million tonnes, according to the general bureau of animal husbandry (*NYJJ*, August 1982, p. 58). For 1983, their level (17% of output in our table) corresponds to piecemeal information available for some provinces (17% of grains in Shandong in 1983, see *Dazhong Ribao*, 30 January 1984). For 1983 and 1984, it seems that the Chinese authorities have rather under-estimated the overall share of fodder grains and over-estimated that of rations.

12. Derived from Xu Dixin, in *JJYJ*, July 1984, pp. 32 ff. Another source (Cai Gennü in *NYJSJJ*, October 1984, pp. 28–31) estimates grain losses through rotting and the depredations of insects at about 15 million tonnes a year, in round figures (30 billion pounds) – no doubt less than the reality.

13. See survey at Bi Xian, Sichuan in (*RMRB*, 7 May 1983).

14. See the excellent analysis and comparisons with Japan by Ishikawa (1967).

15. The production of pork is derived from per capita consumption figures from 1952 to 1983 (published in *SYB*, 1984, p. 477). The totals for slaughtered cattle and pigs are those of the official figures (*SYB*, 1984, pp. 159–60).

16. We assume an average extraction rate of 0.74.

17. Some have wondered, in particular, whether or not the very low consumption of cereals revealed in the sample of urban families included grains consumed in canteens. Even so, it is not very easy to see why this consumption in canteens, counted in the family rations, would not be taken into account in the sample survey.

18. In particular, the figures for actual average overall consumption in Beijing (canteens thus being included) given to Croll (1983, p. 131), are in agreement, at least for the level of recent years, with the series in the urban sample; in net kg (e = sample; *BJ* = Beijing) 1957, 167 (e); 1958, 206 (BJ); 1964, 156 (e); 1966, 184 (BJ); 1970, 176 (BJ); 1975, 163 (BJ); 1979, 150 (BJ); 1981, 145 (e) (urban over-consumption at the time of the Great Leap, followed by a collapse and a slow recovery until 1966; the regular fall in consumption only began subsequently).

19. A check on the validity of our model is made possible by the official figures for rural and urban consumption published for some years by a Chinese source (*NYJJZY*, 1982, pp. 206–9). These figures, expressed in 'trade grains', are (rural/urban consumption): 1952, 192/241; 1957, 204/196; 1965, 177/218; 1975, 187/217; 1978, 193/218; 1979, 203/219.

Weighted by the figures for rural and urban populations that we have used for these same years, these consumption figures correspond well to the official average consumption figures in Table 4.4. The rural population/urban population distribution used in our model is thus the one used by Chinese statisticians.

For the 1960s and 1970s, the official rural consumption figures in unprocessed grains scarcely differ from those of our model (official consumption/model): 1965, 208/205; 1975, 220/220; 1978, 227/235; 1979, 239/240. Except for 1978, the year when the statistical bureau's official figure for grain production was under-estimated (see note 5), the difference between the two series of figures is of the same order of magnitude as the margin of error in our calculations. On the other hand, the official urban consumption figures, for these same years, do not allow us to confirm our hypotheses to the extent that the Chinese figures group together direct consumption and consumption after industrial processing. These figures, however, remain compatible with ours, if it is observed that the total consumption that they imply corresponds, approximately, to the total of urban and industrial consumption in our model: official consumption = raw growth x urb. pop. / model = urb. cons. + ind. cons. × 106t. 1965, 33/34; 1975, 41/40; 1978, 44/45; 1979, 48/48.

For the 1950s, the official Chinese figures are scarcely credible. In fact, the urban consumption figures that they imply are not consistent with the equally official figures of net deliveries: they show a fall of 19% in the urban ration between 1952 and 1957, whereas the deliveries increased at the same time by 21%! For lack of anything better we have therefore retained the overall consumption figures provided by Chinese statisticians (official series in Table 4.4), but have preferred our own estimates based on the samples to their rural/urban breakdown.

20. The sum of urban and rural consumption figures derived from the samples is

slightly below the total supply of meat derived from production. The difference, of the order of 15% of supplies, might arise from the superior diet of urban cadres not surveyed in the sample (families of workers and employees). We have taken account of this for the years incompletely covered by the samples in the estimates that we have had to make.

21. It is not impossible that climatic vagaries may in future precipitate temporary falls in cereal production, with, as a consequence, temporary collapses of fodder supplies.

22. See *RMRB*, 21 November 1984. In Heilongjiang, the state had to make a contract with private families to keep its excess stocks in their warehouses, see *JJRB*, 10 July 1984. It was the same in Jilin (see Radio Jilin, 14 December 1983, in *SWB*, daily 7519).

23. These imports, mainly of wheat, have for the most part substituted for the coarse cereals delivered by the peasants for urban consumption. There coarse cereals were thus made available for the foddering of cattle on suburban state farms.

24. These figures are much lower than the official estimate of the average overall diet: 2,877 calories per person per day in 1983 (*China Daily*, 5 November 1984). It is not clear how this last figure can have been calculated, since taking the total official rations of grains, meat, etc., which are higher than those of the samples, and our coefficients, they give a total of 2,600 calories for the same year (see Table 4.9).

25. Rations calculated from the data in the urban and rural samples and from the estimates of grain and meat consumption in Tables 4.7 and 8 for the missing years.

26. It is not ruled out, however, that part of the grains resold to the peasants were sold to some of them who had, deliberately or not, sold too much to the state at the time of the first delivery (this would often be a matter of speculation: massive sale by the peasant of grains in summer, paid for by the state largely at very favourable over-quota prices, buying back of grains in the autumn by the same peasant, now unable to meet his own needs, grains this time bought from the state at the low quota prices).

27. Letter from a villager of Fengmu, Xihua district, in *JJRB*, 16 July 1984.

28. The case of pork, in the summer of 1984, was quite different from that of grains. Not having benefited from rises as large as those of cereals (see Table 4.14), the prices of live pigs purchased by the state (0.6 to 0.7 *yuan* per pound), remained insufficient compared to those of grains, given the still low productivity of family stock raising. See Chang Jingwei, in *NYJJWT*, August 1984, pp. 44–6.

This insufficiency of the relative price of pork was no doubt not unconnected with the consolidation of the growth of meat production observed in 1983 (see Table 4.1), and explains, retrospectively, the decision in early 1985 (see note 3) to free the purchase prices of pigs.

29. Survey in Nantong, in Jiangsu, in *ZGSHKX*, May 1982, pp. 121 ff; in 26 teams in Jiangxi, in *NYJJWT*, August 1982, pp. 50 ff; in Jiading (Shanghai), in *NYJJWT*, January 1981, pp. 54 ff (the figures for this latter survey are also cited at length by Ishikawa (1982), p. 18.

30. Norms for Anhui, in *NYJJWT*, April 1981, pp. 23 ff; for a county in the district of Yanjin, Henan, see *ZGSHKX*, June 1983, pp. 121 ff.

31. The editorial in the *RMRB*, 19 March 1984, envisages that in the year 2000, of a rural labour force estimated at 450 million people, only 30% will be employed in agriculture.

5 The Implications of Contract Agriculture for the Employment and Status of Chinese Peasant Women

Delia Davin

There has been an enormous amount of debate in China on the implications of the rural reforms. Critics seem to have regarded them as contrary to, or at least threatening, the interests of socialism and the collective. Those who support the reforms have admitted that they may increase inequality, but argue that 'some have to get rich first', that collectivism should not mean 'everyone sharing the same poverty' and that already the reforms have produced a general rise in the standard of living. There has been less interest, at least in China, in the repercussions of the rural reforms on relations within the household and in their implications for the sexual division of labour and women's roles. These issues have however been taken up by students of China in the West (Hazard, 1982, Stacey, 1983, Croll, 1984, Wolf, 1985) and it is with them that this chapter is concerned.

Work and Working Relationships

The introduction of responsibility schemes has involved devolution, usually to the household. The devolution may be more or less limited according to the type of contract being used, but although the degree of power transfer varies, in each system the household gains in importance in relation to the team. The household head, usually the oldest working male, takes over decisions on such matters as the deployment of labour, the amount of labour to be allocated to a particular job, the division of labour between fieldwork, sidelines and domestic labour, the allocation of family members to particular tasks, the amount of leisure time to be permitted to each and so on. Such decisions were formerly in the hands of the team leader.

This strengthening of the household and the household head is a threatening development for women because, despite all the communist efforts at family reform, the household remains a patriarchal institution (Diamond, 1975; Davin, 1976a; Croll, 1981; Stacey, 1983). Indeed, although there has been some effort to make family life more democratic, the concept of the household head has hardly been challenged nor has the assumption that a male should in normal circumstances hold that position. To an extent, moreover, the institution has even been bolstered by both state and collective authorities who follow the tradition of treating the household head as responsible for family members and deal with them through him in such diverse matters as the census, civil registration and the payment of workpoint income. Women's household membership is less stable than that of men's in that they are only temporary members of their natal households and arrive as adult strangers in the households of their husbands. Traditionally this has made it more difficult for them to exercise authority within the household, a problem which revolution has failed to confront. It is true that women occasionally sign contracts directly with the team as individuals or in groups and, if they are successful in their enterprises, obviously benefit from the success (Wu Naitao, 1983). Far more often, however, the contracts are signed by men, usually as the heads of households, so that their wives, daughters, daughters-in-law and other female relatives perform the contract work as part of a family labour force.

Under the collective system women worked on the land alongside peasants from other families, sometimes in women's work-teams, sometimes in mixed ones. Under responsibility systems or in domestic sidelines they are much more likely to work only with members of their own families. Young women will often be supervised by senior family members: fathers or fathers-in-law when the work is performed by both sexes, mothers or mothers-in-law when it is not. Young women are thus losing a chance to communicate at work with their own peer group, with cadres and with people outside the family generally.

In the past, work relationships were especially important to young brides who, given the fairly general persistence of the customs of patrilocal marriage and village exogamy, came as strangers to their new villages and were otherwise constrained in their ability to make contacts outside their husbands' families. These work relationships cannot easily be replaced by other close ones. The double burden ensures that rural women, especially when young, enjoy little leisure. In the off-peak seasons of the agricultural year when men sit around smoking and chatting, women carry on with the normal household routine and busy themselves with home-centred tasks such as mending, sewing, knitting and pickling for which they have too little time the rest of the year.

For very young women, the limitations on regular contacts outside the family will militate against the possibility of establishing even a degree of personal autonomy. Despite a declared policy of ending the system of arranged marriages, the Chinese government had in any case had to settle for a compromise in the countryside whereby young people usually enjoyed at least a power of veto and might even sometimes choose their marriage partners, but parents still had influence and often made the choice, certainly retaining a major say in the financial arrangements and in the timing of the wedding (FLP, 1950; Davin, 1976b; Croll, 1981). This reflects the reality that a marriage involves considerable expenditure on the part of the groom's family and a transfer of labour power from the bride's to the groom's household. It is thus of great concern not just to the principals but also to their families.

Traditionally in China it was considered important to 'match gates' or in other words to ensure that bride and groom were of similar economic status. This preference continued to influence marriage even during the collective period. Marriage connections with the poor or feckless were avoided by the better off and men in impoverished mountain areas found brides only with difficulty, whereas those in suburban communes could take their pick (Croll, 1981; Parish and Whyte, 1978). Young people of 'bad class origin', the children of landlords and rich peasants, also found it hard to marry. As rural class categories have recently been abolished, they presumably no longer feature in marriage choice. However, the much greater spread of incomes now to be found within each village and each district will presumably mean that 'matching doors' narrows choice more than it did under collectivization. The parents of a girl from a specialized household will wish her to marry into a family with a similarly favourable contract, perhaps even one with which they can do business. Moreover, now that the household is left much more to its own devices, prosperous families are likely to eschew marriage connections with poorer ones more actively even than before. A daughter-in-law whose parents have sons or a pension to rely on will clearly be preferred to one whose parents will only have her to look to in their old age.

Although young people in the countryside never really won the right to choose their partners, collective work did sometimes offer a setting in which they could meet, get to know each other and perhaps even arrive at understandings. Within the framework of the production team young people were also able to make their own relationships with outsiders and even authority figures such as team leaders and cadres who might be called on for support in the event of a family conflict over marriage. In a more family-based system this will be more difficult. Even personal identity is affected. As team members, young people could be perceived as individuals and known for their own qualities, characteristics or skills. If they do not work outside a family setting, they are more likely to be known as the son or daughter of such and such a family.

Under collectivization, a young woman, whether married or not, was usually expected to work in the fields. An older woman might accompany her daughter or daughter-in-law as part of a larger work-group or might stay at home to look after children, work on the private plot or take care of the house. Now that labour is deployed by the household, given that men and women frequently work at separate tasks, the women of the house will usually work alone together. Where there are two adult women in one household, they are most frequently mother-in-law and daughter-in-law, a relationship which in Chinese society tends to be characterized by tension rather than female solidarity (Wolf, 1972).

Another factor likely to affect the sexual division of labour is that responsibility systems seem in many places to have produced (or perhaps only exposed) a surplus of agricultural labour. To meet this problem the government has advocated the rapid development of sideline production. Such employment is depicted as especially appropriate for women, so admonitory stories of women thankfully abandoning fieldwork for sidelines in which they rapidly make prodigious sums, now abound in the Chinese press. It is probably often true that women prefer sideline work, which is usually cleaner and lighter, and, unlike fieldwork under the collective when work hours were fixed, fits in comparatively easily with other calls on their time. Nor does all sideline work mean relegation to an inferior, subsidiary sector of the economy. Some such enterprises, for example in recent years the production of angora rabbits for the export market, is so profitable that the women who engage in them become the main income-earners in their households (Wu Naitao, 1983). The producers of cultured pearls have also done well for themselves and have thus attracted media treatment out of proportion to their real importance. Women who live near to important tourist centres take advantage of their location and make what is by rural standards good money by selling souvenirs and craftwork to tourists. But these eye-catching examples should not be allowed to conceal the fact that much sideline production is monotonous, isolated, under-capitalized and, even by Chinese standards, poorly remunerated. Only exceptionally are large amounts of money made. The work is often carried out under sweated conditions and women's enthusiasm for it reflects their lack of alternative opportunities. This is not of course to condemn the strategy of encouraging domestic sideline industry. As investment for it is mostly provided by the household it offers a cheap way to boost certain types of production and to raise incomes. Its bleaker side should not however be overlooked.

Will new forms of cooperation become opportunities for women to form autonomous relations? Some sort of cooperation may again develop in Chinese agriculture. Ironically it has been observed that where the breakdown of the old collective has gone furthest, this is already occurring. As a household's contracted land is made up of scattered strips – to achieve a fair division of good and bad land – a considerable degree of cooperation is needed in order to achieve rational crop management and rotation, pest and water control and even physical access to the strips. But this has produced, according to an eminent Chinese economist, 'mutual aid along kinship lines' (Xu Shaozhi, 1982). The re-emergence of the male-based lineage is not a development likely to further women's interests.

Another report describes the spontaneous appearance of forms of cooperative organization in rural industry and commerce (Watson, 1984). The advantages are obvious: shared equipment, materials bought in bulk, pooled investment and superior borrowing power. Some women have succeeded in forming such groups, but on the whole they are likely to be based on male networks derived from kinship, school attendance, neighbourhood and teashop use. Women's networks do not have the same long-term stability as they are upset by geographical remove on marriage.

Income and the Control of Resources

Even under the collective system, the household head controlled the shared household budget and the income earned by individual household members was paid by the collective to him. It could be argued that the changes in the organization of arable work have hardly affected the situation since, whether income is distributed by the team on the basis of workpoints earned, or whether it comes directly to the household in the form of retained production, it is controlled by the household head. The workings of the centripetal Chinese household economy are such that this obtains to an extent even when households are made up of individual wage-earners, as has been shown in Hongkong (Salaff, 1981). The system does work to women's detriment, although their lack of financial autonomy is of course shared by all the younger members of the household. However, as I have argued elsewhere, even where women do not control the income they have earned, it may 'give them face' or, in more Western terms, enhance their status and thus increase their influence within the family if their contribution is at least clearly perceived. The workpoint system, although it discriminated against women in various ways, did have the advantage of giving each individual's work outside the household a clear and well publicized value (Davin, 1976a).

In family farming the distinct contribution made by each member of the family disappears. Except in cases where the availability of suitable non-agricultural employment for men leaves women as the majority among those working on the land as sometimes happens in suburban communes, women are likely to be seen as 'just helping'. Much of what they do will become as 'invisible' and therefore as incapable of conferring status as is their household labour.

The promotion of household sidelines has rather different implications. Again generalizations are difficult. There are areas in which access to raw materials or to markets is lacking, or where conditions are unsuitable in some other way, so that household sidelines make no significant contribution to household income. Even within the same village, some households may depend for most of their income on 'sidelines' while others, differently endowed with skills, labour or resources, have no involvement in them. However, household sidelines over rural China as a whole had grown to the point where by 1982 they provided 38% of average household income.

The effect of this growth of women's employment and on intra-household relations will vary from one sideline to another according to its place in the sexual division of labour. For example, women are rarely involved in hunting or forestry, take more part in sidelines based on gathering, do the major share of work on private plots, and may be wholly responsible for sidelines such as embroidery, basket-making and raising silkworms.

Women may do better from their involvement in the sidelines seen as 'women's business', even if they are minor, than in those seen as family enterprises. The way a peasant man from Hebei province interviewed in 1970 thought of his family pig enterprise is instructive:

> There's not enough to fatten a second pig when she raises a litter. I'll be needing cash soon for a number of things, so I'll be fattening Big Pig up for the marketing co-op, then I'll feed and fatten Little Pig.

Himself unconscious of the contradiction, the interviewer later reports that it is in fact this man's wife who fattens and cares for the pigs – she even washed Little Pig when he fell into the latrine (Chen, 1973). Although the pigs are the women's responsibility, they are seen as the household's resources and thus decisions about them lie ultimately with the household head, as does the control of the cash raised from them.

Craftwork such as embroidery and basket-making done only by women with no major input of household resources will probably be seen in a somewhat different way. The income from the sale of such goods is perceived as having been earned by women and acknowledged as their contribution to household income. They are thus likely to be able to retain a little cash for personal spending from it. Women are very often responsible for selling sideline produce in the free markets now found all over China. Again, when money passes through their hands, they are likely to retain something. In a society which is still poor and in which most households still produce the bulk of what they consume, small sums can give a disproportionate sense of power. Not only can those with access to cash get themselves small treats, they can please or placate others with little gifts: special food for older people, a ribbon for a daughter, cigarettes for men and so on. Women may also make minor purchases for the household which are important to them, such as an easily cleaned plastic tablecloth or detergent to lighten the burden of laundering clothes.

Property

Legally in the People's Republic, before the Inheritance Law of 1985, women were equally entitled to inherit family property with their brothers and all that was acquired during marriage was the joint property of husband and wife. The *de facto* position in the countryside was somewhat different. The main inheritable property after the collectivization of land was housing, which, in the countryside, was still usually privately owned. This, along with household goods, normally passed to the sons who still lived in their parents' village. In most cases, one of these sons would have stayed with his parents to care for them with the help of his wife, while his brothers made a contribution to their expenses. The share of the co-resident son in the inheritance was larger in recognition of his greater contribution. If challenged, the discrimination against the daughters who inherit nothing would be justified on the grounds that they had not supported the old people. In cases where daughters had remitted money for their parents' support they did sometimes successfully claim their share of any inheritance. The principle of the joint property of husband and wife was put to the test upon divorce or the remarriage of widows, both uncommon events in the rural areas. Divorcees tended to leave their ex-husbands' homes with only their personal possessions and widows leaving to join their second husbands' households seemed often to do no better. However, if the death of a husband had left them as head of household, they sometimes retained the property, even on remarriage.

Women's lack of control over property was thus hardly challenged, even under the collective system; but its injustice became more blatant as households became wealthier and were permitted to own as private property assets which would formerly have been collectively owned. Rising incomes mean that more is now owned in the form of better housing and furnishings but income is also increasingly being invested in quite important means of production both for agriculture and sidelines. Wealthy households can invest in power pumps, wells, vehicles, agricultural machinery, animals, looms, sewing-machines and so on. Moreover, although the outright purchase of land is still impossible, the long-term control of land under contract is now available to the household. As it is normally the male-led household which contracts for land, women's access to it is dependent on their relationship with men.

The law attempts to deal in terms of individual rights, but in peasant society most property is seen as belonging to the family as a unit. When this unit grows in economic importance, the implications of any division of its property also become more significant. When women were given their share of land after land reform in the early 1950s, wives who attempted to assert their right to land and take it with them upon divorce often became the victims of violence; indeed, hundreds of thousands of them were murdered (Davin 1976a). Now that the household again possesses or controls so large a share of the means of production, it is not surprising that inheritance rights in general, and those of women in particular, have become the subject of controversy once more. After much disagreement at the National People's Congress, a new inheritance law was finally passed which became effective in October 1985 (see the chapter by Michael Palmer in this volume). The equal rights of both sexes to inherit are affirmed and indeed the courts are asked to give special protection to the rights of daughters, especially if married or illegitimate (Defend the Rights of Citizens to Inherit Legally Recognized Property, *RMRB*, 14 April 1985). On the other hand, two principles were introduced which could be seen as limiting women's rights. First, property jointly owned by a married couple was henceforth to be considered in two halves upon the death of a spouse. The first half was the absolute property of the widow or widower, while the other half was to be divided between the surviving spouse and the children and parents of the deceased. This appears to weaken the legal claims of widows. Secondly, it is laid down that the greater the family role played by an heir, the greater the entitlement to inherit. This is intended to reward children who have supported aged parents: in most cases of course, males. However, as we have seen, women in the past rarely obtained what they were legally entitled to. It may be that this law, although it seems to entitle peasant women to less, will eventually give them more, since being less remote from rural realities it should be easier to implement. Like other Chinese laws this one is often vague, leaving much to the discretion of the courts. Its implications for women are thus still a matter for speculation; only time will show how, or indeed if, it affects their situation.

For the moment under the household-based economy, women are a sort of proletariat with a use-right to the means of production in the household to which they belong which ceases if they leave it. In this they are clearly disadvantaged. Although divorce is still rare in most villages, this knowledge that she would be able to take nothing from the household which she had helped to build up must clearly inform the behaviour of every married woman. She is not operating on equal terms as she seeks to negotiate the necessary compromises of everyday life with her husband and her in-laws.

Welfare and Education

Even in China, despite a widespread tendency to insist that the rural reforms have been entirely beneficial, some concern has been expressed about their implications for the services provided by the collective. The problem is that as the collective unit becomes weaker, so does its ability to raise money for the welfare fund and for education, both of which have in the past been locally financed. When the responsibility system was first introduced there were many reports that schools, kindergartens and clinics were being closed and that collective welfare funds were no longer sufficient to meet obligations. The state reacted by urging that collective services be sustained at their former level or even improved and it seems they have at least partially recovered (Davin, 1985).

However, some benefits which were particularly important to women may have been lost permanently. Under the collective system the team leader had a specific responsibility to protect pregnant or menstruating women and nursing mothers by given them the lightest tasks. Now that labour is deployed by smaller-scale units this will be more difficult. Women commune members had a right to maternity leave from their production team and in some prosperous communes even received some workpoints for the period of their leave. The degree of care women get will now depend more directly on the labour resources of their households.

Economically disadvantaged households which, in China as elsewhere, are often those 'deviant' households headed by women, retain the right to basic aid but have lost the right to borrow grain from the collective at low interest. This practice has ceased not only as an economy, but also because such loans were used by families with a high dependency ratio and repaid when the ratio went down as children became old enough to earn. They then came under fire as a subsidy to families who ignored the government injunctions to plan their child-bearing and had too many babies.

Education has suffered as children are kept back to help on responsibility land or with sidelines. Primary school attendance is neither free, compulsory nor universal in China; but the 1982 census revelation that, of China's 200 million illiterates 70% were female, reflected the fact that parents had allowed their sons more schooling than their daughters (Women's Congress, 1983). As the belief that female children are more useful, obedient and diligent than their brothers is widespread in China it is likely that a majority of those missing school in order to help their parents are girls. The loss of even the basic education offered by a rural primary school will inevitably have deleterious effects on the future status and employment prospects of these girls.

The Effect of Population Policy

Although the Chinese have been slow to consider the implications of the rural reforms for gender relations, one new factor has focused official attention on women's roles and status and has made complacency impossible: the re-emergence of female infanticide in the wake of the stringent new population policy. The single-child family policy was introduced in 1979 and has since been pushed with great intensity. It is a drastic response to what is seen as the grim threat of demographic explosion as the bulge generation of the 1960s reaches marriageable age. China's population has almost doubled in the past 30 years and could do so again in the next 45 if families average three children (Chen and Tyler, 1982). To comply with the new policy, couples are urged to limit their families to a single child. They come under enormous political pressure to conform, are offered considerable economic incentives and can be heavily penalized for non-compliance. Recently there have been rumours that the policy may be abandoned or made less strict. This has been met with many official denials but it may well be that more exemptions allowing people to have a second child are being granted in the rural areas.

Female infanticide was a traditional method of dealing with unwanted girl babies whose upbringing would be too great an expense for poor parents (Lee, 1981). Campaigns against the practice in the 1950s were successful, probably because peasant parents, once they could afford to bring up their daughters, were quite willing to do so. However, the advent of the single-child family policy means that parents whose first-born is a daughter must either abandon all hope of having a son or pay the high price of defying the policy. A son is regarded as a necessity in every family since he will support his parents in their old age. Daughters, because they marry out, cannot be satisfactory substitutes. Female infanticide, which allows parents whose first-born was a girl to try again for a boy, while appearing to conform to the policy, has again made an appearance on a scale significant enough to have been reflected in some of the provincial sex ratios at birth and in infancy revealed by the 1982 census (Aird, 1983).

That female infanticide could occur in a socialist state of 35 years standing produced profound shock. There is a new concern in both government and party circles as well as among sociologists about the problems of women's status and roles. The recognition that there is a problem has also legitimated more intense and militant activity on the part of the Women's Federation in defence of women's interests and employment than has been seen since the 1950s (Croll, 1984; Davin 1982). It has to be admitted however that no very feasible solutions have yet been produced.

Conclusion

This chapter may seem to present rather a gloomy view of the prospects for rural women in China. I should stress that I am not attempting to argue that the effects of the rural reforms on women have been wholly negative, or even that on balance they are necessarily negative. All observers seem to agree that for the present at least the reforms have raised productivity, stimulated initiative and income and produced a remarkable and fairly general increase in standards of living. While it seems probable that women are disproportionately numerous among the very poorest groups who are being left behind in the race for prosperity, it is certain that most women will benefit, as members of their families and communities, from improved standards of living. However, given the family structure of rural society, the specific effects on women of the rural reforms are not so positive. Since it stimulated the employment of women, taking them out of the age and sex based hierarchy of the household and freed them at least partially from the ties of domestic work and child care, it seems unfortunate that when the collective system was transformed, the repercussions for women were initially hardly considered. This neglect represented a general failure to think through the implications of the reforms for individual and family behaviour. For example, it is now admitted that the general weakening of collective authority which resulted from the responsibility systems caused a temporary rise in the birth rate as families decided 'we have our own land and can decide for ourselves the number of children we can have' (Xu Shaozhi, 1982). The introduction of this pro-natalist economic policy in the same year as the introduction of the anti-natalist single-child policy is an extraordinary example of the failure to make connections.

The contradiction between the rise in the autonomy of the individual household which has come about with the rural reforms, and the government's attempt to assume an unprecedented measure of control over the reproductive plans of individual households, has forced the Chinese authorities to begin to take the Chinese peasant household as a unit of analysis. Population policy, by exposing the degree of discrimination against females which still survives in rural China, has led to more serious attempts to understand the roots of women's subordination. It is possible that these developments will force the government to evolve policies which focus on women's subordination within the household structure as a major problem. Meanwhile however, current rural policies, in strengthening the patriarchal peasant household, seem to be tightening the bonds of women's subordination. Whereas various features of collectivization were consciously designed to improve women's status, such benefits as the new policies offer women seem to be chance by-products rather than carefully planned results.

6 Implementation and Resistance: The Single-Child Family Policy

Lucien Bianco and Hua Chang-ming

China will not be able to modernize itself without slowing down the growth of its population. This growth has been more rapid since 1949 than at any time in the country's history, which is not unusual in the Third World. What is, on the other hand, peculiar to China is the size of the population, which has risen from half a billion in 1949 to over one billion today. As the total cultivated area has slightly diminished over the same period (and it will be difficult and costly to increase it in anything more than a marginal way), the virtual doubling of the Chinese population has led to a halving of the cultivated area per head, which has become one of the lowest in the world. Before the spectacular progress of these last few years, the intensification of yields had just made it possible to maintain food availability per head at its level of 1933. Despite the recent progress, a not insignificant minority of Chinese still do not have enough to eat, if only because of the scale of regional disparities in food resources (see Chapter 2). It is to be hoped that this situation is only temporary and that these persistent pockets of malnutrition will gradually disappear with increased output; but in the long run the modernization of agriculture, which implies increasing productivity as well as yields, will pose acutely the problem of surplus labour. Already it is estimated that there are 100 million surplus workers in the agricultural sector; finding jobs for them elsewhere will take all the longer because there is already an abundance of labour in the secondary and tertiary sectors and because the authorities have enormous difficulty in containing unemployment among young city-dwellers.[1] Leaving aside the absorption of the widespread under-employment that already represents a serious obstacle to economic development, almost 200 million non-agricultural jobs would need to be created between now and the end of the century simply to keep up with the foreseeable increase in the number of job-seekers.[2] Modernizing the Chinese economy involves making enterprises more competitive: they have to produce and sell more more cheaply by reducing not only the cost of using capital but also labour costs. Almost everywhere productivity is low or indifferent, and it can and must be greatly improved; but how to lay off surplus labour when so many new job-seekers have to be absorbed? This is a classic illustration of a commonplace vicious circle: modernization, which would create – and, with luck, will create – new jobs, is handicapped by the excess of labour which slows down improvements in productivity.

After agriculture and employment, we should say a word too about energy and the environment. Well endowed though China is with coal and petroleum, tens of millions of peasant households – not only in north China – are inadequately heated while they are being forced by the shortage of fuel to burn too much wood (more wood than is consumed by construction and paper making) or straw. The rapid deforestation of China (a reduction by a good third in the usable area since 1949) has already led to worrying soil erosion and increased both flooding and desertification (in the north-west, for example), while the use as fuels of roots and stubble deprives the soil of organic matter essential to the maintenance of fertility and water retention.[3] Water is short in north China and in many towns and cities. Even in the regions where it is not in short supply, as in Hubei, reserves are diminishing rapidly, and arable lands are being taken from lakes (the surface of Lake Dongting has shrunk by over a third since 1949 and the water is often polluted).[4] Atmospheric pollution, increased by recent industrialization, is reaching record levels in Beijing, Shanghai and other large cities. China's ecological balance was already precarious before 1949 and it has not stood up well to the waste of energy and other natural resources or the countless errors brought about by ignorance and lack of attention to the environment: in China as elsewhere, human beings are often those most responsible for 'natural calamities'. But the degradation of the environment is, in any case, difficult to counter where the minimum needs of a billion human beings exhaust resources which are not unlimited: however we look at it, there is absolutely no way of evading the population pressure and the planners have no choice but to reduce it whatever the cost. In so doing, they are not working for themselves (for despite their efforts, this pressure will worsen in coming years), but for their successors and the Chinese of the third millennium.

Encouraging a rapid and profound alteration in the behaviour of the large cohorts of reproducers who are growing up and will be growing up between now and the year 2000 is thus a perfectly legitimate goal, even if it has to be done brutally. It does not necessarily follow that such an extreme measure as the single-child policy was the most appropriate. But this chapter does not intend to discuss whether it was the right policy nor to outline its long-term consequences, for example on the age structure of the population (which might end up, if the single-child rule were to be strictly enforced over a long period, with a high proportion of retirees compared to the working population) or on marriage customs (the old predominance of virilocal residence made impossible). Still less does it aim to go over once again the introduction, main phases and regional nuances of a policy that has already been the subject of excellent analyses (for instance, Croll *et al.*, 1985). Our sole purpose is to assess and illustrate the difficulties of enforcing a policy that is very ill received by those at whom it is directed. Cadres responsible for enforcing it are dragging their feet or, on the contrary, being over-zealous; couples are reluctant or run for cover: such is the situation, more or less, revealed by the Chinese press in the 1980s – and not always obliquely.[5] These problems eventually, especially since 1984, extracted substantial concessions from the leadership, that relax the way the single-child rule is applied (without rejecting the principle of it).[6]

Cadres

For cadres at the base, above all rural cadres, responsible for enforcing the single-child rule, it is virtually impossible to secure adequate results and even more to prevent all 'out-of-plan' (*jihua waide*) births without using force. They are thus sometimes criticized for their lack of determination in enforcing a policy that shocks them as much as it shocks those they administer, or the bad example they set by having (or bearing) excess children themselves and sometimes for excessive zeal and the intolerable abuses that they have to commit to get the single-child rule respected at any cost.

Lack of Coordination, Zeal or Equipment

Why did Hua Sanzhen repay the single-child grant? A letter to the chief editor of *Wenhuibao* (26 April 1980) set out the case of Hua, a young female worker with the single-child certificate, who suddenly changed her mind and refunded the three months grant that she had already received. She lived with her husband and her child in an unhealthy $8m^2$ room in a building that was hot in summer and cold in winter and that threatened to collapse at any moment. In November 1979, she went, with her single-child certificate, to the housing allocation bureau claiming that holders of the certificate were entitled to the same accommodation as the parents of two children. The official on duty replied that he was not aware of that rule (the text of which had been published in the paper): he allocated apartments on the basis of family size and paid no attention to the single-child certificate. 'What can I do?', sighed Hua. 'Either you wait for your building, classified as dangerous, to be pulled down, or you increase the size of your family, and then I can act on your request.' Hua went home and talked it over with her husband and they decided to have another child.

In other circumstances, it is the lack of equipment that makes people give up. Most of the time, it is not the fault of local cadres, any more indeed than it is of higher authorities, who, in this area, have made considerable strides since the early 1970s (Chen Pi-Chao in Croll *et al.*, 1985). For lack of sufficient beds, the hospital of the *xian* of Dangyang, Hubei, turned away a woman who had come to be sterilized. She had travelled 25 kilometres with her husband, the hospital in the commune being itself so full that it sent women home as soon as the tubectomy was done. At the headquarters of the *xian*, she would have to wait three days for one of the six gynaecological beds to become available (*Guangming Ribao*, 28 May 1980). She quailed at the cost of accommodation and food. In other cases, responsibility for bottlenecks falls at least in part on local cadres and officials. In October 1983 it was difficult to get pills, coils or diaphragms in Nanchang and virtually impossible in Ganzhou, even in the few pharmacies in the town that carried advertising for contraception. They sold all sorts of other products, but were in no hurry to restock their contraceptive products which were distributed free and brought in nothing (*RMRB*, 22 October 1983).

Bad Example: Over-prolific Cadres

More serious than shortcomings and lack of zeal on the part of poorly motivated cadres, officials, or employees, is the bad example set by cadres who have too many children or, quite simply, one child when it is not their turn. The press returns to this delicate issue all the more often because the Party expects cadres to set a good example and, in theory, punishes them more harshly when they contravene the single-child rule.[7] In fact, the denunciations of prolific cadres, especially common in 1980, sometimes suggest that they are in a better position than others to carry through to its term an 'out-of-plan' pregnancy and do so unscathed. A letter to the chief editor of *Dazhong Ribao* criticized 'the ambiguous attitude' of the Shandong provincial leaders who had taken no sanctions against the assistant secretary of the Tai'an Youth League, who was guilty of having had a second 'out-of-plan' child, only two years after the birth of the first.[8] The breach of the rule is not always so minor. The director of a petroleum refinery in Guangdong who already had three sons and a daughter sent his wife to the other end of the country, to Manchuria, on the excuse of getting medical treatment there; in fact it was a new pregnancy, concealed from the authorities until the birth of the fifth child (*Nanfang Ribao*, 17 May 1980). On the borders of Hebei and Shandong, the local authorities took revenge on an over-zealous female family planning agent who dared to prevent the daughter-in-law of the assistant secretary of the Party committee of the *xian* of Wuqiao (Hebei) from giving birth to an 'out-of-plan' child. Three times a veto by this Party committee prevented her being a delegate to the National Family Planning Congress, a public inquiry was launched against her on the basis of an anonymous letter, etc. (*RMRB*, 14 January 1984).

The norm stressed a hundred times is that model family planning communes and brigades have quite simply followed the good example of local cadres, while when these set a bad example family planning goes by the board. Such was the case in Hainan where there was criticism of numerous cases of fourth, fifth and sixth births in the families of cadres that went unpunished, and where a third of births in 1979 were third or higher parity children (*Nanfang Ribao*, 17 May 1980). Another example, at the level of the village this time, concerns Xikang brigade, Yanzhuang commune, Jinghai *xian*, Tianjin. Of 16 births between January and October 1980 (the brigade had 1,100 inhabitants), only three were in line with the plan: two first births and one authorized second birth. Nine were third or higher parity births (four of them were fifth or sixth). Moreover, among the twelve women pregnant at the time of the report (in October), only six were so for the first time and one of them, aged 48, was having her eighth pregnancy. The rest of the article set out in detail the family situation of the main village leaders, beginning with the head of the brigade, the vice-secretary of the Party cell, whose wife had just given birth to her fifth child, after concealing her pregnancy from the authorities. No one dared to criticize the number one man in the village, but every couple concluded: if the head of the brigade can have five children, then we can certainly have a second one (*Tianjin Ribao*, 26 October 1980)

Excessive Zeal, Abuses and Violence

Cadres, responsible for ensuring that the quota of births allocated to them is not exceeded and, moreover, often paid piece rates according to births avoided (bonuses are given to family planning activists who succeed in keeping the birth rate of their sector below a certain threshold, then getting it down), are likely to do too much rather than too little. Some excessive zeal is mischievous or ridiculous: in one kindergarten, two sweets are given to single children every day and only one to the others. On the institution's festival day single children are entitled to twice as many presents and their parents take them out while other children are assigned to cleaning out the crèche or kindergarten (*RMRB*, 2 August 1981).

The press takes umbrage at such initiatives just as it denounces cadres who throw sumptuous banquets paid for by creaming off the fines paid by two-children parents (*Sichuan Ribao*, 24 August 1982) or ones who falsify the registration of births so as to collect substantial bonuses. Yet it treats as perfectly normal, worthy of imitation even, measures that are not only severe but unfair, if they are seen as being inspired by the general interest (the determination to achieve results). This is how it treats the collective responsibility of the neighbourhood or unit (*danwei*) for any 'out-of-plan' birth that occurs within it. Wide publicity was given to an interview with the vice-secretary of Chanshan commune, Jimo *xian*, Shandong, who achieved total control of the population (*Dazhong Ribao*, 10 February 1984): all the couples of child-bearing age were divided into 424 'groups linked for family planning' (*jihua shengyu lianhuzu*) all headed by a Party member. Within each group, families were detailed to watch each other and 'persuade' defaulting couples to resort to abortion to terminate an unplanned pregnancy. In other cases, the similarity with the old imperial neighbourhood Watch System (*baojia*) is even more obvious, the families of the group being expressly warned that they will be fined if one of them 'produces' an 'out-of-plan' child.[9] Again, the parents-in-law (it is true that their responsibility is generally more direct than that of neighbours) were heavily fined if it was discovered that their daughter-in-law had gone to deliver elsewhere (*Zhengming Ribao*, 28 July 1981).

While he was careful not to mention the practice of *baojia*, the vice-secretary of Chanshan commune was quite happy to resort to the language of guerrilla or civil war: he talked of launching 'surprise attacks' on priority targets (fertile couples who already had one child).[10] Elsewhere, as in the region of Huiyang, Guangdong, the 1981 family planning campaign was compared to the battle of Huaihai which a third of a century before dealt the fatal blow to the forces of Chiang Kai-shek. The goal was no longer to conquer the white armies, it was to prevent 47,000 second pregnancies from reaching their term. Some couples were prepared to pay the fine laid down in the event of a second birth, some pregnant women were ready to risk expulsion from the Party to keep their child, but the authorities, required to respect the quota for abortions fixed by the secretary of the regional committee of the Party, would not tolerate any subterfuge. They resuscitated the study classes (now consisting of a handful of pregnant pupils harangued by a host of masters belonging to various echelons of the hierarchy) and the cow pens (punishment sheds) of the Cultural Revolution. The Public Security of the *xian* of Huidong entrusted the search for pregnant women to armed guards equipped with arrest warrants which identified the delinquent woman with a single word: 'pregnant'. Some of these 'delinquents' were taken directly to the hospital to undergo an abortion, the privileged ones by car, the others simply in chains (like conscripts during the Sino–Japanese war) in lorries surrounded with iron bars that were usually used to transport pigs. Those who succeeded in escaping left behind a husband or family: substitute targets that became the object of attacks intended to wear down the enemy (the recalcitrant wife or daughter-in-law).[11] If the close family succeeded in getting away too, there was always the house and the possibility of cutting off water and electricity, affixing seals or quite simply beginning to take the roof off. Some overseas Chinese who had come from Hong Kong to visit their family had their passports confiscated because some relative or other had fled to avoid an abortion. Launched at the beginning of May, the campaign ended temporarily (a second wave was to be launched in September–October of the same year) eight weeks later: on 26–28 June, all the regional leaders of the CCP were summoned to hear a victory report. The 47,000 (including some eight-month foetuses smothered as soon as they were expelled) enemies had been wiped out, people had shown themselves worthy of the heroes of Huaihai (*Zhengming Ribao*, 27 and 28 July 1981).

We must be careful not to generalize from an almost unique piece of evidence, especially as the manifest indignation of the reporter may have led him to believe in rumours: the forced abortion campaigns have not been so brutal everywhere.[12] Conversely, if such a piece of evidence has reached us, it is obviously because it concerns a region of Guangdong close to Hong Kong.[13]

Another more recent eyewitness account from Hong Kong describes a sterilization campaign conducted with the help of methods comparable to those to which the Huiyang authorities had recourse to impose abortion. When a woman refused to be sterilized, the commune had the furniture removed from her house. She could get it back on payment of a heavy fine, deemed to cover the costs of removal and transport. The tubectomy she had to undergo was, on the other hand, absolutely free (*Zhengming*, March 1984, p. 25). What the Chinese press does on occasion report and deplore are less brutal but nevertheless very effective forms of financial pressure, such as the one in which single-child mothers in Sichuan who refused to be sterilized were victims in 1980: a doctor came and parked himself on the family, which had to turn over 1.60 yuan a day to the commune (for the doctor's time) until it agreed to sterilization (*RMRB*, 13 September 1980, quoted in Tien, 1982, p. 289).

Couples

From what has already been said it can be guessed, or inferred, what the attitude of couples is towards a birth control policy whose harshness sharply contrasts with the general tenor of other 'Dengist' reforms and the place they give to individual initiative. The *de facto* decollectivization brought about by the generalization of responsibility contracts has made the peasants bolder in expressing their hostility to interference by the Party and its representatives in an area (procreation) which in their eyes is wholly private.[14] It also, especially at first, drove them to have more children, so as to increase their labour-power and hence the income from their plots, including the sidelines derived from sale on the market of products of the farmyard or handicrafts. The effects of decollectivization did not, however, uniformly encourage a higher birth rate. Whereas in the collective system bringing up children was the only major investment open to a peasant household, the latter is today tempted to devote its meagre resources to securing the fertilizer or agricultural equipment that was formerly purchased by the commune, the brigade or the team. In addition, the collective system, which encouraged a certain amount of irresponsibility, could even favour having more children since large families gained more workpoints and grain rations were distributed per head. Today, each household has a more direct awareness of the link between the smallness of a plot which cannot be enlarged and the number of mouths to feed: since labour is plentiful, the proportion of people who feel that, when all is said and done, it is short-sighted to go on increasing the amount of family labour indefinitely ought to rise.

But if considerations of this sort gradually reduce the ideal family size desired by farmers, they are obviously not enough to reconcile them to the single-child rule. So the authorities, who previously (before 1979) thought up all sorts of measures to counter the higher birth rate effects of the collective system, are now devoting themselves (since the early 1980s) to doing the same with the effects of the responsibility system: for example, by allocating more land to single-child families and reducing the output quota required of them. Now, as previously, implementing these measures is not at all easy: once the stability of responsibility contracts is solemnly guaranteed and thus the size of the plot allocated, it is difficult to reduce this size later if the family grows.

The relationship between the responsibility system and the single-child policy has been the subject of ample comment and analysis since the early 1980s, both in China and abroad.[15] It has posed many thorny problems to the authorities who are keen to carry out economic reform and family planning together. It has, by the same token, thrown some light on the state of mind of the peasant population and its behaviour in the face of a campaign that it dislikes as much as those of the Maoist era. This behaviour is illustrated even more sharply – sometimes to the point of caricature – by eyewitness accounts. In a village in Hunan, the attitude of a single-child mother who had taken herself to the commune hospital of her own free will to be sterilized and obtain the single-child certificate provoked jeers and sarcasm, that were revealing of a virtually unanimous disapproval (Hunan Radio, 15 June 1982, *CNA*). A rural school in southern Jiangsu had to close its doors since parents were refusing to send their children there. The reason for this refusal, confirmed by several identical complaints emanating from neighbouring localities and *xian*, was that the parents were convinced that the injections given to the schoolchildren by itinerant medical teams made girls and boys sterile (in fact, they were vaccinations against various contagious infantile diseases (*XH*, Nanjing, 6 April 1983)). Soothsayers have been doing a roaring business (and complicating the task of family planning agents) by telling their clients that they are destined to have one son every two births or first a daughter and then a son (*XH*, Nanjing, 13 April 1981, and Perry, 1983, p. 43, n. 87). The faithful flocked to a protestant temple which the Party committee of Yijing commune, Yiwu *xian* (in the centre of Zhejiang) had authorized to be re-opened in accordance, so says the reporter, with the directives of the Third Plenum of the Eleventh Central Committee. Many were convinced that sincere devotion guaranteed the birth of a son and 28 believers purely and simply refused to submit to family planning, pleading their faiths (*Zhejiang Ribao*, 14 December 1982).

The refusal to accept family planning is widespread: the only difference is that these Christians were expressing it collectively whereas ordinarily it is an individual matter. While female cadres or teachers voice it unambiguously, [16] peasant women seek rather to conceal their pregnancy as long as possible and deliver in another locality. In some villages near Guangzhou, the inhabitants mounted guard in turns. As soon as the birth control team was sighted, a clap on the gong would warn pregnant women and they would quickly flee to the hills carrying with them a little dried food prepared beforehand (*Zhengming*, June 1984). That is very like what used to happen under the old regime, when people would mount guard against marauders and bandits or farmers would flee at the approach of the rent collectors, healthy men from recruiting sergeants.

But flight, the usual recourse of defenceless people, did not then (before 1949) exclude occasional outbursts of anger. These are probably rarer today and in any case more rarely reported in the press. The only case known to us is that of a member of the people's commune of Shuanglu, Fengdu *xian*, Sichuan: he insulted the members of the team who had come to organize birth control and, helped by his son and sister, hit the chairwoman of the Women's Federation, who fainted. Tried in public, in the presence of a thousand people, he was condemned to five months' imprisonment for deliberate bodily harm (*Sichuan Ribao*, 7 July 1980).

Children Adopted, Coils Removed

Generally speaking, couples are less inclined to let their resentment explode than to find a means of avoiding the obligations of family planning and, when they succeed, escape the penalties laid down for offenders. The recrudescence of adoptions and illegal sales of children, which people go and negotiate in another province if necessary, is to be explained by the complementary needs that can be satisfied by these deals: the acquirers obtain the son or second child that they are not authorized to produce themselves, the 'suppliers' hope to escape the penalties that fall on large families, since they reduce the size of theirs. As the authorities rightly observe, most of the children adopted are born 'out-of-plan' (*Dazhong Ribao*, 28 May 1980). These children are not all boys: some couples want to have one child of each sex. They are not satisfied with their luck, envied in the neighbourhood, of having a son first time, if this beginning must be an end: '*er nu shuang quan*' (you need a boy and a girl for the couple to be complete) (ibid.). For their part, the parents of two children seek to escape sterilization, which is often automatic in the cities for one of the parents of more than one child, by having one of their children adopted, preferably their daughter if they have a daughter and a son.[17]

Another flourishing business is in the illegal removal of coils, far and away the most widely used contraceptive device in China in the early 1980s.[18] Doctors or *ad hoc* practitioners are making a fortune by removing the coil from a considerable proportion (quite often 30%, sometimes 60% or 80%, in one case all without exception) of the women in their brigade or commune who have had one inserted.[19] In the south-east of Sichuan, on the borders with Hubei and Guizhou, a whole network of planned parenthood saboteurs was uncovered who were operating in 41 districts (*qu*) and 149 communes (*Sichuan Ribao*, 7 August 1981). The charges varied from three to thirty, in some cases fifty, *yuan* per patient.[20] As the removal of coils is carried out by people who are not always skilled and rarely with the correct instruments, some women were injured during the operation and a few died as a result of their wounds. With most of the others, the removal of the coil sooner or later led to an unplanned pregnancy which the authorities sought to terminate.[21] Removal of the coil is responsible for a good number of 'out-of-plan' births, which explains the harshness of the punishments meted out to those guilty. In different provinces, two to four years seems to be a common punishment,[22] including the associated charge of involuntary homicide.[23] There has been a single death sentence, but it was on a man who took advantage of removing coils to rape 16 of his 83 patients (*Fujian Ribao*, 9 January 1983).

At Least One Son!

'It is against the preference for male offspring that a one-child campaign must fight its hardest battles' (Davis-Friedmann 1985, p. 153): that is indeed what makes the current campaign much more difficult to implement than all previous ones. The most recent population control campaign advocated marrying and having children late, spacing births and having fewer children (the famous *wan, xi, shao* fashionable in the mid-1970s), which could, at a pinch, be accepted so long as people were assured of having at least one son. But this possibility is now denied to all who have the misfortune to bring into the world a daughter, thus wasting their sole chance in the births' lottery: it is rather like drawing the wrong number in a country where conscription is done by lot.

The main reason for the persistent preference for sons is economic. It concerns first and foremost old age security and arises above all in the countryside. This preference will become less difficult to eradicate the day the administration is in a position to extend enjoyment of a pension to farmers. But this is not going to happen tomorrow: for the time being, fewer than a fifth of Chinese workers are entitled to a pension and only a tiny fraction of rural residents are thus privileged. Some five million workers on state farms, or less than one-sixtieth of the 320 million farm workers, could look forward to a pension in 1980. In addition to this number there are half a million inhabitants of particularly prosperous suburban villages, to whom their brigade envisages paying a maximum of 50% of their average wage (most retired city-dwellers receive 75% of their last wage) (Davis-Friedmann, 1985, pp. 151–4).

There remain the famous 'five guarantees' (food, clothing, fuel, the bringing up of children and burial), which include a paltry charity to childless elderly poor people without relatives able to help them. As 'the five guarantees have . . . never provided a satisfactory alternative to relying on the support and care of a co-resident adult son' (Davin, 1985, pp. 61–2), the villagers cannot contemplate the end of their days calmly without the help of at least one son (two would be even better). Only a son and not a daughter will do, since a daughter will be looking after her parents-in-law and, usually, living with them in another village, by virtue of the custom of exogamy. Many other reasons, whether of an economic nature (girls earn less than boys, even in towns their chances of a successful and well paid career are much slimmer than those of their brothers) or not (such as the survivals of the 'feudal mentality' deplored by the authorities), combine together in the minds of parents to make a son seem more desirable than a daughter. But none is as decisive as the concern to ensure security in their old age. It is because they cannot give up the son who provides a pension in kind that so many village households welcome the birth of a girl as a calamity: a calamity for which many are tempted to compensate. Whence countless everyday tragedies, precipitated by the most recent avatar of the age-old curse of women: by being born – the single child allowed – a daughter prevents her parents from producing and thus acquiring something more precious than herself.

Mothers Maltreated

Petitions for divorce, made on various grounds (arranged marriage, conjugal incompatibility, etc.) are in fact motivated by the birth of one or two daughters: by remarrying, a divorced man retains a chance of having a son. In January 1983, the tribunal of Zhengzhou refused to grant two divorces sought by the husbands: in the first case, the two partners got on very well; in the second, the couple were already having problems caused by bad relations between the daughter-in-law and her mother-in-law, but the birth of a daughter had worsened tensions (*RMRB*, 7 April 1983). Other husbands take more direct action: a woman in Dandong, Liaoning, who had had the misfortune to bring twin girls into the world, was beaten by her husband, who threatened to divorce her and in the end drove her out (*RMRB*, 31 January 1983). Brutality toward the mothers of girls occurs in all social circles (the husband in Dandong was a Party member), in the cities – city-dwellers, as we have seen, do not have such strong reasons as peasants to want a son at any cost – as well as in the countryside (*RMRB*, 3 March 1983). With the father-in-law or brother-in-law giving the husband a hand on occasion, the 'infertile' wife is beaten up or tortured (can a woman who can do no better than produce girls be considered fertile?), sometimes out of spite, more often to driver her to divorce, or to adopt a son or murder the daughter. Here are three examples, all taken from the north-east, which illustrate these various typical cases.

A miner in Fushun, married in 1977, got divorced in 1979 following the birth of a daughter. When he remarried in 1981, he took care to warn his new wife, 'If you give me a daughter, I'll divorce you.' But that is what happened. He refused to see his daughter or to see his wife again and he cut off her subsistence by forbidding her to set foot in their house again. Four months after the birth, the abandoned wife met her husband and asked him to let her return home; she was beaten up for her pains. She then decided to collect at least her clothes, accompanied by her three brothers and fourteen neighbours who came to protect her. She found the door closed and was fired at by her brother-in-law. She then climbed up on the roof of her former house with one of her brothers. They took tiles off and threw them down from the roof, which earned the woman a suspended sentence of a year in prison for 'assault and pillage' (*RMRB*, 9 April 1983).

The wife of a prominent cadre in Jilin suggested to her daughter-in-law that she adopt the third son of her sister-in-law, passing it off as the twin of the girl to whom the daughter-in-law had just given birth. When she rejected this arrangement, which suited the two brothers (it gave one of them a son and saved the other from being punished for having had three children), she was tormented by her husband and in-laws. Between 1979 and 1983, she escaped death five or six times, then attempted to commit suicide. She was brought round in hospital. Her father-in-law forbade her to reveal the truth, but this became known in the end and the husband was sentenced to two years in prison (*JJRB*, 8 March 1984).

A woman worker in a watch factory in Anshan gave birth to a daughter in March 1983. Her father-in-law pressed her at once to smother the infant. When she refused, the husband and sister-in-law maltreated her baby, then the husband and father-in-law tormented her. She ran away, her husband found her, half-strangled her, and threatened her with an axe:

> 'If you do not agree to a divorce, I'm going to kill you, since you don't want to give me a son. I also want a sum of five hundred yuan, so as to be able to find another wife. If you don't give it to me, I will kill your two brothers, so that your parents realize what it is not to have any sons.'[24]

Girls Killed

The contempt for village women who have no son, the harsh treatment meted out to them by their in-laws, and the husbands' warning threats have led many expectant women in Guangdong to deliver at home, with the help of a woman neighbour, instead of going to the hospital. If it is a boy, they thank the gods; if it is a girl, they drown her in a bucket prepared beforehand (*Nanfang Ribao*, 7 February 1983; *Zhengming*, June 1984). Apart from the bucket, the most widespread methods used in Guangdong appear to be smothering and other forms of drowning or asphyxiation: the baby girl is put in a sack or wrapped up in several layers of clothing and smothered; or she is thrown into a corn mill, a latrine, a river or a pond. Sometimes, she is buried alive (*Nanfang Ribao*, February 1983). During 1982, over 130 corpses of baby girls were found in Jieyang *xian*, near Shantou. In a single commune of Taishan *xian*, situated in the south-west of the province, more than 80 drowned baby girls were found during the first six months of the same year (ibid). Between 1978 and 1979, 195 newborn girls were found to have been drowned in Quanjiao *xian*, in eastern Anhui (*JJRB*, 5 April 1983). And so on. Besides the girls killed, there are those who are simply abandoned and taken in by hospitals: there were 65 in a single *xian* in Liaoning during the two months of January and February 1982 (*RMRB*, 31 January 1983).

In most of the villages and regions concerned, infanticide is an open secret. Many local cadres close their eyes and show great understanding for the murderers: 'Now that one can only have a single child, of course every couple wants it to be a boy' (*Nanfang Ribao*, 7 February 1983). The higher authorities, on the other hand, deplore and combat the recrudescence of infanticides, as is evidenced by the press campaign denouncing the discrimination, lack of care and maltreatment to which baby girls are subjected.[25] During this campaign, Chinese newspapers published or summarized measures and decrees adopted all over the country to combat the abandonment and maltreatment of baby girls and their mothers.[26] They also reported trials of infanticides: the sentences handed down ranged from two years' imprisonment for a mother who threw her nine-day-old baby girl from the second floor of the hospital to thirteen years' given to a father who smothered his four-month-old daughter and then threw her into a well.[27]

So far as we know, the only infanticides carried out at the behest of the authorities were in Shanghai, where it is practically impossible to have a second child, at least if it is delivered in a hospital. A gynaecologist, who described her job as that of a 'murdering midwife', asserted that she had been ordered to inject a lethal product into the fontanelle of any second child, of either sex.[28] Nevertheless it is likely that abortion terminates most pregnancies discovered after the first among women in Shanghai. This is the case in Tianjin, where they even make women who are seven months pregnant abort. If it happens that the foetus expelled is viable, it is killed forthwith.[29] It is, however, almost certain that most infanticides are committed not on orders from the authorities but by parents conscious of breaking the law. These infanticides are almost all of girls and mostly of girls born in the countryside.

Whether direct or indirect (girls neglected, not fed properly or left uncared for in the event of illness), infanticides are sufficiently numerous for many abnormally high sex ratios to appear, at least at the local level. We shall leave aside some local data that are manifestly not representative, or not reliable: in several brigades in Liaoning, 65–70% of babies born in 1982 and still alive in January 1983 were boys (*RMRB*, 31 January 1983); at the other end of the country, the proportion is said to have reached four, five, even seven or eight boys for one girl in a particular brigade in Guangdong (*Nanfang Ribao*, 7 February 1983). Even if it is less glaring, an imbalance becomes even more significant when it occurs at the level of the *xian*: such is the case, often reported, of Huaiyuan *xian*, Anhui, where out of 10,768 babies in 1981 there were 6,266 boys (58.2%) and 4,502 girls (41.8%), a sex ratio of 139:100 (*JJRB*, 5 April 1983). At the level of the whole province, the sex ratio in Anhui at the beginning of 1983 was 111.12 boys for 100 girls under one year old, 110.53 among those under three and 109.84 among those under five (*RMRB*, 19 April 1983). In recent years, other provinces and even whole regions[30] have recorded an abnormally high sex ratio at birth or among young children, though Chinese demographers deny that it is true for the country as a whole. But births in 1981 showed a national sex ratio slightly higher (108.4) than the ratio deemed normal (about 106);[31] this was also the case (ratio of 107.4) for children aged under three in the 1982 census.[32] Defenders of Chinese family planning policy reply that on several occasions in the 1970s the sex ratio at birth was over 109 in the Philippines and South Korea: this is proof, according to them, that the sex ratio at birth is quite different for different ethnic groups (for example *SWB*, 9 November 1985, FE/8104/C/6). But that does not close the case: it would be more to the point to show that the sex ratios at birth observed in the PRC since the beginning of the 1980s are no higher than they were in the same country before the introduction of the single-child policy. But we do not know these ratios precisely and certainly. We know only that the sex ratios of children aged four to twelve in 1982 were all lower than 106.5 and thus less unbalanced than those of children born since 1979 (*Zhongguo 1982* (1983), pp. 64–5). But is this difference to be explained by a more pronounced imbalance in the sex ratio at birth or by a lower death rate of male children in their early years and during adolescence?

We shall leave the argument there. It is better to abandon these unhappy comparisons and calculations and suspend judgement. Exact knowledge of the evolution of the national sex ratio at birth would only make it possible to measure the scale of infanticide; of its recent recrudescence there can, alas, be no doubt.

Concessions

In the end the authorities took account of people's reservations and the fact that it was virtually impossible for cadres, especially in the rural areas, to enforce the single-child policy. Since 1983 and particularly since the spring of 1984, this rule has become less strict. There had, of course, been some exceptions from the beginning, notably with regard to the national minorities. It was also always (and still is) much less rigorously enforced in the countryside than in the cities. But the authorities were, even so, trying to reduce these two categories, which account for almost four-fifths of the total population, to the common norm. Repeated statements were made to the effect that the rural areas constituted the principal area (*zhongdian*) of the work of family planning (Bianco, 1985; p. 15. n. 14). And numerous surveys devoted to the demographic, economic and social evolution of the various non-Han national minorities stressed the urgency of enabling the non-Han populations to benefit from a modified form of birth control (Bianco, 1985, p. 15 n. 15).

For the Han proper,[33] there were extremely few official exemptions to the single-child rule. They varied from province to province, but nowhere was it easy to satisfy any of the conditions making it possible to ask for authorization to have a second child. It was necessary, for example, that the firstborn be seriously handicapped and unable to perform normal work; or that one and only one of the two spouses had a child from a previous marriage; or again that a couple believed to be infertile had ended up adopting a child and that cure of the infertility had then made the wife capable of becoming pregnant, etc (Davin, 1985 pp. 50–1). Other exemptions admitted in some regions concerned mountain people living in sparsely populated, poor and remote areas; uxorilocal marriages, on condition that the wife have neither brother nor sister; couples in which the husband was the only son of a martyr of the revolution, etc. These slightly less strict conditions, granted to rural couples in Shanxi in 1983, were accompanied by a clause foreshadowing the wider exemptions granted in many provinces since the spring of 1984: if both spouses were themselves only children, a peasant couple in Shanxi could be authorized to have a second child (Davin, 1985, p. 51).

But the situation was little changed: this last condition was itself rarely satisfied. Even if they were all added together, the categories of legal exemption affected only a tiny proportion of couples of child-bearing age. Second births 'in conformity with the plan' were far fewer than second – not to mention third – births 'outside-the-plan' among couples meeting none of the minutely catalogued special circumstances. It was precisely the theoretical character of these various very poorly observed rules that led the leadership to attenuate their strictness so as to make them less far removed not only from actual practice, but also from possible practice.

Classically, it was a document emanating from the 'Centre' (in this case, an important directive promulgated by the CCP Central Committee in April 1984) that set off the avalanche of new provincial regulations (or 'supplements' to earlier regulations which they modified) (*SWB* 12 July 1985, FE/8001/B11/8) recorded up to February 1986. This directive condemned and prohibited 'all forms of coercion and commandism' in planned parenthood work. It called on local cadres, held responsible not only for abuses, but also for an 'oversimplified and crude practice' that had caused discontent among the masses, especially in the rural areas, to show more restraint and consideration in future for people's state of mind and wishes: the planned parenthood policy must be applied more sensibly and on the basis of mass support. Which meant: apply the single-child rule less rigidly, do not be universally unyielding towards couples who want a second child.

Since the promulgation of this document, the regulations seem to have been relaxed over most of the country. The conditions for having a second child vary from province to province and within a single province; they have often changed or been gradually spelled out since its promulgation. It would be tedious to go over these regional variations and variants in detail: one provincial regulation lists several conditions which might allow for a second birth for city-dwellers, cadres, workers and staff, then other conditions equally if not more numerous for peasants, others again for the national minorities.[34] It is better to try and appreciate the significance of the changes recently made to the single-child rule for each of the three broad categories: cities, countryside, national minorities.

The concessions granted to city-dwellers are generally quite limited. Care is taken to deny rumours put about that the inhabitants of cities can now have a second child: (FBIS, *Daily Report China*, 1 May 1984, p. 1; 8 July 1985, p. 10), the single child remains the rule for them. Nevertheless, a second child is no longer refused automatically to some couples of city-dwellers who 'have practical difficulties' (a deliberately vague formula) and who meet certain conditions, the most common being that each of both spouses are themselves only children.[35] The single-child rule having on the whole been quite well observed in the cities – which does not mean there was no suffering or complaining – there is no reason to modify it in any very significant way.

The peasants, on the other hand, are much better treated and they are the main beneficiaries of the relaxation of the rule. In May 1984, villagers in Guangdong could ask for permission to have another child when their first child was a girl and was four years old (FBIS, *Daily Report: China*, 1 May 1984, p. 1); since October 1985, peasants in Liaoning have been able to do the same, without waiting for their daughter to be four years old (*SWB*, 9 November 1985, FE/8104/C/8). From February 1986, the inhabitants of a 'pilot' zone in Heilongjiang have been able to have a second child six years after the birth of the first, whether the first is a boy or a girl, and women over thirty can be authorized to have a second child three years after the birth of their daughter (*SWB*, 7 December 1985, FE/8128/B11/10). In poor and/or remote provinces, the right to a second child is apparently not subject to any condition relating to the sex or age of the firstborn.[36]

The more extensive concessions granted to peasants in Hainan, Guangxi and Qinghai are perhaps to be explained by the proximity of these rural people of Han nationality to large non-Han communities: not as a result of contagion but because too blatant discrimination proved to be too difficult or even impossible to impose on the Han within one and the same region. The single-child rule is in fact hardly ever applied to the national minorities: the norm is sometimes two children,[37] sometimes two or three,[38] sometimes two for some nationalities and three for others,[39] sometimes two on certain conditions for city-dwellers and two without restrictions for rural people[40] or again two for farmers, three for nomad herdsmen,[41] etc. It even happens that, exceptionally, no restriction on the number of children is imposed on people of minority groups living in remote border regions:[42] the government is satisfied to 'encourage' them to practise family planning.

This differentiated relaxation (by region and ethnic or sociological categories) of the regulations in force inevitably raised wild hopes, which the authorities endeavoured to deny: the Party was not changing and would not change direction, it was simply improving the mannner of implementation of a policy that could not be abandoned (at least for the next twenty or thirty years). This was the only reason why it was issuing new regulations that were 'reasonable, well received by the masses, and practical for the cadres to enforce' (FBIS, *Daily Report: China*, 23 July 1984). This disguised admission amounts to recognizing that the previous regulations were ill received by those affected and very difficult to enforce: so difficult in fact that in many rural areas the cadres had not waited for the spring of 1984 to refrain from punishing second births 'outside-the-plan'. For some of them 'refrain' is a euphemism: they no doubt felt they did not have – or no longer had, since the implementation of the great 'Dengist' reforms had reduced their means of action and control – the means to do so.

The first part of this chapter described the behaviour of the leaders responsible for enforcing – and on occasion evading – the implementation of the single-child policy. Most of the incidents reported are acts of negligence or abuse committed by cadres and denounced as such by the Chinese press. The campaign waged in Chanshan commune in Shandong (above, pp. 9–10) illustrates the much rarer case of methods deemed perfectly licit, even held up as an example for their effectiveness. Finally, a third category of measures, seen as impossible to admit, is never reported in the Chinese press: we only know about them through comments by persons interviewed or works published in Hong Kong or abroad (for example the late abortions, even infanticides, practised in Tianjin, Shanghai and Huiyang). Some of the techniques used during the campaign waged in Huiyang and other neighbouring *xian* in eastern Guangdong in 1984 (above, pp. 00) are reminiscent of those of the Maoist era: quota of second pregnancies to be terminated fixed at a relatively senior echelon of the hierarchy (regional secretariat of the CCP); balance sheet drawn up after a few weeks of the offensive at a meeting of cadres of the various echelons involved in the campaign; this balance sheet itself followed by a pause that is doubtless used by the leaders to fix objectives and above all the strategy of the next offensive planned for a few months later. These are methods of control and mobilization used by a regime that remains dictatorial – even if the dictatorship has somewhat relaxed – but they also stem secondarily from the choice of objectives which are almost unattainable.

This continuity is that of a communist regime, which embraces both Maoist and Dengist variants. But it overlooks the sharp difference between the chimerical goals of Maoism and the eminently practical goals pursued by Deng Xiaoping. The methods to which communist China has recently resorted, to enforce the single-child policy on a recalcitrant population, have been more brutal than is generally recognized. Without wishing to justify them, we can agree that the dictatorial nature of the regime is, in this area, neither the sole nor even the main reason for recourse to coercion; after much wasted time (in Mao's lifetime and by Mao's doing), China had no choice but to accelerate the demographic transition artificially, without waiting for the socio–economic conditions to mature. Of course, the dilemma already faced Mao himself more or less in these terms, because of the demographic time-bomb he inherited in 1949. But the rapid aggravation of the threat, the corollary of the inaction or ineffectiveness of the birth control campaigns conducted desultorily during the first two decades after 1949 (an almost natural fertility rate, higher than five children per woman, was maintained until the beginning of the 1970s, and now the children of the baby boom of the 1960s have in turn become reproducers), made it even more urgent to put a brake on the growth of the population, by the same token reducing the leadership's room for manoeuvre. Whether or not the single-child policy was a judicious measure, it remains the fact that the choice of draconian measures confronted Mao's successors all the more strongly because they were obliged, in this area as in economic matters, to make up for the shortcomings or mistakes of the Maoist era.

Conversely, the spectacular fall in the birth rate that occurred in the 1970s demonstrates that a strict birth control policy less extreme than the single-child policy would have been less badly received by the population and hence less difficult to enforce. This fall was certainly not obtained without all sorts of coercion and pressure, but the balance between results and costs (in sacrifices imposed on the population and resentment towards the authorities) was pitched at a level that was on the whole more acceptable than the very disappointing balance sheet of the single-child campaign. This campaign was enforced to the letter in the large towns where it was and remains very difficult to have a second child; but it has only secured very uneven results in the rural areas. And couples who have shown themselves ready (especially city-dwellers) to gradually modify their habits in the area of reproduction obstinately jibbed (even the city-dwellers) at the single-child rule which they saw as asking too much. It might have been expected that the inhabitants of the large towns, headed by the intellectuals, would accept the sacrifice required of parents. That is indeed what some of them say when they are asked in China. However, to judge by the comments made abroad not only by couples of child-bearing age, but by single students not yet subject to the single-child rule or professors in their fifties who suffer from it only through their married children, it seems that the majority judge the single-child policy irrational and doomed to failure. Far from being convinced or even resigned, they hope, vaguely, that it will be abrogated in the end and sometimes wonder whether this will be done in time for them or their daughter to have a second child.

Nevertheless, the types of behaviour described in the second part of this chapter will not lead to a revolt. They are in line with tradition: widespread submission (almost nobody contemplates openly opposing the government's plans), combined with a considerable number of individual attempts to evade the consequences of an unpopular policy. In this area, too, there is continuity with the previous period: continuity of a regime against which any revolt seems dangerous and doomed to failure, continuity too in the attitude towards the authorities on the part of a population, especially a rural population, which has long since (since long before 1949) learned to bend before the storm. The absence of revolt – and we cannot rule out the possibility that there have been some isolated revolts of which we are unaware – does not mean, far from it, absence of alienation or discontent. As soon as they were forced to sell their grain at low prices, then as collectivization was introduced (from cooperativization to communization), many peasants had the feeling that the state was taking back with one hand what the other had given them at the time of the agrarian reform and land distribution. It is likely that a similar feeling prevails at present when a reform felt as a liberation (agricultural decollectivization) is accompanied by unprecedented demographic pressure.

It is equally likely that the enormous and endless difficulties raised by the – very imperfect – enforcement of a very unpopular policy were the decisive cause of the concessions mentioned earlier: much more decisive, certainly, than the foreign pressures frequently alleged (American denunciations and financial sanctions), or even than the very legitimate concern raised by the long-term consequences (inverted age pyramid, etc.) of maintaining the single-child rule, especially over a prolonged period. These consequences were, in any event, foreseeable from the outset and we will not insult the Chinese leaders – precisely because the infallible Helmsman is no longer at the helm – by suggesting that they threw themselves behind this policy without taking them into account. It is very likely that the true objective, at the time they launched the single-child slogan, was to bring the birth rate down to below replacement rate. In their forecasts, Chinese demographers usually use an average of 1.5 and even more often 1.7 children per family. A birth rate of 1.8, or even 1.9, might have been an objective that was very ambitious but less inaccessible in a first phase. It is perhaps to an objective of this sort that the authorities provisionally resigned themselves, at the time when they began to retreat. If they were driven to make further concessions, it should not necessarily be seen at once as an agonizing reappraisal. Two steps forward, one step back is a commonplace and clever strategy.

Although it is tactically inevitable at intervals of varying length, the relaxation of the pressure still worries the leadership.[43] What is likely is that a series of forceful 'mobilization' campaigns (call them phases A) will be interspersed with periods of 'consolidation' or relaxation (phases B) during which mobilization is less brutal and more circumspect. Far from implying abandonment or deviation in terms of the chosen path, the present phase B simply illustrates the compromises that the leadership is obliged to make with the population. They have to feel their way and be all the time changing the tempo, since it is impossible to achieve a miraculous balance between the level of coercion supportable by the population and the minimum effectiveness compatible with the urgency of acting today so as to modify tomorrow (in the 21st Century) the overwhelming demographic legacy of the previous generation, added to that of a dozen previous generations (to go no further back than the rapid population growth that was a corollary of, or at least contemporary with, the golden age of the Qing dynasty). In the coming years leaders will be tempted not to wait around in phase B, despite the manifest aversion of the population for phase A, so as to avoid combining the raised birth rate effects of a relaxation of the pressure with the (inevitable) effects of the age structure. The imminent resumed upward march of the birth rate, consecutive on the boom in the marriage rate which has already begun and will increase, threatens to push some leaders to ignore the opposition – which is not about to disappear – of couples and their families. The most varied scenarios can be imagined on condition that one is ruled out: a lowering of tension and a return to calm.

Notes

1. See Michel Bonnin's contribution in this volume.

2. According to calculations by the Chinese demographer Wu Gangping ('The Characteristics of Age Composition of China's Population', paper presented at the International Seminar on China's 1982 Population Census, Beijing, 26–31 March 1984, p. 14), the working-age population (15–64) will increase by 235 million between 1982 and 1997: 337 million entrants to the labour market as against 102 million retirements. In fact, a number of workers and especially women workers will retire before they are 65 and not all adolescents will become job-seekers at 15. But that is also true of the baseline, in 1982: the working-age population (622 million in July 1982) which Wu used as his initial baseline already included many inactives among the oldest and youngest segments of the 15–64 age group. On the other hand, the increase in the labour force will be less rapid between 1997 and 2000 than between 1982 and 1986 (where it was over 2% a year), since the cohorts born in the early 1980s are smaller than those of the 1960s. The increase in the working population will still continue, at a slower rate, until the 21st Century, since retirements will only become large-scale when the cohorts of the 1950s and above all those of the 1960s reach 50 or 55 for women and 60 for men.

3. Aubert, 1983, pp. 23–4; Fabre, 1985, pp. 49–54. For further details, see V. Smil, 1984.

4. Fabre, 1985, pp. 51 and 53–4. The encroachment of fields is not solely responsible for the reduction of the surface of Lake Dongting: alluvia and silt brought down by rivers and streams that feed into it are gradually filling it up.

5. Information in this chapter is mainly from the national and regional press in the PRC. Our thanks to the team on the journal *China News Analysis* (henceforth *CNA*) for making its archives available to us in September 1984. We went through the whole of the *Renkou wenti* (Population) file of the *CNA* from January 1980 to 31 August 1984. The Hong Kong press and monitoring stations also provided some supplementary details.

6. Brief examination of the concessions made by the government also represents the sole concession that we ourselves will make to the study of the single-child policy as such (in the rest of the paper, we shall be concerned essentially with the behaviour that its enforcement has provoked) and chronology (since these

concessions mark the most recent phase of a campaign initiated seven years ago). For the rest, we shall assume knowledge of the introduction and earlier phases of the single-child policy and also of major measures (for example, the new marriage law, the generalization of responsibility contracts, the abolition of people's communes) that have influenced and often encouraged a higher birth rate, thus forcing the authorities to strengthen their anti-birth arsenal.

That would not however have prevented us from analysing the chronological evolution of the behaviour itself – which would have been part of our study – if our main source had allowed us to do so. But the rarely spontaneous nature of the campaigns launched in the Chinese press usually makes it impossible to identify precisely the more or less frequent occurrence of the incidents reported in it. Here is an example: almost all the mentions of maltreatment inflicted on the mothers of a single daughter and on newborn girls themselves appeared between the autumn of 1982 and the spring of 1983, that is at the time when the authorities had decided to give wide publicity to this phenomenon. It can obviously not be concluded either that the problem did not exist in 1980 or that the recent concessions have settled it once and for all.

7. In some communes, cadres are liable to the same penalties for the birth of a second child as ordinary members are for the birth of a third.

8. The local Party committee had recommended that she have an abortion, but she refused saying, 'A leader is not obliged to serve as a model in all areas' (*Dazhong Ribao*, 3 June 1980). A week earlier the same paper (*Dazhong Ribao*, 28 May 1980) had denounced the chairwoman of the Women's Federation of Yinping commune, Youcheng district (*qu*), who had also delivered a second time (on 10 March of the same year). She had gone into hiding for two months to escape abortion and, the height of impudence, she had organized a banquet to celebrate this 'out-of-plan' birth. This time the authorities punished the bad example by excluding the guilty woman from the Party and appointing someone else to head the Women's Federation.

9. Collective responsibility sometimes concerns both the cadres and population. In 1981 and 1982, the five leaders of a work team (or more likely a brigade) in Yunnan visited by Ashwani Saith were entitled to a collective bonus of 200 *yuan* if there were fewer than 15 births per 2,000 inhabitants, but were fined ten *yuan* for every second birth. As for the members of the team (or the brigade), 1,000 workpoints were deducted from their total every time a couple had a second child (Saith, 1984, pp. 354–5).

10. This directive constituted, like the organization of 'linked families' (*lianhu*) into groups, one of the ten points in the detailed programme that the vice-secretary had drawn up beforehand, like a general his battle plan (*Dazhong Ribao*, 10 February 1984).

11. Example: a teacher in Liaoshe commune, Dongguan *xian* (still in the same region, somewhat closer to the estuary of the Pearl river and Hong Kong) had succeeded in fleeing to Shenzhen to avoid terminating her second pregnancy; her husband was immediately imprisoned. Shortly after she was visited by her niece who travelled to Shenzhen to beg her to accept abortion so as to save her husband from torture (*Zhengming Ribao*, 28 July 1981).

12. On the eve of the launching of the single-child campaign it was in Guandong, targeted because of its high birth and natural growth rates, that the idea originated of fixing a quota of abortions to be adhered to, whatever the cost. At the time, the goal was to have 340,000 of the 600,000 pregnant women counted in the province abort by terminating all the third and higher order pregnancies and as far as

possible second pregnancies (Aird, 1981, pp. 184–5).

13. The few other similar eyewitness reports also come from Hong Kong or foreign journalists: *Zhengming*, March 1984, p. 25 and Zafanolli, 1984, pp. 33–4 and notes 154–7.

14. 'I have accepted a responsibility contract for my field, I am bringing up my children myself, the cadres have no business knowing how many I bring into the world' (quoted in Bianco, June 1985a, p. 32).

15. We shall simply refer readers to the recent study by Davin (1985, pp. 54–61 and 63–6). The preceding paragraph is based on her firm but balanced comments.

16. Compare the case of a rural teacher suspended for a year for having obstinately rejected an 'amends-making attitude' that would have put an end to her seventh pregnancy and having finally delivered a seventh child in November 1980 (*BR*, 1 February 1981).

17. *Zhengming*, March 1984, p. 25. Routine sterilization after a second birth was also practised in some rural areas, such as the model *xian* of Shifang, Sichuan: *Renkou Yanjiu*, no. 6, 1982, p. 31.

18. In 1982, coils alone were more used than all other means together, including sterilization, since they accounted for 50.16% of the total. Next came female (25.39%) and male (10%) sterilization, the pill (8.44%) and 'various' means including the diaphragm (6.01%) (Qiu Shuhua et al., 1983, p. 130). Today the coil represents only 40% of the total and is being overtaken by female sterilization (38.1%) (*FEER*, 28 November 1985, p. 24).

19. The most widely used coil in China (a modified Ota ring with no tail) cannot be removed by the woman herself, as it needs a thin metal hook (Ch'en Pi-chao, 1985, p. 139).

20. The reports of trials arising from the illegal removal of coils generally spell out the amount of the illicit gains of the accused. The lowest fee that we have encountered is that of a woman who was content to remove 30 coils in eight years (from 1973 to 1981) in three *xian* in north-eastern Jiangsu, which brought her 91 *yuan*, as well as clothes and food (*RMRB*, 6 October 1981). See in *Guangming Ribao* (11 June 1981), in addition to the single mention of a fee of 50 *yuan*, fees ranging, depending on the localities, from 5 to 30 *yuan* in Hubei and 10 to 30 *yuan* in Sichuan.

21. Example: of 600 women belonging to various national minorities in five communes of the Xinglong autonomous region, Sichuan, who had the coil removed, over 500 were pregnant at the time the authorities discovered the secret. They quickly 'persuaded' them to accept abortion and they and the few dozen others to have the coil re-inserted (*Guangming Ribao*, 22 July 1981).

22. Example: a judgment delivered in the autumn of 1982 by the tribunal of Jinjiang, near Quanzhou, in Fujian. It condemned respectively to one year's (the lightest sentence that we have found), two and four years' imprisonment three accused people who had shared 1,200 *yuan* for removing 112 coils in the two previous years, leading to 61 'out-of-plan' births (*Guangming Ribao*, 8 December 1982).

23. In cases where removal of the coil led to the death of the patient: see *Guangming Ribao*, 27 August 1981.

24. *Gongren Ribao*, 12 May 1983. For examples of women beaten to death or dying as a result of their injuries, see *RMRB*, 31 January and 3 March 1983; *Zhengming*, June 1984.

25. Numerous editorials and reports were devoted to the subject between the autumn of 1982 and the spring of 1983. See an incomplete list, covering the first four

months of 1983, in Bianco, 1985a, p. 21, no. 25.

26. See, for example, the regulation adopted by the Standing Committee of the Fifth Provincial People's Assembly of Liaoning, analysed in *Liaoning Ribao*, 2 April 1983, and discussed at length in *RMRB*, 9 April 1983. In addition to the administrative and penal sanctions inflicted on offenders (parents, husbands, in-laws), this regulation also includes a ban on doctors using ultrasound scans to determine the sex of the foetus.

27. The first case (a 28-year-old peasant woman, who delivered on 25 June 1982, killed her daughter on 4 July and was sentenced on 18 October by the People's Tribunal of the *xian* of Baoshan, Shanghai) was reported in the Shanghai *Jiefang Ribao* of 19 October 1982 (the crime itself had been reported in the same paper on 8 July). The second case (a worker in a radio factory in Dandong, Liaoning, sentenced by the People's Tribunal of the same town on 11 December 1982, a week after the crime) was reported in the *Guangming Ribao* of 12 January 1983. Intermediate sentences (four years for the father, three years for the uncle who killed a girl at birth on 29 December 1982) are mentioned in *RMRB*, 7 April 1983.

28. *Zhengming*, June 1984. See also Zafanolli (1986, p. 33). According to official statistics, almost two-thirds (64.91%) of women in Shanghai born between 1951 and 1955 were mothers of one child at the end of 1981 and almost a third (32.66%) had no children. One in fifty (2.03%) had two children, one in 500 (0.20%) three, none had more than three (*Renkou Yanjiu*, no. 1, 1984, p. 29). The table in *Renkou Yanjiu* has a slight error, since the total comes to 99.80%.

29. Interview with the uncle of a young woman employee in a hospital in Tianjin, whose identity we prefer not to reveal. According to this woman, whose work, she asserted, 'offended virtue' (*que de*), the hospital got rid of several bins full of foetuses every day; some other hospitals in the town did the same.

30. Example: sex ratio (0–4 age group) of 110/100 in the north-east according to the one in one thousand sample fertility survey; ratio at birth of 110.4 in the centre-south in 1981 according to the results of the 1982 census (Liu Chunmei and Li Zhu 1983, pp. 147 and 149).

31. Liu Chunmei and Li Zhu, 1983, p. 149. See also Aird, 1983, pp. 616–7, which also contains other local examples of 'abnormally high sex ratios'.

32. 3,939,000 boys as against 3,669,000 girls under three out of 100,379,000 inhabitants (a tenth of the total population) (*Zhongguo 1982*, pp. 8–9).

33. Except for overseas Chinese, who are in principle allowed to have two children, except in the case of a mixed marriage (one partner born in mainland China, the other from overseas).

34. Five conditions for state cadres, staff members or workers, and urban residents, five conditions 'in addition to the above-mentioned', for rural peasants in Jilin province, August 1984: FBIS, *Daily Report: China*, 23 August 1984, five conditions for rural peasants, three for cadres, staff members, workers, or urban residents, three more for remarried couples in Heilongjiang, August 1984: FBIS, *Daily Report: China*, 5 September 1984. According to a document issued by the Guangdong province CCP Committee and Guangdong provincial government on 12 June 1984, eight categories of people may apply for a second child: *SWB*, 9 November 1985, FE/8104/C/7.

35. Example: Hunan province since 1 January 1985, FBIS, *Daily Report: China*, 17 December 1984.

36. Guangxi: *SWB*, 28 March 1985, FE/7911/BII/4; Qinghai: *SWB*, 3 October 1985, FE/8072/BII/9. In Hainan island, Guangdong province, the first-born must be a daughter, but, as of October 1985, no condition of age was stipulated: *SWB*, 9

November 1985, FE/8104/C/7.

37. A second child after four years if both husband and wife are minority people, after eight years if one of the couple belongs to a national minority; in Jilin province, February 1985 (*SWB*, 7 March 1985, FE/7893/BII/4).

38. In Yunnan province, October 1985: *SWB*, 9 November 1985, FE/8104/C/8.

39. Two children for Zhuang (as well as for Han), three under certain circumstances for other minority nationalities in Guangxi, March 1985: *SWB*, 28 March 1985, FE/7911/BII/4. From one (Manchu) to three children depending on the nationalities in Heilongjiang in August 1984: FBIS, *Daily Report: China*, 5 September 1984.

40. Qinghai province, September 1985: *SWB*, 3 October 1985, FE/8072/BII/9.

42. FBIS, *Daily Report: China*, 23 July 1984, T/2.

43. It should not be forgotten that the authorities had already had recourse to such a relaxation – or had been forced to it – during the summer of 1978, on the eve of the launching of the single-child campaign, then again in 1980–81, following the initial, particularly hard and painful, phase of this same campaign.

7 China's New Inheritance Law: Some Preliminary Observations

Michael Palmer

The study of the legal framework of inheritance may appear rather unexciting in comparison with some of the other contemporary developments in family law and social policy such as the single-child programme, freedom of divorce, adoption and the state's attempt to elevate the social status of the married-in son-in-law (Palmer, 1986a). Moreover, inheritance law might be regarded as occupying only an insignificant position in a socialist society which does not permit individuals to hold heritable proprietary rights in the principal means of production, agricultural land. However, describing China's law of inheritance in these terms seriously underestimates both the intrinsic importance of the corpus of legal rules governing this mode of property devolution and the light which the operation of the law can throw on domestic, kinship and other close interpersonal relationships.

The inheritance of a number of important forms of property has been permitted throughout the period of socialist rule and the new inheritance law which came into effect on 1 October 1985 has recently expanded the range of heritable objects. In addition, it should always be remembered that inheritance is not only a mechanism for the redistribution of property but also a significant influence on the ways in which people conduct their interpersonal relationships. Inheritance in China normally occurs between close kin and, not surprisingly, ties between family members as well as wider kinship bonds are sometimes deeply affected by manoeuvres over inheritance matters. Potential beneficiaries may attempt to enhance their shares in an estate at the expense of other candidates. Testators may wish to reward or punish family members by increasing or limiting the inheritance shares of the various prospective heirs. The PRC's new inheritance law is intended not only to structure the manner in which some of the proprietary rights in material objects, including money, are passed down but also to provide clear and precise norms of property distribution which will assist in the resolution of domestic conflicts over inheritance rights. Accordingly, the present chapter attempts to lay out the main features of China's recently introduced law of inheritance and to examine some of the important social concomitants of this legislation.

China's new inheritance law is, of course, part of a much broader and prodigious shift in legal orientation that has occurred in the PRC during the past few years. Since the demise of the Gang of Four in 1976 the Chinese leadership has committed itself to far-reaching plans for legal development which, *inter alia*, are intended to overcome many of the challenges to authority and social order that were made during the Cultural Revolution when 'there was neither law nor natural justice' (*wufa–wutian*) and 'rule by people greatly outweighed the rule of law' (*renzhi chaoguo fazhi*).[1] Thus arbitrary political rule, factional violence, widespread reliance on personal connections and other perceived shortcomings of the period between 1966 and 1976 are to be rectified by means of a much greater reliance on formal and autonomous legal institutions.[2] As a result, there has been an unswerving and sustained concern to codify law, to extend public knowledge of the law, to revive the legal profession, to expand legal education and so on. Official policies stress the need to protect the legal position of those whose rights are particularly vulnerable to abuse, namely the old, women and children. It is also hoped that the construction of a regular and predictable legal process will encourage the development of China's economy by furnishing clear norms which will both better regulate domestic economic activity and stimulate the role of western and Japanese capital and technology in the PRC's development programme.

A further and highly significant area of change has been in the policies designed to cope with demographic and related problems such as rapid population growth, the need to provide material security for people in their old age and meeting the welfare needs of those unable to support themselves or who are otherwise seriously disadvantaged. In fact, in this area of social life the state is pursuing somewhat contradictory policies by attempting simultaneously not only to restrict family size, but also to place on the family even greater responsibilities in production and welfare matters. This is particularly true in rural areas, where four-fifths of the population are located and where the imperatives of agricultural production under the household responsibility and contract systems encourage expansion of the family workforce. At the same time the very limited state and collective provision of support for the aged and other potential welfare beneficiaries has placed an even greater reliance on households and wider kinship networks themselves to furnish assistance of this nature. Indeed, the state now insists that ageing parents must not be abandoned and has not only enshrined rights of support in the constitution (Article 50) and the marriage law (Article 15), but even introduced a criminal offence into the law by which failure to support parents, grandparents or some other person in need may – under certain circumstances – constitute the crime of abandonment which is punishable *inter alia* by imprisonment of not more than five years (Criminal Code, Article 183).[3] This emphasis in the law on the care of the elderly, which is said to reflect a more general obligation on all members of society to support the senior generation, is also a reaction to the experiences of the Cultural Revolution and the ensuing interregnum. During that troubled period Chinese traditional norms of respecting and caring for the elderly are now said to have been seriously damaged, with some old people forced to leave their home towns in order to beg and a significant number of others resorting to suicide (Zhongguo Renmin, 1980, p. 196).

China's new inheritance law owes a great deal to and is part and parcel of these developments. In fact, the law is not entirely new but, rather, represents a codification of the various kinds of norms which have in general been applied since the early 1950s, with the exception of the hiatus of the Cultural Revolution. Until recently these rules were rarely published, even though they were an important resource for judicial decision-making.[4] The main purpose of the systematization and enactment of these rules in 1985 was said to be the felt need to

> use the law to protect the lawful inheritance rights of citizens. Since Liberation the state has always protected by law rights of inheritance in the personal property of a citizen . . . However, during the Cultural Revolution it was not possible to afford proper protection. In 1982 the Constitution was revised and reaffirmed state protection by law of the rights of citizens to own and inherit personal property. The inheritance code defines the size of the inheritance, the eligible beneficiaries and the rights of citizens to go to court if their inheritance rights have been infringed (Gu Angren, 1985).

The Chinese leadership also hopes that this provision of a set of explicit norms will help to promote social stability by reducing the incidence of intra-family disputes over inheritance matters. At the same time, however, the introduction of an inheritance code is also intended to bolster China's new direction in economic development. The law is designed to furnish a mechanism by means of which the financially successful may pass on the personal wealth that they have accumulated, to promote confidence in investment by enabling contracts to be inherited, and to stimulate overseas Chinese and foreigners to invest in the PRC by safeguarding the rights of these citizens of other countries to give and to receive material objects and financial wealth through inheritance. Thus, for example, the legal recognition and protection of inheritance rights in private property is said to be essential for the successful implementation of the 'wealthy citizens' policy' (*fumin zhengce*) by which it is hoped that encouragement of material inequalities will enhance production and investment.

> In order to stimulate on an extended scale peasant economic reproduction and to encourage peasants to take the road to common prosperity it seems to be absolutely necessary to protect by law the private ownership of property and inheritance rights (Chen Qinyi, 1985).

An additional, explicitly acknowledged, consideration behind the new code is a felt need to strengthen the provisions in this area of the law as they relate to the duties of care and support which inhere in the bonds between parents and their children.

> The use of the law to protect the inheritance rights of citizens in private property promotes the function of the family in providing support for the old and bringing up the young [*shanlao yuyou*] and assists in meeting the need for unity and harmony among family members . . . since parents and children share obligations of support and assistance they also, of course, enjoy mutual inheritance rights in property (Chen Qinyi, 1985).

Indeed, since the fall of the Gang of Four, statements of social policy in the domain of family law have stressed the importance of 'the mutuality of rights and obligations' (*quanli yiwu xiangyizhi*; *xianghujian de quanli yiwu guanxi*). This principle is reported to be 'a basic starting point in our socialist legal system which affirms the legal right of inheritance and is also one of the bases on which cases of inheritance disputes are handled in the course of our judicial work' (Zhu Pingshan, 1981, p. 27). There are, in the new inheritance code, explicit provisions both for bequeathing additional portions in an estate to those children who have special needs and for bequeathing reduced shares to those offspring who fail to carry out their obligations to provide for the comfort of elderly parents even though they possess the means to do so (Articles 13, 19). It is hoped that this approach will strengthen

> the principle of the mutuality of rights and obligations in order that we can ensure an increase in the numbers of those who perform their obligations fully, a decrease in the numbers of those who do not fully meet their obligations and the elimination of those who perform no obligations (Zhang Peilin, 1985).

This link between inheritance and welfare programmes is also strengthened by the PRC's more general policies designed to protect the legal rights not only of the elderly and the young, but also of women (*ZGFZB*, no. 91, p. 2, 23 April 1982; no. 192, p. 4, 30 January 1984). In particular, the state now admits that in the past the inheritance rights of daughters and widows who remarry have frequently been infringed and that this must be corrected, especially as, in recent years, the successful implementation of policies restricting family size has led to an increase in the numbers of young women available for work in industry and other forms of paid employment. At the same time, it is said that the contributions of daughters working, for example, in households engaged in commodity production for the private market, should also be given recognition by affording such women appropriately protected inheritance rights. The new inheritance law attempts to overcome these problems.

> First there should be no discrimination between the sexes in respect of rights of inheritance. Within kin of the same degree male and female enjoy equal rights of inheritance. It is our policy that differences in gender should not be used to justify differences in inheritance rights between, for example, daughters and sons, mothers and fathers, and brothers and sisters. [See Inheritance Law, Articles 9 and 10]. Secondly, the property which wife and husband jointly owned during their marriage should, in the event of a division of the estate and in the absence of an alternative arrangement, be so divided that one half is retained by the surviving spouse and the remaining half becomes the heritable estate of the deceased spouse. Subsequently, this estate is divided among the surviving spouse and other first order heirs [Article 26]. Thirdly, in order to forbid [the practice of] obstructing widows from taking property with them upon remarriage, it is stipulated that following the death of one spouse a surviving spouse has the right to dispose of her or his inherited property when remarrying [Article 30] (Wang Hanbin, 1985).

The need for an inheritance law is also explained in terms of the fundamental constitutional rights of PRC citizens. Legal theorists emphasize that the comprehensive and specific provisions of the new code are, basically, an important elaboration of Article 30 of the Constitution which provides that 'the state protects the inheritance rights of citizens in private property' (*siyou caichan*). Full national legal protection may now be afforded to such rights because contemporary legal views on property stress that,

> In contrast to the inheritance system of the exploiting class, our country's inheritance system is socialist in character. Following the establishment of a People's Republic our country implemented a complete socialist transformation of the private ownership of the means of production, eliminated exploitation of man by man, and established a socialist economic infrastructure. The landlord and capitalist classes, as classes, have already ceased to exist. Workers, peasants and intellectuals became masters of the country, and took over the ownership of the country's entire means of production. China's inheritance system, which has been established on a socialist economic base, eradicates all the conditions involving the use of the means of production by private owners to exploit others or the use of inheritance of the means of production to enable descendants to exploit others (Chen Qinyi, 1985).

Even during the Cultural Revolution, when much criticism was levelled against the 'so-called legal rights of the capitalist class' (*suowei zichanjieji faquan*), *de facto* recognition was given to the inheritance rights of the individual (Wang Hanbin, 1985). Indeed, in the case of certain items of property such as houses, inheritance often proved to be the only politically safe mode of transferring proprietory rights from one person to another (Whyte and Parish, 1984, pp. 81–5). This toleration has now been transformed into a positive acknowledgement that the legal recognition and regulation of inheritance is a necessary right of the PRC citizen. Accordingly, the first article of the inheritance code provides that 'this inheritance law is formulated in accordance with the stipulations of the "Constitution of the People's Republic of China" to protect the rights of inheritance of a citizen in private property'. And one of the major problems against which the citizen needs to be protected is the threat posed by 'ultra-leftist attitudes'. This was made clear at an important seminar on inheritance law held in August 1985 in Sichuan Province and attended by judges from People's Courts located in many parts of the country. In a key speech, the Vice-President of the Supreme People's Court, Ma Yuan, stressed that,

> above all, it is essential to oppose leftist thinking and earnestly to safeguard the inheritance rights of citizens. The most prominent of these problems caused by leftist attitudes is the adverse influence of the slogan 'Regard class struggle as the guiding principle' (*yi jieji douzheng wei gang*]. This principle protects neither the inheritance rights of citizens nor the proprietary rights of citizens in private property. In thoroughly implementing the inheritance law it is necessary to eradicate the influence of leftist attitudes (Xu Jiang, 1985).[5]

In addition, the new inheritance code is intended to play an educative role by assisting the Chinese leadership in strengthening 'socialist spiritual civilization' (*shehui zhuyi jingshen wenming*) and promoting 'social stability and unity' (*shehui de anding tuanjie*). It is hoped that the new law will achieve these ends not only by the performance of the various functions noted above, but also through educating people to handle their inheritance matters in an amicable manner. Thus, the new code is seen as encouraging heirs to deal with such questions as the timing, the mode and the apportionment of a heritable estate through divisions based on 'mutual understanding and accommodation' (*huliang hurang*) and in a 'spirit of unity and harmony' (*hemu tuanjie de jingshen*). Heirs are advised not to attempt to obtain heritable property by methods which infringe the rights of others, nor to fight over the property. A surviving spouse is urged to keep the family of the deceased together by refraining from an immediate division of the household. The small minority whose conduct is not consistent with these principles of socialist spiritual civilization must be subjected to criticism and re-education (Gu Angren, 1985; Chen Qinyi, 1985). Moreover, it is feared that the need to maintain harmony in domestic relations will become much greater in future years 'when the incidence of inheritance disputes will greatly increase following the implementation of further [new] policies and as a result of the constant improvements in the people's living standards' (Yan Rong, Li Ya, Zhong Sheng *et al.*, 1985).

The Testamentary Disposition of Property

One of the most radical developments in the PRC's regulatory framework for inheritance has been the official emphasis given in recent years to the social and legal utility of the will. In traditional China the testamentary disposition of property (*yizhu jicheng*) was unimportant except in extraordinary circumstances.[6] During the first three decades of socialist rule wills only very gradually grew in significance. Since the late 1970s, however, government policies have actively encouraged testamentary inheritance and have acknowledged the unequal division of a heritable estate that is often involved in a will (Li Weiyun 1981, p. 97). In addition, in order to 'safeguard the lawful rights of citizens, avoid disputes and reduce litigation', official certification at public notary offices has been promoted and 'according to incomplete statistics, 2,400 wills were certified in the . . . year [prior to April 1982]' (Zhao Xiaoluo, 1982, p. 36). It is likely that the incidence of testamentary inheritance will increase in the next few years and one of the five chapters of the new inheritance code provides a number of rules which govern the use of wills and related matters.[7]

A central feature of the chapter on wills is the absence of explicit restrictions on the testator to transmit property as she or he thinks fit. The principal justification for the prominent role in both law and social policy afforded to testamentary inheritance in general and testamentary freedom in particular is the notion that the will represents a highly significant component of the property rights of the citizen.

> Testamentary inheritance is a very important aspect of the inheritance system. Our Constitution proclaims and protects the citizen's individual rights of property ownership [*gongmin geren hefa caichan de suoyou quan*]. The citizen possesses the right . . . to use a will to arrange for the disposition of her or his individual property (Li Weiyun, 1981, p. 97).

At the same time, however, the emphasis on testamentary freedom should also be seen as one manifestation of economic policies designed to increase levels of production and which are explicitly acknowledged to inform the new inheritance code. Thus, testamentary freedom should also be viewed as constituting a reward for effort. It affords a means by which the financially successful may be assured that they can use their resources in order to influence the conduct of close kin, affines and friends by the manner in which they dispose of their personal property at death. An additional facet of the will is that it provides the testator with an opportunity to demonstrate that she or he is a good citizen by the donation of property to a public institution. Thus Goody's observation that the binding testament in mediaeval Europe served as 'an instrument for the alienation of property not only to "irregular" heirs (mistresses rather than wives) but also to organizations such as the Church' (1976, p. 15) is echoed in the PRC's inheritance code which provides that 'a citizen may make a will bequeathing his individual property to the state, the collective or a person or persons other than the legal heirs' (Article 16). The concern to promote this 'honourable' mode of transmitting property is reflected in an illustration of a standard form will recently published in the Chinese legal press. The testament provides for a gift of property in housing into public ownership in order to provide a 'home for the young' (*xiaonian zhi jia*) in a certain neighbourhood in Shanghai (*MZYFZ*, 1984, no. 7, p. 38).

The following case summary, taken from the advice column of one of China's leading legal newspapers, illustrates not only the use of a will to disinherit children who have failed to maintain proper relations with their parents, but also the principle that a testator has the right to make more than one will.

> It is a characteristic trait of a will that it gives full expression to the wishes of the testator. It is one-sided legal conduct. Thus, if the testator, while she or he is still alive (that is, before the will takes effect), wishes to change or revoke the original will for whatever reason, then she or he is fully permitted to do so in law (Gao Shi, 1985).

> Mr and Mrs Zhang [who reside in Zhejiang Province] begat two sons and one daughter. They owned four house-rooms (*louwu sijian*). The children jointly supported their parents. In May 1975 the Zhang couple made a will in which they gave two rooms to their elder son and two rooms to the younger son. By March 1977 Mr Zhang's relations with the elder son had deteriorated [because of the son's failure to support the father] and the two men often quarrelled. As a result, Mr Zhang made another will in which he gave instead one of the two rooms originally intended for the elder son to the daughter. In October 1981, again because the elder son would not regularly provide financial support for his father, Mr Zhang made a further will in which he gave two rooms to the daughter and two rooms to the younger son. Earlier this year [1982] the Zhang couple died. The three children each hold a different will and argue over the inheritance. Which will is valid? (Hong Bing, 1982).

Reply by the newspaper's legal advice section:

> Making a will is a form of legal conduct in which certain decisions are made about one's property following one's death. In a will one can designate one or more persons to inherit one's property . . . this choice is protected by law. However, a will cannot transgress the policies of the party and the state. It cannot deprive minors or disabled persons of their legal rights . . . On the basis

of the contents of your letter Mr Zhang's will does not contravene the [relevant] regulations and should be recognized. Since the testator has the right to change her or his mind about a will's contents, the last will is considered to be the final version provided that it has been properly drawn up in accordance with the appropriate legal procedures. Thus, in this case it is the will made in October 1981 which is the accepted will in law (*MZYFZ*, 1982, no. 10. p. 44).

The restrictions on testamentary freedom to which this reply refers indicate that while the new inheritance code contains few explicit limitations on the rights of a testator freely to dispose of property, there may still be fetters on the manner in which she or he distributes property through the will.

The continued existence of limitations on the will-maker in the current situation is immediately apparent from some of the very recent Chinese legal analyses of the new law. Thus it is emphasized that 'a testator has no right to deal with property that is not owned by the testator' (Gao Shi, 1985). Significant restrictions are placed on the disposition of certain types of property and the inheritance of certain forms of proprietary rights. These limitations apply both to testamentary and statutory inheritance and will be considered in greater detail later in the chapter. Suffice to say here that objects such as land which are owned by the state or a collective may not be inherited and if, for example, an individual holds land under a contract, then it is only the contractual right to the income derived from the use of that land and not proprietary rights in the land itself that may be inherited.[8] In addition, a testator may well hold proprietary rights in a jointly owned estate (*gongyou caichan*). Unless the joint owners have agreed on an alternative arrangement for the disposition of the estate, it is possible for the testator to include in her or his will only her or his personal share of the estate. Thus, if the head of a family dies his testament may distribute not the entire family estate but, rather, only his share of the estate (Gao Shi, 1985; Wang Zhenshao, 1982).

In addition, a testator must almost certainly allocate a portion from her or his heritable estate to financially disadvantaged heirs. In fact, Article 19 of the new code provides only that 'a will should [*yingdang*] reserve a necessary share of the estate for those heirs who are unable to work and are without income',[9] and adds that

> if the People's Court, in deciding actual cases, discovers that the testator has not reserved portions for heirs who lack sources of income, then the Court should set aside for such heirs property essential for their basic livelihood. Only then may the remaining property be distributed according to the fixed principles of the will (1985).

In fact, according to Zhang Peilin (1985), the drafters of the law originally constructed this provision in somewhat broader terms by providing that a testator 'cannot [*budei*] cancel the inheritance rights of elderly heirs, minors who are heirs, or heirs who are faced with difficulties in making financial ends meet'. This original wording is, of course, thoroughly consistent with the welfare policies of the state which are intended to place much of the responsibility for providing social aid on to the family. However, during the final stages of the drafting process, the rule was relaxed to a limited extent in the 'interests of accuracy and equity' (*wei zhunque, heli*). The codists were persuaded that this wording was an unnecessarily restrictive binding on testamentary freedom because

> elderly persons and minors . . . lack the ability to work but may not definitely be without sources of income. If they do possess other, dependable, sources of income then it is not necessary to reserve for them their statutory inheritance rights and we should permit a testator to distribute the estate in an alternative manner.

As a result it is essential for the heir to lack both the ability to work and a source of income before she or he is eligible to benefit under this rule. Moreover, although the testator is enjoined to furnish the disadvantaged heir with a necessary share of the inheritance, the law still leaves the testator with room to manoeuvre in determining the size of their portion. She or he is not required to furnish a fixed proportion of the estate but, rather, is compelled to provide only a share sufficient to protect the livelihood of this type of heir.

A further problem in the interpretation of this rule is raised, however, by the shift from the use of the imperative *budei* (must) to the weaker admonition *yingdang* (should) in characterizing the testator's obligations to such an heir. The language used in recent authoritative glosses on the chapter on wills in the new law suggests that this requirement is nevertheless very likely to be interpreted by the people's courts as a near imperative. Thus, Gao Shi's explication of the rule not only uses the compound *yingdang*, but also relies on the term *bixu* ('the will must . . .') and adds,

> if the People's Court, in deciding actual cases, discovers that the testator has not reserved portions for heirs who lack sources of income, then the Court should set aside for such heirs property essential for their basic livelihood. *Only then* [emphasis added] may the remaining property be distributed according to the fixed principles of the will (1985).

Zhang Peilin's exposition of the relationship between wills and duties of care retains the character *ying* or 'should', but also describes the requirement to provide for a disadvantaged heir as an 'essential restriction' (*biyao xianzhi*) on testamentary freedom (1985). Finally, a will which abrogates the inheritance rights of heirs lacking the capacity to work and without income is categorically stated to be null and void (*wuxiao*) in an analysis of the creation of wills made by the Chinese jurist Wang Zhenshao (1985). I suspect that the most satisfactory interpretation of the rule in Article 19 rests on a recognition that a testator cannot be assumed to possess full knowledge of the financial position of her or his heirs. The will-maker is not absolutely compelled by Article 19 to make special provision in the testament because she or he may not know of an heir's difficult circumstances. But an heir in need who is overlooked by the testator in this manner may challenge the will in court and expect the court to rectify the omission by altering the distribution of the estate in her or his favour.

Another important aspect of the problem of testamentary freedom concerns the inheritance rights of dutiful heirs who perform fully their obligations of care but who are nevertheless left out of the will by an ungrateful testator. The chapter on statutory inheritance not only requires provision for such heirs, but also encourages a testator to furnish a larger than average share for the caring person (Article 13). This is another expression of the state's welfare policies which are designed to concentrate welfare responsibilities on the family and household. Immediately before the adoption of the new inheritance code this view was most forcefully enunciated in the Chinese legal press by Zhang Peilin.

> I consider that . . . a will should reserve a necessary share of the inheritance for those statutory heirs who have, throughout their lives, fulfilled their obligation of care. The rationale behind and the advantage of adding this kind of restriction is that it promotes and encourages people to assume [financial] obligations of care towards elderly people. In contemporary Chinese society family members generally help each other and the vast majority of elderly people receive proper [financial] support from their children. However, there are also exceptions, with a minority of children unable satisfactorily to carry out in full their obligations of support to elderly persons. Under these kinds of conditions, we are not only strengthening the principle of the mutuality of rights and obligations in order to ensure an increase in the numbers of those who perform their obligations fully, a decrease in the numbers of those who do not fully meet their obligations, and the elimination of those who perform no obligations. In addition, we give the above-mentioned protection to those statutory heirs who have throughout their lives fully met their obligations of care, and this will certainly benefit greatly the promotion of support for the old and the safeguarding of old people spending joyfully their final years. Some persons consider that making a will is a matter of a testator dealing with personal property – an implementation of personal ownership which the law cannot restrict. In fact, for more than thirty years we have placed a number of restrictions on wills. The exercise of personal property rights in a socialist society absolutely cannot be an 'unrestricted freedom' – it must be consistent with the policies of not harming the social good. If we permit the use of testaments to cancel the inheritance rights of heirs who have throughout their lives fully met their obligations of [financial] support, then this will not encourage children to support the elderly and will harm social morality.

This strongly worded view of the relationship between testamentary inheritance and duties of care does not, however, reflect a general consensus. Zhang concedes that there are jurists who

> assert that supporting [financially] one's parents is a statutory obligation. Children cannot demand to be 'reimbursed' because they have provided such support. It is inappropriate [in this area of the law] to use a policy of obtaining rewards according to one's labour [*an lao qu chou*].

This line of reasoning is criticized by Zhang on the grounds that it over-estimates the possibilities of reciprocity in relations between testator and heir and therefore is misplaced.

> This approach sounds very reasonable when one first hears it, but, in reality, it is a form of specious argument. In our opinion a will cannot be used to eliminate the inheritance rights of those persons who have throughout their lives fully met their obligations of [financial] support. This is absolutely not a way of encouraging people to compete for rewards . . . of demanding the 'obtaining of rewards according to one's labour'. In reality, the money and the physical effort

that one expends in providing care in most situations will not be equal [to the share of] the estate that one obtains. As a result, there is . . . absolutely no question of 'obtaining rewards according to one's work'. The crux of the matter is that heirs who fully and conscientiously meet their obligations of care should be encouraged and rewarded in order to stimulate more heirs fully to meet their obligations of care . . . We firmly believe that protecting a necessary share of the inheritance for those who throughout their lives have fully performed their obligations of care will be beneficial to the promotion of the general good mood of the people in the [financial] support of old persons. It will also benefit the creation of spiritual civilization [among our people] because it is correct (Zhang Peilin, 1985).

These arguments were apparently insufficient to achieve the insertion of a provision in the chapter on wills which would have explicitly compelled a testator to provide a portion for the dutiful heir. In view of the presence of stipulations which favour such heirs in the section concerned with statutory inheritance, it would seem reasonable to conclude that under the PRC's new inheritance law a testator is indeed free to disinherit an heir who has been attentive in her or his duties of care towards the former.

However, it may also be the case that in specific instances of litigation the people's courts will find ways of rewarding dutiful but disinherited heirs and thereby thwart the intentions of an ungrateful testator. On the one hand, the materials on conflicts over inheritance matters contained in the Chinese legal press show that great importance is attached to the provision of care,[10] and this suggests that a court would be favourably disposed to an heir who has proved herself or himself filial. On the other hand, the chapter on wills in the inheritance law also omits to mention certain provisions which, according to the legal press, constitute a highly important restriction on testamentary freedom. In particular, 'the contents of a will may not harm state or collective interests. If a will does infringe these interests, then the part which so offends is null and void' (*MZYFZ*, 1984, no. 4, p. 48). Similarly,

the contents of a will may not transgress the law, public interests or the norms of socialist morality. Any [part of a] will which violates the law, infringes the public interest or runs counter to the norms of socialist morality is null and void.

Now, the problem of testamentary provisions that fall foul of these requirements is illustrated in the Chinese legal press by reference to rather obvious pitfalls such as disposing of family rather than personal property or transmitting property in which the testator holds rights of use only (Wang Zhenshao, 1985). Nevertheless, the principles of balancing rights and obligations and caring for the elderly are so pervasive in social and legal policies relating to family law that the filial but disinherited heir could well find support from the courts. The latter may choose to define the actions of a testator in failing to provide for a filial heir as, in particular, an infringement of the norms of socialist morality and therefore decide to remedy the omission.

A further restriction on testamentary freedom warranting comment here concerns Article 29 of the new code which reads, 'the division of the heritable estate should be favourable to production and the needs of daily life, and shall not harm the usefulness of inheritance'.[11] In fact, legal commentaries on wills do not make any reference to this restriction, but since Article 29 has been placed within a general section dealing with the disposal of the inheritable estate it would seem safe to assume that this provision is intended to apply equally to statutory and testamentary inheritance. The main purpose of introducing Article 29 appears to be related to the shift in legal policy by which the PRC now permits the inheritance of privately owned means of production. This crucial change will be considered in greater detail below. Suffice it to point out here that Chinese legal commentators are concerned to emphasize that since productive property is now firmly included in the sphere of items that may constitute a heritable estate, it is only fitting that the property should be devolved in an economically responsible manner. Thus,

> the law permits the means of production owned by individuals to be inherited and, at the time of the division of the estate, they should be transmitted in a manner that will benefit production and meet the requirements [of heirs who have special needs] as well as avoid harming the usefulness of inheritance (Gu Angren, 1985).

Unfortunately, the various commentaries on the new inheritance law do not provide examples of deviation from this principle. The stipulation that heirs facing hardship should obtain a special benefaction from a will or a statutory inheritance is repeated elsewhere in the code and is not a matter which need be dealt with here. The requirement that personal property in general and the means of livelihood in particular should be devolved in a way that enhances production is, however, rather difficult to assess. It may mean no more than that a portion of the estate should not be passed on to those who exhibit what is considered to be negative behaviour such as lavish expenditure, laziness, and other manifestations of a dissolute life. However, it may also be the case that this provision is intended to strengthen the role of the household as a unit of production by, for example, discouraging the dispersal of an estate in a manner that has an adverse impact on a hitherto successful productive unit. Some evidence for this sort of approach is contained in the commentaries concerning Article 4, which provides that,

> the earnings that an individual is entitled to receive from work carried out under a personal contract [*geren chengbao*] shall be inherited in accordance with the provisions of this law. The law permits an heir to continue working a personal contract but this shall be handled as a contractual matter.

In an important explanation of this measure Wang Hanbin (1985)[12] emphasizes that only the income from a personal contract may be inherited and that, in many situations, an heir may not take up a contract because this would be inconsistent with certain forms of production such as those dependent on the personal knowledge, skills, reputation and so on of the person with whom it has been made. In other types of situation, however, the possibly adverse impact of inheritance on the operation of a contract is avoided or reduced by characterizing the devolution of rights as a matter governed not by inheritance law but, rather, by the rules of contract. Thus, Wang observes, in contracts dealing with barren hill land[13] or tree plantations the benefits are long-term. The contract is long-term. The children of a deceased contracting party are allowed to take over [*jixu chengbao*] the contract. However, the contract cannot be devolved as a heritable estate because several heirs of the same order may want an equal share regardless of whether or not they are in a position to inherit the contract. This would not be beneficial to production.

A similar approach is also used to structure the 'devolution' of rights in a contract with a family or household (*jiating chengbao*). It is stressed that this is a matter of contractual relations (*hetong guanxi*) and that the contracting party is the family and not individual family members. As a result, 'the death of a household head in a family which has entered into a contract will not give rise to problems in the transmission of contractual rights'. In reality, of course, the death of a member of a household in the case of either a household contract or a long-term personal contract, may still have important implications for the operation of such contracts. It will often give rise to such difficulties as family fission, the splitting of proprietary rights in and control over means of production important for the continued operation of the contract, intra-family disputes between avaricious members and so on. Thus, the provision in Article 29 that the division of a heritable estate should be favourable to production may be seen as promoting a certain congruence between the devolution of a contract and the inheritance of property such that, for example, the means of production are not transmitted in a manner that disrupts the operation of that contract.

The power of a testator to dispose of property as she or he thinks fit is also constrained by the provisions of Article 31 which affords legal recognition of inheritance care agreements (*yizeng fuyang xieyi*; *gongyang xieyi*). These agreements have their social origins in customary practices of adult adoption (*RMRB*, 3 June 1985, p. 4), although they are also in part derived from analogous provisions in the Soviet and Bulgarian Civil Codes (Liu Nanzheng and Zhang Peilin, 1985). The customary forms of agreement enjoyed *de facto* state acknowledgement for some years before the introduction of the inheritance law (*MZYFZ*, 1982, no. 11, p. 44) and, indeed, one variant of the adoptive contracts has been care agreements between collective units and elderly people. These latter types of arrangements are also afforded a secure legal position by the provisions of Article 31 of the new law.

The inclusion of inheritance care agreements in the new code raises again the problem of tension between the felt need to promote testamentary freedom and the policy of utilizing private domestic arrangements for the provision of care for the aged. It is a measure of the importance which the state attaches to inheritance care agreements that these contracts cannot easily be revoked by means of a will. The basic position is conveyed in an informed reply to a reader's letter lately published in the Chinese legal press. The reader refers to a dispute between himself and the adopted daughter of a recently deceased neighbour. The reader stood to gain from an inheritance care agreement with the neighbour whereas the daughter, who had married virilocally, was the principal beneficiary in the will which had subsequently been made by her adoptive father. A minor beneficiary in the will was the neighbour's adopted son who had been sent away from the area by the authorities for punishment by 're-education through labour' (*laogai*). According to the reader, Zhi Yuanxing, the elderly neighbour had entered into an inheritance care agreement with him because the two adoptive children were not living at home and could not or would not send enough money to meet the old man's subsistence needs.

> He asked me to subsidize him a little, to be responsible for looking after him when he was ill and to provide a burial for him after death. If I did these things for him he would willingly give me his three-roomed house (*sanjian fangwu*) after his death . . . In May 1978 we asked a cadre to witness the contents of the agreement. The old man and I each kept one copy and a further copy was lodged with the local neighbourhood committee (Zhi Yuanxing, 1985).

However, following the death of the elderly neighbour in 1984 the daughter produced a will written in June 1983 in which she and the adopted son stood to inherit all the old man's property including the three house-rooms originally designated for Mr Zhi. The legal advice section of the magazine to which Zhi had written informed him that the provisions of Article 31 of the new code afforded legal protection for the inheritance care agreement. If Zhi had fulfilled his duties of care under the terms of the agreement he retained the right to inherit the property specified in the agreement despite the subsequent will, 'otherwise there would be no protection for the rights of those persons who enter into inheritance care agreements under Article 31 of the inheritance law'. His position would be less secure, however, if he had failed in his duties of care and thereby infringed the original provisions of the agreement. Under such circumstances testamentary freedom is restored.

> The old man would be permitted to change his original position and to make a will providing a new disposition of his property. [Zhi] would have no right to demand that the beneficiaries of the will implement the provisions of the inheritance care agreement' (*MZYFZ*, 1985, no. 10, p. 46).

Although inheritance care agreements are officially characterized as contractual arrangements they are themselves a form of will which offers a considerable degree of testamentary freedom. They serve as instruments by means of which an elderly person may devolve personal property as she or he thinks fit. A new heir is created and may benefit from the estate of the deceased to the exclusion of the statutory heirs. It should also be noted that the family members of an elderly person who has entered into such an agreement with another person are not themselves relieved of their legal duties to provide care and support for the old woman or man (*RMRB*, 3 June 1985, p. 4). This again raises the possibility of a filial heir being disinherited although, of course, if an heir does provide adequate support, then the elderly person has no real need to enter into an inheritance care agreement.

A final aspect of the problem of freedom of testation that should be considered here concerns the relationship between wills and the welfare institution known as the 'five guarantees' (*wubao*). The latter is a form of rural social security by means of which elderly persons, incapable of supporting themselves and without grown sons to provide for them, are able to rely on the collective for housing, food, clothing, medical care and a decent burial. It is clear that since the 1950s there has been a conflict of attitudes among Chinese jurists regarding the devolution of property belonging to beneficiaries of the five guarantees. Of course, in many cases the five guarantee households are so poor that they have very little property worth devolving. However, the debate is not entirely academic because current policies encourage the return to their rightful owners of property such as houses confiscated during the Cultural Revolution and some five guarantee households will have regained valuable items of property in this manner.

According to Liu Nanzheng and Zhang Peilin (1985), one viewpoint maintains that the heritable property of a five guarantee beneficiary should be devolved according to the provisions of any will that the deceased may have made. In the event of intestacy the property should not devolve according to the rules of statutory inheritance but, rather, should pass to the collective which has given support to the intestate. Proponents of this view argue that enjoyment of the five guarantees is a socially protected right conferred by constitutional and labour law. It is the rural equivalent to the pensions received by retired workers in state enterprises. State workers are not prevented from making wills by virtue of their enjoyment of pensions. Similarly, five guarantee beneficiaries should not be barred from disposing of property as they think fit – otherwise the state would be pursuing a policy of 'favouring industry at the expense of agriculture' (*hougong er bonong*). The alternative viewpoint stresses that the above arguments pay insufficient attention to the empirical realities of contemporary Chinese society and are too idealistic. They ignore the difficulties of eradicating the deep-seated differences between urban and rural China. Moreover, there are significant contrasts in the mode of financing state pensions and five guarantee support. Because the former are issued by the state they do not adversely affect the economic performance of particular units. However, the five guarantees are funded by the collective and if this responsibility is not balanced by a right to receive the property of a deceased beneficiary then the collective's enthusiasm for providing the five guarantees will be seriously undermined. Proponents of the first approach tacitly admit this by providing that in the absence of a testament the deceased's property should not devolve according to the rules governing intestacy but, rather, should pass directly to the collective. They do this because they know that if first order heirs such as daughters married into other villages are beneficially entitled to the intestate's property, then the five guarantees will receive very little support from the collective. The expenditure incurred by the collective in affording this form of welfare assistance would not be offset by any contributions from the estates of deceased five guarantee beneficiaries.

Liu and Zhang report that these two approaches have stood in opposition for a considerable period of time and that the legal authorities have favoured one or the other at different points in China's recent history. The new inheritance code attempts to provide a compromise by both affirming the inheritance rights of five guarantee households and furnishing a mechanism that will enable a collective to have a beneficial interest in the property of a deceased recipient of the five guarantees. Thus, the inheritance law treats equally five guarantee households and the average citizen and permits the welfare recipients to use wills to pass on their property as they think fit. If there is no will an inheritance is governed by the statutory rules. However, as noted earlier, the testator who needs considerable support during her or his lifetime, may enter into an inheritance care agreement with

> a unit of collective ownership. By this agreement, the unit of collective ownership carries the obligation to support that citizen during her or his lifetime and to bury her or him after death and has the right to accept the citizen's gift (Article 31).

Moreover, as also noted earlier, under Article 16 a citizen may make a will passing her or his personal property to the collective and this, too, could function as a means by which the welfare expenditure of a collective on a member may be reciprocated following that member's death.

Statutory Inheritance (*fading jicheng*)

Traditionally, Chinese have not relied on wills in order to structure the inheritance of property and even in present-day conditions the majority of Chinese do not have recourse to such instruments. Intestacy remains the norm and it is governed by Chapter 2 of the new code. The most basic principle in this section is contained in Article 9 where it is laid down that males and females have equal rights of inheritance. This axiom is also generally enshrined in the Marriage Law of 1950 (Article 1) and 1980 (Article 2). Clearly, it is a distinct improvement on the traditional situation in which daughters did not enjoy rights of inheritance in the family estate although, of course, they could expect to receive a fairly generous dowry upon marriage if they hailed from a wealthy family.[14] Article 10 of the new code places daughters in the same category of heirs as sons, parents and the surviving spouse. These constitute the first order of heirs (*diyi shunxu jichengren*) and share the entire estate equally (Article 13).[15] In the absence of heirs in this category all heirs in the second sequence should inherit equally. In line with the emphasis on Article 9 this category comprises not only brothers[16] and paternal grandparents, but also sisters and maternal grandparents.

Another development which reflects the even greater emphasis which the state now gives to the responsibility which adult children are expected to give to their elderly parents is the change which has taken place in the inheritance rights of parents. According to both Article 18 of the Marriage Law 1980 and Article 10 of the Inheritance Law 1985, parents have the right to inherit regardless of whether or not they are dependent for their livelihood on the deceased. In contrast, during the 1950s the Supreme People's Court laid down that only those parents who were unable to support themselves could be included in the category of first order heirs. Parents who were able to maintain their own livelihood constituted a second order and could only inherit in the absence of first order heirs (van der Valk 1961, p. 333). The current writings on legal aspects of inheritance neither emphasize nor explain this apparently important change, but it is consistent with the general requirement that the younger generation should be responsible for the welfare of their seniors.[17]

It should be noted that the provision for inheritance by grandparents in the absence of first order heirs is also in keeping with the general intention of the codists to improve the care and comfort afforded to ageing people. Prior to the introduction of the new code there had been considerable debate among Chinese jurists regarding the inheritance rights of grandparents. Some writers argued that they should be second category heirs whereas others insisted that they should be in a third order category of their own. Still others argued that grandparents should not enjoy any rights of inheritance because they were likely to fritter away the property and their inclusion would also result in significant reduction in the inheritance portion of other heirs. It is now certain that grandparents are placed in the second category and this is thoroughly consistent with the emphasis in legal policies on the importance of the family as a unit of care for China's elderly citizens.[18]

It must also be observed that the rule stating that heirs of the same category should share equally may be modified in order to provide additional support for those who are in need and in order to sanction those charged with duties of care. Thus,

> an heir who has special difficulty in earning a living should be taken note of when the estate is distributed, an heir who has fulfilled her or his principal duty to provide for the deceased or who has lived together with the deceased may be given more when the estate is distributed; an heir who has the ability and who is in a position to provide for the intestate [when the latter was alive] but fails to do so should be given nothing or a reduced share when the estate is distributed;[19] if the heirs agree through consultation, an estate may also be distributed on an unequal basis (Article 13).

The emphasis on obligations of care and support in this provision, which is mainly intended to provide guidelines for the courts in the event of disputes, is also contained in Article 14 which states,

> an appropriate amount of the estate may be distributed to a person who is not an heir but who has relied on the support of the intestate [when the latter was alive], or to a person who is not an heir but who provided more for the intestate.

Furthermore, a son-in-law or a daughter-in-law who fulfils duties of care to support the parents of his or her spouse is especially defined as a first order heir under Article 12.

The chapter of the law dealing with statutory inheritance not only emphasizes the rights of women and the elderly, but also acknowledges the rights of others in socially vulnerable positions such as illegitimate children and adopted daughters and sons. These provisions affirm the principles laid down in the 1980 Marriage Law that the term 'children' should be taken to include those born out of wedlock and those who are adopted into the family (Articles 19, 20). However, the inheritance rights of another marginal category, namely step-children, are dependent on the existence of a relationship of care: step-children are characterized as first order heirs provided that they have supported or have been supported by the deceased (Article 10). This restriction is probably intended to distinguish between situations in which the step-child has been fully incorporated into the family of the step-parent and those in which it has not been incorporated. In an article on inheritance law published in 1981, the legal writer Zhu Pingshan emphasized this distinction.

The children of a former husband or wife . . . should in principle inherit the property of their own parents. They do not have rights of inheritance in their step-parent's estate. But if they have broken off relations with a parent and have actually formed adoptive parent–child relations with a step-parent then they should enjoy rights of inheritance as an adopted child (Zhu Pingshan, 1981, p. 25).[20]

Underlying the distinction between the two types of domestic situation is not only the principle of protecting the rights of those who are in a vulnerable position, such as immature step-children, but also the principle of balancing rights and duties which informs a great deal of family law (Palmer 1986a and 1986c). I have elsewhere outlined the inheritance rights of adopted children. Suffice it to say here that adopted children cannot as a general rule enjoy rights of inheritance in both their adoptive and their natural families. However, an adopted child that contributes to the comfort of its natural parents with the knowledge and approval of the adoptive parents may still receive gifts from the natural parents and thereby inherit a portion of the natural parents' estate and enjoy 'double inheritance' (Palmer, 1986a).

Ideology, Objects and Estates

In a socialist society one of the most important and ideologically difficult issues is the definition of the forms of private property that may be included in a heritable estate. Although the PRC, unlike the USSR, quickly accepted the facts of private property and inheritance of personal property, it is nevertheless the case that in socialist China inheritance has been a highly sensitive issue and sometimes quite difficult to accommodate to basic policy tenets. Severe attacks were made on this institution during the Cultural Revolution (Chen Jialiang and Zhang Peilin, 1980 pp. 11–12).

For many years the principal ideological defence against such strident views was the argument that inheritance in China involved not the 'means of production' (*shengchan ziliao*) but, rather, the 'means of livelihood' (*shenghuo ziliao*). This distinction was based on the axiom, referred to earlier, that property in capitalist societies and property in socialist societies are fundamentally different in nature. According to this view, in capitalist societies inheritance is rigidly based on a system of private property and inheritance rights are, more or less, unearned rights to exploit the labour of others. The main inheritors of property belong to the exploiting class. The broad mass of the proletariat, who possess neither capital nor land, can pass to their children only the means of livelihood and, in many cases, the objects which are passed down cannot really be described as constituting a 'heritable estate'. Indeed, some workers even bequeath heavy debts to their offspring. In capitalist societies, therefore, the inheritance system is established on a private economic base and serves only to promote the interests of private ownership and the exploiting classes. Its main purpose is to provide for the inheritance of the means of production and its nature is the protection of the reproduction of private ownership of the means of production. In socialist societies, however, the system of inheritance is based on an economic structure in which the means of production are held under socialist ownership, that is, either state or collective ownership. Thus, in such societies it is only the means of livelihood that is heritable. Moreover, the subjects of inheritance in socialist societies are primarily the working class and other labouring people. As a result, in socialist societies inheritance does not involve exploitation and therefore has a role to play in the socialist legal system (Chen Jialiang and Zhang Peilin, 1980; Zhu Pingshan, 1981; Chen Qinyi, 1985).

Official and semi-official commentaries on the new inheritance law no longer rely on this kind of argument in order to justify inheritance although they do continue to make the distinction and are rather cautious in their rejection of its importance. Article 3, paragraph 5, of the new inheritance law states that a heritable estate may include the 'means of production owned by the citizen as permitted by law' (also Gu Angren, 1985; Chan Qinyi, 1985). In fact, in recent years the means of production–means of livelihood distinction has become a representation of property relations that is increasingly distinct from the reality of property relations in China.[21] The logic of the economic reforms and the open-door policy has been to encourage further private ownership of 'comparatively important means of production' (*bijao zhongyao de shengchan ziliao*) (Chen Qinyi, 1985). The Chan, Madsen and Unger social history of a southern Guangdong village shows a very considerable replacement of collective by private ownership during the early 1980s.

> The teams had been instructed to distribute not just land but [also] the essential means of production. Farm tools, from shoulder-poles to winnowing baskets, were sold off to all of the families . . . almost all of the larger farm equipment – the team's and brigade's threshers, carts and tractors – were auctioned off to the highest bidders (if need be, as with the brigade's large tractor, on credit). The new owners were gambling that they could more than recoup their losses by renting the equipment out to neighbours or by setting up their own transport businesses. Going a step further, the team and brigade tendered out to the highest bidders all responsibilities for the village's fruit trees and fish ponds. The new managers would be committed to pay each year the sum they had bid, and in exchange they gained total rights over the yields of the trees and ponds (Chan, Madsen, and Unger, 1984, pp. 269–70).

A weighty English language commentary on the new code contained in the *China Daily* (21 April 1985, p. 4) gives great emphasis to the fact that many of these objects may now be legally inherited.

> One important feature [of the inheritance law] is the definition of legitimate private property that can be handed down after death. Such property consists not only of a citizen's personal savings and effects but also of those means of production that they are permitted to own by law. The latter includes gains accruing from a person's productive activities based on contracts that have been signed, such as crops, trees, fish and earning from enterprises. Likewise the means of production that overseas Chinese have invested in China are also inheritable private property. This provision will surely tend to encourage people to develop production, save and invest.

Thus, although private ownership of land is still not permitted, Articles 3 and 4 of the new code provide for the inheritance of a wide range of personal property.

Article 3. A heritable estate is the legal personal property devolved by a citizen upon her or his death and includes: (1) the citizen's income, (2) the citizen's houses, savings and articles for daily use, (3) the citizen's trees, livestock and poultry, (4) the citizen's cultural relics, books and reference materials, (5) the means of production owned by the citizen as permitted by law, (6) the right of property in a citizen's copyright and patent law, and (7) other legitimate property of the citizen.

Article 4. A person's earnings received from work done under a contract should be inherited in accordance with the provisions of this law. If the law permits an heir to continue working under the same contract he may do so by following that contract.

It should be noted that housing, an extremely important form of property, is characterized as heritable by Article 3. Virtually all housing in rural areas is in private hands, urban housing is being subjected to privatization or 'commodification' (*shangpinhua*); privately owned properties confiscated during the Cultural Revolution are steadily being returned to their original owners (see, for example, Fu Lunbo, 1983). Of course, in virtually all societies real estate is an object in which there is a multiplicity of rights and right-holders (Epstein, 1969, pp. 110–37). Contemporary China is no exception. Any observations on the devolution of rights in housing must, in particular, distinguish between three types of estate: family property (*jiating gongtong caichan*), conjugal property (*fu-qi gongtong caichan*) and personal property (*geren caichan*). This plurality of estates, and the enormous significance of the devolution of proprietary rights in houses in the lives of many people, are important factors encouraging disputes over inheritance matters. The Chinese legal press contains an abundance of letters to the comrade editor and readers' requests for advice from legal advice sections which illustrate that inheritance is frequently a contentious matter. Some of the issues involved are conveyed through the following summarized account.

Mr and Mrs Chen who resided in Xuzhou City, Jiangsu Province, had three daughters and one son. During Land Reform in 1950 they received a five-roomed house (*wujian fangwu*). In 1981 the Chen couple died and the four children shared in the funeral arrangements. At that time the second and third daughters suggested that the four children should divide up the five house-rooms among all the children. However, the eldest daughter and the son objected on the ground that the second and third daughters had been married for a number of years and therefore should not return to their parents' home in order to inherit property. As a result, no decision was taken regarding the apportionment of rights in the house-rooms. Subsequently, the eldest daughter and the son moved into the house in which their parents had once lived. In July 1982, the government resumed the land [on which the house stood] from the Chens. The eldest daughter and the son, without informing the second and third daughters, divided the property between themselves and signed a compensation agreement with the reclamation unit. When the second and third daughters learned about the matter they insisted that the house should be shared between them as well. The eldest daughter and the son refused to acquiesce in this demand. What should be done? (Jiao Mingheng, 1982).

The legal advice section's reply tackles a number of issues involved in the devolution of this property including the rights of inheritance of virilocally married daughters and, more significantly, the importance of the distinction between a heritable estate and the family joint estate.

we think that the following three points are important:

(1) We should distinguish between a heritable estate (*yichan*) and the family estate (*jiating gongtong caichan*; [lit. 'family joint property']. The first involves the passing of property from the deceased to the statutory heirs or to the heirs designated in a will. The second is involved in the division (*fenxi*) of the family's joint property. Some people confuse the two matters and upon their parents' death regard the family estate, which belongs to the entire family, as inheritance. This may harm the legal rights of the family estate holders.

According to the information contained in your letter the five-roomed house belongs to the family estate because during Land Reform it was distributed to the family, which at that time contained six members. Each member holds one-sixth of the proprietary rights in the five house-rooms. As a result of the death of the parents one-third of the proprietary rights constitute a heritable estate. Two-thirds of the rights, however, belong to the four children. They are not a part of the parents' heritable estate.

(2) According to Article 18 of the Marriage Law [and now Article 9 of the Inheritance Law], the four children have equal rights of inheritance. As a result of feudalistic influences some people still consider that daughters who are married have no rights of inheritance. This is against the law. Of course, one should look at each inheritance case in terms of its particular circumstances. For example, with reference to the inheritance rights of a daughter one should also look into her share of duties and obligations in order to decide on her rightful inheritance share. Thus, if a daughter does not inquire about inheritance at the time of her parents' death and the property was divided between them in later years, unless she has sound reasons for claiming inheritance rights in the estate any demands that she may make will not be supported. However, if the married daughter has always shared in the provision of the parents' living expenses her claims may well be recognized. In the case under consideration the four children should enjoy equal rights of inheritance unless the second and third daughters agree to waive their rights.

(3) In law, property held jointly (*gongtong caichan*) may be sold only with the approval of all estate members (*gongyouren*). Thus, in agreeing to hand over family property to the reclamation unit without consulting the second and third daughters, the eldest daughter and the son have infringed the property rights (*caichan quanli*) of their sisters. The contracts which they have signed are illegal (*feifa*) and invalid (*wuxiao*). The second and third daughters' request that the contract be abandoned and that the estate be shared between all the children is . . . correct and lawful . . . and should be supported by the unit concerned (*MZYFZ*, 1982, no. 10, p. 45).

This correspondence was published some two years before the promulgation of the new inheritance code. Nevertheless, the sharp distinction which it draws between the personal property of family members and the family estate is reproduced in the new law which now provides that in situations where 'the heritable estate is part of the family estate then, at the time of the division of the heritable estate, the property of other family members should be set aside first'. The characterization of inheritance and the division of the family estate as two related but distinct and separate processes is no longer only important in the context of housing. The increasing emphasis given to the household as a unit of production raises questions regarding the division and inheritance of capital, equipment and so on as the following case summary illustrates.[22]

Following the implementation of the 'production contract responsibility systems' (*shenchan chengbao zerenzhi*) in rural areas, the family of Old Qin jointly made great efforts and set up a piggery. They became a specialized household (*zhuan yehu*). Old Qin and his wife were responsible for rearing the pigs. The eldest son and the wife of that son were in charge of purchasing animal feed, moving the pig dung and cultivating the fields. Old Qin's mother remained at home doing the cooking and looking after her grandson. After three years' hard work Old Qin's family became their village's 'ten-thousand yuan household' (*wanyuanhu*). Sadly, earlier this year, Old Qin suddenly became acutely ill and died. After the funeral the second son, who was working away from home, stated that he wanted to inherit his father's property. He also said that all the property which had been acquired during the past five years belonged to his father. The second son demanded that the property should be divided into four shares which would be distributed to his mother, his grandmother, his elder brother and himself.

Are the demands of the second son reasonable? We analyse the situation in the following terms . . . the proposed demands of the second son blur the boundaries between the heritable estate and the family estate by assuming that inheritance and the division of the family and its property are the same.

The so-called 'division of the family and its property' refers to the division of all the property owned jointly by the family members and its distribution to family members according to shares (*gu*) or portions (*fen*). The second paragraph of Article 26 of the Inheritance Law stipulates that if the estate of the deceased is part of the family estate then other members' property should be set aside first when the inheritance is divided. That is to say, when an inheritance commences and is divided there should first be a division of the family and its estate (*fenjia xichan*). Thus . . . the property involved in the case discussed above belongs to the family estate and has been built up over a period of several years by the united efforts of Old Qin's entire family (with the exception of the second son who has been working away from home). Those individuals who have contributed to building up the family estate including Old Qin's mother all enjoy proprietary rights in that estate. As a result, following the death of Old Qin, the family estate should be divided first in order to establish accurately the property that each family member should obtain. Only after the individual shares of each family member have been allocated can there be inheritance of Old Qin's personal property.

After the heritable estate has been defined the heirs can commence the inheritance. It is thus evident that inheritance and the division of the family estate are two problems which differ in nature. They may not be confused and discussed as if they were the same thing – otherwise the lawful property rights of other family members will be infringed. It should also be pointed out that [another difference between inheritance and the division of the family estate] is that the division of the family and its property is not only resorted to in the event of the death of one of the family members. It may also occur because of the financial needs and living requirements (*shenghuo xuyao*) of family members, or because there is disharmony in the family (De Yi, 1985).

Problems such as those contained in the two cases above arise because, of course, the sharp distinction made by the law between the personal estate of the deceased and the family estate is not reflected in everyday attitudes. The latter owe much more to traditional ideas and practices. In the traditional Chinese situation it was often extremely difficult to distinguish between the two categories of rights (Freedman, 1966, pp. 53–6). Indeed, personal property was so unimportant that apparently it was not even dealt with in the first draft for a civil code in 1910 (van der Valk, 1961, p. 315). In the PRC's inheritance code – and indeed for some years prior to its introduction – the inheritance of the property of the deceased is basically limited to her or his personal property (*geren caichan*). However, it is generally acknowledged that cases such as those outlined above are fairly common. Many people are said still to believe that partition of the family estate – including, in particular, housing – is the same as inheritance. Of course, one important reason why it is difficult to distinguish between the two processes is that in many instances it is on the death of the household head that the family estate is partitioned. In such cases, the heirs-cum-partitioners should receive both their share of their parents' personal property and their share of their family estate. The parents' heritable estate should include not only her or his personal property in some sense acquired independently of the family estate, but also the parents' share of the family estate. It is not altogether surprising that poorly educated peasants are not always fully aware of the different kinds of estate held in the same item of property under contemporary Chinese law.

But the devolution of property may be complicated by another issue which, when tackled by National People's Congress deputies in their discussions of the draft inheritance law, proved to be a source of much debate. I refer to the inheritance rights of, in particular, a widow, and the fate of the conjugal estate (*fu-qi gongtong caichan*) upon the death of her husband. The term conjugal estate refers to property jointly held by the household head and his wife as distinct from the family property and family member's personal property. Items characterized as conjugal property may include

> the property obtained by the labour of one party or both parties [and, presumably, any savings accrued as a result of such work], property accepted as a gift or inherited by either or both wife and husband including presents given at their wedding, and property that was personal property before marriage and which has been renovated or otherwise significantly improved.[23]

The problem which vexed the NPC deputies concerned Article 26 of the new code which provides that

> in the event of a division of a testate's heritable estate and in the absence of any alternative arrangement, a surviving spouse should take one-half of the property which the couple acquired and jointly owned during the course of their marriage. The residue falls into the intestate's heritable estate. If the [intestate's] heritable estate [contains property that is] part of the family estate, the property of other family members should be set aside before any division of the [intestate's] heritable estate.

Opposition to this measure came from deputies who argued that the entire conjugal estate should be inherited by the surviving spouse 'in accordance with Chinese traditions and customs' (*chuantong xiguan*).[24] This approach, it was asserted, would make it easier for children to support their surviving parent, better equip a surviving spouse to support dependant children, ensure a higher standard of living for the spouse in her or his declining years, promote family stability and avoid unnecessary disputes. Such arguments were, however, dismissed on the grounds that they placed too much emphasis on family bonds and would thereby hinder China's prospects for economic development. The inference appears to be that by allowing the surviving spouse to retain only one-half of the conjugal estate a more direct link between labour and reward is maintained (because the half retained represents the product of the surviving spouse's own labour). Moreover, by devolving the property more quickly those children who have aged parents-in-law to support are better able to provide care for their elderly dependants. This is an increasingly important consideration in a country in which by the late 1990s many children will have as many as four 'parents' to support as a result of the rigorous implementation of the single-child policy. It is also clear that because the life expectancy of women is significantly greater than that of men, so this provision will adversely affect widows much more than widowers (for example, Su Werming, 1982, p. 87).

Conclusion

This chapter has considered the main features of China's recent inheritance code.[25] The new law is an important buttress for the PRC's development programmes in general and its readjusted policies on private and personal property in particular. An important concomitant of the change in economic direction has been the rise of new and more varied forms of ownership, including a greatly enhanced role for private property. Indeed, it is possible to detect something of a shift in the official justification for an inheritance law even during the past few years: at the beginning of the 1980s the need for a new code was explained in terms of domestic harmony. Family disputes over inheritance matters were becoming increasingly common and in order to rectify the situation there had to be a code laying out the basic rules (for example Wu Xinyu, 1987, p. 28). Although these grounds have not been rejected, they are nevertheless no longer placed at the forefront of official explanations. Instead, inheritance law is primarily seen as promoting industriousness. The right to dispose of personal property, including earned income, is considered to encourage greater effort and in so doing to expand China's economy. Inheritance is thus part and parcel of the general programme of strengthening the role of direct economic incentives in the PRC's modernization.[26] Hence, as we noted in the section on wills, one of the few explicit restrictions on inheritance in general and testamentary freedom in particular is the requirement in Article 29 that the division of a heritable estate should be favourable to production and the needs of daily life.

In line with these developments there has been a critical shift in the principal ideological argument for the need for an inheritance law. The means of production

-means of livelihood distinction is retained but no longer relied on. For more than 30 years it has been the principal defence for inheritance and inheritance law. The new code now positively embraces inheritance of the means of production and a major question for the future would seem to be whether or not land will come to be defined as one of the means of production that the law will permit to be inherited. There is a sense in which collective ownership of land under the contract and responsibility systems is becoming something of a fiction, not unlike the fiction of earlier periods that only the means of livelihood could be inherited when, in fact, private housing in urban areas rented out to others was characterized as heritable property.[27] A concomitant of this shift is the emphasis currently being placed on the need to safeguard the property rights and interests of the citizen as a basic legal right (Chen Qinyi, 1985; Yan Rong *et al.*, 1985).

The current emphasis in the law on testamentary freedom and the general policy of encouraging the use of wills in order to structure the vertical transmission of property may well have far-reaching social consequences. It seems quite possible, for example, for there to evolve in China one law for the rich and one law for the poor. Successful farmers and prosperous entrepreneurs are increasingly likely to use wills in order to pass on property in a manner appropriate to their interests: the will is 'an outward and visible sign of wealth and a check upon the "wrongful" disposition of property, it enshrines the wishes of the individual holder as against the demands of the potential heirs' (Goody, 1976, p. 15). The state is prepared to encourage the use of the will not only because making a testament is seen as a basic legal right which is conducive to economic development, but also because the state expects that the sort of heirs whose demands will be thwarted are likely to be those individuals who refuse fully to carry out their obligations to support the elderly testator. Statutory inheritance, however, is increasingly likely to be relied on by the less successful. Those who have lost out in the pursuit of riches will have little property to leave their heirs and will therefore be unwilling – and perhaps insufficiently educated – to go to the trouble of entering a notary office in order to have a testament certified.[28]

The official emphasis on the testament is, of course, a sharp break with traditional Chinese ideas and practices regarding transfer of property from one generation to the next. Like the support in the law for inheritance care agreements, it would seem that at the same time that the state is impressing on younger members of the family the need and duty to support their parents, the state is creating the possibility that the children will not be rewarded for so doing. The existence of an inheritance care agreement (itself a form of will) does not release a testator's family members from the obligation to support and provide comfort for the testator. Similarly, the NPC has decided not to afford protection in the code for a filial but disinherited heir. These policies seem to reflect a wider problem, namely the ambivalent attitude of the state to the family. On the one hand the state would like the family to function once more as a unit of production and to persist and even flourish as the major unit of care for China's ageing population. On the other hand, the state does not want to place too much emphasis on close family ties and kinship values lest this 'particularism' becomes an obstacle to China's 'modernization' by, for example, creating unwanted nepotism and even doubtful political loyalties.[29]

Notes

1. See, for example, the comments of National People's Congress Deputy Lin Liyun welcoming the new inheritance code, as reported in *RMRB*, 9 April 1985, p. 3.

2. For a sceptical view of the political attitudes underlying the PRC's renewed emphasis on formal legal institutions, see Ding Yichou, 1986.

3. The circumstances which give rise to the criminal offence of abandonment (*yiqizui*) are outlined in Zhongguo Renmin, 1980, pp. 195–6. In brief, a crime of this nature is committed if a person who is without independent means of support – because, for example, she or he is elderly, very young, seriously ill or disabled – is abandoned by another who bears a legal duty of care (*fuyang yiwu*) towards that person. These legal obligations exist, in particular, between husband and wife, parents and their children, and adoptive parents and their adopted children. The relevant literature gives the general impression that the most important element in the obligation of care owed to the elderly is financial support (*shanyang*).

4. In particular, Chinese legal commentators have recently drawn attention to a major statement of inheritance law made by the Supreme People's Court and contained in an apparently restricted document dated 1963. 'Suggestions for Solving some Problems in Implementing our Civil Policies; Revised Draft' (*Guanyu quanche zhixing minshi zhengce jige wenti de yijian; xiuzhenggao*). These rules, which were amended in 1979 by material contained in 'Suggestions for Implementing Civil Laws and Policies' (*Guanyu quanche zhixing minshi zhengce falü de yijian*), are reported to have provided detailed and systematic statements on the nature and size of the heritable estate available for distribution, classes of heirs eligible for inheritance and so on (Zhu Pingshan, 1981, p. 25).

5. See also the comments of Chen Jialiang and Zhang Peilin who assert that during the Cultural Revolution leftist attitudes led to a serious weakening in inheritance rights, and even to proposals for the complete abolition of inheritance (1980, p. 11).

6. The limited importance of wills in traditional times reflected the fact that private property was held primarily in the form of the family joint estate. The father held this estate in trust and, in theory at least, each of his sons could not be deprived of his expectant interest in the property (Freedman, 1966, pp. 49–50). A will could be set aside by the imperial courts if it differed significantly from the pattern of distribution prescribed by law and custom (see, for example, Alabaster 1899, pp. 581, 582). However, a son whose behaviour was generally considered to be exceptionally reprehensible could be disinherited by a special form of will known as a *yishu* or *yiming* (Boulais, 1924, p. 203).

7. It should also be noted that recent Chinese legal press reports indicate that customary deeds of adoption and documents of a similar nature are often characterized as wills and thereby afforded official recognition (see, for example, *MZYFZ*, 1982, no. 11, p. 44).

8. The Chinese press also contains reports, made several years before the introduction of the new code, that the rights of a citizen in a private plot may not be transferred to others by means of inheritance. See, for example, the editorial reply to Li Shuhua's letter published in *Fortnightly Talks* in which such rights are characterized as strictly usufructuary (*Ban Yue Tan*, 1982, no. 15, p. 5).

9. Compare the *SWB* version of this article which renders *yingdang* as 'must': 'A will must . . .' (22 April 1985, FE/7931/C/1[B]).

10. See Palmer (1986c) for translations and discussions of such cases.

11. It might be added here that this principle of mutuality of rights and obligations is manifested in another very important area of the law, namely responsibility for the tax liabilities and debts of the deceased. According to Li Weiyun

> in our judicial practice of handling the debts of the deceased a principle of limited liability is adopted. That is to say, the legal debts of the deceased are to be repaid from the estate; the heir is not responsible for the settlement of any debts in excess of the total value of the estate. As a result . . . on the one hand the interests of the creditor are protected because the heir, who benefits from the estate, has an obligation to settle the debts of the deceased . . . on the other hand, the obligations of the heir will not be outweighed by the rights which she or he enjoys . . . to require an heir to repay all the debts of the deceased without due regard to the total value of the properties inherited is an obsolete and feudualistic viewpoint, and is incorrect (1981, p. 98; see also Zhu Pingshan 1981, p. 27).

These principles are now enshrined in Article 31 of the new inheritance law which provides that 'heirs to an inheritable estate must pay the taxes and debts the deceased should have paid according to law. Payment of taxes and debts shall not be more than the real value of the inheritance, except when heirs volunteer to pay. The heir who renounces an inheritance is not responsible for paying the taxes and debts the deceased should have paid according to law'.

12. Wang Hanbin is Secretary-General of the Standing Committee of the National People's Congress and Chairman of the Committee for the Legal System.

13. It is worth noting that the practice of rewarding pioneers by transferring special land rights is a long-established arrangement among the Chinese. See Palmer (1986b p. 0) for an extended account of such practices in traditional times.

14. This is not to say, however, that the new code ensures that there will be no gender discrimination in inheritance matters. There are, for example, several indications that the position of daughters may be less secure than Article 9 suggests. Thus, in rural areas in particular, a virilocally married daughter is likely to be overlooked unless she makes a point of asserting her statutory inheritance rights. In addition, the chapter on wills does not contain any specific provision for gender equality. As a result it would seem that a testament may serve as an instrument for disinheriting daughters – although, of course, the various restrictions on testamentary freedom discussed in the previous section of this essay may be interpreted by the courts in a manner that prevents a testator from excluding a daughter from an inheritance. This is an area of the law which I hope to take up in a later publication when the post-code experience has shed more light on the problem.

15. Of course, a testator may choose to dispose of no more than a portion of her or his estate by means of a testament, or may make a will which is valid only in parts. In such cases it is merely the remainder that will be governed by statutory provisions (Li Weiyun, 1981; Inheritance Law 1985, Article 27).

16. In addition, in Article 11 of the new code the principle of gender equality is extended to statutory inheritance by subrogation (*daiwei jicheng*) for 'the sequence of inheritance by subrogation applicable to the paternal side [*fuxi*] is equally applicable to the maternal side [*muxi*]' (Zhu Pingshan, 1981, p. 28).

17. It should be recalled, however, that a similar provision is not contained in the

chapter on wills. We noted at p. 000 that the rigorous wording of the original draft specifying that a testator 'cannot cancel the inheritance rights of elderly heirs' was relaxed because 'elderly persons who lack the ability to work . . . may not definitely be without sources of income'. I would tentatively suggest that the less favourable position of parents *qua* heirs in the testamentary system may well reflect not only the state's desire to promote testamentary freedom but also the drafters' expectation that it will mainly be comparatively wealthy families that utilize testaments. In wealthy families, of course, parents are likely to be able to provide for themselves.

18. See Palmer 1986a, p. 000, for an account of a special form of adoption primarily intended to furnish support for elderly persons and referred to as 'alternative generation adoption' (*gedai shouyang*) in the Chinese legal press.

19. In fact some NPC deputies debating the draft inheritance law wanted to make this rule more rigorous by deleting the words 'reduced share' (*xiaofen*) and thereby penalize an unfilial heir even further (see *ZGFZB*, 15 April 1985, no. 380, p. 2).

20. It is not clear if this phrase 'adoptive parent–child relations' (*yangzi yangnü yangfu-mu guanxi*) refers to the creation of full legal adoption, or whether it merely characterizes the development of close attachments between the step-relatives.

21. For example, private housing in urban areas was (and still is) characterized as a means of livelihood even when the owners rented it out to others for profit.

22. Unfortunately, this is one of the few cases discussed in the Chinese legal press which fails to provide any indication of the place of residence of the disputing parties.

23. Gan Quan, 1985. This article provides a useful account of the three forms of estate. However, it does so primarily in the context of divorce settlements, and the definitions which it offers may not therefore be entirely appropriate to inheritance matters.

24. The NPC debate outlined in this paragraph is drawn from the account provided in *ZGFZB*, 15 April 1985, no. 380 p. 2.

25. It is not possible here to adequately consider all the legal characteristics and social concomitants of the new law. I have not, for example, been able to deal with such matters as notarial certification of wills, inheritance involving a foreign element, the timing of inheritance (a particularly important issue which I hope to take up in detail in a later publication), payment of the tax liabilities and debts of the deceased, the work of mediation committees and other judicial bodies in settling disputes and the development of rules specially applicable to the minority nationalities in the PRC. In addition, the question of inheritance in the family is in reality complicated by other modes of property devolution, such as the transfer of money and goods by means of bridewealth and dowry. Although the Marriage Law 1980 provides that 'the exaction of money or gifts in connection with marriage is prohibited' (Article 4), these methods of alienating property are nevertheless both widely practised and tolerated by the state (Wolf, 1984, pp. 158–60, 175–8; Chan, Madsen and Unger 1984, pp. 194–5). Of course, an accurate assessment of the overall pattern of property distribution within the family and household would only be possible on the basis of proper anthropological field research in China.

26. It should also be noted that some legal writers are now proposing to introduce death duties in order, *inter alia*, to generate income for the state from the devolution of property (see, for example, *ZGFZB*, 1 January 1985, no. 340, p. 3).

27. Indeed, there are indications that in the Autonomous Regions inheritance of land is permitted in order to facilitate land reclamation: 'to encourage farmers to

contract to use anti-erosion methods, Ningxia [Hui Autonomous Region] stipulates that whoever undertakes water and soil conservancy projects can keep the profits from the crops they cultivate. Their children can inherit the land' (*China Daily*, 11 September 1985, p. 3).

It might also be noted here that Chinese legal press reports suggest that 'customary' forms of private proprietary rights in land are emerging in certain areas of present-day China. Thus, for example, it is reported that in suburban areas in particular, collective land is being sold to peasant families for housing and other building purposes. Village- and county-level cadres are apparently turning a blind eye to such irregularities and refusing to take up complaints (*MZYFZ*, 1986, no. 2, p. 45). Clearly, the fairly permanent nature of the construction on this land is likely to create problems of inheritance and devolution in future years.

28. Some idea of the difficulties which a testator may face in the process of authenticating a will may be gained from Zhao Xiaoluo's observations regarding the work of a notary public in this area of the law. Zhao notes that the notary's duties in will certification include propagating the socialist legal system and explaining to testators that a will may not violate the law, transgress official policies, infringe the public interest, harm social institutions and so on (1985).

29. An important concomitant of this ambivalence is the equivocal nature of the state's attitude towards the incorporation of customary concepts into the inheritance law. Where a 'customary' notion such as the need for 'mutuality in rights and obligations' (*quanli yiwu xiang yizhu*; *xianghujian de quanli yiwu guanxi*) may be utilized in order to give support to the law and even to settle disputes it is conveniently characterized as a 'tradition' (*chuantong xiguan*). However, if a practice or customary norm appears to run counter to general policies, it is simply dismissed as feudal superstition (*fengjian mixin*).

8 Urban Employment in Post-Maoist China.

Michel Bonnin and Michel Cartier

After having denied for 20 years even the possibility that there could be a problem of unemployment in a country in which 'the contradiction between the social character of production and the private character of the ownership of the means of production' had been resolved,[1] the Chinese authorities were forced in 1979 to recognize the existence of an 'employment problem' in their country, especially in the towns and cities. Chinese experts who have attempted to explain this problem have generally agreed that the basic cause is the gap between population increase since 1949 (about 2% a year on average) and rather sluggish economic growth. The other reasons mentioned were mainly the 'irrational' structure of the economy, the over-centralized labour management system and the policy of sending 'educated youths' to the countryside at the time of the Cultural Revolution.[2] It is usually estimated that 17 million city-dwellers were sent to the countryside between 1968 and 1978, and 13 or 14 million peasants were recruited in urban areas in the same period. Taking returnees into account there were probably still 10 million young people in the countryside at the end of 1978,[3] when, taking advantage of the political liberalization following the return to power of Deng Xiaoping, vast numbers of them began to return to the cities. The return of these young people and the imminence of the arrival on the employment market of the products of the baby boom of the early 1960s created an emergency situation which led the authorities to envisage and adopt a number of measures. These were aimed at reducing the gap between the employment absorptive capacity of the urban economy and the number of young city-dwellers 'waiting for work' (*daiye qingnian*). They can be divided into three categories that we shall look at separately: 1) 'negative' socio-economic measures, aimed at limiting the number of job-seekers in the cities; 2) 'positive' socio-economic measures, aimed at enlarging the capacity of urban work units to absorb labour; 3) technical measures intended to improve the recruitment system.

Solutions Envisaged, Measures Applied

Measures Aimed at Reducing the Number of Job-seekers
Limiting the recruitment of peasants: Even though it was only revealed in 1980 and above all 1981 that many peasants had been recruited in the cities during the

Cultural Revolution, the need to prevent peasants from obtaining jobs to the detriment of young city-dwellers had been proclaimed as early as 1979 (*RMRB*, 17 June 1979). The open struggle against the recruitment of peasants by urban enterprises and against the more or less fraudulent conversion of agricultural residence permits (*nongye hukou*) into non-agricultural residence permits (*fei nongye hukou*) has been going on since that date. It reflects an exasperation on the part of young city-dwellers and their parents, comparable to that aroused by the recruitment of foreign immigrants in industrialized countries in periods of unemployment. The *Beijing Daily* published several readers' letters denouncing neighbours, colleagues or enterprises in breach of the law, and calling for jobs, even temporary ones, to be reserved for young city-dwellers (4 April 1981, p. 3). The press was quick to reveal the scale of the problem: in Jiangxi, for example, at the end of 1980 there were 400,000 young city-dwellers waiting for work (including 40,000 educated youths still in the countryside) and 220,000 peasants recruited outside the plan in the cities (Radio Jiangxi, 14 October in *FBIS*, 17 October 1980). The government itself announced that, at the end of 1980, 9,310,000 peasants were employed in one way or another by state enterprises, not counting permanent workers (*Guowuyuan*, vol. 27, no. 374, 10 February 1982, p. 883).

Since 1979, central and local authorities have therefore issued a whole series of measures to prohibit the recruitment of labour from the rural areas in the cities and to return as many peasants as possible to the countryside.[4] In August 1980 the National Labour and Employment Conference discussed this problem (*XH*, 12 August in *FBIS*, 13 August 1980), and the decisions taken by the Central Committee and the State Council in October 1981 reiterated the need to 'control the inflow of rural labourers into cities and townships strictly' (*XH*, 23 November in *SWB*, 27 November 1981). But denunciations by the press, in 1982 and 1983, of unhealthy practices in this area show that the effect of these measures has been at best limited.[5] It is true that, of the 24,000 workers of rural origin recruited outside the plan in Wuxi in 1978, more than 20,000 were said to have been sent back by the end of 1981 (*QNJY*, 1983, p. 359), but the press did not conceal the fact that 'some units have continued to employ workers that it had "got rid of", so that, in the end, the number of these workers recruited was higher than that of those removed' (*Yangcheng Wanbao*, 3 August in *FBIS* 13 August 1982). Another practice denounced at the time consisted in an employee of rural origin getting himself replaced by one of his children when he retired, whether at the normal age or early and, instead of returning to his village, as he ought to have done, finding another job in the city. It must be noted that the decree of 3 December 1981 which denounced this practice, still authorized this type of replacement (*dingti*), on condition that the retiree returned to his home village (*Guowuyuan*, vol. 27, no. 374, p. 88). Given that it is very difficult to check on this return effectively, the system of *dingti* constitutes an important channel of rural immigration into the cities. Conversely, the settlement in cities of demobilized soldiers of rural origin – a traditional channel of immigration – seems to have been significantly reduced, and has led to a certain amount of muttering among those concerned in addition to increasing the difficulties of recruitment resulting from the improvement of the economic situation of the peasantry.[6] In order to facilitate the reintegration of these soldiers in the countryside, several measures were taken by the government: the provision of a nest egg to help the demobilized to settle down reasonably (*XH*, 22 January in *FBIS*, 25 January 1983) and, more recently, the insistence on a 'double training' of soldiers during their service,[7] as well as the organization of courses and the grant of various loans and assistance for the newly demobilized. This work has taken on particular importance since the decision taken in May 1985 to reduce the strength of the PLA by a million (*XH*, 25 July, *FBIS*, 30 July 1985, and *China Daily*, 2 August 1985).

It is difficult to say what the real effects of the various measures taken have been. Official figures, probably under-estimated, show that in 1982–3, despite a significant drop, still over 10% of jobs assigned in the cities were assigned to peasants (see Appendix). These are generally unpleasant or dangerous jobs, particularly in construction and public works, which are unpopular with young urban school-leavers.[8]

For several years it has been possible to observe a distinct shift in the policies of the authorities towards the employment of peasants in urban areas. The emphasis is no longer on halting the recruitment of rural labour but on channelling it. The authorities seem to have realized that the drift of rural-dwellers to the cities is irresistible and that measures simply banning it are ineffective. The main reason for this shift is probably the increasingly blatant character of rural under-employment, after several years of implementation of the responsibility system in the countryside. On the other hand the encouragement given to marketing agricultural output implies close exchanges between cities and countryside and peasant enrichment creates possibilities of investment that must be seized on. Thus today peasants are permitted and even encouraged to create their own enterprises in the cities: construction teams, small factories, shops, hotels, etc. (e.g. *Mingbao*, 6 July 1984, *China Daily*, 2 March 1983). It is true that, in line with the views of Fei Xiaotong (1984), peasants are above all encouraged to go and work in small towns without giving up their village residence (*li tu bu li xiang*); but they are also permitted, if they have the means, 'to leave the village' to set up enterprises in large towns, enterprises in which they can take on their children (*Beijing Wanbao*, 4 July 1984).

This change of attitude on the part of the authorities is reflected in the figure of 1,230,000 peasants recruited in the cities in 1984 (almost double that for 1982[9] and almost the same number as in 1980). It can thus be argued that the authorities have acted to contain the drift of rural people towards the cities, then, after 1984, channelled it so as to avoid creating too many employment problems in the cities. The relative drop in unemployment among urban youth has made this shift possible, but the risk of a worsening of this unemployment linked to rural immigration is always present. Any observer of urban society today can in fact see that the old registration (*hukou*) system has lost much of its power to keep the rural population in the rural areas and that, in addition to the legal recruitment of peasants, clandestine or semi-clandestine immigration into the cities is on a significant scale.[10] For the time being, the continued development of urban employment capacities makes this phenomenon tolerable. It might be different if there were to be stagnation or a recession. But, by maintaining the principle of *hukou* and making it very difficult for residents of rural origin to obtain the urban *hukou*, even if they have been settled there for a long time and legally employed, the government retains the possibility of sending superfluous labour back if the situation requires it.

Increase in retirement: A classic means of opening up jobs for the young is to encourage older employees to retire as soon as they reach retirement age or even to take early retirement. In 1958, just before the Great Leap Forward, some economists, anxious to reduce the urban labour surplus, argued for mandatory retirement at the legal age. They were not heeded and, until 1977, retirement had never been considered either as a duty or even as a right, so that very large numbers of employees were continuing to work after the normal age, either from fear of being accused of lack of revolutionary ardour or for economic reasons (Davis-Friedmann, 1983, p. 25–7). The fact is that a worker obliged to give money every month to his child or children sent to the countryside needed all his wages and could not manage with 70% for his pension. Delaying retirement thus exacerbated the ageing of the wage-earning population. To a large extent, it was composed of people who entered the labour market in the early 1950s. This 'raising of the average age of workers and employees' was made particularly shocking by the 'lowering of the average age of the national population and the population of working age' (Zhao Lukuan, in *RMRB*, 2 March 1982, p. 5), and, above all of course, by the problem of youth unemployment. That is why, in 1978, new legislation on retired people was introduced that was more generous financially and contained relaxed eligibility criteria. In addition to these measures designed to encourage retirement, the authorities have sometimes gone so far as to take authoritarian measures against workers who refuse to retire (for an instance see Radio Guangdong, *FBIS*, 17 March 1982). Cadres – with most to lose, because of the 'perks' that go with their jobs – have been persuaded more tactfully to leave their posts in exchange for obtaining a post as an 'adviser' or keeping their salary and many of their perks. (Different words are used to describe the two types of retirement: *tuixiu* for ordinary workers, *lixiu* for the privileged ones). But the persistence of pleas to take retirement show that some of those involved are still resisting.

Easily the most effective measure has been one that is not authoritarian: it has consisted in allowing any worker or employee taking retirement or early retirement to be replaced by one of his children. This system of *dingti* which had begun to be applied in special cases before the Cultural Revolution and had been re-introduced in 1973, was considerably extended in 1978–9. At a time when over half of young city-dwellers – ordered to the countryside – needed the help of their parents to survive, this method of recruitment was above all aimed at 'guaranteeing family income' (Lin Zili, 1980, p. 182). From the end of 1978 and above all in 1979, it served principally to provide jobs for the millions of 'educated youths' returning from the countryside. The social pressure at the time was such – of children on their parents and of parents on their units – that the units accepted replacements with no heed to either the capacities of the replacements, or the age of those being replaced (ibid). While the retirement age is normally 60 for men and 50 or 55 for women, it is not unusual to see employees leaving 10 years prematurely, on the excuse of health problems that are imaginary or exaggerated. Later rules were made to limit abuses (*Guowuyuan*, vol. 27, no. 374, 1982, p. 885), but, on the whole, the system still survives today. This measure enabled a very large number of urban youths to get jobs. In most cases, it is in fact the desire to help one of their children find a stable job that has pushed elderly wage-earners to retire. Thus when, on 21 February 1983, the authorities in Guizhou decided that from the following 1 March cadres taking retirement would no longer automatically have the right to be replaced by one of their children, there was an enormous wave of retirements in the next ten days by 7,005 cadres, almost all of whom were replaced by one of their children. In many cases, these replacements were only made possible by cheating on residence permits, birth dates, the state of health of those involved and so on.[11]

As we shall see below, the system of *dingti* has had negative effects on productivity, but it is undeniable that it was one of the most effective measures – certainly the most effective in the short term – for opening up urban jobs, and thus for solving the serious unemployment of the late 1970s.

Increase of numbers in schools: In order to reduce the size of the working-age population, the retirement of older workers can be accelerated. But it is also possible to delay the entry of the young by prolonging the schooling of as many of them as possible. The calls to extend education usually refer only to the need to improve the quality of the future labour force. But some authors have been quick to suggest that this extension would also make it possible 'to absorb in the schools a large portion of the young of working age and to reduce the pressure on jobs' (Zhao Lükuan, *RMRB*, 2 March 1982). The educational policy that has been implemented since 1978 does not seem to have taken this potential function of education into account. After ten years of developing the quantity of education, there was a brusque shift to a stress on quality with an élitist distribution of available funds (Bastid, 1984; Rosen, 1985). While the universities admitted 384,000 new entrants in 1984 as against 217,000 in 1976 and 278,000 in 1977 (Rosen 1985, p. 312; *BKNJ*, 1980, p. 538), the senior secondary level has considerably reduced its numbers which, on the national level, fell from 1,869,000 in 1977 to 866,000 in 1983.[12] As we do not have any breakdown by cities and countryside for recent years and as the length of schooling at all levels has been extended, it is not possible to calculate precisely the effect of the new educational policy on urban employment. It is clear, however, that it has not made it possible 'to reduce the pressure on employment'.

Reduction of female employment: A common reaction in the event of unemployment is to encourage women to remain in or return to the home. Chinese experts duly thought of this possible solution,[13] especially as the employment of women on a large scale is a recent phenomenon in China and conflicts with traditional views. Two possibilities have been contemplated; either for women to return full-time to housework (which would have the additional advantage of freeing husbands from this sort of worry), or to arrange part-time work for women, especially those with children (Hooper, 1984). Since the first solution has the disadvantage of drastically reducing family income, a system of 'single income allowance' has been suggested

(*China Reconstructs*, no. 3, 1982, p. 23). Part-time work seemed more acceptable from the viewpoint of family income as well as from the ideological viewpoint: it was rather 'a form of consideration for women and not discrimination against them' (Zhao Lükuan in *RMRB*, 2 March 1982).

Neither of the measures contemplated has been implemented by the authorities, who have apparently hesitated before the financial, social and ideological problems they posed. The National Women's Federation opposed the pure and simple dispatch of women to the home to make way for men, and the Central Committee endorsed this stand (*China Reconstructs*, no. 3, 1982, p. 23). But, on the whole, the government has taken a background position on this problem. It has had simply to abandon in part the ideological, and often unrealistic, struggle that the Maoists had been waging in this area of sex equality and let the spontaneous tendencies of society assert themselves to the full. This ideological retreat certainly made it possible to put an end to economic aberrations like the large-scale assignment of women to heavy labour for which they were unsuited (Lin Zili 1980; *XH* in *SWB*, 31 May 1985), but it also left the field free for traditional discriminatory attitudes towards women. Paradoxically, these have been strengthened by the current economic reforms. Thus, enterprise heads concerned with 'economic efficiency' often avoid employing women because they are likely to ask for maternity leave or time off to look after sick children and, in general, because they do most of the work in the home and are thus less available for productive work (Hooper, 1985; Radio Guangdong in *FBIS*, 6 August 1985). It is too soon to assess the effect of this rampant discrimination. The available figures show that it has not prevented a distinct rise in the proportion of women in the employed population: according to the statistical yearbooks, the ratio rose from 33.1% in 1978 to 36% in 1981 and 36.5% in 1983 (*RMRB*, 1 May 1983 and *SYB*). But the fact that young women make up 60 to 70% of young people waiting for work indicates that this rise is not enough to satisfy a growing demand for jobs on the part of young women city-dwellers, and thus suggests that the ideal of the 'housewife' is less and less widespread.[14] The single-child policy certainly plays a role in this phenomenon, as, no doubt, does the consumerism that has gripped city-dwellers in recent years. In addition, the development of sectors traditionally open to women like light industry and services should open up new job prospects for them. It thus does not seem that the authorities can count on a fall in the rate of female employment to solve the employment problem. At most, they can attempt to limit its spread.

Dispatch of urban youths to the countryside and keeping them there: Even if such was not its main function, the massive dispatch of educated youths to the countryside between 1968 and 1978 made it possible to remove from the 'employment market' for varying lengths of time over half the youths then reaching working age (17 million out of a population that can be estimated at between 30 and 32 million). After the Third Plenum of the Central Committee of the CCP in December 1978, in a period of great unrest caused by educated youth, the government could not or would not oppose the large-scale return of most of the 10 million youths who still remained in the countryside. But it endeavoured to reduce the scale of the problem caused by this return by preventing some categories from returning to the cities.

Thus, with variations from city to city and with numerous exceptions, married educated youths, those who had left before the Cultural Revolution and those who had secured a paid job in the countryside were not permitted to return. The gains in urban jobs obtained in this way were not very large (probably between 500,000 and a million today) and were paid for by a sporadic social unrest which was still continuing in 1985.[15] The authorities also attempted to set up a new system of settlement more acceptable than the previous one. Throughout 1979, the press urged that a large number of young secondary school graduates should still leave for the countryside each year. A figure as great as one million was put forward (*Beijing Information*, 26 November 1979, p. 77). 'Farms' and 'educated youth brigades' were set up in the suburbs of the cities, often by urban enterprises anxious to find a niche for the children of their employees. They enjoyed various sorts of loans and assistance. The settlement grant for educated youths was raised to 500 yuan in 1979, then to 600 in 1980, and a fixed wage was guaranteed, sometimes close to that in the cities.

But this policy was not a success and it has today been totally abandoned. After the disastrous experience of their elders during the ten previous years, urban youths had no desire to leave. The new system no longer has the compulsory power of the old one. It was, moreover, much more expensive and managers preferred to invest in the creation of urban collective enterprises.[16]

Export of labour: If dispatch to the countryside is today no longer a means of removing part of the urban labour force and appears to be an out-dated policy, the export of labour abroad on the contrary is seen by some as a method for the future. China has entered the era of international exchanges and, possessing 'the world's largest manpower resources', it was natural that, like many Third World countries, it should envisage this means of solving the employment problem, while simultaneously earning foreign exchange and stimulating its foreign trade (*QNJY*, 1983, pp. 366–7; Zhao Lükuan, in *RMRB*, 2 March 1982). In China it is a matter of an organized export of contract labour, either the simple loan of workers to foreign companies or the taking over of a specific project by a Chinese team. Experts endeavour to show that the game is worth the candle and that the exploitation of labour by foreign capital, the risks of ideological contamination and flight of qualified personnel, are small compared to the advantage that can be drawn from it for the fulfilment of the 'four modernizations'. This export began in the late 1970s, and since 1980 it has been one of the normal tasks of those responsible for external trade (*QNJY*, 1983, p. 367). Despite that, ideological inhibitions and administrative red tape have prevented the real flowering of a trade that the world economic crisis was already making difficult. In 1981, only 17,000 people were 'exported', and 47,000 in 1984, which is not many for a country that has 600 million inhabitants of working age.[17] It is true that the defenders of this practice have never thought that it might be 'the main means of resolving the employment problem' (*QNJY*, 1983, p. 371). But, for the time being, it can be said that their hopes, modest as they were, have been disappointed. The facilities granted to Chinese citizens to go abroad either as legal migrants or on 'family visits', on 'study travel' or as 'tourists' have as yet had only a very limited effect on relieving the congestion of the urban labour market and increasing the inflow of foreign exchange. Moreover, the international economic situation gives little ground for believing that in the near future there will be any possibility of significant expansion of the export of labour, whether organized or free.

Birth control: Considering that, as we have seen, the root of the employment problem is the gap between population growth since 1949 and economic growth, Chinese experts feel that the radical solution to the problem involves strict birth control (Feng Lanrui, 1981). Birth control has, of course, been rigorously enforced by the authorities and, despite resistance from the population, this policy has achieved major results, above all in the cities. Unfortunately, it is a measure whose effects are only felt in the long term (16–18 years). It can thus have no immediate influence on the demand for jobs.[18]

However, the policy of family planning first began to be effectively implemented in the cities of the early 1970s (despite the very anti-Malthusian language used by the then leaders). The significant drop in the size of the urban cohorts reaching working age will thus begin to be felt in the late 1980s, which will reduce the tension on the employment market.[19]

In short, it can be said that since the late 1970s the government and Chinese experts have contemplated virtually every possible means of reducing the demand for work in the urban sector. These measures are very similar to those being implemented in other countries in the world faced with the problem of unemployment, with the difference that in China the *hukou* system, instituted in the 1950s, established a relationship between cities and countryside that is reminiscent of the one that exists in the western world between industrialized countries and economically peripheral countries. The measures actually implemented have not yet succeeded in solving the problem; at most they are temporarily containing the number of competitors for jobs.

Measures Aimed at Enlarging Employment Capacities

This other aspect of the employment problem is directly linked to the economic reforms put into effect since 1978. At that time the correction of some aspects (denounced as 'irrational') of the former economic system took on an urgent character because of their negative effects on employment and, consequently, on the social and political climate. The concern with enlarging employment capacities in the cities thus precipitated the adoption of major economic reforms.

Reform of the economic structure: The problem of the leadership being to create the maximum number of jobs with the available capital (Yu Guangyuan, 1984, vol. 2, p. 223), a reform was envisaged to give more weight to sectors of activity that are labour-intensive than to those that are capital-intensive. Experts calculated that for an investment of a million *yuan* in state enterprises, 94 jobs could be created in the heavy industrial sector, 257 in the light industrial sector and between 800 and 1,000 in the commerce and services sector (*RMRB*, 16 November; *FBIS*, 20 November 1981). It was for this and other reasons decided to alter the balance among the three sectors, in favour of the latter two. The results, while not spectacular, are clear-cut.

Whereas at the end of 1978 wage-earners in the 'commerce restaurants services' sector representated only 12.4% of the total number of wage-earners, at the end of 1984 they accounted for 13.9%, their numbers having grown by 40%. (If we take into account the 2,820,000 individual workers in this sector, the advance is even more striking.) Conversely, wage-earners in the industrial sector represented only 44.3% of the total in 1984 as against 44.8% in 1978 and their numbers had only increased by 24% (*SYB*, 1985, pp. 26–7). The meaning of this change only becomes apparent if it is recalled that in 1957 the proportions were 33% in industry and 21.1% in commerce. It was thus a matter of fighting against a deep-seated systemic tendency that is to be found in all 'Soviet-type' economies. It was the same with the balance between heavy industry and light industry. It is clear that the powerful heavy industry lobby did everything it could to prevent a significant redistribution of investment funds and labour towards light industry. It is true that the share of light industry in industrial output rose from 43.1% in 1978 to 48.5% in 1983; but it was 51.5% in 1981 (*JJNJ*, 1981–4). Since 1982, the growth of heavy industry has been more rapid than that of light industry despite the contrary targets of the plan (9.9% in 1982, 12.4% in 1983, 14.2% in 1984, as against 5.7%, 8.7% and 13.9% for light industry). The proportion of wage-earners employed in light industry increased slightly between 1980 and 1983, but with some slowing down in the latter year. This proportion rose from 39.1% at the end of 1980 to 40.9% in 1981, 41.3% in 1982 and 41.1% in 1983. Thus the reformers have succeeded in stopping, and even reversing overall, the tendency for the less labour-intensive economic sectors to grow more rapidly. But the results achieved remain modest and can certainly not constitute a radical solution to the employment problem.

Reform of the ownership structure: The employment justification for this reform is the same as the reform of the economic structure: the creation of one job in a collective enterprise costs on average only 2,000 yuan whereas it takes 9 to 10,000 *yuan* in a state enterprise (*RMRB*, 16 November; *FBIS* 20 November 1981). A shift in the balance was thus deemed necessary to favour the collective sector and also the individual, that is private, sector, which costs the state nothing. Considered under the Gang of Four as a shameful survival of capitalism, the private sector is now described as an 'indispensable complement' to the two other forms of ownership of the means of production (*XH*, 28 November; *FBIS*, 25 November 1981). This reform complements the previous one since the collective and individual sectors mainly concern light industry, commerce and services. Their development should help not only to solve the employment problem but also to make the everyday life of city-dwellers easier, thanks to the provision of services and consumer items which had been in desperately short supply since the Cultural Revolution and even since the nationalization of 1958. The development of the collective and individual sectors sought by the reformers has run up against resistance on two fronts; from their rival – the state sector – and from the young job-seekers.

In fact, in many cases, state enterprises found themselves competing directly with the new collective or individual enterprises to obtain raw materials and for outlets. In this case, the cadres usually came down strongly on the side of the state enterprises and used every means available to them to secure the closure of the 'unsettling' enterprises (e.g. *XH* 16 August; *FBIS*, 18 August 1980; *Jiushi Niandai*, no. 9, 1984, pp. 88 – 90). For their part, the young hesitated or declined to take a job that was socially ill viewed, offering few or no social advantages, and less well paid or less stable than a post in the state sector.

Despite these obstacles, the central authorities' perseverance in their policy made possible some revival in the proportion of wage-earners in the collective sector which, after falling from 24.7% in 1965 to 20.9% in 1976, rose to 21.6% in 1978 and 23.8% in 1983. The 1965 rate was only surpassed in 1984 with a leap to 27% (see Table 8.1). But this leap does not reflect a sudden change of direction in the assignment of new employees, if one is to believe the official figures on this (Tables 8.2 and 8.3). According to the figures – which, although 'inflated', do give an order of magnitude – the proportion of wage-earners placed in the collective sector fell slightly between 1979 and 1983, falling from 36% to 31% and stayed practically unchanged in 1984 (Table 8.2). The leap in the collective sector in 1984 was apparently due to the transfer of a significant number of wage-earners from the state sector to the collective sector, as the diminution of the number of employees in the state sector compared to 1983 shows. Given the new assignments in 1984, this loss of almost a million employees must reflect a transfer of at least three million people whom we find in the figures for the collective sector. We are thus dealing here with a not insignificant phenomenon but one that is perhaps not as significant as the figures might lead one to believe. In fact, the collective sector is extremely varied. There exist 'new collectives', which are cooperatives or cooperative groups wholly responsible for their profits and losses. They are particularly valued by the reformers because they cost the state nothing and their employees' zeal is stimulated by the direct relationship between work and pay (*Beijing Information*, 20 August 1979, p. 14). But there are also what some experts call 'bogus collectives' (*jia jiti*), which are created by state enterprises and remain in fact dependent on those enterprises. This is the case with many collective units obliged to recruit the children of wage-earners in the public sector. The same is likely to be true of collectives that have taken on transferred employees. But the enterprises which create them do get something out of it: they get rid of excess employees who reduced their productivity and get them useful jobs in branches of activity that do not require heavy investments. Thus, a hundred or so superfluous employees of a metallurgical factory in Chongqing have been organized to produce food and drinks intended for the staff. Subsequently they were employed in recycling the waste materials of the factory to make hardware products (*XH*, 27 May; *SWB*, 31 May 1985). Transfer to the collective sector involves not only employees, but also the state enterprises themselves. Some small-scale enterprises have been contracted or leased to collectives or even to individuals. It is too soon to predict the future of this type of collective enterprises and the effects they will have on the capacities for employment of the urban economy. For the time being, outside this phenomenon of transfer, it seems that recruitment into the collective sector is stable rather than rising (Table 8.2).

The change has been much sharper in the individual sector which, starting with 150,000 members at the end of 1978, is reported to have reached 3,390,000 at the end of 1984 (Table 8.1). However, the absolute figures remain tiny compared to the whole wage-earning sector. At the end of 1984, the number of individual workers represented only 2.85% of the total number of wage-earning workers whereas it represented 3.44% in 1965. But it is possible that the official figure is an under-estimate (see Appendix). In addition, the advance accelerated in 1983 and especially in 1984, a year when over a million jobs are said to have been created in this sector. This advance reflects a change of mentality that is very perceptible among some of the urban youth who are not afraid to look to the future (*xiang qian kan*), 'looking to money' (*xiang qian kan*), according to a popular pun in China today. In many cases, individual entrepreneurs (*getihu*) earn much more than the average wage. Monthly incomes of several hundred *yuan* are not uncommon. This type of job also makes it possible to escape from the tight system of social control that is found in all work units, more and more young Chinese are seeking this relative independence. Despite the reverse of the coin (lack of guarantee for the future, social security and access to cheap housing, persistence of a degree of social contempt), the individual sector should continue to provide jobs for a not insignificant number of urban youths in the years to come.[20]

On the whole, the measures to readjust the system of ownership of the means of production and the economic structure have had a real effect, beneficial but limited, on the employment situation in the cities. These particular reforms were in line with the whole direction of reform sought by the new leaders to give the Chinese economy the dynamism and efficiency it lacks. Despite the resistance at the base that we have mentioned, a broad consensus among experts and the central leadership exists on the importance of these reforms. It is not the same with the other two measures envisaged for job creation, both of them presented by their advocates as basic solutions.

The reduction of work time: The general reduction of work time has never been part of the reformers' programme, but it has been advocated by orthodox supporters of

Table 8.1
Numbers of Wage-earners and Individual Workers (in 000)

Year		Wage-earners				Individual
	Total	*State*	*%*	*Collective*	*%*	*Workers*
1952	16,030	11,870	98.6	230	1.4	8.830
1957	31,010	21,030	79.0	6,500	21.0	1,040
1965	49,650	37,380	75.3	12,270	24.7	1,710
1978	94,990	74,510	78.4	20,480	21.6	150
1979	99,670	76,930	77.2	22,740	22.8	320
1980	104,440	80,190	76.8	24,250	23.2	910
1981	109,400	83,720	76.5	25,680	23.5	1,130
1982	112,810	86,300	76.5	26,510	23.5	1,470
1983	115,150	87,710	76.2	27,440	23.8	2,310
1984	118,900	86,370	73.0	32,160	27.0	3,390

Source: *SYB*, 1985.

Table 8.2
Distribution of Wage-earning Jobs Created and Persons 'Found Jobs' (1978–84) (in 000)ᵃ

Year	1978	%	1979	%	1980	%	1981	%	1982	%	1983	%	1984	%
Jobs created *state sector:*	2550	66	2420	52	3260	68	3530	71	2580	76	1410	60	-970	
persons found jobs	(3920)	(72)	(5675)	(64)	(5722)	(67)	(5210)	(66)	(4093)	(65)	(3737)	(69)	(4156)	(68)
Jobs created *collective sector:*	1320	34	2260	48	1510	32	1430	29	830	24	930	40	4720	
persons found jobs	(1524)	(28)	(3181)	(36)	(2780)	(33)	(2671)	(34)	(2223)	(35)	(1706)	(31)	(1973)	(32)

Table 8.3
Distribution of Wage-earning and Individual Jobs Created and 'Persons Found Jobs' (1978–84) (in 000)ᵃ

Year	1978	%	1979	%	1980	%	1981	%	1982	%	1983	%	1984	%
Jobs created *wage-earning sector:*	3870	100	4680	96	4770	91	4960	94	3410	91	2340	74	3750	78
persons found jobs	(5444)	(100)	(8856)	(98)	(8502)	(94)	(7881)	(96)	(6316)	(95)	(5443)	(87)	(6129)	(85)
Jobs created *individual sector:*	—	—	170	4	490	9	320	6	340	9	840	26	1080	22
persons found jobs	—	—	(170)	(2)	(498)	(6)	(319)	(4)	(334)	(5)	(840)	(13)	(1086)	(15)
Jobs created *total:*	3870		4850		5260		5280		3750		3180		4830	
persons found jobs	(5444)		(9026)		(9000)		(8200)		(6650)		(6283)		(7215)	

ᵃ The gap between the number of jobs created and that of 'persons found jobs' cannot be explained solely by the replacement of retirees. There is an unexplained 'inflation' of the figures in brackets, perhaps due to multiple counting of temporary and contractual jobs. This problem is dealt with in the Appendix.

Sources: Statistical yearbooks.

the need for full employment in a socialist regime (*Beijing Ribao*, 18 September 1979, p. 3). Since 1979, however, it has been presented as a basic solution only in a distant and vague future, paying homage to the dogma according to which the increase in productivity in a socialist system does not lead to unemployment but creates the conditions for the full development of workers (*JJYJ*, no. 7, 1982, p. 79–80). Supporters of this measure have been content for the time being to propose specific measures designed to increase the possibilities of employment without harming productivity. In 1981, the Ministry of Labour announced that a beginning had been made on introducing a system of 'four teams, three shifts' in the textile industry and that the six-hour day would be introduced for underground miners (*La Chine en Construction*, February, 1981, p. 27). More general measures do not appear to have been introduced since then. These measures have thus certainly created few jobs.

Increasing the growth rate of the economy: If the root of the employment problem is indeed the gap between population growth and economic growth, as the reformers think, then increasing the growth rate of the economy is a basic solution to the problem, complementary to birth control (Feng Lanrui, 1981). For the reformers, the best means of stimulating growth is to increase labour productivity, which implies, for enterprises, the right to dismiss excess or incompetent labour (Feng Lanrui 1983; Lin Zili, 1980, pp. 182–3) and, for the state, the duty to close redundant or loss-making enterprises, in the framework of the readjustment launched in late 1978. But, in the short run, does not the cure risk seriously worsening the disease? 'Some comrades think that there is a contradiction between raising labour productivity and employment', Feng Lanrui recognizes (1983). Given the scale of under-employment in urban enterprises and units, it is in fact hard to see how productivity could be significantly raised without getting rid of large numbers of employees.[21] At the time of the first readjustment, following the Great Leap Forward, the problem was solved by the dismissal of millions of peasants recruited over the previous years and by the dispatch of thousands of urban youths to the countryside. But the situation then was entirely different (see Ma Hong in *RMRB*, 29 December 1981) and, as we have seen, the timid attempts made in this direction since 1979 have run up against resistance from the masses.

Figure 8.1
The Chinese economy's vicious circle

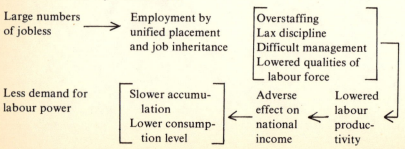

There is thus a contradiction between an ideal long-term solution and its practical short-term effects. The Chinese economy is caught in a vicious circle which experts put schematically, as outlined in Figure 8.1.

How to escape from this vicious circle? The point of attack chosen by the reformers is the job allocation system (Feng Lanrui *et al.*, 1983, p. 13). The basic solution to the inadequacy of the supply of jobs thus involves a reform of this system.

Reform of the Job Allocation System

The system under attack from the reformers was the system of unified labour allocation (*tongbao tongchou*) by labour bureaux at all levels. According to them, this bureaucratic and authoritarian system was harmful to productivity for several reasons: it did not take any account of the preferences of employees, thus reducing their work motivation; neither did it always take account of the requirements of enterprises, but forced them to take on employees who did not meet their needs, leading to over-staffing and lack of skills, essential causes of the low growth of productivity since 1949. It granted all employees in the state sector (and even in the 'large collective' sector) lifelong employment with promotion by seniority: this 'iron rice-bowl' system was detrimental to workers' zeal and incompatible with any degree of job mobility. In recent years, things had become even more 'irrational' with the development of the practice of the replacement of those retiring by their children, whatever their qualifications. This method amounted to the massive replacement of qualified labour by unqualified labour, leading to a significant loss of productivity and work quality. In some places, as we have seen, even the posts of cadres were thus inherited.[22] Moreover this inheritance was not limited to the replacement of one person by another, since enterprises were also encouraged to provide employment to the children of their employees who were still working (e.g. *QNJY*, 1983, p. 153).

For the reformers, this situation had become intolerable. It was necessary 'to break the iron rice-bowl' (*zhai tiefanwan*). In contrast to the 'arranged marriage' between employer and employee, which is what the system amounted to, the reformers proposed 'freedom of marriage and divorce' (Xue Muqiao in *JJGL*, no. 11, 1979 p. 10) i.e. the right for the employee to choose his job and for the employer to select his staff himself and fire them if necessary. As regards 'freedom of marriage', effective measures have been adopted in many municipalities with the creation of a system of examinations. In some cases, these are organized by the enterprises themselves (see *La Chine en Construction*, February 1981, p. 28). In others, labour bureaux organize a single examination for all job-seekers in a single city (see *QNJY*, 1983, pp. 118–19). These apply for a job in a unit that they choose from a list; the result of their application depends on the recruitment criteria of the unit in question and their marks in the examination. If they are rejected, they can apply to another unit, until all the positions are filled. This is a freedom that is still tightly controlled since the number and type of positions offered in each unit are decided by negotiations between the unit and the municipal labour bureau and the final appointment is always the province of this latter. Furthermore this system does not solve the problem of the numerous rejects.[23]

Despite these shortcomings, 'freedom of marriage' between employers and employees has certainly advanced. 'Freedom of divorce', on the other hand, has met with strong resistance. The proposals for the liberalization and decentralization of dismissals envisaged supervision by higher bodies, notably labour bureaux, and workers' organizations (trade unions and workers' congresses). They still provoked strong criticism from those who felt that dismissing a worker was incompatible with socialism and the socialist solution to the problem lay in reducing working hours and following a low wage policy, so as to share the available work (*Beijing Ribao*, 10 January, 1979). They also caused great concern among workers who were afraid of finding themselves at the mercy of heads of enterprises. The *Workers' Daily* echoed this concern by publishing a particularly sharp reader's letter; but it tried to defuse it by adding a reply by the well known economist Yu Guangyuan (*Gongren Ribao*, 10 January in *FBIS*, 23 January 1981). Yu assured readers that the right to dismissal for disciplinary reasons could only be granted to heads of enterprises on two conditions: that a powerful trade union existed, capable of defending workers' interests against arbitrary decisions and that workers' congresses had the power to supervise and discuss these matters. In addition, any employee dismissed should be able to enjoy social security and help from a job agency. He stressed the need for prudence in carrying out this reform. This debate concerned dismissals for serious misconduct or incompetence. In the case of dismissals for economic reasons, the reformers also envisaged a system of social insurance to look after dismissed workers, the help of a job agency and retraining courses (see Lin Zili, 1980, p. 192).

Let us say straightaway that this reform has never been implemented. None of the conditions necessary for its realization exists today. Neither the trade unions nor the workers' congresses are empowered to oppose the arbitrariness of heads of enterprises. As for the system of unemployment insurance, it has remained no more than a proposal. The reformers recognize that they have not succeeded in 'breaking the iron rice-bowl', but they are sticking to their views and renew their proposals when the climate is favourable. Thus during the summer of 1985, Li Chengrui declared that there should be no hesitation in declaring enterprises that could no longer pay their debts bankrupt and that workers who thus lost their jobs should receive social assistance. The system he proposed was based on western ones: full pay for a period, then reduced pay, then the minimum wage; the funds would come from contributions paid by the employer and the employee. Since his proposal guaranteed a minimum wage for all, Li felt that he too was a defender of the 'iron rice-bowl'; but on condition that the amount of rice in the bowl varied depending on whether one worked well, averagely or not at all (*RMRB*, 26 July; *FBIS*, 9 August 1985).

Two weeks later another writer called for the creation of a true employment market so as to meet the needs of enterprises to take on and lay off labour according to the variations in the volume and type of their output. The first condition for the establishment of this market was, according to the writer, to solve the problem of 'understanding', i.e. explaining that it did not contradict the public ownership of the means of production and that it did not transform labour into a commodity (*Guangring Ribao*, 10 August; *FBIS*, 21 August 1985). A month later, the *People's Daily* asked that the increase in the number of jobs be subordinated to raising productivity (*RMRB*, 9 September; *FBIS*, 20 September 1985).

The very fact that these proposals are being made proves that, for the time being, the reformers have not succeeded in overthrowing the stronghold represented by the 'iron rice-bowl'.[24] The entrenched supporters of 'sharing the cake in small parts' strong in popular support, will not be easily dislodged. Nevertheless, the reformers are not content with an interminable and ineffective siege. They have used what Chevrier (1985) calls the 'bypass strategy' so as to create, around the stronghold, a space in which a different logic prevails.

In fact, one of the criticisms made of the 'unified allocation' system was its monopoly character. For the heads of enterprises, the only way to escape this monopoly was to recruit peasants outside the plan. Urban youths had no choice but to wait until they were allocated by the labour bureaux. That is why the reformers have not simply sought to improve the normal recruitment system by introducing examinations, but have tried to create new means of access to jobs outside the area covered by the labour bureaux. Thus young workers have been encouraged to help themselves by creating individual private enterprises or by associating together to set up cooperatives with their own funds. Again, units of the state sector have been invited to set up collectively owned enterprises to slot in the children of their staff. Loans and tax holidays for several years have been granted to these new types of enterprise that have made it possible to mop up a significant proportion of youths awaiting work. In addition, in order to help the young unemployed and avoid them being left to their own devices, the authorities have invented a flexible and multi-functional structure: the work and service companies (*laodong fuwu gongsi*). These companies can be created by other units than the labour bureaux. At the end of 1982, a third of them came under these bureaux (essentially at the base level: neighbourhood, district), and two-thirds were managed by enterprises, departments, schools and even units of the army (*JJNJ*, 1984, pp. iv–54). Their role is to set up collective enterprises to take on unemployed youths, organize pre-vocational training courses and offer temporary jobs to those who do not yet have any permanent job. These companies are now part of everyday life in Chinese cities. Their number rose from 800 at the end of 1979 to over 20,000 at the end of 1983. They have served to stimulate the development of small collective enterprises and absorb part of the urban labour force. At the end of 1983, three million young people were working in units coming under these companies whose turnover exceeded ten billion *yuan* (*JJNJ*, 1984, iv–54).[25] In addition, they were giving a pre-vocational training to 800,000 young people and had enabled 800,000 others to find temporary jobs in 1983. By controlling, at least partly, the market for temporary labour, they have probably also helped to limit the recruitment of peasants. It is in any case one of the functions that experts hoped to see them assume (*QNJY*, 1983, p. 359). In 1983, the reformers launched a new attack on the stronghold by introducing a new system of recruitment through fixed-term contracts. According to the Minister of Labour and Personnel, this system should, eventually, replace the 'iron rice-bowl' (*China Daily*, 3 February 1983, p. 1). But the number of people recruited in this way is still modest (650,000 in June 1984, 2,140,000 at the end of August 1985 in the state sector where most of the contract workers are to be found) (*China Daily*, 20 June 1984; *XH*, 26 September; *SWB*, 1

October 1985), and these are only new entrants into the labour market. For the time being, the contract system seems rather to be an improvement of temporary recruitment than a substitute for permanent recruitment; but it is still too soon to say what role it may play in future.[26]

The system of job allocation has not undergone the radical reform advocated by some economists, but it has changed in two directions; in the state sector, while the allocation of labour remains part of the planning process, freedom of choice for employer and employee have made some progress within this framework. Nevertheless, labour mobility remains very limited. By contrast, in the private sector (individual enterprises and cooperatives) and in the mixed sector (various companies created jointly by state or collective enterprises and individuals), freedom of choice and mobility are much greater. They remain, however, limited by administrative regulations such as the one that forbids individual entrepreneurs to recruit more than two employees and five apprentices.[27] There are not yet very many people involved in these sectors but they are expanding all the time and their existence introduces an element of flexibility that influences the state sector. Thus, employees in conflict with the managers of their unit or who feel themselves underemployed and underpaid can resign and find another job. This phenomenon, which is not uncommon today, was unthinkable before 1978. It cannot but be beneficial to the dynamism of the economy.

Present Situation and Prospects

The result of the various measures taken to resolve the employment problem is not easy to assess precisely because the figures supplied by the authorities are inconsistent. As we have already observed about Tables 8.2 and 8.3, the statistics on the number of jobs provided cannot be used as they are. Those concerning people waiting for work are equally difficult to use. Thus, the figures provided for 1979, when unemployment was at its peak range from 6 to 10, to 15, to 20 million.[28] It may be that these differences are to be explained by the time of year when the counts were taken (there are no 'seasonally adjusted figures') and by the criteria used (minimum length of time spent waiting to be considered as 'without employment', whether those temporarily employed are included or not). It seems that the figure of 20 million provided by the Labour Bureau was revised downwards by the Statistical Bureau for unspecified reasons.[29] It is possible that, as in many countries, the authorities demanded that, for reasons of prestige, very narrow definitions be used. It is known that Chinese experts are not unanimous about the criteria used in the 1982 census (*QNJY*, 1983, p. 44).

The figures put forward today on the supply and demand for jobs in the urban sector are shown in Table 8.4.

It may be wondered, seeing the figures for 'persons without employment at year end' why employment has been seen as one of the most serious problems facing the new regime in the post-Maoist era. In fact the relative lowness of these figures is the corollary of the number of those found jobs. But it is quite obvious that these figures are heavily inflated (see Table 8.3 and Appendix). There is also the question of the

Table 8.4
Supply and Demand for Urban Jobs (1978–83) (in millions)

Year	A^a Persons for whom a job had to be found	B^b Persons found jobs	C Persons without employment at year end	D^c Proportion of those without jobs/working-age population
1978	11.31	6*	5.31	5.3% (5.3%)
1979	15.38	9.02	6.36	5.5% (6.0%)
1980	13.09	9	4.09	3.6% (3.7%)
1981	11.05	8*	3.05	2.6% (2.7%)
1982	(9.69)	6.65	3.04	2.6% (2.6%)
1983	(8.99)	6.28	2.71	— (2.3%)

(N.B. The number of persons waiting for employment provided by the census of 1 July 1982 was 3.4 million, a proportion of 3.75% of the non-agricultural working-age population of cities and townships.)

Sources: *Beijing Information*, 27 September 1982, p. 19, and 28 March 1983, p. 23; *BKNJ* 1983 and 1984.

a We have calculated the figures in brackets from columns B and C.
b The figures marked * are markedly different from those provided by the statistical yearbooks.
c Our sources do not give the definition of working-age population. We have added in brackets the percentage of the workless in the working-age population calculated as the sum of all wage-earners, urban individual workers and young people waiting for work. This definition is used, for example, in *RMRB*, 9 September 1985 (*FBIS*, 18 September 1985, p. K9). *Beijing Information* refers without further explanation to an even larger population, whereas our definition is already too broad as a base from which to calculate the proportion of the unemployed among only urban workers. Some wage-earners do not live in the cities. The proportion of wage-earners working in the countryside has never, so far as we are aware, been calculated, but it is not impossible that it is as high as 20–25%. Therefore, the total wage-earning population working in the cities is markedly smaller than the total featured in this table. The proportions in brackets are thus under-estimates.

reliability of the figures on persons for whom a job had to be found. We do not know whether they have been obtained simply by the addition of columns C and B (in which case they are almost useless), or whether, on the contrary, they formed the starting point for the subtraction that results in the total of persons without employment at year end. In this case, we would like to know how they have been calculated and, for example, why the figure of 20 million for 1979 has been reduced to 15 million. A total of 20 million, not of unemployed but of persons for whom a job had to be found, does not seem excessive. It would include the 2 million persons allocated by the state (rural people, graduates, demobilized soldiers and rehabilitated cadres) (*Beijing Information*, 28 March 1983, p. 25), plus the 5 million without employment in 1978 (including, probably, a good proportion of the educated youths who had returned several months or several years previously), as well as the 9 or 10 million remaining in the countryside at the end of 1978 and, finally, the 3 or 4 million young people leaving secondary school that year. If this figure is approximately accurate, and even if we accept the inflated figure of 9 million jobs provided, there would remain 11 million without employment at year end, plus more than 2 million persons placed temporarily (*Beijing Information*, 27 September 1982, p. 20 and Yu Guangyuan 1984 p. 213), for an unemployment rate of 10% or 11.5% depending on whether the temporarily employed are included or not, and of 8.3% if the two million or so educated youths who had not yet returned from the countryside at the end of 1979 are excluded. We are not claiming that these rates are the real rates; but they are certainly closer to them than the official rates.

Even the results of the 1982 census concerning the number of persons waiting for employment seem to us to under-estimate the true situation. The census pre-tests had given very different results. According to these sample surveys (*dianxing diaocha*), the unemployment rate was 15% if only those with a permanent or individual job were counted as employed, 9% if those with a temporary job provided by units other than the neighbourhood work and service companies were also included and 6% if all temporary jobs were included (*Renkou Yanjiu*, no. 2, 1982, p. 36). It is possible that this survey was not carried out on a sufficiently representative sample. It does, however, point to the importance of temporary work in the economic life of Chinese cities. Informal surveys carried out in China have shown that temporary jobs are often sporadic: standing in for sick employees for one or a few days or supplementing the permanent workforce for urgent and irregular work. There are many young people who left secondary school one, two, three or more years ago who are scraping a living as best they can in this way with occasional ill-paid petty jobs (1 *yuan* a day in 1981; 1.20 *yuan* in 1984; 1.50 *yuan* in 1985), while waiting to find a permanent job. Although they are still dependent on their parents for housing and, partly, for food and clothing, they are not counted in the statistics as without employment. It is true that other young people, many fewer it seems, work in the black economy in the private sector, but do not register so as to preserve their chances of obtaining a permanent job. These, on the other hand, must be counted as young people waiting for employment, even if what they earn is enough for them to live on.

Generally speaking, our surveys, confirmed by official sources,[30] show that most general secondary school graduates have to wait from a few months to up to several years before obtaining a permanent job. During this period, the young unemployed are rarely left to their own devices: the neighbourhood organizations and the work and service companies try to find them temporary jobs or pre-vocational training. In this case we are dealing with primary unemployment, affecting only young people coming out of the education system. Unemployment after a period of permanent employment seems for the present to be much rarer. In the state sector, the 'iron rice-bowl' means the continued payment of wages to workers and employees temporarily outside the production process because of redundancies or closure of enterprises. Conversely, in the cooperative and individual sectors, financial responsibility might well lead to failures. Although the Vice-minister of Labour has recognized that, in these sectors, 'hundreds of thousands of people must be re-employed each year' (Radio Beijing, 28 April in *SWB*, 4 May 1985), we lack detailed information on this phenomenon. The authorities obviously have an interest in avoiding a public acknowledgement of unemployment that could not be classified as primary and more like structural unemployment in capitalist countries. That is surely one of the obstacles standing in the way of the suppression of the 'iron rice-bowl'. However, if a political and social consensus could be found on this, the resources of Marxist–Leninist casuistry would certainly be wheeled in to justify it. The ideological factor thus seems secondary, but it might serve as a supplementary weapon to opponents of this reform.

Whatever the exact scale of unemployment, it is clear that the authorities have so far succeeded in containing it within politically tolerable limits. The ten million or so educated youths who have returned to the cities have been absorbed as best they can be, despite the arrival of very large cohorts in the early 1980s. The explosive situation of 1979 has thus been defused, at the price, it is true, of a rather slow growth in productivity and a latent discontent among many young people dissatisfied with their jobs. But the problem has not been solved. According to official estimates, there is still a hardcore remainder of two or three million unemployed and every year six million jobs have to be found. If temporary employees are included, the leadership thus regularly have to find jobs for ten million people in the urban sector – no small problem. For the time being, it seems that the forecasts of the Sixth Plan in the area of job creation will be achieved or almost achieved. It is true that the goal of 29 million people to be found jobs only aims to solve the problem 'overall'. Other estimates spoke of more than 30 million jobs to be found (Zhuang Qidong and Sun Keliang, 1981). Table 8.5 compares the forecasts with the jobs actually provided according to the statistical yearbooks. The slight gap is perhaps due to under-estimating figures for the individual sector. In the absence of contrary reasons, we have accepted the number of retirements used in the forecasts. This number seems to be consistent with the results of the census if account is taken of the early retirements occurring today, but on a much smaller scale than in 1979–80.

From the demographic angle things should begin to improve by the end of the current decade. But as visible unemployment disappears, it is likely that hidden unemployment will appear. The fact is that, on the one hand, rural pressure on the urban job market can only increase from now to the end of the century since 100

Table 8.5
Targets of the Sixth Plan for Employment and Achievement, Year end 1984 (in millions)

Forecasts 1981–5		Average over 4 years (1981–4)		Jobs provided (1981–4)	
New jobs: state sector:	11	8.8		6.18	
New jobs: collective sector:	11	8.8	} 18.8	7.91	} 16.67
New jobs: individual sector:	1.5	1.2		2.58	
Replacement of retirees:	5.5	4.4		4.4*	
Total	29	23.2		21.07*	

* Estimate

Sources: *RMRB*, 13 December 1982 (*FBIS*, 20 December 1982, p. K36), and *TJZY*, 1985.

million peasants will have to find non-agricultural employment between now and then (*XH*, 13 March; *FBIS* 16 March 1984, pp. K17–18). On the other hand, if the reformers are still in power, they will certainly endeavour to use the demographic breathing space to raise productivity and hence reduce over-manning. But this was already estimated at about 20% in 1985 and it can only grow as a consequence of the technological modernization of enterprises.[31]

In these conditions, urban employment is likely to remain a delicate problem for the Chinese leaders and a subject of concern for the people for many years.[32] Since 1978, it has acted as both a stimulus for some reforms and an obstacle for others, an obstacle still unsurmounted today. In fact the shift from an extensive development logic to an intensive one which requires problems of profitability to be taken into account, does not happen without creating difficulties in the field of employment. It would be interesting, in this perspective, to compare the Chinese experience with that of Hungary or Yugoslavia. In China, the problem has been aggravated by the massive return of educated youths – itself the consequence of a shift from one policy to another – and, more fundamentally, by the demographic boom of the 1950s and 1960s. What was China's strength in the Maoist conception ('Six hundred million, that is our strength!') has become with the change of policy a terrible burden, dragging the economy in a vicious circle from which it has still not escaped.

But the coming improvement in the demographic situation in the cities will not solve every problem. Even if the new leaders succeed in controlling rural immigration – and it is not at all certain that they will[33] – the contradiction between their will to modernize and the constraints of their politico–economic system threatens to prevent the realization of reforms that they see as essential. Thus, their proposal to 'break the iron rice-bowl' and create a true labour market would require profound socio–political changes to become reality. This reform would in particular call into question the system whereby the individual is looked after and cared for by his unit; this is one of the pillars of present urban society. It would also require the appearance of a new type of relationship between employees and management within enterprises. Yu Guangyuan has recognized that reform would not be acceptable without the introduction of a trade union counter-power and effective legal rights. But the historical examples, including that of Poland, show that a workers' state cannot tolerate an autonomous workers' power, even a limited one, and that individual or group legal rights count for little in the face of the decisions of representatives of the government. On the other hand, it is difficult to see what the reformers could offer workers and employees in exchange for their lost job security. In these conditions, the prevailing social harmony that reigns between the working class, 'mistress of the country', and the regime might very well be jeopardized by the generalization of jobs without security. Moreover, unrest here and there among labour so far has generally been the work of temporary or contract workers.[34] On the other hand, it is obvious that the modernization of China demands improved economic efficiency. The 'rationalization' of the employment situation thus constitutes a real challenge for the Chinese reformers in their programme of modernization. Novel methods to respond to this challenge have yet to be discovered.

Notes

1. 'Workers in the new China are not worried about unemployment!', *Xinhua*, 30 April 1976.
2. See, particularly, Feng Lanrui and Zhao Lükuan, 1982, pp. 123–38; 'Le problème de l'emploi en Chine', *La Chine en Construction*, February 1981, pp. 25–9; 'Un célèbre économiste parle du problème de l'emploi', *Beijing Information*, no. 33, 20 August 1979, pp. 13–15.
3. According to *RMRB*, 25 January 1978, some ten million educated youths remained in the countryside at the end of 1977. We estimate that departures and returns in 1978 must more or less have balanced each other out.
4. *Guowuyuan* vol. 27, no. 374, pp. 885–6; Radio Jiangxi, 14 October 1980 (*FBIS*, 17 October 1980); Radio Guandong, 12 September 1981 (*SWB*, 25 September 1981); Radio Yunnan, 4 January 1982 (*FBIS*, 8 January 1982); Radio Shaanxi, 28 December 1981 (*FBIS*, 8 January 1982).
5. *RMRB*, 23 June 1982; Radio Zhengzhou, 11 July 1982 (*FBIS*, 20 July 1982); Radio Hainan, 6 August 1983 (*SWB, 10 August 1983); Yangcheng Wanbao*, 3 August 1982 (*FBIS*, 13 August 1982).
6. The introduction of compulsory military service may be a response to this crisis of recruitment. See *AFP*, 30 October 1985 and *XH*, 29 October 1985 (*SWB*, 1 November 1985).
7. See for example, the interview with Yu Qiuli distributed by *XH* 30 March 1985 (*FBIS*, 31 March 1983).
8. Interview with Feng Lanrui, 24 August 1985.
9. See Appendix. The real difference is however not so high because the change in the criteria used to define townships makes comparison impossible. A number of peasants recruited in formerly rural enterprises are today classified as employed by township enterprises.
10. The 'Provisional regulations of the Ministry of Public Security on the control of short-stay residents in towns and villages', issued on 13 July 1985, are an attempt to deal with the problems of control posed by the increase in rural–urban exchanges. See *XH*, 7 September 1985 (*FBIS*, 12 September 1985).
11. See *RMRB*, 6 February 1984, p. 4; also Davis-Friedmann, 1983, p. 27. This author gives an average of 80% of retirees replaced by one of their children in the eight factories she visited.
12. These figures include general and technical education; Rosen, 1985, p. 320.
13. Particularly Lin Zili, 1980, p. 193; Zhao Lükuan, *RMRB*, 2 March 1982; Zhuang Qidong and Sun Keliang 1981, C4.
14. Zhuang Qidong and Sun Keliang, 1981, p. C/5; *QNJY*, 1983, p. 329; *Gongren Ribao*, 7 March 1982, p. 1. The 1982 census gives a rate of 53.36% of women among youths 'waiting for work' and a proportion of 40.8% of female labour in the non-agricultural sector in cities and townships. The use, for the census data on employment, of categories and criteria quite different from those used by the statistical yearbooks prevents any comparison between the two series of figures.
15. For instance, the week-long sit-in by young people from Beijing sent to Shanxi in 1968, who, 17 years later, had still not been permitted to return home (*XH*, 29 April 1985 and 4 May 1985).
16. It was calculated in a region of Sichuan that it took 1,900 *yuan* to create one job in a farm for educated youths and only 500 in a collective township enterprise (*Gongren Ribao*, 30 July 1980).

17. *JJRB*, 20 July 1985 (*FBIS*, 1 August 1985). The holding of a national conference on this subject in June 1985 shows however that the government is seeking to improve results in this area (*XH*, 13 June 1985 in *FBIS*, 19 June 1985).

18. In the short term, however, it may have had a beneficial influence on the supply of jobs in so far as the savings achieved by the reduction in the number of children to be fed, cared for and educated can be invested in new jobs (*RMRB*, 19 August 1980 in *FBIS*, 4 September 1980, p. L26).

19. According to the statistical yearbooks, the urban cohorts were regularly below 3 million after 1972 and even below 2.5 million from 1974–9.

20. However, this sector is at the mercy of even the least recovery of power by conservatives, as is shown by the fall in the number of *getihu* in Beijing during the few months of intense 'struggle against spiritual pollution' (*RMRB*, 20 May 1984).

21. There is, however, one way of improving the quality of labour and hence productivity without harming employment: this is the development of education and especially vocational education, which all the experts call for. The undeniable improvements in the quality of education certainly have benefical effects on labour productivity; but these are probably limited by the fact that gains in quality have as their counterpart reductions in quantity. In addition, while vocational secondary education is experiencing a renaissance today, its cost prevents any spectacular progress. See Bastid (1984) and Rosen (1985).

22. See, for example, Xue Muqiao in *Beijing Ribao*, 18 July 1979, and the State Council decree no. 137 in *Guo wuyuan*, no. 415, 20 November 1983, p. 931. See also Note 11 above.

23. Thus, in Tianjin in 1983, of 46,000 youths who passed the recruitment examination, only 13,303 were selected (*JJNJ*, 1984Y, p. iv–55).

24. We must be careful here not to confuse what the reformers say they want to do and what they are actually doing. Thus, we feel it is quite premature to say 'now that the "iron rice-bowl" has been broken'; See Saich, 1984, p. 155. The same is true of the alleged rescinding of the *dingti* system, to which D. Davis-Friedmann refers in an otherwise excellent article (1985b, p. 184).

25. The yearbook (*BKNJ 1984*) gives a figure of 3,940,000 youths employed at the end of 1983.

26. In fact contract workers enjoy social and political advantages superior to those of temporary workers (*Zhongguo Xinwenshe*, 21 February; *FBIS*, 22 February 1983).

27. Decision of 17 October 1981 on employment (*XH*, 23 November, in *FBIS*, 23 November 1981). It is true that in practice this regulation is often ignored or side-stepped.

28. *Beijing Information*, 27 September 1982 and 28 March 1983; *QNJY* 1983, p. 4; *Kyodo*, 11 October, *SWB*, 13 October 1979.

29. Interview with Feng Lanrui, 24 August 1985.

30. Until 1983 the municipal and provincial authorities quite regularly published data on the maximum waiting time in their area. This generally varied from two to four years. See for example, Radio Hunan, 24 November 1981 and Radio Xinjiang, 25 November 1981 (*FBIS*, 2 December 1981); Radio Nei Monggol, 13 December 1981 (*FBIS*, 15 December 1981); *Beijing Review*, no. 39, 1982, p. 20, and *China Reconstructs*, no. 6, 1983, p. 33.

31. Interview with Feng Lanrui, 24 August 1985.

32. . . . as well as being an interesting object for study for foreign researchers. Among the specialized articles on this subject, see especially: White, 1982, Emerson 1983 and Anderson, 1984.

33. Nationally, the demographic situation as regards employment will not improve before the beginning of the 21st Century. According to the data in the 1982 census, between now and 2000, 400 million young people will enter the employment market whereas only 150 million old people will retire. Thus 250 million jobs will have to be created, essentially for young rural people. There is thus likely to be heavy pressure by the countryside on the cities between now and the end of the century.

34. For a recent example of a demonstration organized by temporary workers in Tianjian, see *Le Monde*, 23–24 June 1985, p. 3; for an example of riots caused by the closure of factories, see White, 1982, p. 626.

Appendix

Remarks on Employment Policy (1966–84)
Michel Cartier

Some have thought that the policy of 'departures for the countryside' was a response to an economic necessity. The arrival at working age of young city-dwellers born in the 1950s would have exceeded the capacities of the industrial and service sectors to absorb them; the unexpected return of the 'educated youths', the result not of a political decision but of a relaxation of controls, would have been bound to create a crisis situation. Moreover this interpretation seemed to be confirmed by the pessimism of Chinese demographers themselves about a situation that was bound to worsen in the 1980s because of the imminent arrival on the labour market of the adolescents born in the mid-1960s. The recent publication of retrospective statistical series leads us to question the strictly demographic interpretation which was so easily accepted. It is necessary to go back and analyse employment policy in the light of the detailed information that is now available.

The number of wage-earning jobs created – which can be deduced by calculating for each year the difference between its total of wage-earning jobs from those in the previous year – affects above all the urban population. A detailed study of the way in which new jobs have been allocated would presuppose being able to compare year by year the number of these new jobs with the proportion of the population reaching the legal working age (18), after deducting the number of retirements (so as to compare 'job offers' with 'job-seekers').

Not all this information is available and we must be satisfied for the present with four independent series: 1) age distribution of the urban population; 2) urban births; 3) jobs created; and 4) age distribution in non-agricultural jobs at the time of the 1982 census. The attempted reconstruction that follows is limited to the period between the beginning of the Cultural Revolution (1966) and the end of the 1970s, a key period for understanding how things have developed in recent years. It is almost impossible to reconstruct the evolution over the previous 15 years because of the considerable upheavals brought about both by the socialist transformation of industry and commerce and by the disorders of the Great Leap Forward. Table 8.6 makes it possible to grasp a particularly complex reality.

Table 8.6
Urban Demography and New Jobs (1966–80)

Year	Urban-dwellers I	Urban births II	New jobs III
1966	2,971,000		2,330,000
1967	3,002,000		1,010,000
1968	3,601,000		1,990,000
1969	3,481,000		2,100,000
1970	3,943,000		5,020,000
1971	4,072,000		5,710,000
1972	4,480,000	3,500,000	3,470,000
1973	4,723,000	3,370,000	2,230,000
1974	4,445,000	3,480,000	3,140,000
1975	4,638,000	4,420,000	5,470,000
1976	4,966,000	3,600,000	4,750,000
1977	3,811,000	3,640,000	4,350,000
1978	3,994,000	3,660,000	3,870,000
1979	3,173,000	2,750,000	4,680,000
1980	3,453,000	4,130,000	4,770,000

Sources: *Statistical Yearbook of China 1984* and the 1982 Population Census. The totals of urban-dwellers aged 18 at various dates are obtained by combining the age pyramids of cities and townships; urban births are calculated by applying the urban birth rates to the urban populations of the corresponding year. Thus the total of urban residents in 1982 reaching the age of 18 during the year concerned was compared with the number of urban births 18 years earlier. It should be noted, however, that the two series do not wholly coincide.

Table 8.6 can be summarized as follows.

Table 8.7
Comparison of Jobs Created and New Entrants (1966–80)
(in 000s)

Period	Cumulative total I	Cumulative births II	Jobs created III	Number engaged in non-agricultural activities IV
1966–70	16,860		12,450	19,600
1971–75	22,375	(18,300)	20,020	26,200
1976–80	49,365	17,800	22,420	22,300

Comparison of these four separate series suggests a number of observations. Comparison of columns I and II reveals the moderate character of peasant immigration. Given the likelihood of survival (over 90%), the young born in the cities surely comprised the vast majority of the urban totals in 1982. The number of new jobs is definitely lower than the total of young reaching the age of 18 during the first years of the Cultural Revolution (1966–9). After 1970, on the other hand, job supply was much higher than the specifically urban demand. Finally, inasmuch as the two sets of figures can be compared (census definitions are broader than those used in the yearbook) comparison of columns III and IV confirms that entry into the working population does not necessarily coincide with the legal age. The difference between the number of new jobs and the totals of wage-earners entering theoretically during the corresponding period is particularly great during the first half of the Cultural Revolution: 19.6 million wage-earners in 1982 aged 30–34 for 12.5 million jobs created between 1966 and 1970. There is a marked gap for the 25–29 age group: 20 million new jobs for 26 million wage-earners. Conversely, the two figures are very close for the 20–24 age group: 22.3 and 22.4 million. The gap between the two series obviously reflects a delay in entry into the wage-earning population as a result of the crisis situation of the late 1970s. It might also be partly explained by the fact that the non-agricultural jobs counted in the 1982 census are more numerous than the wage-earning jobs in the statistical yearbooks.

To conclude, it is thus quite clear that the dispatch of the 'educated youths' to the countryside did not reflect an economic necessity but was rather the outcome of a political decision to encourage the mixing of labour from different parts of the country.

The Treatment of Unemployment

It is well known that the Chinese authorities have taken pride in practically abolishing unemployment and having provided jobs for most of the 'youths waiting for work'. According to the yearbooks, the total number of people who secured a wage-earning job between 1977 and 1984 was over 57 million, an annual average of over 7 million. Compared to the cumulative total of the urban cohorts reaching the age of 18 – some 35 million people – this number of jobs was more than enough to solve the problem of urban under-employment, even though the urban population continued to grow at the same time through immigration. The yearbooks make it possible to go beyond this simple observation: in fact they provide the data for a double entry table giving the breakdown of new wage-earners by categories of origin and by destination.

This table in fact raises far more questions than it answers since, in general, the total of wage-earners that can be deduced from it in no way corresponds to the figures provided by the yearbooks. The two tables below make it possible to measure the degree of divergence between the information on the increase in the total numbers of wage-earners and those relating to young people supposed to have secured a job between 1977 and 1984.

Visibly the shortfall in jobs provided for 'educated youths' is the counterpart of a

Table 8.8
New wage-earners in Categories of Origin and Destination (in 000)

Category	1977	1978	1979	1980	1981	1982	1983	1984
Waiting for work	2,263	1,597	4,995	5,340	5,343	4,081	4,065	4,497
Educated youths	840	1,152	1,890	885				
Diploma holders	499	377	334	800	1,070	1,174	934	817
Young rural people	1,206	1,484	708	1,274	920	660	682	1,230
Various	396	834	1,099	701	858	735	602	671
Destination								
State enterprises	?	3,920	5,675	5,722	5,210	4,093	3,737	4,015
Cooperatives	?	1,524	3,181	2,780	2,671	2,223	1,706	1,973
Individual sector			170	498	319	334	840	1,086
Total	*5,204*	*5,444*	*9,026*	*9,000*	*8,200*	*6,650*	*6,283*	*7,215*

Table 8.9
Summary by Origins of Job-seekers and Jobs Provided Between 1977 and 1984 (in 000)

Category	Job seekers	Jobs provided
Educated youths	c. 10,000	4,700
Awaiting work	35,600[a]	32,200
Diploma holders	4,760	6,000
Young rural people	121,000[a]	9,400
Various	—	5,900

[a] These figures represent the total of the eight cohorts reaching 18 between 1977 and 1984, and thus include some diploma holders.

Table 8.10
Summary by Destinations of Jobs Provided Between 1978 and 1984 (in 000)

Sector	Jobs provided	Increase in total numbers
State enterprise	32,500	14,800
Collective sector	16,100	13,000
Private sector	3,200	3,200

possible excess of jobs assigned to young unemployed. The final rate of employment for 25–29 year-olds is 98.5% men but only 88% for women. We know indeed that after 1980 no distinction was made between these two categories. The gap gives the impression that the eradication of unemployment was long and difficult while rural immigration in no way diminished.

We should note the striking difference between the number of jobs provided and the increase in the total number of wage-earners: 31 million against 51 million. This phenomenon relates essentially to the nationalized sector which grew by only 14.8 million units whereas the statistics indicate 32.5 million jobs provided. Of course retirements and deaths have to be included in our reconstruction of the movement of the working population. But, if we refer to the results of the census the number of non-agricultural workers able to activate their right to retirement (men reaching 60 and women 50 to 55) did not exceed 900,000 a year. The total of the retired was 11.5 million in mid-1982. It is thus difficult to accept that, even taking account of early retirements, more than 10 million people left their jobs during the period. There is thus a gap, difficult to explain, of some 12 million jobs. It is very likely that this curious phenomenon is due to a counting of temporary jobs plus a significant under-estimate of the private sector.

9 Urban Housing Policy after Mao

Richard Kirkby

Forty-odd years ago, the Chinese Communist Party found itself on the threshold of nationwide power. That the Party's leaders viewed their new, urban-centred tasks with trepidation was no secret (Mao, 1961, pp. 361–75). They were ill prepared for their new role as arbiters of industrial and commercial complexities in the great cities. They were fearful of dealing with urban class relationships which bore scant resemblance to those which had become familiar, and manageable, in the countryside. And they had in the long years of rural exile given next to no thought to the question of the city as a physical and spatial entity.

In many ways, the sheer chaos of the newly liberated cities, and the evident remedies immediately required, hindered the emergence of any grand philosophy of urbanism for the new age. The response demanded by the vast squatter areas, the miles of stagnant ditches, and the millions of tons of street debris of decades of national decay, was self-evident. On the other hand, even more obvious was the necessity of restoring and mobilizing the machinery of production, circulation and communication; it was these over-riding tasks that figured long in the communist programme for national reconstruction. We will recall that Mao's strategic prescription for the cities was to transform them from slothful, corrupt centres of consumption (*xiaofei chengshi*) to purposeful socialist 'producer cities' (*shengchan chengshi*). With this productionist ethos in command, speculation about the form and spatial weave of urban society appropriate to the new socialism was not ruled out of order – it simply never arose in the China of the Mao era.

The new regime immediately inaugurated vast programmes of slum clearance and housing construction, especially in the large coastal metropolises. These efforts stemmed from a subjective desire on the part of the leaders of New China to better the lot of the urban masses; but in terms of socialist ambition, of the kind suggested by the great debates on the urban question which had been a feature of the Soviet Union of the 1920s they were unremarkable. The CCP in power evidently regarded urban planning and urban construction as identical. As for urban citizenship, throughout the Mao era, a reductionist equation was to predominate: urban citizen = urban producer.

Interpretations by Western observers that the PRC's development process was 'anti-urban' are no longer tenable; the Chinese experience has been – and to a lesser degree, remains – a variant on the theme of urban–industrial bias (Leeming, 1985; Kirkby, 1985, pp. 1–20). Within the dominant ethos of the Mao era, central to which was the hegemony of production and of accumulation over consumption, all those in the tightly delineated and controlled urban sphere have been beneficiaries of this bias. The early adoption of the eight-grade wage system, the almost unbreakable 'iron rice-bowl', was the underlying guarantee of urban supremacy. Welfare in the broad sense (*shehui fuli*), including employees' health care, pre-school care, and, most costly of all, the provision of basic shelter, was to be part of a social wage in an economy which was expressly 'low-wage' as far as monetary remuneration was concerned. Workers' welfare was essential to the grand purpose of rapid industrialization, the *raison d'etre* of Communist Party power.

From the early 1950s on, therefore, urban housing provision was considered the responsibility of the state. This, of course, was a novel departure in China; now the government, through local municipal housing bureaux, or through the urban enterprise system, would take on the primary responsibility for housing investment, construction and rehabilitation, allocation, maintenance and repair and general management. By 1956, 95% of urban land had become state property and less than 5% of rented sector accommodation remained in private hands (Yu Xinyan, 1981, p. 45). Though owner occupation was upheld (in the mid-1950s comprising just over two-thirds of all the private sector), by and large it was assumed that private urban housing was a residue from the old society and that ultimately it should all be taken over by the state.

As a component of state welfare, housing provision was to follow the broad principle of equity in supply. This meant that within a certain range, unequal distribution of the social wage was sanctified: officials, technicians, and the 'higher intelligentsia' were to be treated differently from the common masses. A survey of the mid-1950s demonstrates this mild inequity – while only 17% of ordinary workers' households had four or more m² of 'living space', 40% of white-collar workers (including government officers) had more than this.[1] And appropriations for new housing construction for those of a superior station in society were considerably differentiated. For example, in the Nanjing of the 1950s, workers received apartments at around 30 *yuan* per 4 m², while college professors' housing cost more than 60 *yuan* (Howe 1968, p. 80).

At the bottom of the pile were the single workers, usually male, recruited by urban units from the villages. In the early days, the People's Republic vowed to eradicate the dormitory system – seen as a hangover from the feudal crafts society and the foreign-imposed factory system. But the temptations of continuing – indeed institutionalizing – the dormitory idea were too great. At a time when the Soviet-inspired norm for newly built family apartments was nine square metres per person, the 2–2.5 m² of the dormitories represented a considerable saving in investment, a saving which factory managers considered they could put to better, more productive uses (Kwok, 1973, p. 241).

In short, by the mid-1950s, the parameters of urban housing policy had been established. Housing had become primarily the responsibility of the state, either directly through municipal government, or indirectly through the enterprise or institution. Just as for health care, educational and recreational services, the consumer was to pay only a nominal fee for housing, a basic element of the collective welfare system was the concomitant of the low wage economy.

Now, however, in the 1980s, the reformers who are at the apex of the party have already overthrown many of the previously inviolable tenets of China's post-1949 polity. Urban housing has not escaped their attentions. The first objective here was a drastic transformation of the immediate supply basis of housing, premised upon a revolution in macro-economics which would cast out the Stalin–Mao model and its ruling nexuses.[2] The aspect of this transformation which most concerns us here is the dramatic increase in non-productive capital investments as a part of all capital construction funds. Nevertheless, the housing crisis persisted – largely because of other externalities. The reformers were thus driven to challenge the entire edifice of China's urban housing provision.

The next section of this chapter will, therefore, consider the crisis in housing supply which was the legacy of the Mao years, and which has occasioned radical measures in the housing field. The subsequent sections describe the revolution in the housing supply picture. Largely because of its limited impact in the face of extraordinary urban population growth, new, more market-oriented policies began to appear in the early 1980s, with their inevitable ideological trimmings. The final section speculates on the future for housing policy, and for the basic provision of urban shelter in a period of development which promises enormous expansion of China's non-agricultural population.

The Emerging Housing Crisis under Mao

The extensive industrialization programme of the First Five-Year Plan (1953–7 – hereafter 1FYP) was accompanied by considerable attention to the question of housing the new cohorts of factory workers. Yet even with 9.1% of total 'basic capital construction funds' (*jiben jianshe touzi*) annually devoted to housing (*SYB*, 1984, pp. 333, 339), the sheer scale of urban population growth outpaced housing supply. On the eve of the 1FYP, China's global urban population stood at almost 72 million. Average per capita floorspace available was 5.4m². Just seven years later, because of the injudicious migration policies of the Great Leap Forward and a neglect of housing after 1957 (in the 2FYP it averaged only 4.1% of total capital construction funds), the 130-odd million urban-dwellers had only 3.5 m² of housing each (Kirkby 1985, p. 173; *RMRB*, 8 May 1981). There is evidence that the larger the urban place, the less available housing space there is per person (Chao Kang, 1966, p. 393).

The ensuing 15 years saw a more marked neglect of non-productive urban capital investments – utilities, roads and above all housing. It is not surprising in view of the anti-consumption ideology of the Cultural Revolution that the 3FYP (1966–70) saw all time lows in both housing investment (4% of all capital construction funds) and in floorspace produced (annual average of 10.8 million m²). This gross neglect of urban infrastructure and housing coincided, of course, with a retardation of urban growth due to mass expulsions of city youth and other sections of society. From 1964 to the end of 1976, it is estimated that China's cities grew only around 12% (from above 99 to 112 million). With increased resources to housing during the 4FYP (1970–75), the overall average at the end of 1978 had increased to 5.3 m² (Kirkby 1985, p. 176).

Yet this figure concealed much variation, principally between the smaller, non-municipal urban settlements (almost all of which were under 100,000 in population), and the designated municipalities. A survey in 1978 of these municipalities (at the time numbering 192) found that here the average space was only 3.6 m^2 per person, in contrast to the 4.5 m^2 of 1952. Further, this survey discovered that of the approximately 23 million households in the 192 municipalities, around one-third had severe housing problems. For example, 1.83 million families were housed in warehouses, corridors, factory workshops, classrooms and offices, 1.89 million families had three generations sleeping in the same room and several million young people were unable to marry because they had no place to live (Zhang Jun, 1985, p. 32). In Shanghai, 800,000 people of a total urban population of around five million were judged to be in severe housing difficulty (with per capita housing space under 2 m^2 or grown-up children of different sexes sharing the same sleeping space or two couples of different generations sharing the same room or young people of marriageable age – at that time 27 for men and 25 for women – still on the housing waiting list) (Wang Fengwu, 1985, p. 22).

As for the condition of the urban housing stock, a wander off the main highways in any city would reveal the parlous state of housing after decades of neglect. The absence of routine repairs and maintenance during the Mao years was partly the result of lack of funding and of building materials for the domestic sector and partly of peasant attitudes to the city. Between 1949 and 1980 the official figures show that the gross urban housing floorspace stock grew by 469 million m^2. Yet 675.4 million m^2 of new housing was put up in these 31 years. With very little being deliberately demolished to make way for new projects – for this was definitely not the policy of the urban authorities – we can estimate that upwards of 150 million m^2 was lost due to neglect of simple repairs (Kirkby 1985, p. 173).

A survey in 1955 had shown that 50% of all municipal housing stock was in need of rehabilitation (Kwok, 1983, p. 226). While in certain cities (particularly Beijing) much effort was put into repairs in the 1950s, the ravages of time meant that the overall physical state of China's urban housing by the end of the Mao period was much worse than in the mid-1950s. It was especially bad in the fifty or so cities of over 500,000 in population, where over 40% of all China's urban population resided (Kirkby 1985, p. 150). Take the example of the great metropolis of Wuhan in Central China: here, of the 6.37 million m^2 of housing floorspace administered by the municipal housing bureau, some 9% was in a 'highly dangerous' state, 77% was broken-down or damaged and only 14% was considered up to standard (He Gongjian, 1980, pp. 13–14).

City housing managers complained that they neither had the financial resources nor the trained staff to cope with matters more efficiently. In 1977, a national housing conference heard that in all the designated municipalities (*she shi*) as a whole, the average annual repair bill (let alone management, maintenance and additions to the housing stock) per m^2 of public housing stood at 2.1 *yuan*, whereas the rental income was a mere 1.09. For Wuhan, on average in the 1970s, 830,000 m^2 (roughly 13%) of the municipal housing stock required 'large or medium-scale' repairs. Yet the funds available for repairs could only be stretched to just over one-third of this area (He Gongjian, 1980, p. 14).

This problem of disparity between costs and rental income continues. The extraordinary expansion of the housing programme (described in the following section) has seen a large rise in unit cost of construction. Some of the first of the new wave of building in China was along Beijing's Qiansanmen Avenue. But here, the disparity between relatively high rental income and the costs of running the new multi-storey buildings was even more remarkable. One report claimed that while the annual rental income for the 19 high-rise blocks of the project came to 500,000 *yuan* in 1980, the cost of maintaining and running the lifts alone came to 750,000 *yuan* (*RMRB*, 8 May 1981). It was calculations of this order and the despair amongst those responsible for administering a housing finance system which had become almost inoperable, which provided the political basis for a complete rethinking of the housing supply system in recent years.

The Post-Mao Housing Programmes and their Impact: Mass Problems and Mass Solutions

The transformation of many aspects of economic life in China since the end of 1978 has, not unexpectedly, had its accompaniments in the realm of theory. Often these have seemed rather hollow justifications for pragmatic action. A rather more edifying debate, however, has centred on the proper objectives of work and life in a socialist society. While the new regime by no means eschewed stark output targeting, there was now general agreement that the purpose of socialist production is not simply to enhance future production. As usual, the discussion was couched in Mao's own terminology and directives – specifically his observation that planners must not give way to the temptation to build up the 'skeleton' (*gutou*) at the expense of the 'flesh' (*rou*). (*RMRB*, 8 May 1981). But the Cultural Revolution rule of thumb, *xian shengchan, hou shenghuo* ('first production, then livelihood') came under heavy fire. In urban policy, complaints against the neglect of the Mao years began to be aired. The concept of the cities as primarily places of production, in which consumption aspects were regarded as unworthy of attention by socialist planners, was thoroughly rejected.

All this presaged a change in those policies which most closely determined the state of the physical fabric of urban China. In September 1978, during the last days of the Hua Guofeng interregnum, the State Capital Construction Commission convened a special conference on housing. Here it was declared that in the coming seven years (1979–85), more urban housing was to be built than in the previous 28 years, that is to say at least 550 million m² (*Ta Kung Pao* 28 September 1978). In the five years before the conference, a mere 28 million m² per annum had been achieved (Kirkby 1985, p. 173) and the prospect of increasing annual output by a factor of three seemed most unrealistic. Targets such as these would demand the mobilization of millions of construction workers, an enormously expanded construction materials industry and a rebirth of rudimentary urban planning at central and municipal levels. But most difficult of all, they demanded a revolution in central investment policies.

That this revolution actually occurred is one of the unsung achievements of post-Mao China. In 1978, non-productive funds constituted 20.6% of all capital construction investments, and housing took 7.8%. A dramatic climb in these figures peaked in 1982 at 45.5% and 25.4% respectively. That is to say, one-quarter of all capital investments in 1982 went to urban housing construction, compared with the PRC's historical low of 4% per annum in the early years of the Cultural Revolution (*SYB* 1985, p. 304). As Table 9.1 illustrates, the amount of housing floorspace produced in China's towns and cities reflected this staggering escalation in funding – from 37.5 million m² completed in 1978 to around 100 million m² in 1984.

We will only briefly comment on the nature of the housing produced in this enormous programme of construction. On the whole it has meant an abandonment of previous building methods and designs (principally the four/five storey walk-up block using a mixture of traditional and modern structural techniques). The revolution in housing output has necessitated the adoption of the mechanized construction techniques which were seen in the West in the late 1950s and 1960s. Much of what has been produced is, of course, of dubious structural and social quality. But as a mass solution to an immediate problem of vast proportions, the post-1978 developments have been an outstanding achievement. A key organizational factor was the re-institution of the approach developed in the 1950s – *tongjian (tongyi) jianshe* – 'integrated construction'. The 'six integrateds' cover planning, investment sources, design, construction, allocation and management. The results – extensive high-rise estates – are to be seen today in every city in China.[3]

This mass construction programme has endeavoured to help those in greatest need. But with housing the most pressing problem of urban existence, it has inevitably created ample opportunity for abuse of official positions. Newspapers and radio broadcasts of the early 1980s regularly featured cases of corruption in the housing sphere; commissions of enquiry were set up in many localities, and most cities promulgated special by-laws in an attempt to curb the worst excesses. In 1984, the Party's Central Consolidation and Guidance Commission issued a directive stating 'the distribution of housing should be decided by honest and upright people with no leading Party cadre allowed to make decisions if personally involved'. One immediate outcome was the releasing of tens of thousands of purloined flats around the country by Party officials (*Ta Kung Pao*, 23 February 1984).

Nevertheless, in the short term at least, and in quantity if not quality, the brave and unprecedented efforts on the urban housing front have had tangible results. But these have been far less than anticipated in 1978, for the transformation in the sphere of housing has coincided with a considerable wave of rural–urban migration and an upturn in the natural rate of increase of the urban population. At the end of 1977, China's global urban population stood at 116 million. By the end of 1982 it was up to 153 million. Had there been no net migration to the urban areas during this period, a natural rate of increase of 11 per thousand would have meant a total increment on the 1977 figure of just 6.5 million rather than the actual 37 million (Kirkby 1985, p. 121). A low order of urban increase (consonant with the experience in the previous 15 years) would have meant considerable improvements in the average per capita space standards – from the 5.2 m² of 1977 to 7.8 m² at the end of

1982. Instead, the improvement was confined to just 1.1 m² per person on average (1982 = 6.3 m²).[4]

Table 9.1
Non-productive Investment, Housing Investment and Floorspace produced, 1949–84

Period	Investment %		Urban housing floorspace (m²)
	Non-productive[a]	Housing	
Rehabilitation 1950–2	34.0	10.6	4.5
1st FYP 1953–7	33.0	9.1	18.9
2nd FYP 1958–62	14.6	4.1	22.0
Readjustment 1963–5	20.6	6.9	14.2
3rd FYP 1966–70	16.2	4.0	10.8
4th FYB 1971–5	17.5	5.7	25.2
5th FYB 1976–80	26.1	11.8	47.0
1976	18.8	6.1	24.2
1977	20.6	6.9	28.3
1978	20.9	7.8	37.5
Readjustment 1979	30.3	14.8	62.6
1980	35.7	20.0	82.3
6th FYB 1981–5	42.4	22.0	88.3
1981	43.0	25.1	79.0
1982	45.5	25.4	90.2
1983	41.7	21.1	82.5
1984	42.0e	22.0e	100.0
1985	40.0e	21.0e	90.0e

[a] Non-productive investment (*fei shengchanxing touzi*) is that part of the state's 'basic capital construction' funds devoted mainly to urban utilities, cultural, educational and social services installations, public buildings, commercial enterprises and transport and communications construction and housing. Here, the figures in the first column represent non-productive investment's proportion of all capital investments. Column 2 is that part of all basic capital construction investments going to housing. Column three is the average annual output of urban housing floorspace (*juzhu mianji*) in millions of square metres. In the period rows, all data are annual averages for the respective period. Some of the 1983 and 1984 figures are estimates (e).

Source: *SYB*, 1984, pp. 323, 339, 357; *SYB*, 1985, pp. 304, 331; for 1984's urban housing completions, *BR*, no. 12, 25 March 1985, p. VIII; for 1985's urban housing completions, estimated from figures in *China Daily News*, 26 November 1985.

The Ideological Shift and a New Housing Policy

The Development of the Debate on the Housing Question
By 1980, the ideological climate had veered further towards the concepts of market guidance and market regulation in the planned economy. This was a natural development of the reforms inaugurated in rural production after 1978; it was considerably spurred on by outside advice. In 1980 China became a member of the World Bank; an examination of the Bank's latest overview, *China: Long Term Issues and Options*, and comparison with current policy directions as enshrined in the recently published Seventh Five-Year Plan indicate a high degree of correspondence between the official Chinese view and outside opinion.

Housing has become one of the most important spheres of the urban economy in which radical new measures are now being tested. There are particular reasons for this: first, despite the efforts described above, the outcome in terms of overall betterment of urban housing conditions has been marginal. In the largest cities there was no end in sight to the housing crisis: while the average urban per capita floorspace at the end of 1982 stood at 6.3 m², for the 20 so-called million cities, it was just over half this figure. Indeed, official statistics show that for Lanzhou, Chengdu, Shenyang, Chongqing and Tianjin the average was well under 3 m² per person (Kirkby 1985, p. 275).

After three decades in which central bureaucratic planning had become over-rigid, unwieldy and in many areas of the economy a deadening influence on productivity, the market backlash of the early 1980s was hardly unexpected. Naturally, in a climate in which the market was suddenly invested with magic powers – like Monkey's jade sceptre – this theoretical reassessment was soon to encompass the intractable problems of urban housing supply. The immediate catalyst was the enormous state budgetary deficit (17 billion *yuan*) which confronted the nation in 1979. Major causes were the downturn in enterprise profits remitted to the government, which resulted from changes in management and accounting requirements, and the unparalleled increase in agricultural procurement prices which were implemented without due consideration of the ability of urban wage-earners to absorb them. In 1979, the government was obliged to subsidize these transfers in part by a supplement to the urban wage packet (*BR*, no. 12, 25 March 1985, pp. 16–17).

Economists calculated that in 1981, on average each urban resident paid 0.1 *yuan* per m² for housing; the actual cost (taking into account depreciation, repair, maintenance and management) came to 0.38 *yuan*. Thus the state subsidized each m² to the tune of 0.28 *yuan*. The total call on the state budget by the existing housing stock (not including new construction) was therefore 3.5 billion yuan – a figure greater than the entire national budget deficit for 1982 (*BR*, no. 39, 25 October 1982).

Housing ownership and rent in the early 1980s: At this point let us summarize the overall situation regarding housing ownership and rent levels. By 1980, 250 million m² (31%) of the total urban housing stock of 810 million m² was owned and managed directly by municipal housing bureaux (variously titled, but most usually *fangchan guanli ju*). Urban enterprises held 360 million m² – 44% of the total. Two hundred million m² (25%) remained in private hands, the majority of this being in owner occupation, but with a significant part still in the private rented sector. As for the most important urban centres, the municipalities, the situation in 1981 is shown in Table 9.2.

Table 9.2
Housing and Rentals in 200 Municipalities, 1981

Ownership	Total floorspace (million m²)	Percentage	Average monthly rent (yuan/m²)
Municipal housing bureaux	203.4	28.7	0.08–0.12
Enterprises	380.3	53.6	under 0.08
Private	125.8	17.7	0.10–0.14 (rented sector)
Totals	*709.5*	*100.0*	—

Source: *Zhang* Jun, 1985, Table 2, p. 27.

From this Table, we can see that the state, either directly or indirectly, owned around 82% of all municipal urban housing stock, somewhat more than for all urban areas (75%) and rather less than in the largest cities. For example, the figures for Shanghai in 1981 were 42% under the Municipal Housing Bureau and 43% under the enterprises, giving a total state ownership of housing of 85% (Zhang Jun, 1985, p. 27). The general picture, then, is that the larger the urban settlement, the greater the proportion of state-owned housing stock.

In the years immediately after the Liberation, household rents were relatively high (e.g. in Wuhan they represented 14% of household income – see *JHLT*, no. 5, 1980, p. 31). This was deemed too great and in the mid-1950s leading economists proposed that the appropriate level for rents in the New China should be 6–10% of household income (He Gongjian, 1980, p. 14). There were two factors, however, which made rentals a diminishing proportion. First and most importantly, the labour participation rate in the urban sector climbed dramatically, from around 20% in the early 1950s to today's 58.6% (municipalities only – see *SYB*, 1984, p. 470). Second, rents experienced a real fall, mainly but not exclusively because of the expanding enterprise welfare sector. For example (again in Wuhan), in 1974 all municipal housing bureau stock had rents cut by one-third. In that city, therefore, rents fell from 14% of household expenditure immediately after Liberation, to 8% in 1957 and 5% in 1970; by 1978 they represented just 2.3%. Now they had become merely 'token rents' (*xiangzhenxing fangzu*) – though the situation described earlier of declining per capita space standards and deterioration of the housing fabric must, of course, be borne in mind (*JHLT*, no. 5, 1980, p. 31).

Recent data for China's urban population as a whole indicates this steady decline in rents, though starting at a lower point altogether (Table 9.3).

Table 9.3
Rents and Household Utilities as a Proportion of Household Expenditure[a]

Year	Rent (%)	Water and Electricity (%)	Food (%)
1957	2.32	1.46	58.43
1964	2.61	0.97	59.22
1981	1.39	0.97	58.66
1983	1.52	1.14	59.20

[a] Re the upturn after 1981 in rental and utilities proportions, the *World Bank Report* (1985, Annex E, p. 88, Table G2a) puts urban rentals and fuel/power proportions higher – at 4.9% and 4.5% respectively of household expenditures.

Source: *SYB*, 1985, pp. 463–4.

The ideological onslaught on low rents: The first serious and cogent attack on the traditional housing supply system came in an article by Su Xing, in the Party's theoretical journal, *Hongqi (Red Flag)*. Having reviewed the problems at the end of the Mao era, and roundly criticized their causes, Su Xing then endeavours to develop a theoretical case to prove that under the socialist system, housing is a commodity. In doing so he enlists Engels to his cause, for in his arguments with Proudhon Engels refuted any suggestion that the relationship between landlord and tenant was equatable with that between capitalist and worker. Therefore,

> In a socialist society, housing is an individual consumer item and remains a commodity. What is different is that here it is no longer a transaction between individuals; instead, the state, representing the system of ownership by the people, rents or sells the houses to the individual labourers, making this a form of the principle of to each according to his labour . . . The difference between housing and other consumer goods is that the duration of its consumption is relatively long . . . Is it permissible to sell some of the housing to workers and staff? It should be.

Su Xing then goes on to praise the Romanian state mortgage system, which requires down-payments of 20–30% and repayments over 15–25 years at low rates of interest (3–5%). He argues that in theory, rent levels should be based on the total value of the labour power expended in the creation of a given housing unit. He concedes that in practice, given the structure of incomes in urban China and the 'low-wage' policy, the average difference between household incomes and expenditures is very small. Therefore immediate all round increases in family housing budgets would be impracticable. Nevertheless, he asserts, rents should not be further reduced, and excessively low and 'irrational' rents should be raised forthwith:

> In the current stage, the rental should at least cover depreciation, maintenance and management expenses and land taxes. Otherwise, it will be impossible to retrieve not merely the cost of reproduction of housing, but also the cost of minimum maintenance.

Su Xing recommends the removal of housing from welfare and from the control of enterprises. The public housing stock should be placed under the control of special corporations, with their own internal profit-and-loss accounting, thus creating the 'reproduction and expanded reproduction' of housing through their own income generation. Only in this way will the 'objective economic laws' of socialism be honoured.

The editor of *Hongqi* chose in the ensuing issues of the journal to carry a number of articles which were more or less in favour of Su Xing's proposals (e.g. *HQ*, no. 7, 1980, p. 49; no. 9, 1980, pp. 27–8). Meanwhile, however, an obscure Wuhan social sciences publication, the *Jianghan Luntan* (*JHLT*) became a forum for both the pro-commodification (*shangpinhua*) position and, more interestingly, for well argued appeals in favour of maintaining the status quo in China's urban housing system.

The *JHLT* debate was initiated by Gu Zhiming, in an article entitled 'Housing's Fundamental Character and the Problem of Return on Investment' (*Zhuzai de xingzhi he touzi shouhui wenti* in *JHLT*, no. 5, 1980, pp. 3–7). The case which Gu rehearses here is much the same as that of Su Xing, except that his contribution endeavours to be more theoretical, liberally referring to the Marxist classics and their critique of housing under capitalism. Indeed, the entire *JHLT* housing debate was couched in highly theoretical formulae, in many cases to justify quite prosaic conclusions. Since the official case for commodification has already been reviewed, we will concentrate here on the opposing viewpoints, which rest on both 'theoretical' and practical lines of argument. Those extracted from a number of issues of *JHLT* between 1980 and 1983 are summarized below.

1. It is broadly accepted that in the era of socialism, commodity production is still the rule rather than the exception; however, commodity production is of a special nature and is subordinate to planning. It should therefore not be regarded as an end in itself, or as an article of faith.

2. Though housing may be a commodity, it is no ordinary one, for its period of consumption is very long, and, if privately owned, it represents a form of personal wealth and savings, and is thus a basis for speculation or private gain incompatible with socialism.

3. Various contributors resurrected the Mao bogey of a 'return to the small peasant economy' (i.e. 'capitalism' in the Cultural Revolution polemics) which the communists had been trying to eliminate for three decades. If the present housing supply system were privatized, it would not be in keeping with the social progress demanded by a society which called itself socialist. Indeed, generalization of the commodity principle could threaten the very basis of China's socialist system.

4. Other writers against commercialization ridiculed their opponents' use of 'theory'. They pointed out that theoretical arguments by their nature must maintain consistency. Thus, if state support to housing were to be withdrawn, so should the myriad of subsidies provided by the central and local state, including many from work units. For example, heating allowances, the whole range of supports to urban food prices, health, cultural and educational facilities, and so on and so forth (with many of these areas now, in the mid-1980s, receiving the attention of the commercializers, proponents of this line of argument may now wish they had held their fire).

5. One writer hi-jacks the theoretical underpinnings of the commodifiers and

turns these against them. He notes Engels' opposition to home ownership under capitalism, on the grounds that it fetters the working class to one place, thus preventing labour mobility and the full development of capitalism, in which socialism is seen as immanent. Since the new economics of the 1980s claims that the current stage is one of almost universal commodity production, it must acknowledge the necessity of a mobile labour force to the further development of China's productive forces.

6. Technical reasons are also highlighted – principally the practical difficulties of splitting up existing publicly owned apartment blocks into private units.

7. The most forceful arguments rest on the universality of the low-wage system. One writer examines both household income and expenditure, and finds that the balance between the two (with the latter comprising universally acknowledged necessities) is very narrow. In Wuhan in 1977, for example, the municipal authorities determined the per capita basic subsistence requirement to be 22.74 *yuan* monthly. Yet 40% of the employed population (including their dependants) had less than 20 *yuan* per head. As one commentator remarked, if the government did not want a mass rebellion, it would have to raise urban incomes to pay for higher rents. This would be a pointless exercise – taking money out of one pocket of the state and simply placing it in another.

Despite frequent use of highly contrived positions, on the whole this grand controversy over housing policy represented a healthy departure from the 'one-line' debates of the 1970s. Yet given the 'gale of commodification' which began to sweep the board in the early 1980s, the opponents of commercialization were unlikely to prevail. By May 1984, the whole debate was effectively foreclosed through the direct intervention of Deng Xiaoping himself. The *People's Daily* (15 May 1984) reported Deng's exchanges with the 'central comrades responsible for the construction industry and housing policy' of the previous month. Here, Deng called for an enhanced role in the economy for the construction industry, noting that in the western capitalist nations it constituted one of the 'three main pillars' of the economy, and that it should therefore be capable of making good profits. Housing should be built for sale, and existing public housing privatized or at least made to return realistic revenues. Individual savings should be put into housing, and land and housing costs should be made to reflect differential locational attributes (that is, a quasi-urban land market might be utilized). Nevertheless, low-income groups should continue to enjoy state housing subsidies for the time being. Deng's own declared views in fact reflected developments towards commercialization which were already well underway.

Commercialization in Practice

By the end of the 6FYP (1985), there had been no fundamental change for the vast majority of urban dwellers in traditional parameters surrounding housing supply. Rents remained more or less at the same level, though price rises for domestic electricity and water had been implemented in selected areas.[5] Yet as the policy changes heralded by the great debate began to be realized, for a rapidly growing minority, the all important factor of shelter in the cities was taking on a novel character.

A precursor of this experiment lay in the revival of the 'overseas Chinese new village' arrangements of the 1950s. In order to secure foreign exchange, and more importantly, to play for the allegiance of the overseas Chinese communities, the government now made possible the extensive involvement of Hong Kong and Singapore property companies in the development of housing projects. These were to be sold off to those who wanted to acquire a relatively inexpensive second home in their native areas. For example, in 1979, the Dongshan development in Guangzhou was placed on the market, and demand was such that prospective purchasers had to draw lots for the 150 flats of its first phase (*Ta Kung Pao*, 22 October 1979). By 1985, Shanghai had completed several luxury developments and had plans for 50 large blocks to be built in conjunction with overseas Chinese interests. Such projects have been used not only as a test bed for new high-rise construction methods; they have also provided many localities with an exposure to the technicalities of financing and marketing of a commercialized housing project.

Like all the policy innovations of the present period, the commercialization of housing for citizens of the People's Republic was initially started on an experimental basis and without great fanfare, in a small number of selected localities. The earliest reported pilot projects were begun in 1979 in Shenyang and in Fuzhou. In the latter, the emphasis was on the use of private resources for the construction of new housing; the experiment was conducted on some scale, for it was reported that in 1980, as much new private housing was constructed as under Fuzhou's public municipal programme (*BR*, no. 32, 10 August 1979, pp. 7-8; no. 42, 20 October 1980, p. 5). It is probable that a good proportion of the funds for this private construction came from relatives abroad. In Shenyang, however, where such possibilities are limited, the experiment took the form of selling off existing public housing stock to individual purchasers. According to newspaper reports, demand greatly outstripped supply (e.g. *Ta Kung Pao*, 9 October 1980).

In April 1980, Gu Mu (then Vice-Premier) announced that in Nanning, Xi'an, Fuzhou, Wuxi and a number of other cities, schemes for the sale of public housing would be initiated. Both outright purchase and instalment plan methods (15 years, at 1–2% interest) would be utilized (*BR* no. 21, 26 May 1980, p. 7). Encouraged by the popularity of such schemes – at least amongst the minority of urban households that had accumulated sufficient savings to find the scheme attractive – in late 1981, the National Housing Construction and Development Corporation (*Zhongguo fangwu jianshe gongsi* – hereafter CHCDC) was established.[6] The CHCDC selected the four cities of Zhengzhou (Henan), Changzhou (Jiangsu), Shashi (Hubei) and Siping (Jilin) as testing grounds for an expanded scheme. The package offered by the CHCDC was a repayment period of from 5 to 20 years at interest rates of up to 5%. Where outright purchase was opted for, a 20–30% discount on market price would be offered. Significantly, the standard purchasing arrangements represented a considerable retreat from the more extreme commodification proposals suggested by Party theorists. In CHCDC projects, only 30% of an apartment's cost was to be repaid by the purchaser, and that through instalments if necessary, with low rates of interest. The *danwei* (work unit) and the local municipal government would undertake joint responsibility for the balance of the purchase price. After the amortization period, a flat would become the property of its occupier; it could not legally be sold, but could be passed on to children (*Ta Kung Pao*, 1 March 1984, p. 6; 26 July 1984, p. 6).

On the face of it, commodification of this mildness does not seem to offer important savings to the central state budget, except in cases in which the prospective purchaser is able to hand over the 30% in a single down payment (in Beijing, around 5,000 *yuan* for the typical self-contained unit of around 50 m² – elsewhere as little as half this figure). There may be some accounting advantage, also, in that part of the remaining 70% would come directly from the *danwei*. With enhanced autonomy and increased retention of surplus now practised by the individual enterprise, funds could thus be recouped by the state exchequer which it otherwise would never see. Despite the favourable terms of purchase, the *People's Daily* claimed that on average, in applying the CHCDC's programme in Xiamen, Wuxi and Changzhou, the rate of return on every *yuan* it invested in its housing projects was 10 *yuan* (17 December 1984).

What is the reason for the moderation of this version of bringing 'objective economic laws' to bear on China's urban housing stock? Since 1979, the urban consumer has experienced general price inflation on a scale unprecedented in the People's Republic (the main causes being firstly, the 1979 raising of state agricultural procurement prices, and secondly the post-1984 deregulation of food prices). If the CCP has a constituency to which it must bear some regard – both within and outside its own ranks – then it is an urban one. The price rises which have hit the urban areas have given rise to considerable disenchantment with the overall programme of reform. Any more substantial adjustment to the housing supply system would have added greatly to this incipient opposition. Indeed, calculations by the World Bank economists conclude that should state housing subsidies be totally removed from rented housing, the required urban income increases would be on average between 30% and 50% for the poorest households (*China*, 1985, p. 150). In the present, still tight, circumstances of the urban family budget, this would clearly be unsupportable.

In its second full year of operation, 1983, the CHCDC provided housing units to 7,000 households and extended its operations to 19 cities. Its activities were supplemented by both the People's Bank of China and the Industrial and Commercial Bank, which began to experiment with the issuing of house repair and purchase loans.[7] In 1984, the State Council approved the CHCDC's extension of its activities to 80 more cities, including Beijing, Shanghai and Tianjin, and made provision for contributions from purchaser, work unit and local government which varied from the three-way division of the pilot scheme, 'depending on the financial situations of the buyers and their work units' (*Ta Kung Pao*, 25 October 1984). By its third national conference at the end of 1984, the CHCDC had become a nationwide institution, with branches in every major urban centre. It pledged to enormously increase its role in the coming year, from less than three-quarters of a million m² of housing floorspace in 1984 to over 18 million m² in 1985. Reports at the end of 1985 confirmed that through its 102 branches the Corporation had met this ambitious target. To place it in perspective, the 18 million m² was around one-fifth of all state urban housing construction in 1985, and was sufficient to accommodate 350,000 households. Each apartment was around 51 m², making a per capita average of around 12 m², almost twice as much as the current average available for the urban population (*XH*, 15 December 1984; *China Daily News*, 26 November 1985). Commodification of a kind, at least, was now firmly entrenched. But what of the demand and supply situations for urban housing floorspace, and what of the fifteen years until 2000 AD, when massive urban growth is anticipated?

Conclusion

The first two sections of this chapter reviewed the declining attention accorded to the urban fabric during the Mao years, and the serious condition of the housing stock at the beginning of the present era of reform. We will recall the State Capital Construction Commission's national housing conference of September 1978, at which it was pledged to build more housing floorspace in 1979–85 than had been achieved in the previous 28 years. At the time, this seemed to be yet another extravagant target of the Hua Guofeng interregnum. Yet, as we have seen, against all expectations, from 1979 on, a transformation in macro-economic planning has brought a remarkable rise in the level of non-productive capital expenditures. Housing has been the single most important beneficiary: between 1949 and 1978, around 554 million m² of housing floorspace was constructed in China's towns and cities. For the seven years from 1979 to 1985 year end, the cumulative total comes to almost 600 million m² (Table 9.1 above).

Yet despite this stupendous achievement, the simultaneous rise in the urban population has meant only a marginal improvement in per capita space standards. And China's architects and planners are already wondering whether the new high-rise buildings represent a qualitative improvement over the overcrowded but human-scale dwellings which seem more appropriate to tradition and to family structure.

The impetus towards a commodified housing system has gathered in the 1980s, though it should be pointed out that the more extreme measures of market orientation advocated by some Party theorists have not been implemented. Interestingly, the compromise arrangements now practised by the most prominent new national organization in the field, the China Housing Construction and Development Corporation (CHCDC), have been very much in line with the Romanian model applauded by Su Xing in his theoretical appraisal of 1980.

In many areas, and particularly in the largest cities, the housing crisis remains. Indeed, preliminary analysis of the provincial figures for 1984 indicates an inverse relationship between level of per capita urban housing investment and the proportion of the urban population accounted for it cities of over 500,000. For example, Liaoning, Jiangsu, Shandong and Heilongjiang are amongst China's most highly urbanized provinces. Yet they experienced some of the lowest urban housing investment rates (Kirkby 1985, pp. 257, 268; *SYB*, 1985, pp. 84, 316, 318, 332). In Shanghai, where especially poor housing conditions persist, it was reported, for example that in 1985 almost all newly married couples (half-a-million) still lacked their own apartment. The 1984 per capita housing investment was only around two-thirds of Tianjin's figure and half of that of Beijing (*SYB*, 1985, pp. 84, 316, 318, 332).

There is much evidence from the Chinese press that certain sectors of society, particularly the intelligentsia, are still in dire housing difficulty despite the positive action of the new regime on their behalf. Take as an instance the recurring articles and correspondence in the *People's Daily* (e.g. *RMRB*, 24 September 1983, 19 November 1983) concerning the plight of Beijing staff members of the Chinese Academy of Sciences. Their average per capita floorspace was just 3.7 m^2, or around half the average for Beijing. Several thousand households were still accommodated in single rooms. The leaders of the Academy did not hold out great hope for improvement in the immediate future.

For the overwhelming majority of urban dwellers still renting accommodation from municipal housing bureaux and their enterprises, the reform period has brought little change in cost of housing to the family budget. None the less, the mood in 1985 is still to increase rentals across the board, bringing them up to perhaps 8% of household expenditure by the 1990s. One of the methods currently being floated is to remove indirect state subsidies, raise rents and pay each wage-earner a housing supplement with his monthly income. The justification for this proposal is firstly, that it would represent a saving for the central state, as the overall level of housing support funds would be reduced. Secondly, by paying the subsidy directly, greater consumer choice would be permitted (each household could decide its requirement for housing – quantity and quality, rented or private sector, etc.). Thirdly, direct payments would reduce the tendency towards abuse of official position in the housing sphere: Party and state officials – who are not necessarily very well paid but nevertheless have access to perquisites – would be confronted by the full financial cost of above-norm housing space. It is suggested that they would not be so tempted to misappropriate apartments and those currently occupying excessive space would thus be encouraged to release it onto the market (this is an interesting case in which the connection between economic liberalization and enhanced democracy is persuasive). For the time being, attempts (begun in earnest back in 1979) were continuing in every city to rematch apartments where the journey to work of employed households, or changes in family structure, had made premises inappropriate to their occupiers' needs. Indeed, Beijing's home exchange organization (under the Municipal Housing Bureau) has set up its first computer database in order to speed up housing swaps (*China Daily News*, 30 May 1985).

What of the future? In the short term, extension of the home purchase schemes (arranged through the CHCDC and the growing number of banks involved in the housing loans market) can be anticipated. Efforts are underway to consolidate this reform: for instance, Beijing's Municipal People's Government in 1985 published a directive stipulating that henceforth, at least 20% of the *danwei* housing stock should be privatized (including newly built and existing units) (*RMRB* 2 January 1985).

There is also a move to curb the 'excessive' space standards now being seen in many new private sale projects. The Ministry for Urban–Rural Planning and Environmental Protection proposed that the average new unit should not exceed 50 m^2 (approximately 12 m^2 per person), yet a national housing construction and design conference held in Nanjing in May 1985 heard that 'in some big cities . . . the average had gone up to 60 or over 70 m²' (*RMRB*, 10 May 1985). Moves to reform and rationalize the housing construction industry continued, the purpose being to save on money, materials and time. Here, the introduction of a 'responsibility system' was seen as the best method (experiments in Liaoning were reported in *RMRB*, 6 April 1985). Meanwhile, Shanghai, with its penchant for free marketeering, and still with some of the worst of the nation's housing problems, inaugurated a housing lottery for those opening a special banking account (*Guardian*, 13 November 1985).

In October 1985, the special national conference of the CCP laid out the programme for China's 7th Five-Year Plan (1986–90). According to Premier Zhao Ziyang, a strategic principle of the Plan will be the continued commercialization of urban housing, at the same time making the construction industry a 'pillar of the national economy'. Again, the state's low return on housing investments was bemoaned, and 'well considered methods . . . to gradually commercialize housing' were promised (*BR*, no. 40, 7 October 1985). An important step towards the formulation of a new national urban housing strategy was the national census of housing which took place, with the assistance of one million enumerators, on 31 December 1985 (*RMRB*, 30 July 1985). But the prospects for urban housing in the medium term (say the coming 15 years) do not appear good.

China's urban population at the end of 1985 stood at around 170 millions (see Kirkby, 1985, Chapters 3 and 4). Yet with structural changes in agriculture, and an ever-growing rural population, it is anticipated that this figure may increase by at least 100 million and – if the World Bank's recommendations for overall (balanced) growth are successfully pursued – by as much as 230 million by 2000 AD (Kirkby, 1985, p. 205, Zhang Jun, 1985, pp. 3–4). At present, the central authorities responsible for housing plans hope that by 1990, the present over-6 m² per capita standard will be maintained in the face of a swelling urban population. This would, by their calculations, require an annual production of floorspace of 120 million m² – rather more than has been averaged over the 6FYP (1981–5). Between 1990 and 2000, the rate of construction would have to be stepped up to 180 million m² annually in order to meet a target of 8 m² per person by the end of the century (derived from *China Daily News*, 27 May 1985).[8] Whether this ambition can be attained rests on two great unknowns. The first concerns the financial prognosis – both the fiscal health of the People's Republic in the coming years (whether or not reforms and balanced economic growth can be sustained) and the rate of increase of disposable incomes in the urban sector. The second unknown concerns the fascinating scenario for future urbanization, in a nation in which over 800 million still reside in the rural areas and depend for their livelihood on agricultural production.

Notes

1. *Juzhu mianji* – the general Chinese measure which excludes corridors, kitchen and lavatory space, etc.

2. Namely, high accumulation rate, low consumption rate in the national income, heavy industry over light industry, productive investments over non-productive.

3. For instance the Beijing Tuanjie Hu scheme on the east side of the city, visited in August 1979. Tuanjie Hu is an integrated neighbourhood development of 300,000 m² in total, 260,000 being for housing.

4. See Kirkby, 1985, Table 6.3, p. 176; these figures differ somewhat from those of *BR*, no. 40, 7 October 1985 in which it is stated that per capita living space at the end of 1984 was 6.32 m² compared with 1980's 4.96 m². The disparity probably arises because these figures refer to the municipalities only; around a hundred small cities with relatively good housing conditions were designated as municipalities in the four years concerned. Also, see *Zhonghua renmin gongeheguo xingzheng quhua jiance, Administrative Divisions of the People's Republic of China* (Beijing, Ditu Chubanshe, published annually).

5. *XH*, 8 April 1983, stated that before the end of that year, 15 cities would abolish the system whereby electricity, water and gas were heavily subsidized by work units: in future, charges would be paid directly by households and each flat would have meters installed.

6. Under the general aegis of the newly formed Ministry for Urban–Rural Planning and Environmental Protection.

7. The Industrial and Commercial Bank's scheme applied to '16 provinces and cities' and assisted 9,100 households – *Ta Kung Pao*, 26 January 1984 and *RMRB*, 11 January 1984; according to *XH*, 20 December 1985, the People's Construction Bank had also begun assistance to land development and housing schemes as early as 1980.

8. I estimate that this would be sufficient to accommodate an urban population of around 360 millions if historical rates of depreciation are continued.

Bibliography

Abelson P. (ed.), (1975), *Food, Politics, Economics, Nutrition and Research*, American Association for the Advancement of Science, Washington.

Ahn B.-J. (1975), 'The Political Economy of the People's Commune in China', *Journal of Asian Studies*, 3.

Aird J. S. (1981), 'Fertility Decline in China', in N. Eberstadt.

Aird J. S. (1982), 'Population Studies and Population Policies in China', *Population and Development Review*, 2.

Aird J. S. (1983), 'The Preliminary Results of China's 1982 Census', *China Quarterly*, 96, December.

Alabaster E. (1899) *Notes and Commentaries on Chinese Criminal Law*, Luzac, London.

Anderson D. (1984), 'Youth Waiting for Work in China', *The Australian Journal of Chinese Affairs*, 12 July.

Ashton B., K. Hill, A. Piazza and R. Zeitz (1984), 'Famine in China, 1958–61', *Population and Development Review*, 4.

Aubert C. (1983), 'La Chine est-elle surpeuplée? Révolution agricole et explosion *Chinoises*, Survey Report, October.

Aubert C. (1983), 'La Chine est-elle surpeuplée? Révolution agricole et explosion démographique (1952–1982)', paper presented to the colloquium on Techniques Agricoles et Population – du Passé au Present, Collège de France, Paris, May.

Aubert C. (1984), 'La nouvelle politique economique dans les campagnes Chinoises', *Le Courier des Pays de l'Est*, 286, July–August.

Aubert C. (1986), 'Le triple echec de la collectivisation ou le piège de la tradition', in C. Aubert et al.

Aubert C. et al. (1986), *La Sociéte Chinoise Après Mao: Entre Autorité et Modernité*, Fayard, Paris.

Aubert C. and Y. Chevrier (1982–3), 'Réformer ou ne pas réformer? Le dilemme de l'expérience chinoise (1979–81)', *Revue française de gestion*, Winter.

Bailes K. (1978), *Technology and Society under Lenin and Stalin: Origins of the Soviet Technical Intelligentsia, 1917–1941*, Princeton University Press.

Banister J. and S. H. Preston (1981), 'Mortality in China', *Population and Development Review*, 1.

Banister J. (1984), 'An Analysis of Recent Data on the Population of China', *Population and Development Review*, 2.

Barker D. and Allen S., (eds) (1976), *Sexual Divisions and Society*, Tavistock, London.

Bastid M. (1984), 'Chinese Educational Policies in the 1980s and Economic Development', *China Quarterly*, 98, June.

Bergère M.-C. (1986), *L'Age d' Or du Capitalisme Chinois, 1911–1937*, Flammarion, Paris.

Berliner J. (1968), *Factory and Manager in the USSR*, Harvard University Press, Cambridge, (Ma.)

Berliner J. (1983), 'Managing the USSR Economy: Alternative Models', *Problems of Communism*, January–February.

Bernstein T. P. (1985), 'Reforming Chinese Agriculture', *The China Business Review*, March/April.

Bianco L. (1985a) 'La transition démographique en Chine populaire et à Taiwan', *Revue d'études comparatives Est-Ouest*, vol. 16, no. 2.

Bianco L. (1985b), 'Family Planning Programmes and Fertility Decline in Taiwan and Mainland China: A Comparison', *Issues and Studies*, vol. 21, no. 11.

Boulais G. (translator), (1924), *Manuel du Code Chinois*, Variétés sinologiques, no. 55, Shanghai.

Butler W. E. (ed.), (1986), *Year Book on Socialist Legal Systems*, Transnational Books, New York.

Chan A., Madsen R. and Unger J. (1984), *Chen Village: The Recent History of a Peasant Commune in Mao's China*, University of California Press.

Chao Kang (1966), 'Industrialisation and Urban Housing in Communist China', *Journal of Asian Studies*, vol. 25, no. 3.

Chen H. C. and C. W. Tyler (1982), 'Demographic Implications of Family Size Alterations in the People's Republic of China', *China Quarterly*, March.

Chen J. (1973), *A Year in Upper Felicity*, Harrap, London.

Chen Jialiang and Zhang Peiling (1980), 'Correctly Understand the Nature of our Country's Inheritance System and the Necessity for its Continuation' (in Chinese), *Faxue Yanjiu*, 4.

Ch'en Pi-chao (1985), 'Birth Control Methods and Organisation in China', in E. Croll et al. (eds).

Chen Qinyi (1985), 'The Importance of Protecting Citizens' Inheritance Rights in Accordance with the Law' (in Chinese), *ZGFZB*, 21 October.

Chevrier Y. (1983), 'Les politiques économiques de la démaoisation (1977–1983)', *Revue d'études comparatives Est-Ouest*, vol. 14, no. 3.

Chevrier Y. (1985), 'Les réformes en Chine ou la stratégie du contournement', *Politique étrangère*, 1 March.

Chevrier Y. (1986a), 'Une évolution infirme: la société chinoise dans la transition "modernisatrice"', in C. Aubert et al.

Chevrier Y. (1986b), 'Gestation et modernisation l'entre prise chinoise face à l'Etat' to be published in a forthcoming issue of *Tiers-monde*.

China 1985: Long-term Development Issues and Options, World Bank, Washington and Johns Hopkins Press, Baltimore.

China 1985 – Agriculture to Year 2000, Annexe 2 to *China 1985*.

China – The Health Sector (1984), World Bank, Washington.

China's Economic Structure in International Perspective, Annexe of *China – 1985*, Report No. 5206 – CHA May 1985.

Chinese Finance Society (1981), *Lun Caizheng Fenbei Yu Jingji de Guanxi* (Concerning relations between economy and financial distribution), Beijing.

Cohen, S. (1974), *Bukharin and the Bolshevik Revolution: A Political Biography, 1888–1938*, Wildwood House, London.

Croll E. (1981), *The Politics of Marriage in Contemporary China*, Cambridge University Press.

Croll E. (1982), 'The Promotion of Domestic Sideline Production in Rural China

1978', in J. Gray and G. White (eds.).

Croll E. (1983a), *The Family Rice Bowl: Food and Domestic Economy in China*, UNRISD, Geneva and Zed Books, London.

Croll E. (1983b), 'Production versus Reproduction; A Threat to China's Development Strategy', *World Development*, vol. 11, no. 6.

Croll E. (1984), *Chinese Women After Mao*, Zed Press, London.

Croll E. Davin D. and Kane P (eds.), (1985), *The Single Child Family Policy in China*, Macmillan, London.

Davin D. (1976a), *Woman–Work: Women and the Party in Revolutionary China*, Oxford University Press.

Davin D. (1976b), '"Free-Choice" Marriage in China: The Evolution of an Ideal', in D. Barker and S. Allen (eds.).

Davin D (1982): 'Women in China', *China Now*, March/April.

Davin D. (1985), 'The Implementation of the Single-Child Family Policy in the Chinese Countryside', in E. Croll, et al. (eds.).

Davis-Friedmann D. (1983), *Long Lives – Chinese Elderly and the Communist Revolution*, Harvard University Press, Cambridge, MA.

Davis-Friedmann D. (1985a), 'Old Age Security and the One-Child Campaign', in E. Croll, et al. (eds.).

Davis-Friedmann D. (1985b), 'Intergenerational Inequalities and the Chinese Revolution', *Modern China*, vol 11, no. 2.

De Y (1985), 'Inheritance and Division of the Family Property' (in Chinese), *ZGFZB*, 31 May.

De Koninck R. (1985), 'La persistance territoriale du travail paysan, exemples chinois', *Espace Geographique*, vol. 14, no. 2.

Dernberger R. (1982), 'The Chinese Search for the Path of Self-sustained Growth in the 1980s: An Assessment', in US Congress.

Diamond N. (1975), 'Collectivisation, Kinship and the Status of Women in Rural China', *Bulletin of Concerned Asian Scholars*, January–March.

Ding Yichou (1986), 'Dictatorship by the "rule of law"' (in Chinese), *Jiushi Niandai*.

Dixon J. (1981), *The Chinese Welfare System*, Praeger, New York.

Donnithorne A. (1984), 'Sichuan's Agriculture: Depression and Revival', *The Australian Journal of Chinese Affairs*, 12 July.

Eberstadt N. (ed.), (1981), *Fertility Decline in the Less Developed Countries*, Praeger, New York.

Emerson J. P. (1983), 'Urban School Leavers and Unemployment in China', *China Quarterly*, 93, March.

Epstein A. L. (1969), *Matupit: Land, Politics and Change Among the Tolai of New Britain*, Australian National University Press, Canberra.

FLP (1950), *The Marriage Law of The People's Republic of China*, FLP, Beijing.

FLP (1982), The Marriage Law of the People's Republic of China, (unofficial translation), FLP, Beijing.

Fabre G. (1985), 'Une crise ecologique majeure', *Le Courier des Pays de l'Est*, 298, September.

Fei Xiaotong (1984), 'Small towns, big problems' (in Chinese), *Liaowang*, 2–5 January.

Fei Xiaotong et al. (1986), *Small Towns in China – Functions, Problems and Prospects*, FLP, Beijing.

Feng Lanrui (1981), 'On Factors Affecting China's Labour Employment', in *RMRB*, 16 November, *FBIS*, 20 November.

Feng Lanrui and Zhao Lükuan (1982), 'Urban Unemployment in China's, *SSC*, 1.

Feng Lanrui, Zhou Bilong and Su Chongde (1983), 'On the Relationship Between Employment and Economic Growth', *Selected Writings on Studies of Marxism*, 4, Chinese Academy of Social Sciences, Beijing.

Feuchtwang S. and A. Hussain (eds.), (1983), *The Chinese Economic Reforms*, Croom Helm, London.

Fewsmith J. (1985), *Party, State, and Local Elites in Republican China: Merchant Organisations and Politics in Shanghai, 1890–1930*, University of Hawaii Press, Honolulu.

Freedman M. (1966), *Chinese Lineage and Society: Fukien and Kwangtung*, London School of Economics Monographs on Social Anthropology, no. 33, Athlone Press, London.

Fu Lunbo (1982), 'Some Legal Problems Concerning the Implementation of the Policy of Private Housing' (in Chinese), *Faxue*, vol. 14, no. 1.

Gan Quan (1985), 'Family Property, Conjugal Property and Personal Property' (in Chinese), *ZGFZB*, 28 January.

Gao Shi (1985), 'Correctly Recognize the Legal Effectiveness of Wills' (in Chinese), *ZGFZ*, 4 October.

Gittings J. (1984), 'From Blossoms to Bricks', *China Now*, Summer.

Gold T. (1985), 'After Comradeship: Personal Relations in China since the Cultural Revolution', *The China Quarterly*, 104, December.

Goodman D. (ed.), (1984), *Groups and Politics in the People's Republic of China*, University College Cardiff Press.

Goody J. (1976), 'Inheritance, Property and Women: Some Comparative Considerations', in J. Goody et al. (eds.).

Goody J., Thirsk J. and Thomson E. P. (eds.), (1976), *Family and Inheritance: Rural Society in Western Europe, 1200–1800*, Cambridge University Press.

Gray J. and White G. (eds.), (1982), *China's New Development Strategy*, Academic Press, London.

Grigg D. (1985), *The World Food Problem – 1950–1980*, Basil Blackwell, Oxford.

Gu Angren (1985), 'An Explanation of the PRC's Inheritance Law – 1' (in Chinese), *RMRB*, 10 May.

Gu Zhiming (1980), 'Housing's Fundamental Character and the Problem of Return on Investment' (in Chinese), *JHLT*, 5.

Guisso R. W. and S. Johanssen (eds.), (1981), *Women in China: Current Directions in Historical Scholarship*, Philo Press, Youngstown, NY.

Halpern N. (1985), 'China's Industrial Economic Reforms: The Question of Strategy', *Asian Survey* vol. 25, no. 10.

Hazard B. (1982), 'Socialist Household Production: Some Implications of the New Responsibility System in China', *IDS Bulletin*, vol. 13, no. 4.

He Gongjian (1980), 'The Realities of the Housing Problem and Ideas for its Solution' (in Chinese), *JHLT*, 6.

Hinton W. (1967), *Fanshen – A Documentary of Revolution in a Chinese Village*, Monthly Review Press, New York.

Hong Bing (1982), 'Which One of the Three Wills Should Be Recognized?' (in Chinese), *MZYFZ*, no. 10.

Hooper B. (1984), 'China's Modernization – Are Young Women Going to Lose Out?', *Modern China*, vol. 10, no. 3.

Howe, C. (1968), 'The Supply and Administration of Urban Housing in Mainland China: The Case of Shanghai', *China Quarterly*, 33.

Hsu R. (1984), 'Grain Procurement and Distribution in China's Rural Areas', *Asian*

Survey, 12.

Hua Chang-Ming (1986), 'Le troisième age', in C. Aubert et al.

Hussain A. (1983), 'Economic Reforms in Eastern Europe and Their Relevance to China', Feuchtwang and Hussain (eds.).

Ishikawa Shigeru (1967), *Factors Affecting China's Agriculture in the Coming Decade*, Tokyo.

Ishikawa Shigeru (1982), *Labour Absorption and Growth in Agriculture; China and Japan*, Bangkok.

Jiao Mingheng (1982), 'Following the Death of Parents, How Should We Handle the Devolution of Housing Distributed at the Time of Land Reform of the Basis of Family Size?' (in Chinese), *MZYFZ*, no. 10.

Keyfitz N. (1977), *Applied Mathematical Demography*, Wiley, New York.

Keyfitz N. (1984), 'The Population of China', *Scientific American*, 2 February.

Kirkby R. J. R. (1985), *Urbanisation in China: Town and Country in a Developing Economy 1949–2000 AD*, Croom Helm, London.

Kong Keqing (1980), 'Problems Facing Women in China', *SWB*, 31 October.

Kornai J. (1980), *Economics of Shortage*, North Holland, Amsterdam.

Kwok R. Y. (1973), *Urban–Rural Planning and Housing Development in the People's Republic of China*, PhD Thesis, Columbia University, Xerox University Microfilm, Ann Arbor, 1974.

Lardy N. R. (1983), *Agricultural Prices in China*, World Bank Staff Working Paper, no. 606.

Latham M. C. (1975), 'Nutrition and Infection in National Development', in P. Abelson. (ed.).

Latham M. C. (1984), 'Strategies for the Control of Malnutrition and the Influence of Nutritional Science', *Food and Nutrition*, vol. 10. no. 1.

Lee B. J. (1981), 'Female Infanticide in China', in R. W. Guisso and S. Johannsen (eds.).

Lee P. N.-s. (1986), 'Enterprise Autonomy Policy in Post-Mao China: A Case Study of Policy-making', *The China Quarterly*, 105, March.

Leeming F. (1985), *Rural China Today*, Longman, London.

Lew R. (1986), 'Un état ouvrier?' in C. Aubert et al.

Lewin M. (1968), *Lenin's Last Struggle*, Pluto Press, London.

Li Chengrui (1983), 'On the Results of the Chinese Census', *Population and Development Review*, 2.

Li Weiyuan (1981), 'Several Problems in the Handling of Inheritance Cases' (in Chinese), *Zhejiang Xuehan*, 3.

Li Zhenying (1983), 'On a Chicken Farm', *Women of China*, July.

Lin Zili (1980), 'Initial Reform in China's Economic Structure', *SSC*, 3.

Liu Chunmei and Li Zhu (1983), 'Sex Composition of the Population' (in Chinese), in 'Analysis of the national one in one thousand sample fertility survey' (in Chinese), special issue of *Renkou Yu Jingji* (Population and Economy), July, Beijing.

Liu Fanrong (1983), 'A Hill Family Goes All Out', *Women of China*, July.

Liu Nanzheng and Zhang Peilin (1985), 'A Preliminary Study of Inheritance – Care Agreements' (in Chinese), *Faxue Yanjiu*, 3.

Ma Ping (1983), 'A Challenging Leader', *Women of China*, April.

Mao Zedong (1961), 'Report to the Second Plenary Session of the Seventh Central Committee of the Communist Party of China', in *Selected Works of Mao Tse-tung*, vol. IV, FLP, Beijing.

Maxwell N. and Nolan P. (1980), 'The Procurement of Grain', *China Quarterly*, 82.

Maxwell N. and McFarlane B. (eds.), (1984), *China's Changed Road to Developmment* Pergamon Press, Oxford.

Michio Morishima (1982), *Why Has Japan 'Succeeded'? Western Technology and the Japanese Ethos*, Cambridge University Press.

Myers J. (1985), 'China – the "Germs" of Modernisation', *Asian Survey*, vol. 25, no. 10.

Nove A. (1969), *An Economic History of the USSR*, Penguin, Harmondsworth.

Nove A. (1977), *The Soviet Economic System*, Allen and Unwin, London.

Paarlberg R. L. (1985), *Food Trade and Foreign Policy – India, The Soviet Union and the US*, Cornell University Press.

Palmer M. (1986a), 'Adoption Law in the People's Republic of China', in W. E. Butler (ed.).

Palmer M. (1986b), 'The Surface-Subsoil Form of Divided Ownership in Late Imperial China: Some Examples from the New Territories of Hong Kong', *Modern Asian Studies*.

Palmer M. (1986c), 'Civil Adoption in Contemporary Chinese Law: A Contract to Care', unpublished paper.

Parish W. P. and M. Whyte (1978), *Village and Family in Contemporary China*, Chicago University Press.

Parish W. and M. Whyte (1984), *Urban Life in Contemporary China*, Chicago University Press.

Perry E. J. (1985), 'Rural Violence in Socialist China', *China Quarterly*, 103, September.

Piazza A. (1983), *Trends in Food and Nutrition Availability in China – 1950–81*, World Bank Staff Working Paper, no. 607.

Preston S. H. (1976), *Mortality Patterns in National Populations*, Academic Press, New York.

QNJY (1983), *Qingnian Jiuye de Tansuo yu Shijian* (Youth employment exploration and practice), Beijing.

Qiu Shuhua, Wu Shutao and Wang Meizeng (1983), 'Contraception among women of child-bearing age' (in Chinese), in 'Analysis of the national one in one thousand sample fertility survey' (in Chinese), special issue of *Renkou Yu Jingji* (Population and Economy), July, Beijing.

Rosen S. (1985), 'Recentralization, Decentralization and Rationalization – Deng Xiaoping's Bifurcated Educational Policy', *Modern China* vol. 11, no. 3.

Rossi A. S. (1985), 'Growing Old in China', *Items* vol. 39, no. 3.

Rowe W. (1984), *Hankow. Commerce and Society in a Chinese City, 1796–1889*, Stanford University Press.

Saich T. (1984), 'Workers in the Workers' State: Urban Workers in the PRC', in D. Goodman (ed.).

Saith A. (1984), 'China's New Population Policies: Rationale and Some Implications', *Development and Change*, vol. 15, no. 3.

Salaff J. (1981), *Working Daughters of Hong Kong: Filial Piety or Power in the Family*, Cambridge University Press.

Schell O. (1984): 'A Reporter at Large (China)', *New Yorker*, 23 January.

Schmitt B. A. (1979), *Protein, Calories and Development; Nutritional Variables in the Economics of Developing Countries*, Westview, Boulder, CO.

Schram S. (1984), '"Economics in Command"? Ideology and Politics Since the Third Plenum, 1978–1984', *The China Quarterly*, 99, September.

Schurman H. E. (1961), 'Peking's Registration of Crisis', *Problems of Communism*, 5.

Selden M. (1971), *The Yenan Way in Revolutionary China*, Harvard University Press, Cambridge, MA.

Selden M. and V. Lippit (eds.), (1982), *The Transition to Socialism in China*, M. E. Sharpe, Armonk, NY.

Shao Liang (1983), 'Is the Commodification of Housing a Step Forward or a Step Backwards?', *JHLT*, 5.

Sen A. K. (1981), *Poverty and Famines – An Essay on Entitlement and Deprivation*, Oxford University Press.

Skilling H. and F. Griffiths (eds.), (1971), *Interest Groups in Soviet Politics*, Princeton University Press.

Skinner G. W. (1985), 'Rural Marketing in China: Repression and Revival', *The China Quarterly*, 103, September.

Smil V. (1984), *The Bad Earth: Environmental Degradation in China*, New York and London.

Stacey J. (1983), *Patriarchy and Socialist Revolution in China*, University of California Press.

State Statistical Bureau (1983), *Sample Survey of Peasant Household Incomes and Expenditure* (in Chinese), Beijing.

Su Wenming (1982), *From Youth to Retirement*, Guoji Shudian, Beijing.

Su Xing (1980), 'How to Solve the Housing Problem More Quickly?', *HQ*, 2 January.

Szirmai S. (ed.), (1961), *The Law of Inheritance in Eastern Europe and the People's Republic of China*, Sythoff, Leiden.

Tang Jianzhong and Laurence J. C. (1985), 'Evolution of Urban Collective Enterprises in China', *The China Quarterly*, 104, December .

Tien H. Y. (1982), 'Sterilization Acceptance in China', *Studies in Family Planning*, vol. 13, no. 10.

Timmer C. P. (1976), 'Food Policy in China', *Food Research Institute Studies*, no. 1.

Travers L. (1982), 'Bias in Chinese Economic Statistics', *China Quarterly* 91, September.

Travers L. (1984), 'Post-1978 Rural Economic Policy and Peasant Income in China', *China Quarterly*, 98, June.

Ts'ai Ming-ch'in (1984), 'The Burden of the Peasantry: An Analysis of Mainland China's Rural Economy', *Issues and Studies* vol. 20, no. 4.

UN (1984), *Mortality and Health Policy*, New York.

US Congress, Joint Economic Committee (1982), *China Under the Four Modernisations*, US Government Printing Office, Washington, DC.

Vandermeersch L. (1965), *La Formation du Légisme*, Paris.

van der Valk M. H. (1961), 'China' in S. Szirmai (ed.).

Vermeer E. B. (1979), 'Social Welfare Provisions and the Limit of Inequality in Contemporary China', *Asian Survey*, vol. 19, no. 9.

Vermeer E. B. (1982), 'Income Differentials in Rural China', *China Quarterly*, 89.

Vogel E. (1965), 'From Friendship to Comradeship', *The China Quarterly*, 21.

Walder A. (1982), 'Some Ironies of the Maoist Legacy in Industry', in M. Selden and V. Lippit (eds.).

Walker K. R. (1984), 'Chinese Agriculture During the Period of Readjustment 1978–83', *China Quarterly*, 100.

Wang Fengwu (1985), *Urban Planning in Britain and China*, unpublished MSc thesis, University of Wales Institute of Science and Technology.

Wang Hanbin (1985), 'An Explanation of the Draft of the PRC's Inheritance Law' (in Chinese), *Falu*, 4.

Wang Zhenzhao (1985) 'How to Establish a Valid Will' (in Chinese), *MZYFZ*, vol. 11, no. 30.

Watson A. and O'Leary G. (1982), 'The Production Responsibility System and the Future of Collective Farming', *The Australian Journal of Chinese Affairs*, 8.

Watson A. (1984), 'Agriculture Looks for "Shoes that Fit": The Production Responsibility System and its Implications', in N. Maxwell and B. McFarlane (eds.).

White G. (1982), 'Urban Employment and Labour Allocation Policies in Post-Mao China', *World Development*, vol. 10, no. 8.

Whyte M. K. and W. L. Parish (1984), *Urban Life in Contemporary China*, University of Chicago Press.

Wolf M. (1972), *Women and the Family in Rural Taiwan*, Stanford University Press.

Wolf M. (1985), *Revolution Postponed: Women in Contemporary China*, Stanford University Press.

Women's Congress (1983), 'Report of the Preliminary Meeting of the Fifth National Women's Congress', *BR*, vol. 19, no. 9.

World Bank, see *China*.

Wu Gangping (1984), 'The Characteristics of Age Composition of China's Population', paper presented at the International Seminar on China's 1982 Population Census, Beijing, 26–31 March.

Wu Naitao (1983), 'Rural Women and New Economic Policies', *BR*, vol. 7. no. 3.

Wu Xinyu (1982), 'Explanations on the Marriage Law (revised draft) and the Nationality Law (draft) of the People's Republic of China', in FLP.

Xiao Ming (1983), 'What the Responsibility System Brings', *Women of China*, November.

Xiu Ling (1983), 'Once Poor, Yanbie Is Prospering', *Women of China*, January.

Xu Dixin (1981), 'On the Agricultural Responsibility System', *NYJJ*, 11.

Xu Jiang (1985), 'The Seminar on the Implementation of the Inheritance Law Points Out: Eliminate the Interference of Erroneous Thinking and Handle Cases in Strict Accordance with the Law' (in Chinese), *ZGFZB*, 30 August.

Xu Shaozhi (1982), 'To Control Population Growth We Must Emphasise Responsibility' (in Chinese), *Renkou Yanjiu*, (Population Research), 4.

Yan Ron et al. (1985), 'We Have the Strong Support of the Inheritance Law' (in Chinese), *ZGFZB*, 23 October.

Yanov A. (1983), interviewed in *Le Monde*, 9 October.

Yanov A. (1984), *The Drama of the Soviet Sixties: A Lost Reform*, University of California Press, Berkeley.

Yu Guangyuen (ed.), (1984), *La Modernisation Socialiste de la Chine*, 2 vols. Beijing.

Yu Xinyan (1981), 'Some Views on the Housing Question' (in Chinese), *JHLT*, 1.

Zafanolli W. (1985), 'Chine: de la transition socialiste à la transition capitaliste?', *Revue d'études comparatives Est–Ouest*, vol. 16, no. 4.

Zhang Huaiyu (1981), 'Population, Economy and Population Control in Rural Areas', *JJYJ*, 20 December.

Zhang Jun (1985), *China 1980–2000: Urban Construction and Financing*, unpublished background paper prepared for World Bank, Washington, October.

Zhang Peilin (1985), 'A Will Should Not Eliminate the Inheritance Rights of Those Who Throughout Their Lives Have Fully Met Their Obligations to Support [the Testator]' (in Chinese), *ZGFZB*, 4 March.

Zhao Lükuan (1982), 'On China's Employment Problem under Conditions of Relative Oversupply of Labour', in *RMRB*, 2 March, *FBIS*, 11 March.

Zhao Xiaoluo (1982), 'A Crucial Problem in the Notarial Certification of Wills' (in Chinese), *Faxue Yanjiu*, 4.

Zhao Ziyang (1985), 'Reorganising Agriculture and Loosening Price Control', *SWB*, 2 February.

Zhi Yuanxing (1985), 'The deceased entered into an inheritance-care agreement with me when he was still alive, But he also made a will to handle property covered by the agreement. How can the matter be dealt with?' (in Chinese), *MZYFZ*, 10.

Zhongguo 1982: nian renkou pucha 10% chouyang ziliao (10% sample tabulation of the 1982 population census of the PRC), State Statistical Bureau Beijing, October 1983.

Zhonghua Renmin Daxue Faluxi Xingfa Jiaoyanzu (The Criminal Law Teaching and Research Group of the People's University), (1980), *A Guide to the Criminal Law of the PRC* (in Chinese), People's Publishing House, Beijing.

Zhu Pingshan (1981), 'Preliminary Research into Statutory Inheritance' (in Chinese), *Faxue Yanjiu*, 6.

Zhuang Qidong and Sun Keliang (1981), 'The Problem of Urban Employment During the Period of Readjustment', *HQ*, 11 in *SWB*, 15 July 1981.

Periodicals

Abbreviations and translations of Chinese periodicals.

AFP: Agence France Presse
BKNJ: *Zhongguo Baike Nianjian* (China's Encyclopaedia Yearbook), Shanghai
BR: *Beijing Review*
Ban Yue Tan   (Fortnightly Talks)
Beijing Ribao   (Peking Daily)
Beijing Wanbao   (Peking Evening News)
CNA: *China News Analysis*
Caimao Jingji   (Financial and Commercial Economy)
China Daily News   Beijing
Dazhong Ribao   (Dazhong Daily)
FBIS: *Foreign Broadcasts Information Service*
FEER: *Far Eastern Economic Review*, Hong Kong
FLP: Foreign Languages Press, Beijing
Falü   (Law)
Faxue   (Legal Studies)
Faxue Yanjiu   (Legal Research)
Fujian Ribao   (Fujian Daily)
Gongren Ribao   (Workers' Daily)
Guangming Ribao   (Enlightened Daily)
Guowuyuan: Zhonghua Renmin Gongheguo Guowuyuan Gongbao (PRC State Council Bulletin)
HQ: *Hongqi* (Red Flag)
JHLT: *Jianghan Luntan* (Jianghan Review), Wuhan
JJGL: *Jingji Guanli* (Economic Management), Beijing
JJNJ: *Zhongguo Jingji Nianjian* (China Economic Yearbook), Beijing and Hong Kong

JJRB: *Jingji Ribao* (Economics Daily)
JJYJ: *Jingji Yanjiu* (Economic Research)
Jiefang Ribao   (Liberation Daily), Shanghai
Jiushi Niandai   (The Nineties), Hong Kong
Liaowang   (Outlook)
MZYFZ: *Minzhu yu Fazhi* (Democracy and the Legal System)
Ming Bao   (Bright News), Hong Kong
Nanfang Ribao   (Southern Daily)
NCNA: *New China* (Xinhua) *News Analysis*
NYJJ: *Nongye Jingji Wenti* (Problems of Agricultural Economics), Beijing
NYJJZY: *Zhongguo Nongye Jingji Zhaiyao* (Summary of the Chinese Agricultural
   Economy) Rural Policy Research Centre, Ministry of Agriculture, Beijing
NYJSJJ: *Nongye Jishu Jingji* (Economics of Agricultural Technology)
NYNJ: *Zhongguo Nongye Nianjian* (Chinese Agricultural Yearbook)
RMRB: *Renmin Ribao* (People's Daily)
Renkou Yanjiu   (Population Research) People's University, Beijing
SSB: State Statistical Bureau (Zhongguo Guojia Tongji Ju)
SSC: *Social Sciences in China*
SWB: *Survey of World Broadcasts*, Far East, British Broadcasting Corporation,
   Caversham, England
SYB: *Statistical Yearbook of China 1981–85 (Zhongguo Tongji Nianjian)*, SSB,
   Beijing, and Economic Information and Agency, Hong Kong
Shehui   (Society)
Sichuan Ribao   (Sichuan Daily)
TJZY 1984:   *Zhongguo Tongji Zhaiyao* (Statistical Abstracts of China), Beijing
Ta Kung Pao or *Da Gong Bao* (Enlightened News), Hong Kong
Tianjin Ribao   (Tianjin Daily)
WDR 1985:   *World Development Report*, World Bank, Washington
Wenhui Bao,   Shanghai
XH: *Xinhua* (New China) *Daily Report* – in English
Yangcheng Wanbao (Yangcheng Evening News)
ZGFZB: Zhongguo Fazhi Bao (China Legal System News)
ZGNMB: Zhongguo Nongmin Bao (China Peasant News)
Zhejiang Ribao (Zhejiang Daily)
Zhejiang Xuehan   (Zhejiang Studies)
Zhejiang Ribao (Zhejiang Daily)
Zhengming   – monthly
ZGSHKX: Zhongguo Shehui Kexue (Social Sciences in China)
Zhongguo Xinwenshe   (China News service)

Index

Page references followed by 't' refer to tables.